DATE DUE

RESTRUCTURING
SOVEREIGN DEBT

RESTRUCTURING SOVEREIGN DEBT

The Case for Ad Hoc Machinery

LEX RIEFFEL

BROOKINGS INSTITUTION PRESS
Washington, D.C.

Library of Congress Cataloging-in-Publication data
Rieffel, Lex.
    Restructuring sovereign debt : the case for ad hoc machinery / Lex
Rieffel.
    p. ; cm
Includes bibliographical references and index.
    ISBN 0-8157-7446-X (cloth)
    1. Debt relief—Developing countries. 2. Loans, Foreign—Developing
countries. 3. Debts, External—Developing countries. I. Title.
    HJ8899.R52 2003
    336.3'6—dc22   2003015470

9 8 7 6 5 4 3 2 1

The paper used in this publication meets minimum requirements of the American National Standard for Information Sciences—Permanence of Paper for Printed Library Materials: ANSI Z39.48-1992.

Typeset in Minion

Composition by OSP, Inc.
Arlington, Virginia

Printed by R.R. Donnelley
Harrisonburg, Virginia

Reinventing the Square

The seven brothers (Canada, France, Germany, Italy, Japan, United Kingdom, and United States), led by Sam, had overcome many obstacles during sixty years in the business of delivering global financial stability. Their truck had survived rough terrain, violent storms, and occasional collisions. One day a large pothole caused a blowout. Instead of replacing the tire with the familiar brand, their favorite repair shop proposed a new prototype that would never wear out. It was guaranteed to withstand potholes, nails, and all other perils. Their customers, however, worried that a square tire would make the truck bounce too much and jostle their merchandise. Could it be that, as usual, the customers are right?

Contents

Preface

The international financial system in place in 2003 is the tree that has grown from seeds planted at a conference in Bretton Woods, New Hampshire, in 1944. World prosperity was the intermediate objective; world peace was the ultimate objective.

Sixty years later, progress on the economic front, measured in the consumption of goods and services, is easier to see than progress on the political front, measured by the frequency and intensity of armed conflict. Yet the road to relative prosperity has been far from smooth. A third of the world's population appears mired in poverty. Economic growth has been interrupted by several cataclysms, including the breakdown of the fixed exchange rate system in the 1970s and the developing country debt crisis in the 1980s. A series of financial crises in emerging market countries in the late 1990s was still roiling the waters in mid-2003, and concerns about a period of global deflation emanating from the United States, Japan, and the European Union were beginning to surface.

Even if the momentum of global growth resumes and restores a sense of stability to the system, debt problems among emerging market and other developing countries are likely to wreak hardship on innocent populations for years to come. These problems will also inspire more proposals for "permanent machinery"—some kind of formal international institution like a bankruptcy court—to ensure speedier and more orderly debt workouts.

I have written this book in the belief that the more sensible policy response is to continue relying on ad hoc machinery, such as the Paris Club and the London Club, for arranging sovereign debt workouts. My views have been shaped by forty years of experience that began as a student of economic development, followed by short stints as a Peace Corps volunteer in India and as an economist for the U.S. Agency for International Development in Indonesia, and long years of policy mongering in the U.S. Treasury Department and the Institute of International Finance (IIF).

A villageful of people has encouraged and helped me write this book. I am most indebted to three of them. In 1983, as a member of the Lazard-Lehman-Warburg "troika," Christine Bogdanowicz-Bindert proposed that I write an essay on the Paris Club for a journal issue devoted to the subject of debt restructuring. This challenge launched me into the avocation of writing for publication. I drafted what turned out to be two essays while sitting in the library of the North Shore Community Hospital (Long Island, New York), where my mother was recuperating from cancer surgery.

On a whim, I sent my draft to Professor Peter Kenen, who was heading the International Finance Section of the Department of Economics at Princeton University at that time. He suggested a way of dividing the text into two essays, and he published one of them in the highly regarded series of *Essays in International Finance*. Since then, even though our views on policy approaches to debt problems diverge substantially, Professor Kenen has been a guiding light for my work and thinking on debt. He agreed to review the first draft of this book, and his detailed comments were enormously helpful in organizing the material I had collected into a more digestible structure.

Michael Atkin, a former colleague at the IIF now working in the fund management industry, was the hero who galloped up at the critical moment to save the project at the edge of a cliff. His thorough and timely comments on the second draft boosted my book into the publications queue at the Brookings Institution Press.

Two industry associations provided essential financial support: EMTA (formerly the Emerging Markets Traders Association) in New York, and the International Primary Markets Association in London. Michael Chamberlin at the former was the lead venture capitalist for the project; Robert Gray and Cliff Dammers at the latter were his stalwart partners. Their support made it possible for me to interview key officials and senior industry executives in New York, London, and Paris, and to engage a summer research assistant. Prashant George, a student at the Maxwell School, Syracuse University, helped me sustain the pace of work when I was close to getting bogged down in details.

My examination of the Paris Club benefited enormously from conversations with debt experts in the U.S. government and Delphine d'Amarzit, the current secretary general of the Paris Club. Important historical points and marvelous encouragement came from three former Paris Club chairmen: Jacques de Larosière, Michel Camdessus, and Jean-Claude Trichet. On the London Club side, Harry Tether (formerly with Chase Manhattan Bank) and Rick Bloom (formerly with Bank of America) performed yeoman service clarifying points of procedure, filling in blanks in my experience, and referring me to other experts. Other bankers, too numerous to mention individually, helped me flesh out the picture. At the IIF Sabine Miltner kept me up to date on the status of the public-private dialogue on crisis resolution, and Yusuke Horiguchi suggested a way to set the policy issue into the framework of economic theory.

Bob Litan was instrumental in allowing me to make Brookings my institutional home for this project. Linda Gianessi and Eileen Robinson handled the details and made me feel like a member of the family. The support I received from the Brookings library was beyond imagining. The admiration I have for Eric Eisinger and his crew is beyond words. The editorial team at the Brookings Institution Press—Chris Kelaher, Janet Walker, Marty Gottron—steered me in my first passage through the intricacies of book publication with commendable patience.

I have labored to avoid mistakes of fact or opinion, but have difficulty imagining that I have been entirely successful. The blame for any mistakes rests squarely with me and not with any of the individuals or institutions cited above.

List of Acronyms

ADB	Asian Development Bank
APEC	Asia-Pacific Economic Cooperation
BAC	Bank Advisory Committee (a London Club forum)
BIS	Bank for International Settlements
CIBL	Citicorp International Banking Ltd.
CIEC	Conference on International Economic Cooperation
COMECON	Council for Mutual Economic Assistance
CRS	Creditor Reporting System (OECD)
CTLD	convertible Turkish lira deposit
DAC	Development Assistance Committee (OECD)
DIP	debtor-in-possession (bankruptcy financing)
DRF	dispute resolution forum
DRS	Debtor Reporting System (World Bank)
EBRD	European Bank for Reconstruction and Development
EC	European Commission
ECU	European currency unit
EEC	European Economic Community
EIB-EIF	European Investment Bank-European Investment Fund
EMCA	Emerging Markets Creditors Association
EMS	European Monetary System
EMTA	formerly the Emerging Markets Traders Association
ERM	exchange rate mechanism (European Union)
ESF	Exchange Stabilization Fund (U.S. Treasury Department)

EU	European Union
FBPC	Foreign Bondholders Protective Council
FSF	Financial Stability Forum
G-5	Group of Five
G-7	Group of Seven
G-8	Group of Eight
G-10	Group of Ten
G-20	Group of Twenty
G-22	Group of Twenty-Two
G-77	Group of Seventy-Seven
GAB	General Arrangements to Borrow (IMF)
GATT	General Agreement on Tariffs and Trade
GDP	gross domestic product
GKO	Russian treasury bills
HIPC	highly indebted poor countries
IBRD	International Bank for Reconstruction and Development (World Bank)
IDA	International Development Association
IDB	Inter-American Development Bank
IDC	International Debt Commission
IFC	International Finance Corporation
IIF	Institute of International Finance
IMF	International Monetary Fund
IMFC	International Monetary and Financial Committee (IMF)
IPMA	International Primary Markets Association
ITO	International Trade Organization
JEXIM	Export-Import Bank of Japan
LIBOR	London Inter-Bank Offer Rate
MIGA	Multilateral Investment Guarantee Agency
MYRA	multiyear rescheduling agreement
NAB	New Arrangements to Borrow (IMF)
NATO	North Atlantic Treaty Organization
NGO	nongovernmental organization
NIEO	New International Economic Order
NPV	net present value
ODA	official development assistance
OECD	Organization for Economic Cooperation and Development
OPEC	Organization of Petroleum Exporting Countries
PRSP	Poverty Reduction Strategy Paper (IMF/World Bank)
PSI	private sector involvement
ROSC	Report on the Observance of Standards and Codes (IMF)
RTA	retroactive terms adjustment
SDDS	Special Data Dissemination Standard (IMF)

SDR	special drawing right (IMF unit of account)
SDRM	sovereign debt restructuring mechanism
SRF	Supplemental Reserve Facility (IMF)
TIAS	Treaties and Other International Acts (U.S. State Department)
UDROP	universal debt rollover with a penalty
UNCITRAL	United Nations Commission on International Trade Law
UNCTAD	United Nations Conference on Trade and Development
WTO	World Trade Organization

RESTRUCTURING
SOVEREIGN DEBT

1

Sovereign Default in the Bretton Woods Era

The purposes of the International Monetary Fund are: (i) To promote international monetary cooperation through a permanent institution which provides the machinery for consultation and collaboration on international monetary problems. . . .

Article I, Articles of Agreement of the International Monetary Fund

The machinery for sovereign debt workouts is part of a complex financial system within a more complex global political system. Many basic features of the international financial system predate World War II, but the current structure is the product of the United Nations Monetary and Financial Conference at Bretton Woods, New Hampshire, in July 1944. The principal architects, Harry Dexter White representing the United States and John Maynard Keynes representing the United Kingdom, designed a pair of institutions to anchor the system: the International Monetary Fund (IMF) and the International Bank for Reconstruction and Development (IBRD, or World Bank). Created as specialized agencies of the United Nations, they promote four systemic principles: the rule of law, market-based growth, removal of barriers to trade and payments, and stability.

The Bretton Woods system has not been a rigid one. Indeed, adaptability has been one of its hallmarks. The monetary system based on fixed exchange rates was recast as a floating-rate system in the 1970s. Regional development banks were created. Special programs and facilities were put in place to alleviate poverty in low-income countries. Changes in the system were also made in response to breakthroughs in communications and information technology, the creation of innovative financial instruments, and the emergence of global financial conglomerates.[1]

One measure of the success of the system has been the historically rapid growth of living standards recorded after 1944. Another was the decision by almost all of the communist countries in the 1980s and 1990s—which had opted out of the Bretton Woods system when it was first established—to abandon central planning in favor of market-based growth strategies.

The system has experienced a number of problems, however. Persistent poverty among a large portion of the world's population has been one of the biggest concerns, and frustrations, over the years. Another problem has been instability, manifested in financial crises in the developing countries that have seemed to grow worse in each succeeding decade. Informal and ad hoc machinery has been developed to restructure international debt when necessary to recover from these crises. The Paris Club was created in the 1950s to restructure debt owed to government agencies in the wealthier and more advanced countries. The London Club was created in the 1970s to restructure debt owed to commercial banks. Debt in the form of international bonds issued by developing country borrowers became significant—for the first time in the Bretton Woods era—in the early 1990s. Toward the end of that decade, several countries were unable to avoid restructuring their bond debt along with debt owed to Paris Club and London Club creditors. That situation sparked a lively policy debate about the kind of machinery that should be used to restructure bond debt, with one side favoring ad hoc machinery and the other favoring permanent machinery.

This study views the current debate about bond restructuring as the fourth global debate about the machinery for sovereign debt workouts in the Bretton Woods era. The policy issue at the core of each debate has been burden sharing—how to share the costs of a workout among the debtor country, private creditors (primarily bondholders and commercial banks), Paris Club creditors, and the multilateral agencies (the IMF, the World Bank, and the regional development banks). Protagonists in the current debate often refer to past experience to support particular arguments. Some of these references are factually wrong, and some of the arguments overlook

---

1. The liberal financial system was designed to support and be reinforced by a liberal trading system managed through a sister institution to be called the International Trade Organization (ITO). Cold war politics blocked the establishment of the ITO, but the General Agreement on Tariffs and Trade (GATT)—adopted in 1947 by the noncommunist nations—was quite successful in liberalizing trade in goods and services. Following the end of the cold war, the World Trade Organization (WTO) replaced the GATT in 1995. Most of the former communist countries became members of the IMF and the World Bank in the early 1990s and began to join the WTO later in the decade.

relevant experience. The hope is that this study will help participants in this debate—and future ones—be better informed. The belief is that the lessons of the past fifty years point the way toward a pragmatic, middle-of-the-road approach. Ad hoc machinery can continue to produce sensible bond restructuring arrangements that enable sovereign borrowers either to avoid a default or to cure one.

The first debt debate took place in the 1970s as part of the North-South Dialogue. The less developed countries of the South, organized in the United Nations as the Group of Seventy-Seven (G-77), tried to leverage their numbers in various forums to rewrite the rules of the Bretton Woods system in their favor. The more economically advanced countries of the North fought to defend the existing system, where weighted voting works to their advantage. The North prevailed but made a number of concessions to defuse the tension and reinforce global support for the Bretton Woods system.

The G-77 campaign included a frontal attack on the Paris Club. The developing countries demanded a process that would be more sensitive to debtor country interests and proposed the creation of permanent machinery in the form of an International Debt Commission to ensure speedy and fair debt relief. The advanced countries resisted this proposal but agreed to make the Paris Club's operating principles transparent and to invite the secretary general of UNCTAD (United Nations Conference on Trade and Development) to send an observer to all Paris Club negotiations.

The second debt debate was fueled by the 1980s debt crisis that struck Latin American countries with particular force. This time the focus was on debt owed to commercial banks, and it was a "systemic" crisis. The outstanding loans of the world's biggest banks to developing countries were a multiple of the capital on the banks' balance sheets. Writing down these loans at the onset of the crisis to reflect their current market value would have reduced bank capital to the point of risking serious disruption in the international financial system and a global economic depression. The financial authorities in the major creditor countries adopted a strategy to buy time until the banks were able to accumulate enough capital to absorb these losses.

For seven years following the Mexican crisis in August 1982, the commercial banks repeatedly rescheduled principal payments and extended new loans sufficient to enable the countries concerned to stay current on their interest payments. These arrangements were negotiated in the London Club, an informal process loosely resembling the Paris Club process. Politicians, academics, and financial industry representatives advanced numerous proposals during this period for more rapid and definitive workouts. Most of the proposals involved shifting the risk of future defaults to public sector institutions in return for slashing the size of the claims. Instead, beginning in 1989, a cooperative approach was adopted that involved sharing the burden among debtor countries, commercial banks, creditor countries, and multilateral agencies on a case-by-case basis.

The third debt debate began toward the end of the 1980s and extended well into the 1990s. The debt reduction deals with commercial banks generally succeeded in restoring the creditworthiness of the major debtor countries. Repeated Paris Club reschedulings for a group of forty to fifty low-income countries were not achieving the same result, however. These countries had large debts to multilateral and bilateral agencies but owed relatively little to commercial banks. The Paris Club reached the point of rescheduling everything it possibly could on increasingly generous terms, and even writing off some debt, but still these poor countries had difficulty meeting their debt-service obligations. The crux of the problem was the practice of treating multilateral agencies as preferred creditors, meaning that they never rescheduled or reduced their claims.

Public pressure to ease the burden of debt on the HIPCs (heavily indebted poor countries) escalated until the major creditor countries—which also held a majority of the votes in the multilateral agencies—finally launched a program in 1996 to fix the problem. The HIPC Initiative was a generalized approach to debt reduction designed to ensure that excessive external debt-service obligations would not prevent the poorest countries from meeting the basic needs of their people. Fundamentally, this debate was more about the world's "aid machinery" than about the machinery for restructuring debt. Nevertheless, it was a major preoccupation of financial officials in the 1990s, and a major source of confusion in the latest debt debate. Consequently, the story behind the HIPC Initiative must be told to complete the history of sovereign debt workouts in the Bretton Woods era.

The fourth and current debt debate began in 1995. The Mexican peso crisis at the end of 1994 sparked the debate. To prevent a default that might ripple through other major developing country borrowers and become a systemic crisis, the United States and its major creditor country partners mobilized an exceptionally large package of official financing to tide Mexico over until a program of economic reforms restored the country's ability to borrow in international capital markets. The package was sharply criticized for "bailing out" private creditors and thereby creating an incentive for more imprudent lending. Importantly, the private creditors involved were no longer commercial banks. Much of the banks' exposure had been converted to bonds that were actively traded in secondary markets and held by a broad community of investors. Moreover, developing countries started to issue new bonds in international capital markets on a large scale in the early 1990s, ending a period of almost sixty years when they had borrowed very little in the form of bonds.

A series of financial crises and defaults between 1994 and 2001, culminating in Argentina's spectacular default, prompted an intense global debate about how to prevent crises and how to share the workout burden in those that could not be avoided. The debate naturally focused on the Paris Club and the London Club. On one side were those who advocated making incremental improvements in this machinery, supported by other reforms such as introducing clauses in bond covenants that would facilitate restructuring. On the other side were those who advocated establishing some form of permanent machinery for ensuring orderly workouts. Remarkably, the IMF became the leading advocate of the second, more radical approach. In November 2001 First Deputy Managing Director Anne Krueger gave a speech proposing the creation of a Sovereign Debt Restructuring Mechanism (SDRM) to facilitate the restructuring of bond debt. Representatives of the private sector reacted with horror for the most part. The debate intensified in 2002 as the IMF refined its proposal and the private sector sharpened its criticisms. In April 2003, however, the debate moved into a less intensive phase when the U.S. position changed from support for studying all options to making incremental improvements in the existing system.

The thrust of the argument in this study is that permanent workout machinery is not necessary or desirable at this time. The Paris Club and London Club were both created "organically" in a series of negotiations over several years. First the bilateral donor agencies developed the Paris Club process; subsequently commercial banks developed the London Club process. In neither case were these pieces of machinery designed ex ante by the IMF or any official body and presented to the creditors to be used in future workouts—as the IMF is seeking to do with the SDRM. Past experience suggests that the bondholders themselves, represented by leading asset managers and institutional investors, can develop effective workout machinery for bond debt by themselves. Indeed, they will have a strong incentive to do so in 2003 if a new government in Argentina initiates serious negotiations with its creditors.

The subject of sovereign debt workouts is highly technical. Consequently, the book begins with three chapters explaining the jargon, describing the main players, and examining several basic policy issues. Readers who are familiar with the international financial system can skip these chapters. Chapter 2 on fundamental concepts touches on certain economic aspects of lending across borders. The legal systems for enforcing loan agreements and bond contracts are a critical part of the story and are introduced here. This discussion leads into an examination of domestic bankruptcy regimes and how they differ from various sovereign bankruptcy regimes that have been proposed. In today's system, specific categories of debt are restructured in the Paris Club, other categories in the London Club, and a few are exempt from restructuring. A chart is provided to explain what goes where. The extensive and sometimes confusing vocabulary associated with the business of restructuring is reviewed. Finally, the major sources of debt statistics are noted.

Chapter 3 focuses on the main players, beginning with the finance ministers from the seven major industrial countries (Group of Seven, or G-7), who collectively have assumed responsibility for the design and management of the international financial system. They dominate the process of establishing policies related to sovereign debt workouts and implementing strategies for dealing with specific cases. In this study they are usually referred to as the G-7 architects. Brief descriptions of the major categories of lenders and borrowers are also provided.

Chapter 4 on fundamental issues is a series of short essays on critical or controversial aspects of the workout business. It begins with a discussion of the way respect for contractual obligations relates to the rule of law, one of the four principles of the Bretton Woods system. The efforts made in recent years to prevent crises are noted, and the work that remains to be done in this area is stressed. Approaches to restructuring in specific cases often turn on assessments of a country's ability and willingness to meet its external payment obligations. That in turn relates to a policy choice between financing and adjustment and reveals a paradox at the heart of the workout process. All sovereign workouts have a political dimension that is largely absent from domestic workouts. Finally, the latest debate has been driven by concerns about using public sector resources to "bail out" private creditors, but a greater concern may be that private creditors will end up "bailing out" the public sector.

Chapters 5 and 6 respectively focus on the origins and operations of the Paris Club and the London Club (or Bank Advisory Committee process). A pair of essays on the Paris Club published by this author in 1984 and 1985 have been expanded and updated here, with special attention paid to the Paris Club's approach to burden sharing. The origins and operations of the

London Club process have never been thoroughly documented. As a consequence, the material in chapter 6 may be of particular value. For both these chapters, the author has drawn heavily on first-hand sources. In this connection a list of the chairmen, cochairmen, and secretaries general of the Paris Club is published for the first time, together with a corresponding list of selected Bank Advisory Committee chairmen and cochairmen.

The next three chapters examine each of the first three debt debates in the Bretton Woods era. Chapter 7 focuses on the North-South Dialogue, where an earlier attempt was made to establish permanent machinery for sovereign debt workouts. Chapter 8 examines the debt crisis of the 1980s, with particular emphasis given to the close cooperation between finance officials and the commercial banking community that was a hallmark of this period. Chapter 9 looks at the debate about how to alleviate the debt burdens of the poorest countries and seeks to differentiate the HIPC Initiative from the business of sovereign debt workouts.

The current debt debate is addressed in the following two chapters. Chapter 10 briefly reviews the financial crises that occurred from 1994 through 2002. Chapter 11 tracks how the approach of the G-7 and the IMF to "private sector involvement" (PSI) evolved during this period, and how the private financial community responded.

The final chapter addresses two questions: what is broken in the current system, and what needs to be fixed. The major problem found is the absence of a clear and predictable workout process for cases where much of the debt that must be restructured is in the form of bonds. The recommended solution is for the G-7 and the IMF to actively support efforts by private creditors to develop new machinery through a series of actual cases, building on the foundations of the London Club experience, and in the context of a "tools-based" approach to sovereign debt restructuring. A smaller problem is the Paris Club's approach to burden sharing. Here the recommendation is that the Paris Club adopt a more flexible and forward-looking approach.

From beginning to end, this book is about policy choices, not economic theories or financial principles. The international financial system, as well as the machinery for sovereign debt workouts that is embedded in the system, are the product of political compromises. The science of economics and the art of finance have not advanced to the point where the "right" answer to a problem can be clearly identified. Reasonable people and well-informed experts can find strong arguments for quite different approaches. Even when a consensus is reached on a course of action, the results can be disappointing due to misunderstandings, miscalculations, or unintended consequences. Experience, then, can be especially important in selecting among policy options. The hope is that this study will help policymakers and policy advocates make substantial and lasting improvements in the machinery for sovereign debt workouts.

2

Fundamental Concepts

D ebt contracts have existed for generations. Economic theories about debt have been developed, and procedures for restructuring the debt of borrowers to avoid or cure a default have been refined. Along the way a rich vocabulary of workout terms has been created. This chapter provides lay readers with a short guide to the concepts and technical terms used in the pages that follow.

Economic Aspects

For the purpose of economic analysis, national economies are divided into three distinct groups of economic agents: households, businesses, and governments. The behavior of individual agents in each group follows certain laws and observes certain relationships (microeconomics), and the behavior of all agents aggregated together conforms to other laws and relationships (macroeconomics). Economists generally assume that each agent or collection of agents seeks to maximize the *net present value* (NPV) of its consumption, from the present to the infinite future.[1] In the process of doing

---

1. NPV is a mathematical technique used to compare streams of value, such as consumption, income, or repayments of debt, over periods of time. For example, the NPV of a twenty-year stream

so, each agent decides how to divide its income (from working, from selling goods and services, from taxation) between consumption and investment. Goods and services that are consumed provide immediate value, but will not be available in the future. Those that are invested are not consumed and therefore retain value and can be resold. In addition, each agent decides whether to consume less than its income (save) or more than its income (dissave).

Agents that save are potential lenders; agents that dissave are potential borrowers. Both will enter into a debt contract if they believe that by doing so they can increase their future consumption. For a lender this increase comes in the form of the interest received over the life of the debt contract. For a borrower this increase is the difference between the income produced using the goods and services procured with the borrowed funds and the interest that must be paid on these funds.

Difficulties arise because of uncertainties about the future. Each agent assigns probabilities to these uncertainties in a subjective manner, and these probabilities are reflected in the pricing structure of the debt contract (for example, a risk premium charged by the lender). When the expectations of both the lender and borrower turn out to be accurate, both gain. When they turn out to be inaccurate, one or the other or both lose.

An endless variety of instruments and institutions has evolved over hundreds of years for intermediating between savers and dissavers. In particular, financial markets have been created that work perfectly in theory but have certain inherent weaknesses in practice. One of these is asymmetrical information. It is often the case that one of the parties to a transaction possesses material information that the other party lacks. This asymmetry gives rise to certain market failures. Two that are particularly relevant to this study are *moral hazard* and *herd behavior*. Moral hazard refers to "distorted incentive structures that induce borrowers and/or lenders to engage in risky financial behavior or inadequately monitor the risks they assume, in the expectation that they will be insulated from the adverse consequences of their activities by the public authorities."[2] Herd behavior arises because market investors

---

of consumption is found by discounting each year's consumption back to the present using a common discount rate and adding up these amounts. To illustrate, the NPV of $1,000 received at the end of Year 10 is $386 at the beginning of Year 1 using a 10 percent discount rate. Reversing the calculation, if $386 at the beginning of Year 1 grows at a rate of 10 percent compounded (the base amount is 10 percent greater each year), it will amount to $1,000 at the end of Year 10. The NPV of $1,000 in Year 20 is $149 in Year 1 using a 10 percent discount rate. The NPV of $1,000 in Year 10 is $614 in Year 1 using a 5 percent discount rate.

2. Group of Ten (1996, p. 5).

tend to follow certain leaders in the belief that they have superior information. The result is a pattern of lending where a period of rapid credit expansion is followed by a cessation of new lending and even a contraction of credit. When such behavior occurs at the international level, the reversal can create a financial crisis that leads to a sovereign default, widespread private sector defaults, or both.

On balance, the benefits of financial markets outweigh the costs associated with payment problems. High standards of living in a national economy are inconceivable without a high degree of financial intermediation. Financing oils the gears of economic activity. Practical ways have evolved over a long time to resolve the problems associated with financial transactions. The rights and obligations of agents are spelled out in formal contracts. Institutions have been created to ensure that contracts are enforced. Procedures have been developed to restructure or settle the claims of creditors when borrowers are unable to meet their obligations.

Legal Enforcement and Sovereign Immunity

Debt contracts are worth more than the paper they are printed on because of the framework of laws and institutions that support them.[3]

Typically creditors deliver cash when contracts take effect and receive repayment in cash (interest and principal) during the ensuing months and years. As a consequence, enforcement is commonly a concern for creditors and only rarely for debtors. In particular, enforcement becomes an issue in the context of a default. Broadly, a default is any failure by a debtor to meet its contractual obligations. The main *event of default* is missing a scheduled payment of principal or interest. According to standard contract provisions, when a payment is missed, creditors have the right to "accelerate" the entire debt that remains outstanding. This amount becomes due immediately and the creditor is then free to seek a judgment from a court against the debtor to recover whatever assets may be available.

Contracts in some countries and communities are enforced directly by the parties involved without involving a judicial system. For example, a creditor makes arrangements with someone who physically threatens a nonperforming debtor or forcibly removes assets in the debtor's possession.

---

3. For this discussion of sovereign debt workouts, the principal forms of debt are loan agreements with lending institutions such as banks or government agencies and bond covenants with individual bondholders.

At times in the past, nonpayment of debt has been a serious crime enforced by governments through imprisonment.

In the more civilized world we now live in, such means of enforcement are unthinkable. As a substitute, countries have adopted laws spelling out in considerable detail how debt contracts will be enforced, and institutions have been developed to implement these laws. The laws are known as bankruptcy or insolvency laws, and the institutions are part of each country's judicial system. Together they enable creditors to take possession of assets belonging to delinquent debtors to satisfy claims. At the same time, the laws establish certain protections for debtors, enforced by the courts, to discourage predatory lending and to preserve social order.

Naturally, over time, creditors have sought ways of strengthening laws or revising the terms of contracts to make enforcement easier. Debtors have sought to make laws more debtor-friendly or introduced clauses in their contracts to facilitate renegotiation. As might be expected, the laws of countries vary widely, as does the institutional capacity to enforce debt contracts. In countries with authoritarian governments, contract enforcement can be relatively strong even though the judicial systems are weak. Generally speaking, countries with strong enforcement capacities tend to have more-developed financial systems that contribute to steady (but usually unspectacular) rates of economic growth.

At the international level, extreme forms of enforcing debt contracts have been seen in the past. In the late 1800s and early 1900s, it was considered reasonable for powerful countries to use military force to extract payments on delinquent debt. This was done, for example, by collecting taxes on trade. War reparations (a form of debt) levied on Germany at the end of World War I were a heavy burden, which contributed to the rise of the Nazi government and ultimately World War II.

By contrast, the global political system embodied in the United Nations was designed to discourage the use of force to settle international disputes.[4] The notion of forcible collection of international debt is anathema. The United Nations could in theory adopt a global bankruptcy law or convention, but that would intrude on national sovereignty beyond the limits of what is currently acceptable. As a result, enforcement of debt contracts with sovereign borrowers is relatively weak.

Another basic reason why debt enforcement is weak at the international level is the doctrine of sovereign immunity. This is the concept in interna-

4. The IMF and the World Bank are counted among the specialized agencies of the United Nations.

tional law that sovereign nations cannot be sued by private parties (or other sovereign authorities) against their will. It is derived from the meaning of sovereignty. A nation forced to submit to another is not truly sovereign. Creditors have strengthened their rights in the event of a default by a sovereign borrower by including waivers of sovereign immunity in most loan contracts and bond covenants. Creditors attempting to use litigation to enforce claims against defaulting sovereigns have rarely been successful, however.

Given this experience, commercial creditors would appear to be the main beneficiaries of an international bankruptcy regime. In fact, however, commercial creditors have been more inclined to oppose than support steps in this direction. One fundamental reason is the difficulty of designing an international bankruptcy regime that is apolitical. The devil is in the detail here. Ultimately any such regime will vest enforcement powers in a new governmental body of uncertain ability. Creditors prefer the certainty associated with existing procedures. Another fundamental reason is that countries would have to give up certain sovereign rights to make an international bankruptcy regime effective, and few countries appear eager to take this step. Without any means of compelling sovereign borrowers to transfer assets in their possession to satisfy the claims of creditors, any international bankruptcy procedure tends to look like a one-edged sword directed at creditors.[5] In short, commercial creditors generally prefer to negotiate an ad hoc debt restructuring arrangement to avoid or cure a sovereign default. They hope that official institutions (such as the IMF) will normally facilitate such arrangements and at least not impede them.

Default in a National Context

A debtor may fail to meet its obligations under a debt contract for endless reasons, but the core reason typically is that its income is insufficient to meet a scheduled payment of interest or principal. In most cases the debtor has a number of obligations outstanding and has to decide as its cash runs short which creditors to pay and which ones to ignore. Alternatively, it can propose either a comprehensive or limited restructuring of its obligations. If the problem is temporary, certain payments can be deferred and repaid later with a premium acceptable to the creditors, or the money required to

---

5. Judgments against a sovereign borrower that has waived its immunity can only be enforced with respect to assets located outside its borders. Airplanes and ships can be seized and bank accounts frozen, but the scope for meaningful action of this kind is quite limited.

make the payments due on old debt can be obtained from a new loan. Such a situation is generally termed a *liquidity* problem. If the problem is an unsustainable amount of debt, then some reduction of the principal or the stream of interest payments is required to restore the debtor's creditworthiness. That is called a *solvency* problem. In rare cases, a single unexpected event can make a solvent borrower insolvent overnight. More often, debt problems begin as liquidity problems and become solvency problems when the borrower fails to take steps to restore its creditworthiness or when these steps prove to be inadequate.

National bankruptcy regimes have been designed to deal with a large volume of insolvencies in an efficient manner. By definition, every bankruptcy is associated with a financial loss. As a result, creditor claims are worth less than their nominal value—and the loss must be absorbed by the country's economy in some manner. Bankruptcy regimes determine how such losses will be "socialized."

Taking the bankruptcy regime in the United States as a model, several options are available. The most extreme is liquidation of a company at the initiative of its creditors pursuant to Chapter 7 of the U.S. Bankruptcy Code (Title 11, U.S. Code). In such a case, the assets of the company are distributed among the creditors according to well-established conventions, and the company disappears. Loosely speaking, creditors absorb losses in proportion to their exposure, taking into account any special protections built into their debt contracts.[6] That is not the end of the socialization process, however. Banks, for example, share the burden of losses with their employees and shareholders in the form of reduced profit sharing and reduced dividends. Another portion is passed on to the broader society in the form of reduced tax payments. Bondholders, similarly, lighten the burden of their losses by deducting them from gains on other assets in calculating their tax liabilities. Former employees of the liquidated company suffer a loss of income.

An alternative to liquidation is debt restructuring initiated by the company in distress pursuant to Chapter 11 of the U.S. Bankruptcy Code. The company's managers must prepare a plan for reorganizing their business, which usually involves selling off assets that generate insufficient income, discharging nonessential employees, and reducing fixed costs. In addition, creditors are asked to write down their claims to the extent required to make

6. More specifically, a bankruptcy judge supervises the disposition of assets by an administrator and the satisfaction of creditor claims, taking into account the circumstances of each case and legal precedents.

the reorganized company financially viable. If the plan is accepted by a majority of creditors and approved by a bankruptcy court, it becomes binding on minority creditors opposed to accepting losses on the scale proposed. The economic losses in these cases are again shared among all the parties involved, but the total loss is generally smaller than would result from liquidating the company.

Two variations on the Chapter 11 bankruptcy process are worth mentioning. First, companies in distress can negotiate a debt-restructuring arrangement with their creditors "in the shadow of the law." This means that they do not formally enter the Chapter 11 process. But all involved understand that the company will have recourse to Chapter 11 if agreement is not reached on a viable plan. Second, a distinct procedure for bankrupt municipalities is set forth in Chapter 9. Liquidation is obviously not an option in these cases. Essential services provided by the municipality are protected, and the views of residents are taken into account.[7]

A key feature of all national bankruptcy regimes is a careful balancing of the interests of debtors and creditors. The first bankruptcy law in the United States was enacted in 1800, and there have been five major revisions since then, the latest being the Bankruptcy Reform Act of 1978. Bankruptcy experts in the United States remain divided between those who believe the law is too creditor-friendly and others who believe it is too debtor-friendly. The 1978 law has been tweaked several times to improve the balance. The latest tweak was in the direction of making it more creditor-friendly. The domestic bankruptcy regimes of other countries share many of the principles and procedures of the U.S. regime, but each has its idiosyncrasies. As more corporations have become global, work has been undertaken to harmonize bankruptcy laws across countries.[8]

Differences in enforcement, however, generally have a bigger impact on business behavior than do differences in law. The advanced countries tend

---

7. In this respect, the Chapter 9 approach is a more appropriate model for sovereign workouts than the Chapter 11 approach.

8. The United Nations Commission on International Trade Law (UNCITRAL) has produced a Model Law on Cross-Border Insolvency, and a working group on insolvency law is drafting a Legislative Guide on Insolvency (see www.uncitral.org). In addition, the International Federation of Insolvency Practitioners, based in London, recently produced a set of principles to guide multi-creditor out-of-court workouts (see www.insol.org). The World Bank is in the process of launching a Global Forum on Insolvency Risk Management. The International Insolvency Institute, incorporated in Canada, is another organization seeking to improve international cooperation in the insolvency area (see www.iiiglobal.org). See also the report of the Contact Group on the Legal and Institutional Underpinnings of the International Financial System on "Insolvency Arrangements and Contract Enforceability," September 2002, available on the IMF website.

to have domestic regimes that are strongly and consistently enforced, thereby achieving a high degree of legal certainty. Certainty helps creditors assess probable recovery values in the event of a default, which helps them price risk accurately and tends to lower the cost of lending. Enforcement is generally weaker in developing countries, a situation that contributes to the high cost of borrowing in these countries.

Default in the International System

Default at the international level is more complicated because of the differences between local currency and hard currency debt, the differences between sovereign and private sector borrowers, and the absence of a formal international bankruptcy procedure.

Local Currency Debt

Default on obligations denominated in local currency is primarily an issue for the private sector. Private companies default on local currency borrowing for any number of reasons. When that happens, they are liquidated or reorganized under the domestic bankruptcy regime, as described above.

Sovereign governments are largely immune to default on borrowing in their own currency; they can always print more money and inflate their way out of a debt problem. This solution entails heavy social costs, however, either when it leads to hyperinflation or when action is taken to stop inflation. Borrowing is a policy choice, and some governments make themselves immune to default by keeping their budgets in balance, thereby avoiding the need to borrow. Local currency debt becomes an issue in sovereign workouts for two reasons related to burden sharing—that is, how losses are shared among the parties involved. First, a country that is unable to meet the payment obligations on its hard currency debt to foreign creditors may also have substantial local currency debt. In a workout foreign creditors would object to a restructuring that gives unduly favorable treatment to holders of local currency debt. The second reason is that in some cases foreigners may be substantial holders of local currency debt. Discrimination between foreign and domestic holders of the same local currency instruments can be problematical.

Hard Currency Debt

Governments and companies are attracted to foreign borrowing for several reasons. One is when they can use the resources more productively than can borrowers in other countries. The whole world stands to gain when countries with the potential for rapid growth borrow from slow-growing countries. Another reason is that some financing is available on below-market terms from multilateral and bilateral agencies seeking to promote economic development and alleviate poverty. A third reason is that the cost of foreign borrowing often appears to be less than the cost of domestic borrowing, and that is where many problems originate.

Generally loans from foreign sources have to be repaid in foreign currencies. These currencies may not be available when they are needed, either because the exchange rate is different than assumed when the loans were made or because the national government has imposed rationing. Typically, a debt crisis begins with an imbalance in the supply and demand for foreign exchange. If the government has adopted an exchange rate regime that allows the rate to fluctuate according to market forces, the local currency will begin to depreciate. As a result borrowers must find more local currency to purchase the same amount of foreign exchange as before the depreciation. For private sector companies with substantial foreign loans, a rapid depreciation would soon make them illiquid and then insolvent. Each company decides when to resort to the domestic bankruptcy regime or to negotiate a consensual restructuring with its foreign creditors. For the government, the burden of debt service on the budget will at some point become intolerable because it would require politically unacceptable cuts in government services or investment or inflationary financing. At this point, the government must either default or seek a consensual restructuring of its foreign debt.[9]

If the government has adopted a fixed exchange rate regime, the route to default is somewhat different. Excess demand for scarce hard currency at the fixed rate must be met by drawing down reserves. When those are exhausted, all foreign loans will go into default. Governments, however, normally stop using reserves when they fall to some minimally acceptable level and begin to impose exchange restrictions to ration hard currency. These restrictions establish priorities among competing uses, with essential imports such as food and fuel given preference over debt service. In such circumstances, many private sector borrowers still have sufficient local currency to purchase the hard currency needed to service their foreign debt at the fixed

9. This step would generally have the immediate effect of stabilizing the exchange rate because the government is no longer competing for scarce hard currency. In some cases the government may take this step before it is technically necessary to reduce payment strains on private sector borrowers. In other cases the country's banking system will be vulnerable to a sharp currency depreciation, as a consequence of borrowing by the banks themselves or by their clients. The government can intervene in various ways to prevent a banking system collapse.

rate. They deposit this amount in the central bank but do not receive the corresponding amount of hard currency or are not allowed to transfer it to their creditors.[10] By intervening in the payment process, the national government has in effect nationalized private sector obligations. As a consequence, the government assumes the job of negotiating restructuring arrangements with foreign creditors. In the process of rationing the available hard currency, the government in these circumstances could give priority to servicing its own debts, and even remain current on these at the expense of private sector borrowers. In cases where the government's payment obligations are large, or even larger than those of the private sector, the government may negotiate restructuring arrangements for both private sector and public sector obligations.

In short, for countries with fixed exchange rate regimes, default occurs when foreign exchange reserves fall to a critical level and the government imposes exchange restrictions on debt service payments by private borrowers and suspends payments on its own obligations. The government restructures both private sector and public sector obligations in negotiations with Paris Club and London Club creditors. For countries with flexible (floating) exchange rate regimes, the timing of default is determined either by the budget burden of servicing the government's foreign debt or by the extent to which the private sector is vulnerable to a sharp exchange rate depreciation. The government restructures its own obligations in Paris Club and London Club negotiations. Private sector obligations are restructured under the country's domestic bankruptcy regime.

The Workout Machinery for Sovereign Defaults

A basic reason why there is no international bankruptcy regime equivalent to domestic bankruptcy regimes is that there is no world government. No world parliament exists to enact a law establishing procedures for sovereign workouts. No international judicial system exists to enforce such laws and to consider appeals from creditors and debtors.

One alternative to an international bankruptcy law—an alternative used for a large number of global causes—would be to adopt an international bankruptcy treaty. Several proposals along these lines have been advanced in the past. The IMF in 2001 proposed the adoption of an international bankruptcy treaty indirectly by amending its charter (Articles of Agreement). There are at least three fundamental objections to moving in this direction.

10. Creditors can purchase insurance against this "inconvertibility and transfer risk," either from private companies or from export credit agencies.

One is the limited number of countries in the world: no more than 200. Historically the rate of sovereign defaults in any one year is a small fraction (1–2 percent) of that number.[11] By contrast, domestic bankruptcy regimes are essential because there are many thousands of private companies in most countries and the same fraction of defaults represents a large number. Arranging workouts for bankrupt companies in an ad hoc manner would be highly inefficient. Moreover, liquidating bankrupt companies is a positive feature of a market system that helps to encourage innovation and to ensure that resources are used productively. Liquidating countries is out of the question. Another fundamental objection is the difficulty of distinguishing between a liquidity problem and an insolvency problem at the international level. A third objection is that whereas domestic bankruptcy regimes are designed to depoliticize the process of company workouts, it is impossible to take politics out of sovereign workouts.

In the absence of an international bankruptcy law or treaty (permanent or formal machinery), ad hoc creditor groups (informal machinery) have been created to work out (or resolve) sovereign defaults, either imminent or actual. The first of these was the Paris Club, developed in the 1950s and 1960s to restructure debt owed by both public sector and private sector borrowers to official agencies in the economically advanced, high-income countries.

In the 1970s developing countries began to borrow heavily in hard currencies from commercial banks in the advanced countries, and by the end of the decade a number of the borrowing countries were experiencing severe debt-servicing difficulties. The banks developed similar ad hoc machinery—the Bank Advisory Committee process—that was labeled by the press as the London Club. Seventeen emerging market countries entered the 1990s with a substantial stock of bond debt created when commercial bank loans were exchanged for bonds under the Brady Plan, a major initiative undertaken to resolve the developing country debt crisis in the 1980s. These and other emerging market countries began to issue new bonds in international capital markets at a rapid clip. Bondholders are now in the process of developing

11. Seventy-eight countries concluded 364 agreements with the Paris Club between 1956 and 2002. Assuming each country had only one distinct crisis, that is an average of less than two new crises each year. At the other extreme, assuming each agreement represented a distinct crisis, the average comes to fewer than five per year. Focusing on potential cases of bond defaults, about 30 stable democracies are virtually immune from sovereign default. Another 120 countries have negligible amounts of bond debt. The universe of candidates for a serious default is on the order of 30–40 countries. The odds that half or more of these will default during the next ten years must be very low. That leaves an average of two cases a year at most.

new machinery for restructuring sovereign bonds in the face of an imminent or actual default.

Which Debts Are Treated Where

Much of the confusion surrounding the subject of sovereign workouts is related to the numerous categories of creditors and borrowers that exist and the large variety of debt instruments in use. Figure 2-1 shows which kinds of sovereign debt are treated in the Paris Club, which are treated in the London Club, which are exempt from restructuring, and which are dealt with in ad hoc fashion.

The Vocabulary of Debt Restructuring

This study uses the term *workout* for any process of restructuring (reorganizing) a stock of debt that has become too big for the borrower to manage. More formal synonyms are *bankruptcy* (favored in the United States) and *insolvency* (favored in the United Kingdom). They all involve a set of procedures, formal or informal, for resolving or settling the claims of creditors established in their loan contracts when a borrower is unable to meet its obligations in full.

The jargon associated with the workout process can be quite confusing. Box 2-1 defines some of the most frequently encountered terms, but it is by no means exhaustive. One difficulty is that the same term can be given different meanings by different segments of the financial community. An example is the term *debt relief.* Among finance officials, that term has been used for many years as a catchall for any kind of change in a country's debt obligations for the purpose of easing balance-of-payments strains, avoiding an imminent default, or implementing a workout after a default. Among many financial industry practitioners, however, debt relief is synonymous with debt reduction: a reduction of contractual principal or interest. This study uses terminology as defined in a guide for statistical compilers produced jointly by eight international organizations. It is fifty-one pages long and is available online.[12]

12. *External Debt Statistics: Guide for Compilers and Users* (November 2001). The index is located at www.imf.org/external/pubs/ft/eds/Eng/Guide/index.htm (February 5, 2003). The organizations that prepared the guide are the Bank for International Settlements, the Commonwealth Secretariat, Eurostat, the International Monetary Fund, the Organization for Economic Cooperation and Development, the Paris Club Secretariat, the United Nations Conference on Trade and Development, and the World Bank.

Figure 2-1. Creditor and Debtor Categories and the Restructuring Forums

Creditors

Debtors	IMF	Multilateral development banks	Bilateral agencies	Commercial banks	Bond investors	Suppliers
Sovereigns	Preferential treatment		Paris Club	London Club	To be determined	Ad hoc
Public sector enterprises	No such debt exists	Special treatment	Paris Club	London Club	To be determined	Ad hoc
Banks	No such debt exists	Special treatment	No such debt exists	Special treatment	To be determined	No such debt exists
Private companies	No such debt exists	National corporate bankruptcy regime[a]				

Source: Author's illustration.

a. In the context of a debt crisis where companies are denied access to hard currency by exchange restrictions, certain debt-service obligations of private companies may be assumed by the government and rescheduled in the Paris Club and the London Club.

Major Sources of Debt Statistics

There are three major sources of data on the debt of developing countries: the Bank for International Settlements (BIS), the Organization for Economic Cooperation and Development (OECD), and the World Bank. In the late 1990s, in response to requests for dissemination of more timely external debt indicators, the three organizations collaborated with the IMF in producing the *Joint BIS-IMF-OECD-World Bank Statistics on External Debt*. At the end of 2002 a new quarterly report covering 176 developing and transition countries was initiated. These statistics are available on the websites of all four organizations. From the BIS, these statistics can be found at www.bis.org/publ/r_debt.htm (February 5, 2003).

Locational Banking Statistics and Consolidated Banking Statistics. The BIS began to collect data on international banking in 1963 with eight European countries. Since then the BIS system has steadily expanded the number of reporting countries and banks and the number of analytical breakdowns. For example, in 1974 banks began to report full country breakdowns. Reg-

Box 2-1. A Lexicon of Debt-Restructuring Terms

Terms defined in the *Guide for Compilers and Users* are identified by (G).

Debt reorganization—Debt reorganization arises from bilateral arrangements involving both the creditor and the debtor that alter the terms established for the servicing of a debt. Debt reorganization includes debt rescheduling, refinancing, forgiveness, conversion, and prepayments (G). *Debt restructuring*, the term preferred in this study, is given as a synonym for debt reorganization.

Debt relief—Any form of debt reorganization that relieves the overall burden of debt (G). The guide goes on to elaborate on this concept by reference to net present value and duration, which is not very helpful. In commercial usage, debt relief tends to mean a restructuring that contains an element of forgiveness or reduction. A simpler definition would be any reduction of the cash payment requirement in a defined period, either by deferral (temporary relief) or reduction (permanent relief), in the context of debt-servicing difficulties.

A large number of variations on these terms are found in the literature on sovereign debt workouts. The most general terms, essentially equivalent to debt restructuring/reorganization, include *rearrangement, readjustment,* and *rephasing.* Narrower terms include the following, beginning with the least burdensome from the creditors' perspective to the most burdensome:

ular publication of maturity breakdowns began in 1978. The BIS *Guide to the International Banking Statistics (July 2000)* is available at www.bis.org/publ/meth07.htm (February 5, 2003).

The Creditor Reporting System (CRS). The OECD compiles data submitted by its member countries, which account for the vast bulk of all bilateral lending to developing countries. These data are supplemented by data from the major multilateral lending institutions and from several non-OECD donor countries. A definition of the CRS can be found at www.oecd.org/EN/document/0,,EN-document-58-2-no-8-4684-58,00.html (February 5, 2003). The OECD also publishes an annual report on *External Debt Statistics.* The December 2002 edition is available at www.oecd.org/EN/document/0,,EN-document-61-2-no-15-3497-61,00.html (February 5, 2003).

Refinancing—The conversion of the original debt including arrears into a new instrument (G). This definition is inconsistent with commercial usage, where refinancing generally refers to a new loan that is used to meet payment obligations in arrears or coming due on old loans.

Rescheduling—The formal deferment of [scheduled or contractual] debt service payments and the application of new and extended maturities to the deferred amount (G). Rescheduling can be executed by amending an old contract or signing a new contract that overrides an old one. Synonyms are *deferral* and *reprofiling*.

Forgiveness—The voluntary cancellation of all or part of a debt (G). Two common synonyms are *cancellation* and *reduction*.

Conversion—The exchange of debt for a nondebt liability, such as equity, or for counterpart funds that can be used to finance a project or program or policy reform (G). Conversion typically involves an element of debt forgiveness.

Repudiation—A unilateral disclaiming of a debt obligation by a debtor (G).

Certain debt transactions are undertaken not because of any payment strains but to take advantage of a market opportunity to lower the carrying cost of outstanding debt. For example, countries able to borrow at historically favorable rates have used the proceeds to retire Brady bonds. The term *refunding* is used with this meaning, but it is sometimes used confusingly as a synonym for rescheduling or refinancing at an early stage in a debt crisis when a premium has to be paid for new financing.

The Debtor Reporting System (DRS). The World Bank established the DRS in 1951 to collect debt data from developing countries on a loan-by-loan basis. Private unguaranteed long-term debt was incorporated into the DRS beginning in 1970 on the basis of aggregate data and for a smaller number of countries. The data are summarized and published in the World Bank's annual report on *Global Development Finance*. The data are also available on the CD-ROM edition of *Global Development Finance*. More information can be found at http://publications.worldbank.org/ecommerce/catalog/product?item_id=979840 (February 5, 2003).

3

The Main Players

Apart from the two debt restructuring forums described in chapter 2, the parties involved in sovereign workouts can be grouped into three categories: the multilateral policy community, lenders, and borrowers. Short sketches of the parties in each category follow.

The Multilateral Policy Community

The finance ministers from the G-7 countries—the G-7 architects—bear the primary responsibility for the policy framework for sovereign debt workouts. The IMF is their principal instrument for implementing the framework. Other multilateral agencies play supporting roles.

The G-7 Architects

Management of the Bretton Woods system rests squarely on the shoulders of the finance ministers from Canada, France, Germany, Italy, Japan, the United Kingdom, and the United States, collectively know as the G-7 finance ministers. Their responsibility is directly related to the economic weight of their countries in the global economy and also to the political weight of their heads of state and government, who have been meeting in annual summits since 1975. As a group these seven finance ministers direct the activities of the IMF and the multilateral development banks. They are called the G-7 architects in this study because from the early days of the Bretton Woods era, they have designed the changes required to keep the system up to date. In addition, they led the initiative after the financial crisis in Asia in 1997 to reform the "architecture" of the international financial system.

The United States is naturally the chief architect. In addition to leading the victorious allied forces in the Second World War, it possesses the world's largest economy. The United Kingdom and France joined the United States at the outset as "senior partners," while the communist and socialist countries opted out of the Bretton Woods institutions. The United Kingdom, because of its linguistic and political affinities with the United States and London's role as a center of international finance, has had an influence on international financial issues far beyond its weight in the global economy. France capitalized for many years on its diplomatic skills to secure a disproportionate share of the top leadership positions in the multilateral institutions.

Postwar reconstruction transformed Germany and Japan into cold war allies and dynamic industrial economies with stable and democratic political systems. In 1973 their finance ministers were invited to join their counterparts from the United States, the United Kingdom, and France in a series of meetings to discuss the design of a new international monetary system based on floating exchange rates to replace the fixed-rate system that had collapsed in 1971 when the U.S. dollar's link to gold was broken. This effort represented the first major architectural exercise since the founding of the Bretton Woods system in 1944, and it culminated in the adoption of the second amendment of the IMF's Articles of Agreement. The reform of the monetary system at this time also led to the first summit meeting (at Rambouillet, France, in 1975), which brought Italy into the finance ministers' group. Canada was brought in a year later. Thus from a group of two in 1944 the informal directorate for the international financial system became known as the Group of Five, or G-5, in 1973 and the G-7 in 1976.[1]

1. Russia was invited to the annual G-7 summits in the 1990s as an observer and in 1998 became a full participant. Thus at the heads-of-state level, the G-7 became the G-8. Since then, the regular spring, fall, and winter meetings of the G-7 finance ministers and central bank governors have continued without Russian participation. The Russian finance minister has participated only in presummit meetings of the G-8 finance ministers (and none of the G-8 central bank governors has been included in these meetings). Putnam and Bayne (1984) mention the origins of the G-5 finance

The G-7 finance ministers are at the heart of two somewhat larger groups of finance ministers: the G-10 (Group of Ten) and the G-20 (Group of Twenty). In 1962 a backup line of credit for the IMF was established in the form of the General Arrangements to Borrow (GAB). Three more partners, member countries of the OECD, were enlisted to contribute to the GAB (Belgium, Netherlands, and Sweden), thereby constituting a G-10. Switzerland joined later, although the name of the group was not changed. The G-10 countries hold a majority of the votes in the IMF and World Bank and have constituted an effective voting block for all major policy changes over the past four decades.

The G-20 is much newer. Following the Asian crises in 1997 the United States launched an initiative to reform the architecture of the international financial system to reduce the incidence and severity of future crises. Fifteen of the most important developing countries from Asia and the other regions were invited to join the G-7 in designing specific reforms. This Group of Twenty-Two (G-22) produced a set of reports in 1999 establishing an agenda for reform that continues to be relevant. At the end of 1999 the G-22 was reorganized to include a more representative group of "systemically significant" developing countries and relabeled the G-20. It remains to be seen whether the G-20 will assume an important role or whether it will join the G-22 as a historical footnote.[2]

Central bank governors also participate in these leadership groups. Whenever the G-7, G-10, and G-20 meet, the central bank governors from the member countries are seated next to their finance ministry counterparts.

Since the G-7 finance ministers have domestic responsibilities that usually take priority over international issues, they have all appointed deputies to concentrate on international matters. The deputies are responsible for orchestrating the most sensitive policy debates. They generally meet in advance of each ministerial meeting. They set the agenda and vet the options to be presented to the ministers for a decision. Between meetings, they are in almost daily contact.

Crisis management has been a top priority for the G-7 architects for thirty years. They decide when the international financial system is threatened by developments in a particular country, and they develop a strategy for

ministers group in their account of G-7 summitry. A capsule summary of growth of the group can also be found on the website for the 2003 summit in Evian, France. See www.g8.fr/evian/english (May 17, 2003).

2. Apart from the G-7 countries, the members of the G-20 are Argentina, Australia, Brazil, China, India, Indonesia, Korea, Mexico, Russia, Saudi Arabia, South Africa, Turkey, and the European Union.

defusing the threat or mitigating its impact. When a crisis leads to an imminent or actual sovereign default, they determine the amounts and forms of official support that will be mobilized to finance the country's recovery program. When they conclude that the machinery for sovereign debt workouts is in need of repair, they consider alternative fixes and work with the other players in the international financial community to adopt and implement the most attractive approach.

The International Monetary Fund as a Main Player

The IMF plays a central and multifaceted role in almost all sovereign debt workouts. Its main function in the global system is to establish and enforce rules to promote exchange rate stability. In performing this function, it monitors the economic health of the global economy as well as the economies of its member countries. It actively seeks solutions to both systemic and country-specific problems, and it applies its financial and staff resources to implementing those solutions that are adopted by its members.

The IMF was built on the implicit understanding that international peace and economic growth can best be pursued in a world of market-oriented, rather than centrally planned, economies. Nothing in the IMF's Articles of Agreement explicitly prevents countries with centrally planned economies from becoming members, but some of the obligations of membership are difficult to reconcile with central planning. Because the rule of law is part of the bedrock of a market economy, the IMF has been committed from its inception to reinforcing "the sanctity of contracts." As a creditor and as an institution dominated by creditor countries, it could hardly take any other position. Nevertheless, the IMF is also sensitive to the concerns of its developing country members about how debt problems are resolved and favors approaches that are balanced and growth-oriented.

More than any other institution, the IMF is responsible for preventing country defaults, protecting other countries from the consequences of defaults that inevitably occur, and helping countries recover from financial crises. The IMF goes about the task of preventing defaults primarily through regular surveillance missions to member countries. Staff assessments of each country's economic performance and policies are considered by the IMF's twenty-four executive directors, who represent all 184 members. Since 2001 the IMF has operated on the presumption that all of these assessments (known as Article IV consultation reports) will be made public.

IMF surveillance focuses on the three pillars of macroeconomic policy: fiscal (budget) policy, monetary (central bank credit) policy, and exchange rate policy. The staff assesses the "sustainability" of these policies as a package. A country with "unsustainable" policies, in the view of the IMF, is likely to experience balance-of-payments problems in the medium term unless it changes these policies. Since the mid-1980s the IMF has found it necessary to look beyond the macroeconomic policies of member countries and consider their "structural" policies. These run the gamut from the operation of legal systems to energy pricing to the privatization of state-owned enterprises to the soundness of banking systems. In recent years the IMF has developed a sophisticated methodology for assessing debt sustainability.[3]

The surveillance process prevents crises by pointing out vulnerabilities and suggesting steps that country authorities can take to strengthen their balance of payments. The IMF also provides technical assistance in the form of training for officials or visits by experts who can help analyze alternative policies and implementation techniques. The IMF is currently taking a more proactive stance with regard to the financial sector weaknesses that are prevalent in emerging market countries.

Blaming the IMF for the problems of developing countries has been a popular sport for certain groups ever since the IMF began to provide policy advice and condition its financial support on specific reforms. For example, one often-voiced opinion is that the IMF forces countries to adopt harmful policies. This charge represents a grave distortion of how the IMF operates. A sovereign country, by definition, is one that sets its own course. Countries do not give the IMF the power to determine their economic policies when they join the IMF.

Still, the IMF does have considerable leverage when a country decides to borrow IMF resources. It can withhold financing if a country fails to adopt specific policies considered to be essential for recovery, effectively leaving the country no alternative to default. Furthermore, the IMF is not perfect. It has been too optimistic generally about the ability of countries to implement policy reforms, about the impact specific reforms will have on economic performance, and about the external context in which the reforms are carried out.

The IMF's critics make two common mistakes. One is to view the IMF as a fixed object. Actually it attaches a remarkably high priority to evaluating its own performance and learning from experience. It arguably does a better job in this area than any other international or national public sector body of significance. The other mistake is to view the IMF as an independent

3. IMF (2002a).

authority. The IMF is an instrument of the G-7 countries. There is no example that comes easily to mind of a position taken by the IMF on any systemic issue without the tacit, if not explicit, support of the United States and the other G-7 countries.

Despite the IMF's intentions and efforts, payment crises have continued to occur. Every crisis that reaches the point of default represents a failure of the system to some degree. Every workout is a challenge to the international community, which has a stake in seeing the default cured quickly and permanently. The IMF also plays a central role in the recovery process. In broad strokes, the international community depends on the IMF to determine when a defaulting country is ready to implement credible policy reforms, to provide the first dollops of new money to fuel the recovery, and to use its good offices to facilitate the restructuring of the country's debt obligations to official and private creditors.

From the IMF's perspective, the existing machinery for sovereign workouts has three serious deficiencies. One is the pressure from its major stakeholders to provide more IMF financing to some crisis countries than appears prudent. A second is the reluctance of Paris Club creditors to provide debtor countries enough debt relief. A third is the time it takes for private creditors to organize themselves and reach agreement on a viable debt-restructuring plan. These concerns prompted the IMF toward the end of 2001 to put forward a proposal for ensuring more orderly workouts by creating a Sovereign Debt Restructuring Mechanism, despite the lack of precedents for taking such an initiative. The controversy it provoked is examined in chapter 11.

The World Bank Group as a Main Player

The World Bank is the foremost development institution, which leads many people to assume it must be deeply involved in developing country debt workouts. In fact it plays a prominent role only in the debt problems of the poorest countries, and even here it shares this role with the IMF. In 1996 the World Bank launched the HIPC Initiative for the benefit of a group of forty-one highly indebted poor countries. The initiative was designed to lighten the burden of multilateral debt on these countries without jeopardizing the "preferred creditor status" of the multilateral agencies (see the section below on lenders). The HIPC Initiative concerns the machinery for development assistance rather than the machinery for debt workouts. Nevertheless, this program is examined in chapter 8 because it was a product of the third great debt debate in the Bretton Woods era.

Since its creation the World Bank has made loans to finance infrastructure improvements (roads, ports, electric power) and institutional modernization (school systems, health care systems, agricultural extension services). In the 1980s the World Bank gave a higher priority to "structural adjustment" or "policy-based" lending—lending linked to specific macroeconomic reforms and institution-building activities in countries in the process of averting or recovering from financial crises. Such lending was invariably tied to IMF lending in some fashion, in effect a form of cofinancing. More recently, the World Bank has given a high priority to strengthening weak banking systems and addressing other areas that make countries vulnerable to crises, as well as tackling poverty more directly.

As a country approaches a crisis, the World Bank may suspend lending to demonstrate its discomfort with current policies. Reducing flows in this fashion may push the country closer to default, not only by withholding scarce foreign exchange, but also by signaling to other donors and to private investors that the country's prospects are deteriorating.

After a default World Bank lending is usually limited to projects that address critical social needs until the country adopts a stabilization and recovery program. Once this happens the World Bank can be counted upon to join the IMF in providing financial support. Whereas IMF lending supports macroeconomic reforms, World Bank lending targets key structural changes, such as agricultural pricing, privatization, or social safety nets to mitigate the impact of the crisis on poor families.

Another important World Bank activity is to organize and chair meetings of aid donors (called consultative groups or aid consortiums). Following a crisis a Bank-led donor meeting can be a key step in mobilizing fast-disbursing balance-of-payments loans to close a financing gap in the recovery program.

In the late 1980s the World Bank began to finance, at a deep discount, "buy backs" of defaulted commercial bank debt owed by low-income countries, using the Debt Reduction Facility of the International Development Association (IDA). The operations of this facility have been controversial, however. Nongovernmental organizations (NGOs) have criticized the World Bank for forcing countries to buy back debt at too high a price. Commercial lenders have objected to the World Bank's use of unilateral offers instead of engaging in consensual negotiations.

Finally, the World Bank for decades has helped countries to establish and upgrade debt management systems. It is also one of the main compilers and disseminators of data on developing country debt.

Regional Development Banks and Other Official Bodies as Main Players

The Inter-American Development Bank, Asian Development Bank, and African Development Bank by and large follow the pattern set by the World Bank for countries going into and coming out of a crisis. They tend to cut back balance-of-payments financing (budgetary support) as concerns about a country's prospects grow, to suspend commitments and disbursements when the World Bank does, and to participate in new money packages in the recovery phase. The linkage is not surprising considering that the G-7 countries are the major shareholders in each of these banks.

Two nonfinancial organizations play bit parts in the sovereign workout drama:

—The OECD was established in 1961 to promote cooperation among the leading market economies. From its early days it has tracked flows of financing to developing countries. It maintains the Creditor Reporting System, one of the three main sources of data on developing country debt. It also has a long history of analytical work on development strategies, development assistance, and financial sector issues.

—The UNCTAD Secretariat played a major role in the first global debate about the machinery for sovereign debt workouts, which took place in the context of the North-South Dialogue in the 1970s. This role is examined further in chapter 7.[4]

Lenders and the Debt Hierarchy

The process of restructuring developing country debt is complicated in part because it involves a wide variety of lenders and borrowers. Different classes of debt are treated differently, yielding in effect a debt hierarchy. At the top is debt owed to multilateral agencies.

Loosely speaking, the IMF, each of the multilateral development banks, and a few other multilateral lending institutions are all treated as *preferred creditors*. This means that in a situation of default, payment obligations to these agencies are not restructured. Any accumulated arrears to these agencies must be cleared in full before any further financial support from these

4. The UN Center on Transnational Corporations provided some advisory services in the debt area in the 1980s. The center was merged into UNCTAD in 1994, and its work in this area was discontinued as UNCTAD focused increasingly on direct investment issues. The UN Institute for Training and Research has a program on "Debt, Financial Management, and Negotiations" that includes a training package with chapters on the Paris Club and the London Club process, available at www.unitar.org.

agencies can be provided. Because of the central role of the multilateral lending agencies, financial support from most other sources is normally blocked until either these arrears have been eliminated or a plan for eliminating them has been adopted and is being implemented satisfactorily.[5]

At the bottom of the hierarchy is debt owed to suppliers that may become uncollectible in a workout situation. This section describes the six main creditor categories—the IMF, multilateral development banks, bilateral lending agencies, commercial banks, bond investors and asset managers, and suppliers.

The IMF as a Lender

The International Monetary Fund is the most senior of all lenders. This is not a legal fact, but an observation. From a narrow legal point of view, the claims of the World Bank Group and the other multilateral development banks on debtor countries may be just as strong as the IMF's. Its claim to greater seniority rests on several features:

—Most IMF financing is not in the form of a loan. The IMF operates like a cooperative. When a country becomes a member, it deposits with the IMF a mix of its own currency and hard currencies equal to its quota.[6] When a member requests IMF financing, it obtains the currencies of other members in exchange for depositing more of its own currency. This "exchange of assets" is unique to the IMF.

—The terms of IMF financing are governed by the policies of the IMF. The basic document involved is a request signed only by the borrowing member, known as a letter of intent, not a loan contract.

—The IMF is a monetary institution, not a financial institution. Implicit in this distinction is the notion that the IMF should not be exposed to the risk of default any more than the central bank of a member country is. Another factor is the IMF's practice of not borrowing from capital markets,

5. Market participants occasionally snipe at the preferred creditor status of the multilateral agencies. Academics have questioned its value, and poverty activists have viewed it as a policy that impoverishes poor countries. Nevertheless, the practice is not seriously under assault for some practical political reasons.

6. The U.S. dollar and the currencies of other advanced countries are termed *hard* because of their wide use in international transactions and low probability that they will experience sharp depreciation or be subjected to exchange restrictions. Each member country is assigned a quota when it joins the IMF. Quotas are calculated by a complex formula, which reflects the size of each member's economy and its external payments activity, and are adjusted periodically. Each country's vote in the IMF is a function of its quota, and the amount of financing it can obtain under different facilities is expressed as a fraction or multiple of its quota.

as the multilateral development banks do. To the extent possible under international law, the IMF is the quintessential "risk-free lender."

IMF financing comes in a variety of forms. The basic form (under a standby arrangement) is a "drawing" of hard currencies that must be "repurchased" within five years and that accrues interest at a quasi-market rate linked to the money market rates for the four most important currencies (U.S. dollar, euro, Japanese yen, and pound sterling). Other forms include a ten-year repayment period at a similar interest rate for countries with more complex problems, a two-and-a-half-year repayment period and a higher interest rate for exceptional amounts of financing, and ten-year, low-interest credits for poor countries. These different forms are not important in the context of country workouts because they are all treated as exempt from restructuring.

Multilateral Development Banks and Other Preferred Creditors as Lenders

The oldest and most important multilateral development bank is the World Bank, the IMF's sister institution. The World Bank is more difficult to describe than the IMF due to the vast scope of its objectives and instruments. To begin with, it is an amalgam of four distinct balance sheets referred to collectively as the World Bank Group:

—The International Bank for Reconstruction and Development, at the core of the World Bank Group, makes loans to developing member countries at market-based interest rates and long maturities.[7]

—The International Development Association, created in 1960, is a "soft loan" window funded by grants from donor countries in three-year replenishment cycles. Its loans go exclusively to low-income members and are repayable in thirty-five to forty years. No interest is charged, but a service fee of 0.75 percent is levied on disbursed balances. IDA is now in the process of committing more of its resources in the form of grants.

—The International Finance Corporation (IFC) was established in 1956 to provide financing to private sector companies in developing countries. It

---

7. The World Bank's interest rates are better than most countries can obtain from private sources for two reasons. Backed by the "callable capital" of its shareholders, the IBRD enjoys a AAA credit rating and is an active and familiar issuer of bonds in the international capital markets. Consequently its bonds are priced favorably relative to other issuers. (The regional development banks are funded in the same way and pay only a few basis points more than the IBRD.) In addition, the IBRD charges the same rate of interest to all of its borrowing countries, a rate sufficient to cover the World Bank's costs and generate a modest amount of net income.

provides equity as well as loan financing. The IFC created a syndicated loan product that extends its preferred creditor status to commercial banks and other commercial lenders.

—The Multilateral Investment Guarantee Agency (MIGA) was established in 1988 to promote foreign direct investment in developing countries. It insures cross-border investment, in both equity and loan form, against three classical political risks (war, expropriation, and inconvertibility).

The first regional multilateral development bank to be established was the Inter-American Development Bank (1959), followed by the African Development Bank (1964), the Asian Development Bank (1966), and the European Bank for Reconstruction and Development (1991).

The boundaries of the multilateral category of lenders are fuzzy. One source of fuzziness is a group of multilateral lending institutions with restricted regional membership that claims preferred creditor status. The biggest of these is the European Investment Bank. Among a dozen smaller institutions in this category are the Nordic Investment Bank, the Andean Fund, and the Islamic Development Bank.

Another source of fuzziness is the Bank for International Settlements, located in Basel, Switzerland. Established in 1930 to handle post–World War I reparations, the BIS now undertakes financing operations of particular interest to the national central banks that are its shareholders. Such operations are not everyday affairs, however, and the BIS is better known for its nonfinancing operations. In particular, the Basel Committee on Banking Supervision, a committee of banking regulators supported by the BIS, has developed international standards for the minimum capital that banks should maintain.

The BIS has played an important role in country workouts over the past twenty years by providing bridge loans to countries in crisis. Typically, the BIS disburses financing after a country has reached agreement with the IMF on a recovery program but before the IMF begins disbursing. Such financing is always short term (less than one year) and is always repaid with IMF disbursements.

BIS bridge financing has sometimes been accompanied by parallel loans from national central banks. Although central bank bridge financing is bilateral, not multilateral, it enjoys the same preferred creditor status that the BIS financing does. In some cases, this kind of bridge financing has been used to help countries clear arrears to the IMF and the World Bank.

Bilateral Lending Agencies

Export credit agencies are the most important of the bilateral lending agencies. Simplifying considerably, they serve two distinct functions. The better-known function is to make national exporters competitive by matching subsidized financing terms available to exporters in other countries. The less obvious function is to mitigate risks that deter commercial lenders from providing financing for projects on terms consistent with financial viability in countries where political risks are substantial.[8]

Bilateral agency (public sector) loans have a significant political dimension, which distinguishes them from commercial (private sector) loans. Export credit agencies lend on near-market terms, but an element of subsidy in their operations remains despite efforts by the OECD to squeeze out trade-distorting practices. Other bilateral lending programs are even more political, such as programs to finance military equipment sales.

More generally, bilateral lending programs can be divided into two groups: nonconcessional and concessional. Nonconcessional lending tends to be directed to the most advanced emerging market countries and to revenue-generating projects such as airports and toll bridges. Concessional lending targets the poorest countries and social sector projects such as education and health. To count as concessional, official development assistance (ODA) loans must have at least a 25 percent grant element.[9]

In a sovereign workout all debt owed by or guaranteed by the national government is restructured in Paris Club operations. In these operations an important distinction is made between short-term credit and long-term loans.[10] Trade credit and interbank credit, the most important form of short-term lending, are generally excluded from debt-restructuring arrangements because they function as the lifeblood of a country's trade and financial relations with the rest of the world.

8. Export credit agencies can bear this risk in part because they have political leverage that commercial banks lack. When a problem arises, ambassadors representing their countries can make high-level demarches, and other forms of diplomatic pressure can be exerted.

9. The definition for ODA was set by the Development Assistance Committee (DAC) of the OECD. The grant element is calculated by comparing the present value of the repayment stream, using a 10 percent discount rate, with the face value of the loan. Thus, a loan at 6 percent interest repayable in twenty years has a 25 percent grant element. For many years U.S. aid loans were repayable over forty years with interest charged at 2 percent during a ten-year grace period and 3 percent during the remaining thirty years. The grant element of these loans was 70 percent.

10. The conventional definition of "short term" is maturity of one year or less.

Commercial Banks

Moving from public sector lending to private sector lending, commercial banks have been the most important source of private lending to developing countries since World War II. Bank lending has been volatile, however. A binge of bank lending in the mid-1970s and another in the mid-1990s were followed by periods of sharply reduced lending. Bank lending is now giving way to bond financing as the dominant form of private lending.

Three distinct features of commercial bank loans relevant for this study are the banks' clients, their tax and regulatory regimes, and their form. The bulk of the financing from the official lending agencies goes to governments or public sector enterprises. Commercial bank lending is more naturally directed to private sector borrowers. Banks, however, made loans on a large scale to governments in the oil-importing countries in the 1970s as part of the process of recycling petrodollars. Since the debt crisis of the 1980s and the write-offs associated with the conversion of bank loans to bonds under the Brady Plan, banks have been more cautious about lending to governments.

With respect to regulatory and tax regimes, some harmonization has occurred in recent years, but regimes still vary considerably from country to country. This variation has implications for how individual banks assess risks associated with cross-border exposures and for how they view alternative workout techniques following a country default.

With respect to the form of loans, it is sufficient here to mention syndicated loans and short-term revolving credit.[11] For efficiency reasons governments prefer one large loan to many small loans. Banks seek to avoid concentrations of risk. A syndicated loan spreads risk among a group of banks. A lead bank arranges the loan and sells participations to other banks. Most syndicated loans to sovereign borrowers range from $50 million to $500 million.

In a sovereign workout, debt to commercial banks owed or guaranteed by the national government is restructured in the London Club process, which

---

11. Revolving credit is a form of loan financing that allows the borrower to make new drawings as old drawings are repaid, within an overall ceiling on the same terms each time. It is used routinely for trade financing (provided to exporters and importers while their goods are in transit) and for interbank financing (to smooth the daily ebb and flow of balances). The sale of derivative products by banks exploded during the 1990s, and a sizable share of the market relates to emerging market transactions. While derivatives are distinct from loans, they can create cross-border obligations that may have to be settled in the context of a country workout. The issues raised by derivatives in these situations lie at the cutting edge of international finance and are in a state of flux.

makes the same distinction as the Paris Club between short-term and long-term debt.

Bond Investors and Asset Managers

Bond investors are the stars of this study. The treatment of bonds in sovereign workouts is more complex than the treatment of bank loans for several reasons: bond investors are newcomers to emerging market countries; bonds have a different financial character; and the machinery for restructuring bond debt is in the process of being developed.

At the end of the 1980s bondholders were hardly visible on the landscape of emerging markets finance. The exchange of commercial bank loans for tradable bonds under the Brady Plan to resolve the 1980s debt crisis created a substantial secondary market for developing country bonds at the beginning of the 1990s. This market sparked a burst of bond issuance by emerging market borrowers, followed toward the end of the 1990s by a series of defaults in which bond debt played a key role. During 2002 bond financing for developing countries was in a state of suspended animation, in part because of the high-level debate about the machinery for sovereign debt workouts.

From a strict legal point of view, bonds and bank loans represent equally valid claims, unless they contain explicit provisions that make them secured (backed by collateral of some kind) or subordinated to other claims. Generally, commercial banks are not prepared to yield seniority to bond investors, and bond investors are not prepared to see banks receive preferential treatment. Nevertheless, there is a general impression that bonds are senior to bank loans. This perception arises from differences in the nature of the instruments, how they are marketed and managed, and how they were treated in past workouts. For example, bond investors expect a borrower to approach its bank lenders for refinancing or restructuring support before it has recourse to restructuring its bonds. Some bonds, especially those issued under English law, have features that facilitate restructuring, but most bonds issued under New York law cannot be restructured without the consent of 100 percent of the holders.

Bond covenants are just as specific as bank loan agreements about payment terms and spell out creditor rights in roughly the same detail. Bond prospectuses typically contain as much information on the borrower as offering circulars for syndicated loans. Bonds, however, tend to have different maturity structures and payment profiles from bank loans. Bonds typically mature in more than five years and sometimes as long as thirty years. Banks prefer to make shorter-term loans. Bonds typically get repaid in a single "bullet" payment when they mature; bank loans usually amortize after a short grace period.

Bonds are different from bank loans primarily because of how they are sold and who holds them. These are critical differences.

Commercial banks engaged in cross-border lending provide a broad range of financial services. Loans are just one. Others include payment services (such as travelers checks), trading services (making markets in foreign exchange), and advisory services (arranging project finance). Moreover, commercial banks provide these through overseas branches and subsidiaries, as much as or more than from their headquarters. Accordingly, banks have a "relationship" interest in sovereign borrowers that is totally absent among bond investors. Banks may participate in a loan to a sovereign borrower, even when the prospective return is not commensurate with the risk, if they can gain a business advantage by doing so. Bonds are underwritten by investment banks and priced to sell immediately at issue to institutional and individual investors, thereby transferring all of the default risk. They are designed to be resold easily in secondary markets.

The source of profit in the two forms of debt is quite different. Firms that underwrite bonds make profits through front-end fees; firms that trade bonds earn trading fees and trading profits. Firms and funds that hold bonds make profits by buying at a low price and holding to maturity, or selling at a higher price. Profits on bank loans come from the spread between the interest paid for funds (on deposits, for example) and the interest paid on the loans. Since loans are disbursed upfront while interest and repayments are spread over a number of months or years, banks are exposed to a funding risk that is absent from bonds.

Bonds are carried on the balance sheets of investors at their daily market value. In the language of the financial community, bonds are "marked to market." Banks carry loans on their balance sheets at their face value.[12] Banks are required to maintain provisions against potential losses. Provisions are charged against income as a business expense that is generally not taxed. They rise and fall in response to changing assessments of risk and write-offs or write-downs of specific loans.

The most important aspect of bonds is that they are held by portfolio investors seeking higher returns through diversification and well-timed buy-

12. Bank loans that are taken out of a "hold to maturity account" and placed in a "trading account" or an "available for sale account" are marked to market.

ing and selling.[13] The dominant holders of emerging market bonds are investment funds. In the universe of such funds (known as mutual funds in the United States), relatively few are dedicated to investing exclusively in emerging market bonds. A larger share of emerging market bonds is held by thousands of other funds that are allowed to invest a small portion of their assets in high-yield securities. Critically, most of these managers are not taking risks, as banks do when they make loans. They are managing a pool of savings invested by many people, directly or indirectly through pension funds or employee-sponsored savings plans. They have a fiduciary responsibility to manage their assets in strict conformance with the criteria set forth in their prospectuses. Losses experienced in the course of observing those criteria are passed on to their clients. By contrast, bank depositors are almost totally protected against losses arising from bad loans. Other significant asset managers that invest in emerging market bonds include insurance companies, endowment funds, and hedge funds.[14]

From the perspective of the borrower, bond financing often appears to be an unattractive option compared with bank financing. One reason is that bond investors tend to be fickle. In periods when global liquidity has tightened for reasons beyond the control of the borrowing country, the cost of bond financing may become prohibitive. Banks can usually be found in tough circumstances to provide financing on acceptable terms. Another concern is that the underwriting fees associated with bond financing may look stiff relative to the fees charged for bank loans. In practice, however, both markets are highly competitive, and fees for each form of debt rise and fall to reflect changes in supply and demand.

In favorable market circumstances, bonds can be used to obtain a larger amount of money in a single operation with a longer maturity and at a lower interest rate spread than would be possible by means of a syndicated

13. Emerging market bonds offer yields close to those in the junk-bond category, the opposite end of the spectrum from the investment-grade category.

14. Hedge funds are vehicles for achieving exceptionally high returns by taking exceptional risks, often of a short-term speculative nature. They tend to be highly leveraged, meaning that their equity capital is small relative to the funds they have borrowed from banks and other sources. Hedge funds sometimes take large positions in a single bond issue or the bonds of a particular country. Although institutional investors hold most sovereign bonds, some issues are designed to be marketed to retail investors, especially in Europe where there is a stronger appetite for bonds relative to equity securities. In a restructuring of Ukraine's bond debt in 1999, it became apparent that one issue of bonds denominated in deutsche marks was widely held by thousands of retail investors in Germany. Special efforts were required to get these investors to exchange old bonds for new bonds. The multitude of retail investors holding Argentina's bonds will contribute to the complexity of the workout under way in mid-2003.

bank loan. In addition, the secondary market for bonds performs an important signaling function. Virtually every emerging market bond issue is traded every day, thereby establishing a yield curve for any sovereign borrower that has floated a number of issues. This curve defines a "country risk premium" that can be a highly sensitive indicator of investor sentiment.[15]

As a result of the many differences between bonds and bank loans, the attitudes of bondholders and banks in a sovereign workout tend to diverge. Banks are most concerned with maintaining a flow of interest payments and are relatively relaxed about deferring principal payments. Bond investors are primarily concerned with liquidity. They want to be able to sell today, even if it means selling at a loss relative to yesterday's market value.

Bond investors found themselves in awkward situations in the workouts that transpired after 1997. There was no established process—such as the London Club process—for negotiating the parameters of a bond restructuring with the sovereign debtors seeking relief. In the case of Russia in 1998, bondholder interests were informally taken into account by the bank steering committee formed to restructure Russia's Soviet-era debt. In the cases of Pakistan, Ukraine, and Ecuador in 1999, bonds were restructured by means of exchange offers prepared by investment bank advisors. The advisors consulted to varying degrees with bondholders, but there were no negotiations. The core policy issue addressed in this study is how to organize bond investors to negotiate timely and sound workouts in the future.

Suppliers and Other Claimants

A great deal of trade between companies in the industrial countries is financed without any backup insurance or guarantees because the parties involved have established strong track records of payment. By contrast, many trade transactions involving importers in emerging market countries depend on protection from export credit agencies or other third parties. When a borrower defaults, the insuring party or guarantor participates in the workout, not the supplier (exporter).

Suppliers sometimes view the cost of such protection as too expensive or unnecessary and therefore extend credit to the buyer instead of demanding payment in advance. This practice can lead to a situation where unguaran-

15. The country risk premium, measured in basis points (each equivalent to a hundredth of a percent), is the difference between the current yield on a risk-free, long-term benchmark bond (such as the ten-year U.S. Treasury bond) and the market yield for an emerging market bond of similar maturity. A widening spread can signal a weakening of confidence in the country's prospects. Well-managed countries react to such signals by implementing policy reforms designed to bolster confidence.

teed supplier credit accounts for a significant amount of the debt of a country in default. The treatment of suppliers in a financial crisis is less of an issue today than it was in the early 1990s because the buyers are less likely to be public sector entities or to be caught up in exchange restrictions. As a consequence, most supplier claims are worked out in the context of a country's domestic bankruptcy regime.[16]

The only other private sector claimants in a sovereign default worth mentioning are guarantors and leaseholders. Guarantors assume a claim when they pay off the original lender. This claim is then treated in the Paris Club if the guarantor is an official agency or in the London Club if it is a commercial bank. Leaseholders seldom account for a substantial amount of a national government's external debt. They do not normally participate in debt-restructuring negotiations but are sometimes required to restructure lease payments on comparable terms.

The Borrowers

Creditors have different motivations in a sovereign workout. Multilateral creditors are primarily concerned about preserving their preferred creditor status. Bilateral donor agencies have mixed objectives. Some are preoccupied with maximizing their recoveries; others are more concerned about protecting a market or advancing a specific political or humanitarian objective. Private creditors—banks, bond investors, and suppliers—tend to give priority to a single objective: minimizing their losses.

Borrowers are harder to categorize by motivation. Loosely, they appear to fall into two groups. Borrowers in the first group are preoccupied with access to future credit flows and will go to great lengths to reach a settlement consistent with market standards. Borrowers in the second group view workouts as a zero-sum game; the bigger the loss they can get creditors to accept, the better off they will be.

More conventionally, borrowers can be divided into four categories: sovereign authorities, other public sector borrowers (public sector enterprises and subsovereign entities), banks, and private companies.

16. The one outstanding case of suppliers organizing to pursue their claims involved Nigeria in 1983–84. A steering committee of suppliers was formed to negotiate a restructuring deal with the government. Outstanding supplier debt was exchanged for promissory notes issued by the Central Bank of Nigeria. See Clark (1986, p. 860).

Sovereign Authorities

Strictly speaking, there is only one sovereign borrower in each country: the government. In most countries the finance ministry is vested with the responsibility to enter into debt contracts on behalf of the government and to manage the stock of both internal and external debt.[17] Governments come and go, however. One of the risks associated with developing country debt is that a new government may have violent objections to debt contracts entered into by its predecessor. Some reflections on "odious debt" are presented in chapter 4.

Public Sector Enterprises

National governments everywhere have established enterprises that undertake commercial activities. These enterprises can be wholly owned by the government, or the government may be a majority or minority shareholder. They are found in every sector: mining, oil and gas, electric power, telecommunications, airports, plantations, strategic industries (steel, armaments, automobiles), and even hospitals. Most are able to borrow externally only if repayment is guaranteed by the government, but some are legally empowered to borrow independently. A few are considered to be more creditworthy than their national governments.

The treatment of debt owed by public sector enterprises can vary from case to case. In some situations the foreign debt of these enterprises is restructured on the same basis as strictly sovereign debt. In other situations the foreign debt of public sector enterprises is restructured under the country's domestic bankruptcy regime on the same basis as the debt of strictly private companies.

Subsovereign Entities

Generally speaking, administrative regions (provinces, municipalities, and the like) within countries do not borrow externally and often are barred from such activity by law. The trend, however, is toward more borrowing of this kind, as more jurisdictions are able to get rated by an international credit rating agency. The treatment of subsovereign borrowing following a sovereign default has not been well established because the amounts involved so far have been negligible.

---

17. In a number of countries, the central bank acts as the government's agent in entering into and managing foreign loans.

Banks

Moving from the public sector to the private sector, banks have a role in every country's payment system that makes it impractical to treat them like other corporate borrowers in a financial crisis.[18] The impact of such a crisis on domestic banks depends critically on the extent that they have been allowed to engage in foreign currency transactions. Banking regulations, capital controls, and exchange restrictions differ widely from country to country. In the most restrictive countries banks are not allowed to borrow or lend in foreign currency, nor are they allowed to accept foreign currency deposits. Consequently, when a crisis occurs, domestic banks are affected only to the extent that their borrowers are.

More typically, banks are deeply impacted when a country experiences a financial crisis. A sharp depreciation of the domestic currency in the course of a crisis causes companies to default on their loans from domestic banks as well as from foreign creditors. These defaults leave banks with insufficient cash flow to pay interest to their depositors or to service their own external obligations.

The critical difference between banks and nonbank businesses is that insolvent banks cannot simply be sold off at a loss to the highest bidder. Their loans back up their deposits. A bank's loans can only be written down without jeopardizing depositors to the extent of its equity and retained earnings. When this happens to an isolated bank, it can be taken over by the deposit insurance system, if one exists, or be sold to a strong bank. When a financial crisis affects a substantial segment of the banking system, the government must intervene to recapitalize the affected banks so that they are in a position to pay depositors in full. Otherwise, the entire banking system will be vulnerable to a collapse as depositors lose confidence in one bank after another and rush to withdraw their deposits. In extreme cases, private banks are effectively nationalized to prevent such a collapse.

Private Companies

Private companies are not directly affected by a sovereign default, but they can be seriously affected indirectly in two ways. One is through the broad impact on the economy. As government spending is slashed to avoid an unsustainable budget deficit, many companies experience a drop in their

18. Most developing countries have prominent banks that are wholly or majority-owned by the national government. In some countries these state-owned banks dominate the banking system. For the purposes of this discussion, ownership is not an important distinction.

sales. Another impact is through their funding costs. Domestic interest rates are often raised as part of an economic recovery program. For private companies that rely on foreign financing, the spreads they must pay also tend to escalate and can quickly become prohibitive.

As noted in the section on banks, a financial crisis that produces a sharp depreciation of the country's currency can render a large segment of the corporate sector insolvent. In such cases workouts are carried out in the context of the country's domestic bankruptcy regime. That sounds simple, but it is usually a complex process because of the deficiencies in many regimes and the various steps that governments can take to accelerate workouts and restore normalcy to the country's economic and financial life.

4

Fundamental Issues

Why is sovereign default such a big deal? What makes it so difficult to prevent financial crises in developing countries when they occur so rarely in the most advanced countries? Does debt relief provide an incentive for countries to postpone economic reforms essential for sustainable growth? How do global political interests affect sovereign debt workouts? In what sense are private creditors being bailed out when they are reporting huge losses?

The answers suggested in this chapter highlight the author's orientation toward the policy issues discussed in the chapters that follow.

Respect for Contracts

The current debate about workout machinery is being carried out at a stratospheric level of abstraction. At this height, it is easy to lose sight of the bedrock of the international financial system. Respect for contractual obligations is part of the bedrock.

A modern market economy is a system based on rules (the rule of law). It is the antithesis of a discretionary system where power is exercised without constraints. The financial dimension of a market economy depends on the rules adopted and the manner of enforcing them. After all, money is not something you can eat. It is a symbol of a claim, a form of debt. Its value derives from the faith people have in it. Financial instruments of all kinds are variations on money. They range from a simple IOU to complex derivatives designed to extract specific risks from a transaction and assign them to a third party. Financial instruments serve their intended purpose only as long as people have confidence in them. The confidence level is above 95 percent in a modern economy. This means that the parties to financial contracts fully meet their contractual obligations almost 100 percent of the time.

The global economy is an extension of the market economies that evolved over the past 200 years in Europe and North America. The efficiency of the global economy depends just as much on the confidence people place in cross-border contracts. Indeed, respect for contracts may be more important at the international level because enforcement mechanisms, as pointed out in chapter 2, are inherently weaker.

The conventional view is that effective contract enforcement requires a fully developed judicial system such as those found in the United States and Europe. The evidence is not so clear. China offers a fascinating example of a country with strong enforcement despite having an unreliable legal system. China's judicial system is clearly weak by the standards of OECD members. For example, China's banking system is extremely fragile because of deficiencies in China's bankruptcy laws and enforcement mechanisms. A large fraction of the system's loans are to public sector enterprises that have been losing money, but banks cannot carry out successful bankruptcy proceedings against these borrowers. Consequently, they tend to roll over principal payments and capitalize interest payments. Yet China surpassed the United States in 2002 as the world's largest destination for foreign investment.[1] China could not have achieved this result without providing investors a high degree of confidence that their contracts would be respected. In effect, the political authorities at various levels in the country provide the enforcement that Chinese courts are unable to provide.

Every sovereign workout tests the bedrock of the international financial system. Every workout is triggered by a failure (sometimes imminent, not actual) to meet contractual obligations and entails an effort to cure this failure. Changes in the machinery of workouts can have an impact far beyond the individual countries that have recourse to it. Conceptually, any change

1. Dan Roberts and James Kynge, "Comments and Analysis: China," *Financial Times*, February 4, 2003, p. 13.

will either strengthen respect for contracts internationally or weaken it. Changes in the direction of strengthening should encourage the growth of productive capital flows and hence global growth and welfare. Changes in the direction of weakening carry risks for the global system. It is easy to exaggerate these risks, and they are impossible to quantify. But ignoring them would be foolish.

The instinct to establish rules for sovereign workouts is understandable because discretionary approaches at the level of the firm or household are associated with huge inefficiencies and inequities. As discussed in more detail later, however, the sovereign workout process depends ultimately on political judgments much more than the kinds of technical analyses used in workouts for bankrupt or insolvent companies under national regimes. A discretionary approach at the international level that reinforces respect for contractual obligations may be more viable even if it appears to be biased against sovereign debtors and in favor of their official and private creditors.

Preventing Crises

Before plunging into the thickets of the Paris Club and the London Club and the thornier debate about bond restructuring, it is appropriate to underscore the importance of crisis prevention. A starting point is the adage that an ounce of prevention is worth a pound of cure. That is as true for national economies as it is for men and women and children. The social costs of a sovereign debt crisis to the country concerned can be staggering. The secondary effects on other countries can be terrible and conceivably larger in some circumstances. By contrast, the losses ultimately borne by private investors and lenders are relatively small. They are taking calculated risks in their search for yield or profit. If their gains over time did not exceed their losses, they would not in theory be engaged in this business. Few, if any, banks or institutional investors have gone out of business in the Bretton Woods era because of sovereign defaults.

The G-7 architects have labored diligently since 1995 to identify measures that can help to prevent financial crises in developing countries, and many of these are being actively implemented. The IMF has been at the center of this effort. All the multilateral development banks are making contributions and so are many bilateral donor agencies. Success, of course, depends mostly on actions taken by the developing countries themselves. Some have made remarkable progress. Mexico and Korea come to mind immediately. Others are advancing slowly, and some are falling behind.

The *sustainability* of a country's debt (internal as well as external, private sector as well as public) comes up in this context. A country's stock of debt is said to be sustainable if the burden of servicing it is not producing any strains and if current policies and trends indicate that the debt-service burden will not increase in the future relative to the borrowers' capacity to pay. In theory, a country with a sustainable stock of debt will not suffer a default. In practice, however, sustainability is a judgment reflecting probabilities. There is always a risk that a shock will come out of the blue and sharply reduce a country's capacity to pay.

As part of the IMF's work to prevent crises, it has developed a sophisticated methodology to assess debt sustainability by means of quantitative indicators.[2] This is a huge challenge because in the final analysis sustainability hinges on the ability of a country to implement policy reforms in a timely fashion. This ability depends above all on the political forces at play at some point in the future. Private and official creditors are also assessing debt sustainability continuously, implicitly if not explicitly, in the process of extending new credits and deciding whether to hold or sell their outstanding claims. When private creditors conclude that a country's debt has become unsustainable, they will unload what they are holding. Most official creditors do not have this option or obligation, but they can cut back on new commitments and they can exert political pressure on the country to undertake policy reforms that will restore sustainability. Debtor countries that do not make their own assessments of sustainability, do not monitor the sentiment of creditors, and do not respond to signs that confidence is eroding should not be surprised to find themselves on a path to default.

Still, the G-7 and the IMF could do much more in the area of crisis prevention. In particular, more could be done to head off looming crises before the point of default. It is hard to believe that the only alternative to Argentina's messy default at the end of 2001 was a massive infusion of official financing. Surely some kind of cooperative strategy along the lines of the Brady Plan (for reducing sovereign debt owed to commercial banks at the end of the 1980s debt crisis) stood a chance of reducing the damage to Argentina's economy and advancing its recovery.

Thus it is puzzling and somewhat unsettling to see how much time and effort the G-7 and the IMF have been devoting to developing better workout machinery. Reallocating attention from workouts to crisis prevention would seem to hold out the prospect of larger benefits for the global system.

2. IMF (2002a).

One useful step would be to help politicians and the broad public understand why economically advanced countries seem to be immune to sovereign default. Box 4-1 represents a possible starting point.

Adjustment versus Financing

One of the basic policy choices in a workout situation is the trade-off between *adjustment* and *financing*. Adjustment, in this context, represents the debtor country's share of the workout burden. It consists of policy reforms that will push the balance of payments back toward equilibrium, make it possible for the country to resume servicing its external debt obligations, and restore its creditworthiness. These reforms fall into four major categories: fiscal policy, monetary policy, exchange rate policy, and structural policies. Cuts in budget expenditures and actions to raise revenues serve to reduce the country's budget deficit and its claim on scarce domestic savings. Higher interest rates help to slow down an unsustainable expansion of credit and bring inflation under control. Devaluation or depreciation of the domestic currency helps by discouraging imports and encouraging exports. Structural reforms remove barriers to productive investment and job creation. They cover a vast range of activities including strengthening banking systems, improving public sector and corporate governance, and reinforcing the rule of law.

Financing, in this context, represents money (foreign exchange) the country may receive from external sources in myriad forms. One form is *new money*—new loan commitments from official and private sources. Another is debt relief. The trade-off occurs because the more adjustment a debtor country undertakes, the less financing it requires from the outside. In other words, the bigger the adjustment effort, the less debt relief it will need. This paradox exists at the heart of every sovereign debt workout. It complicates the use of debt relief as a carrot to reward front-loaded recovery programs.

Since the social costs of adjustment—in the form of unemployment and lower income—can be substantial, countries in distress have an incentive to seek as much financing as possible to lighten the burden of adjustment. Creditors, just as naturally, are always pressing countries to adjust more in order to lighten the burden of financing (new money, debt relief) they must provide. There is no objectively definable degree of appropriate adjustment in these circumstances. Clearly there are practical limits to how far and fast a country can adjust without precipitating a breakdown in social order, but

Box 4-1. How Do Countries Become Immune to Default?

None of the mature democracies in the world have come close to a sovereign default in the Bretton Woods era. From time to time, warnings that the United States is headed toward a default—or Japan or Italy or some other country—capture headlines for a brief moment. But a default by one of these countries on its foreign debt is almost inconceivable. Why is this, and what prevents developing countries from acquiring a similar immunity?

Three major features of mature democracies militate against sovereign defaults:

A deep domestic capital market. All of the mature democracies have borrowed extensively from internal sources; their borrowing in foreign currencies is small relative to their domestic borrowing or nonexistent (for example, the United States). The less advanced developing countries by and large do not have domestic capital markets that they can tap to finance budget deficits or infrastructure investment. The more advanced developing countries are all working to deepen their domestic capital markets, and they are expected to become less dependent on external borrowing in the years ahead.

An abiding commitment to macroeconomic stability. Part of the "social contract" in mature democracies is avoiding high levels of inflation that would discourage investment and erode the value of savings. Governments viewed as fiscally profligate tend to get voted out before serious damage is done. One device for reinforcing this stability is central bank independence. Central banks in the mature democracies have established strong track records of monetary discipline. They will not print money to validate a government's

it is hard to make a convincing case that one additional reform at the margin would be catastrophic.

Another trade-off works in the other direction. A workout that leaves a country little room for error may have to be repeated in another year or two if the adjustment program does not achieve its objectives because of flaws in design, weaknesses in execution, or events beyond the control of the government. At the extreme, a failed program can make creditors worse off by requiring them to accept less favorable terms in a second round of restructuring. In every sovereign workout, the creditors perform a technical analysis to measure the country's "ability to pay." By providing somewhat more financing than technically required, creditors may improve the odds that the country will regain its creditworthiness quickly and permanently.

unsustainable spending habits. Another device is a floating exchange rate. Together these and other devices form a system of automatic stabilizers that helps to prevent a sovereign debt crisis (or a financial crisis of the kind that the United Kingdom experienced in 1992). Most of the advanced developing countries have a strong commitment to macroeconomic stability, but they have not established track records that are long enough to bring country risk spreads down to negligible levels.

A political system that makes transitions smoothly. The most difficult feature for developing countries to match is long-term political stability. Contrast the financial crises in Mexico from 1976 to 1994, linked to presidential elections, with the absence of a crisis in the 2000 election year. Recall the troubled leadership transitions in 1997 in Thailand, Indonesia, and South Korea. Look at the anxieties in 2002 associated with election cycles in Argentina, Brazil, and Turkey. A country that can elect liberal and conservative governments in succession without a major change in its macroeconomic orientation belongs to a special club. Policymakers who think they can achieve durable economic and financial stability without a political system that delivers smooth transitions from one government to the next are not being realistic.

Each of these features is difficult for a developing country to achieve and all are interrelated. For example, it is next to impossible to create a deep capital market when the underlying inflation rate is above 10 percent a year. The benefits associated with these features are so great that the citizens of every emerging market country should be pressing their governments to solidify them.

A corollary of the adjustment-financing trade-off is that debt relief by itself does almost nothing to improve a country's growth prospects. Policies make all the difference. As long as a country's policies discourage productive investment and employment, no amount of debt relief will put the country on a path of sustainable growth. That is a basic reason why creditors have little interest in entering into debt-restructuring negotiations before they see a credible reform program. In their eyes the quality of the program reveals the country's "willingness to pay." Experience suggests that good policies cannot be purchased with debt relief. Granting such relief makes sense only as a reward for good policies. By the same token, enlightened governments struggling to recover from a crisis do not start by trying to obtain as much debt relief as possible. They understand that their future economic prospects depend more on the success of their adjustment programs than the amount of debt- and debt-service reduction they extract from external creditors.

Odious Debt and the Political Dimension of Workouts

Much of the literature produced on sovereign debt workouts ignores or downplays political factors. That is unfortunate because sovereign workouts are intensely political exercises. Some of the public misunderstanding that surrounds workouts may be attributable to the exaggerated emphasis on economic and technical factors.[3]

It is hard to find a near default or an actual default that has been caused primarily by economic factors such as a rise in import prices or the loss of an export market. Economic factors loomed large in the debt crises of the 1980s, but a number of countries (especially in Asia) managed to avoid debt restructuring. Their successes were directly related to their capacity to implement reforms—a political factor, not an economic one. Several crises have had purely political origins. The crisis experienced by Pakistan in 1998–99, for example, was directly related to the suspension of aid flows following nuclear weapons tests.

In extreme cases new governments have repudiated the debt of predecessor governments. Over the past century, that occurred most often in the context of a communist takeover (Russia in 1917, China in 1949, Cuba in 1959). These episodes and the current case of Iraq have called attention to the concept of "odious debt"—the idea that a country should not be expected to honor the payment obligations associated with debt that was used for "odious" purposes such as suppressing the population by force or lining the pockets of the ruling elite. In the Bretton Woods era, there has been an implicit quid pro quo. As long as the new government accepts responsibility for debt of dubious benefit that it has inherited, creditors will restructure this debt on generous terms. The most remarkable illustration of this quid pro quo was the restructuring of Indonesia's debt following the collapse of the Sukarno regime in the late 1960s (see chapter 7).

Another manifestation of the political dimension of debt workouts is the campaign led by an NGO coalition under the banner "Jubilee 2000" to persuade multilateral and bilateral donor agencies to write off debts owed by the poorest countries. This campaign had a religious-ethical orientation rooted in a biblical practice of debt forgiveness on special occasions, and related to

---

3. Macmillan (1995, p. 78) is one of the few writers who have squarely addressed this aspect of sovereign workouts: "A debt crisis is a highly political event."

the doctrines of several religions that view debt (especially in usurious forms) as an evil. The pressure generated by Jubilee 2000 succeeded in obtaining some forgiveness that otherwise would probably not have been granted. Such pressures are not always healthy, however. In cases where a country does have the capacity to service its debt, populist appeals for cutting payments—usually to free resources for social programs—may lead governments to take steps that damage their creditworthiness and thereby have an adverse impact on living standards.

The recovery stage of a workout is also loaded with political factors, starting with the design of the debtor country's adjustment program. The content of all such programs is critically shaped by each government's ability to withstand pressures from politically powerful groups (vested interests) that would be adversely affected by specific reforms. Furthermore, the amount of exceptional financing provided by multilateral agencies and bilateral donors is only loosely related to the strength of these programs. It is driven as much or more by geopolitical considerations, such as breaking out of the Soviet bloc (Poland in 1991) or supporting the campaign against terrorism (Jordan in 2002). Even the level of financing by the "apolitical" IMF is influenced by the political objectives of the G-7 (as with Turkey after 2001).

People who overlook political factors will miss early signs of most crises. People who ignore political factors will have difficulty designing effective recovery programs or negotiating successful workouts.

Who's Bailing Out Whom?

The most confusing phrase encountered in the business of sovereign debt workouts is *bail out*. The public interest would be well served by a ban on the phrase in this context. It is normally used to characterize financing provided by official agencies to defaulting countries as a misappropriation of scarce taxpayer resources for the benefit of private sector creditors. Specifically, these funds allegedly allow private creditors to escape or limit their losses.

One problem with the phrase is factual. The IMF and the other providers of emergency financing to debt-distressed countries have not lost a penny of taxpayer money in these operations since the first multilateral workout in 1956.[4] Every penny has been repaid, and in some cases the official agencies

4. This is a slight exaggeration. In the 1956–94 period bilateral donor agencies provided some emergency assistance in a number of cases, and some of this assistance was restructured in subsequent Paris Club operations, occasionally with some element of net present value reduction. The bilateral agencies have virtually stopped making loans of this kind.

have booked a profit relative to their regular lending operations or cost of borrowing funds. The basic reason why no money has been lost is that the multilateral agencies are treated as preferred creditors.

If anyone is being bailed out, it is the debtor country.[5] Emergency financing helps to mitigate the shock of adjustment. Instead of experiencing a 10 percent contraction in its gross domestic product (GDP) and a 50 percent increase in unemployment in the year following the crisis, for example, the country may get by with only a 5 percent contraction of output and a 25 percent increase in unemployment. Secondary effects on other countries are also attenuated. It is true that in the process of helping the debtor country some private creditors may be able to exit without a loss and others may experience a smaller loss than would be the case without any emergency financing. So long as the country recovers and pays back its emergency financing in full, however, taxpayers should not object to having their funds used for this purpose. The nightmare that people should worry about has yet to happen. That would occur if a country receiving a large package of emergency assistance did not recover and the emergency assistance was not repaid.[6]

Efforts by the G-7 and the IMF to ensure burden sharing by private creditors in sovereign debt crises since 1995 have provoked the opposite concern. The private sector may be bailing out the public sector. To illustrate this concern, imagine a country that has defaulted. Half of its debt is owed to the World Bank, which is a preferred creditor and therefore does not forgive debt. The other half is owed to private creditors. A technical and judgmental analysis concludes that the country's debt must be reduced by 25 percent to achieve sustainability. Because the World Bank does not forgive debt, the private creditors will have to accept a 50 percent "haircut" (write-off of their claims). In effect, half of their loss represents a gift to the World Bank that saves the bank from seeking more capital (taxpayer money) to shore up its

5. This point was made as far back as 1969, in the section on debt relief in the Pearson Commission's report: "The primary objective of debt refinancing or consolidation has been to 'bail out' the borrower by providing strictly short-run accommodation." Commission on International Development (1969, pp. 156–57).

6. Something close to this happened in the 1980s, when the IMF provided relatively large amounts of financing to Sudan, Zaire, Liberia, and several other small countries that experienced extreme political instability and consequently lost the capacity to repay this financing. These exposures are being reduced without a loss by means of complex operations largely funded by grants from the major donor countries. The G-7 and IMF expose themselves to a similar risk each time they organize emergency financing for a major borrowing country such as Russia or Turkey or Argentina or Brazil.

balance sheet. This is a gross oversimplification of the issue, but it reflects a legitimate concern.

This discussion is not intended as an argument for ending the preferred creditor status of the multilateral agencies and making them take haircuts along with all other creditors. The rich hierarchy of creditor claims that has evolved over generations contributes to the resilience of the international financial system. Treating all claims as equal would weaken the system. It is, rather, an appeal to the G-7 and the IMF to promote better public understanding in two ways: first, by linking the commitment of emergency financing to mitigating the direct impacts of a crisis on the residents of the country concerned and the indirect impacts on the rest of the world; and second, by pointing out that the risks of losses associated with such commitments are relatively low, and probably lower than the risks historically associated with domestic rescue efforts.

Nor is this an argument that official financing should be used more often or in larger amounts to mitigate the impacts of a crisis. Concerns that a generous attitude toward such financing will encourage imprudent lending by private creditors are legitimate. By the same token, concerns that an "easy" workout procedure will encourage countries to seek debt restructuring as an alternative to policy reforms (adjustment) are legitimate. Much of the power of complex systems comes from a delicate balance of opposing forces.

In the area of sovereign debt workouts, the challenge for the G-7 architects and the IMF is to find an approach in each case that divides the burden—the losses absorbed or the efforts contributed—among the debtor country, its commercial creditors, its bilateral official "friends," and the multilateral agencies in some appropriate fashion. There are no formulas to facilitate this task, nor can there be. The political variables are different in every case. They will determine what can and cannot be done. They will determine how well or poorly the chosen approach will be received. And they may well determine the results.

5

The Paris Club

For most people a club is a fixed place for social interaction with a restricted membership. In the world of international politics and finance, however, clubs have been small groups with a much more ad hoc character. Several groups of creditor countries formed spontaneously in the 1950s to restructure debt owed by a particular country and, following conventions of the time, were called "clubs." One of them, the Paris Club, evolved to become part of the machinery of the international financial system, although it remained largely ad hoc.[1]

1. Much of the material in this chapter is drawn from Rieffel (1984) and Rieffel (1985). Despite the passage of time, the Paris Club continues to operate largely along the lines described in these essays. Two prominent Paris Club chairmen have written accounts of its operation at critical points in time. See Camdessus (1984) and Trichet (1989). A somewhat more recent account can be found in Sevigny (1990). A discussion of current practices from the U.S. government's perspective can be found in U.S. Department of State (1999). IMF (2001c) contains a short primer on the Paris Club, a list of all restructuring operations by bilateral official agencies from 1976 to 2000, a glossary of terms, and other useful information. Other accounts of Paris Club operations can be found in Bitterman (1973), Nowzad and others (1981), Hardy (1982), Hawn (1984), Dillon (1985), UN Center on Transnational Corporations (1989), Kuhn and Guzman (1990), and Kearney (1993).

The Paris Club grew organically out of a series of negotiations with countries experiencing balance-of-payments problems in the 1950s and 1960s for the narrow purpose of restructuring debt owed to bilateral donor agencies.[2] Its principles and procedures were codified at the end of the 1970s in the context of the North-South Dialogue. The number of Paris Club negotiations grew exponentially in the 1980s, and they were generally completed quickly and smoothly. A serious problem emerged toward the end of the 1980s when the Paris Club exhausted the relief it could provide by rescheduling payments one year at a time for a group of slow-growing, low-income countries. It began to negotiate debt-reduction agreements with these countries.

In the 1990s the Paris Club moved in two contradictory directions. For roughly forty heavily indebted poor countries, the Paris Club departed from its normal rules to grant progressively more generous debt reduction with a view to reducing the burden of foreign debt below an agreed threshold. For the non-HIPCs (mostly middle- and upper-income developing countries), especially those that had borrowed substantially from private sources, the Paris Club maintained its policy of not engaging in debt reduction but began to apply its principle of burden sharing more broadly and more unilaterally to force bondholders to reduce their claims on individual countries. In effect the G-7 architects used the Paris Club to cut back on the commitment of public sector resources required to resolve financial crises in non-HIPCs by increasing the losses absorbed by bondholders and other private creditors.

This chapter focuses on the origins of the Paris Club process and how it operates today. The emphasis is on cases of sovereign debt restructuring involving non-HIPCs. Since Paris Club operations with HIPCs are viewed here as aid exercises rather than debt exercises, they fall outside the scope of this book. They are, however, a source of confusion in the current debate about debt relief for developing countries. Consequently chapter 9 is devoted to explaining the HIPC Initiative and why HIPC-style debt reduction is not being considered for non-HIPCs like Argentina.

The G-7 architects have confronted two basic challenges in the course of their recent burden-sharing campaign. One has been to preserve the respect for contractual obligations that is part of the bedrock of the international financial system, while also promoting economic growth in developing countries. The other has been to maintain a multilateral approach to restructuring

---

2. These include agencies that provide financing for exports (machinery, agricultural commodities, military hardware, and the like), for development projects, and for other foreign policy activities.

debt owed to bilateral donor agencies without unduly restricting the ability of individual donor countries to advance their foreign policy objectives.

The Young Paris Club, 1956–75

The Paris Club process was born in the Hague in 1955.[3] Six leading European countries decided to pursue a multilateral approach to clearing imbalances that had built up under their bilateral payments agreements with Brazil.[4] These agreements were a product of the inconvertibility of the European currencies that continued after World War II. Each agreement had different terms, which led to a pattern of inequitable treatment in settling the imbalances. The effect of the Hague Club agreement was to allow Brazil to pool credit balances acquired in transactions with the six participating countries and then to use these credits to settle debit balances with any of the six. As a result, a source of trade distortion was eliminated. The system of bilateral payment agreements evaporated as the European countries made their currencies fully convertible during the 1950s, but the practice of multilateral negotiations with debtor countries endured. A similar negotiation between an enlarged group of European countries and Argentina took place in Paris in 1956, shortly after the overthrow of the Peron regime. This negotiation is now cited as the first Paris Club operation.[5]

More than a decade was required, however, for France to establish an effective monopoly over the process for restructuring debt owed to bilateral donor agencies by developing countries and to firmly attach the "Paris Club" label to this process. In the meantime Brazil went back to the Hague Club in 1961 and 1964 for more debt restructuring. Four debt negotiations with Ghana were held in London between 1966 and 1974. Peru convened meetings with creditors in Brussels and Lima in 1969 but was unable to reach a consensus and proceeded to conclude a set of bilateral restructurings. The Paris Club also had some short-lived competition from the aid consortiums

3. The material in this section is drawn largely from Friedman (1983, pp. 108–110). See also U.S. National Advisory Council (January–June 1956, p. 9).

4. The countries were Austria, Belgium, Germany, Italy, Netherlands, and the United Kingdom. The first Paris Club negotiation in which the United States participated appears to be with Brazil in 1964. The United States made a series of "exchange and stabilization" agreements with ten different Latin American countries plus the Philippines in the 1950s and early 1960s. Most were designed to help these countries avoid arrears on debts owed by private sector borrowers to private creditors. Many were concluded in conjunction with IMF standby arrangements. U.S. National Advisory Council (FY1958 to FY1962).

5. Denmark, France, Luxembourg, Norway, Sweden, and Switzerland joined the six creditor countries participating in the Brazil negotiation.

for India and Pakistan, where debt relief was negotiated six times for India and three times for Pakistan between 1968 and 1976. With these exceptions, all of the debt-restructuring negotiations by developing countries with bilateral donor agencies since 1956 have taken place in Paris and have followed Paris Club rules.[6] The case of Argentina, summarized in box 5-1, illustrates the fuzzy relationship between export credit agencies and commercial banks in sovereign debt workouts during the 1956–65 period.

The point of this brief history is that the Paris Club was not the product of an "architecture" exercise by the G-7 countries, the IMF, or any other official body. It began as a pragmatic solution to a specific problem. Although it had no formal principles or rules at the beginning, it was imbued with the spirit of international cooperation that has been a hallmark of the Bretton Woods system.

The Middle-Aged Paris Club, 1975–95

Debt problems among developing countries began to occur with increasing frequency in the late 1960s and early 1970s. At this point, the principles and rules of the Paris Club were still unwritten but had become firmly established in the practices of the creditor countries (and the IMF). During the course of the North-South Dialogue in the 1970s, developing countries attacked the Paris Club for being opaque, inequitable, and insensitive to development goals. In the first of three global debt debates over the next thirty years, they proposed the establishment of permanent machinery for restructuring debt, to be known as the International Debt Commission. The creditor countries successfully resisted this and other radical solutions but did agree to codify in a UN resolution the principles and procedures that had guided Paris Club negotiations during its first twenty years. The resolution represented a major step toward institutionalizing the Paris Club.

The Paris Club emerged from the North-South Dialogue as a mature institution, a familiar and reliable piece of machinery. During the 1980s it met the challenge of a much heavier caseload without any major changes in its principles and rules. The Paris Club also moved out of the limelight, as the machinery for restructuring debt owed to commercial banks took center stage.

6. In a small number of cases the negotiating forum was given a different label (for example, the OECD Consortium for Turkey in the late 1970s), or the document setting forth the rescheduling terms was called a Memorandum of Understanding instead of an Agreed Minute. These were purely cosmetic changes.

Box 5-1. The Case of Argentina in the 1950s and 1960s

Argentina emerged from World War II as one of the few developing countries that did not default on its bonds during the Depression of the 1930s, although it did convert some bonds to lower coupon rates and longer maturities. By 1950, however, substantial arrears had accumulated on debts owed by Argentine private sector borrowers to U.S. banks and suppliers. The U.S. Export-Import Bank made a four-year refinancing loan in 1950 to clear these arrears.

Following the regime change in 1955, Argentina's debit balances under bilateral trade agreements with a "club" of European countries were consolidated in 1956, rescheduled over varying terms up to ten years, and made payable in the currency of any club member. This arrangement was subsequently designated as the first Paris Club operation. At the same time, the U.S. Export-Import Bank extended two credit lines to ease Argentina's payment strains.

In 1958 a group of U.S. banks extended a refinancing loan to clear a new pile of arrears. A year later a more substantial round of refinancing was organized, including an IMF standby, a repurchase (swap) agreement with the U.S. Treasury, and refinancing loans from a consortium of nine U.S. banks and another of fifty-four European banks. The terms of this arrangement were extended again in 1960 and a third time in 1963.

Toward the end of the 1980s, however, a problem developed with the Paris Club's operations involving a group of more than forty low-income countries that were dependent on financing from official sources. After successive rescheduling operations over a number of years with many of these countries, the Paris Club exhausted the relief it could provide in this form and began to move into a debt-reduction mode.

A bigger problem developed in the 1990s. The Mexican peso crisis at the end of 1994 was the first in a series of financial crises over the next seven years that focused attention on burden sharing among debtor countries, the multilateral agencies, Paris Club creditors, and private creditors. In a nutshell, large packages of official financing of the kind mobilized for Mexico were attacked for bailing out private creditors. Bond debt was replacing bank debt as the dominant form of long-term financing for the more advanced developing countries, but many bond investors objected to using the commercial bank–oriented London Club machinery for negotiating

In 1960 the terms of the 1956 Paris Club agreement were extended, but Argentina's payments situation remained precarious. An even bigger refinancing exercise took place in 1962–63, at which point Argentina had about $2.6 billion of sovereign debt and $1 billion of private sector debt owed to external creditors. After protracted negotiations with the IMF, the related financing arrangements included a third extension of the 1956 Paris Club agreement, a new repurchase agreement with the U.S. Treasury, a balance-of-payments loan from the U.S. aid program, and a refinancing of payments due to the U.S. Export-Import Bank.

In 1965 another refinancing was organized, centered on a Paris Club operation that included the United States as a full participant for the first time. A new stabilization program, built around a 25 percent devaluation in 1967, was supported by another IMF standby and new credit lines from a consortium of U.S. and European banks. Argentina began the 1970s with a weak balance of payments but was able to manage without further Paris Club support during the decade despite the oil crisis and global recession. This achievement did, however, depend on IMF arrangements concluded in 1972, 1975, and 1976, and an abundance of commercial bank financing provided on attractive terms. These chickens came home to roost after the Mexican crisis in 1982.

Source: Drawn from Bitterman (1973, pp.108–18).

bond workouts. The G-7 began experimenting with various ways to achieve private sector involvement, its new euphemism for burden sharing. These experiments provoked a strong reaction from the financial industry, and part of this reaction was directed at the Paris Club's policy of not reducing debt in operations with non-HIPCs.

During 2002, pushed in large part by the controversy surrounding the IMF's proposal to create permanent machinery for sovereign debt workouts (chapter 11), the Paris Club considered various ways to adapt its principles and rules to facilitate sensible workouts with countries that depend primarily on private capital flows. These deliberations culminated in "a new Paris Club approach to debt restructuring" unveiled by the G-8 finance ministers in the communiqué for their meeting on May 17, 2003, preceding the Evian summit in June. The new, staged approach went clearly in the direction recommended in this study (chapter 12). In particular, it expanded the options for treating the unsustainable debt of non-HIPCs to include debt reduction, and it stressed the importance of coordination (not simply cooperation) between the Paris Club and private creditors.[7]

The "Personality" of the Paris Club

The chairman of the first Paris Club negotiation (with Argentina in 1956) was André de Lattre, in his capacity as deputy to the directeur des finances extérieures (director of external finance) in the French finance ministry.[8] Over the next ten years either this director or his deputy served as the chairman of the Paris Club. In 1966 Finances Extérieures was merged into the Trésor (Treasury), and for most years since then the chairman of the Paris Club has been the directeur du Trésor, who also has served as the G-7 finance deputy. From early days the responsible official at the next level down was designated as a cochairman of the Paris Club and presided over some of the negotiations. As the pace of work intensified at the end of the 1980s, a third official was selected to share the burden of chairing negotiations and given the title of vice chairman. The leaders of the Paris Club since its inception are listed in table 5-1.

The Paris Club has been supported administratively by members of the staff of the French finance ministry headed by a secretary general. This arrangement is in effect the quid pro quo for keeping the Paris Club in Paris. Debtor countries do not have to pay a fee to the creditors when they negotiate restructuring terms, so there are no revenues to cover the expenses of operating the Paris Club. At the current level of activity, these expenses are considerable. The secretariat deals with a large volume of correspondence, meets with a constant stream of visitors from debtor countries and the private sector, arranges for simultaneous translation (into English and French at least) during the negotiations, finds meeting space, and manages public relations. The French finance ministry bears the entire load, a feature that explains some of the idiosyncrasies of the process discussed below. The officials responsible for this work have struggled for years to stay on top of their workload, which has been hard to do with the natural turnover of personnel. As a result, less information about the evolution of the Paris Club is available than analysts and scholars would wish.[9]

7. The key sentence in the communiqué was: "Given the need to preserve access to private capital, the Paris Club should tailor its response to the specific financial situation of each country rather than defining standard terms under this new approach." www.g8.fr (May 18, 2003).

8. De Lattre (1999).

9. Most of the members are represented in Paris Club meetings by mid-level officials from their finance ministries. The rate of turnover among these representatives also contributes to the weak institutional memory.

Table 5-1. Paris Club Leadership

Position and officer	Dates of service	Position and officer	Dates of service
Chairman		Ariane Obolensky	1992–94
André de Lattre	1956–58	Francis Mayer	1995–97
Jean Sadrin	1959–60	(unfilled)	1997–99
André de Lattre	1960–66	Stéphane Pallez	2000–present
Claude Pierre-Brossolette	1966–67		
Daniel Deguen	1968–71	*Vice chairman*	
Claude Pierre-Brossolette	1971–74	Anne Le Lorier	1989–93
Jacques de Larosière	1974–78	Bertrand de Mazières	1993–96
J. Y. Haberer	1978–82	Philippe de Fontaine-Vive	1996–2000
Michel Camdessus	1982–84	Bruno Bézard	2000–01
Philippe Jurgensen	1984–85	Ambroise Fayolle	2001–present
Jean-Claude Trichet	1985–93		
Christian Noyer	1993–97	*Secretary general*	
Francis Mayer	1997–99	Elisabeth Cheyvialle	1980–81
Jean Lemierre	1999–2000	Elisabeth Guigou	1981–82
Jean-Pierre Jouyet	2000–present	Pierre de Lauzun	1982–84
		Patrice Durand	1984–86
Cochairman		Jean-Marc Pillu	1986–88
Guy Nebot	1970–75	Nicolas Jachiet	1988–91
(unfilled)	1975–78	Jean-François Cirelli	1991–94
Michel Camdessus	1978–82	Jérôme Haas	1994–96
Philippe Jurgensen	1982–84	Odile Renaud-Basso	1996–99
Jean-Claude Trichet	1984–85	François Pérol	1999–2001
(unfilled)	1985–87	Ambroise Fayolle	2001
Denis Samuel-Lajeunesse	1987–92	Delphine d'Amarzit	2001–present

Source: The Paris Club Secretariat provided a preliminary version of this list. It was refined through conversations and correspondence with five Paris Club chairmen who served before 1993.

Note: The chairman of the first Paris Club negotiation (with Argentina in 1956) was André de Lattre, who became the deputy director of Finances Extérieures in 1957. From 1959 to 1960 Mr. de Lattre served on the staff of the president of France, and the director of Finances Extérieures, Jean Sadrin, became the nominal chairman of the Paris Club. Mr. de Lattre resumed the chairmanship in 1960, and in 1962 he became the director of Finances Extérieures. In 1965 Finances Extérieures merged with Trésor, and the director of Trésor became the senior official in the Ministry of Finance responsible for international issues. Since then, with the exceptions noted, the *directeur du Trésor* has assumed the additional title of Paris Club chairman. On five occasions, the director delegated the responsibility of being the Paris Club chairman to the *chef du service des Affaires Européens et Internationales*, one level down: Claude Pierre-Brossolette (1966–67), Daniel Deguen (1968–71), Philippe Jurgensen (1984–85), Jean-Claude Trichet (1985–87), and Francis Mayer (1997–99). It has not been possible to establish exactly when the secretariat was formalized or when the title of secretary general was first adopted. Further research in the archives of the French Finance Ministry or the U.S. Department of State might yield this information.

Membership

During the North-South dialogue on debt in the 1970s, the North fought accusations that the Paris Club was an exclusive group of powerful industrial countries created to increase their leverage over weak developing countries. The G-7 countries and their OECD partners stressed that negotiations with any specific debtor country were open to any creditor country having a substantial exposure and agreeing to abide by the established principles and procedures of the Paris Club.[10] This view prevailed until the early 1990s, when Paris Club documents began referring to "nineteen permanent members." A dozen other creditor countries have been invited to participate in negotiations with individual countries where they had substantial exposure.[11] The main benefit of being a full member is participation in the Paris Club's "methodology" discussions (see below) and in negotiations with countries where they have no exposure.

With the exception of Russia, all of the permanent members of the Paris Club are members of the OECD. The same countries are also the dominant shareholders of the IMF and the multilateral development banks and are the world's leading aid donors. They thus share the same broad view on how the international financial system should function. The differences that arise among the members during negotiations tend to reflect historical economic and political interests in specific debtor countries or variations in national budgeting and risk management systems more than they represent diverging views of the role of the Paris Club. The number of permanent members is likely to grow slowly in the future. Possible candidates are Brazil, Israel, Korea, and Portugal.

Observers

Representatives from a small number of international institutions participate in Paris Club negotiations as observers. By far the most important of

10. Camdessus (1984, pp. 125–26) underscores the lack of "fixed members" and the ad hoc nature of the Paris Club. Sevigny (1990, p. 13) describes the Paris Club as having an open membership. The shift to permanent members may have occurred in the context of Russia's request in the mid-1990s to become a full participant in all Paris Club business. Before the 1990s the Communist bloc countries as a group, which were major creditors for many developing countries, did not participate in the Paris Club because they were not members of the IMF and therefore were not comfortable with the rule requiring debtor countries to have an IMF arrangement as a prerequisite for negotiations.

11. The nineteen members are Austria, Australia, Belgium, Canada, Denmark, Finland, France, Germany, Ireland, Italy, Japan, Netherlands, Norway, Russian Federation, Spain, Sweden, Switzerland, United Kingdom, and United States. Other creditor countries that have participated in selected negotiations are Abu Dhabi, Argentina, Brazil, Israel, Korea, Kuwait, Mexico, Morocco, New Zealand, Portugal, South Africa, Trinidad and Tobago, and Turkey.

these is the observer from the IMF, because of the link between Paris Club agreements and the adjustment programs that debtor countries must negotiate with the IMF. A World Bank observer is always present, and representatives from the Inter-American, African, and Asian development banks attend negotiations with countries from their region. An official from the European Commission participates as an observer in most negotiations, reflecting the EU's role as a major source of financing for some countries. The only nonfinancial institutions represented are the OECD (because of its role in tracking development assistance) and UNCTAD (for historical reasons explained in chapter 7).

Transparency

Until 2001 the Paris Club was one of the most mysterious, nontransparent pieces of machinery in the international financial system. Although countries restructuring debt in the Paris Club would generally announce the results domestically, and reports on Paris Club activities appeared regularly in the financial press, the press releases traditionally issued by the secretariat at the conclusion of negotiations contained no information about the amount of debt treated or the restructuring terms. In the late 1990s a sea change took place in the IMF, the World Bank, and other international institutions. As they became more transparent, the Paris Club's secrecy became less defensible. The Paris Club finally responded by launching a website in April 2001 that explained its principles and rules and provided basic information on the agreements concluded since 1956.

HIPC Cases versus Non-HIPC Cases

Paris Club operations began to move down two separate tracks in 1988. Along one track was a series of operations with low-income countries that involved progressively more generous amounts of debt reduction in net present value terms.[12] Along the other track was a smaller number of operations with lower-middle-income or middle-income countries that were limited to rescheduling without any explicit debt reduction.

While using the same machinery and bearing a close resemblance on the surface, the operations along the low-income country track were function-

---

12. In a typical debt-rescheduling operation, principal payments are deferred, but the interest charged on these payments protects the creditor from any loss in value. In a debt-reduction operation, either a portion of the principal is written off (forgiven) or the rate of interest is set below the creditor's cost of funds; either action results in a measured net present value after restructuring lower than the NPV of the scheduled payments before restructuring.

ally distinct from those along the other track, which are the subject of this study. The low-income-country operations were not workouts related to an external payments crisis. They were operations in which debt relief was being extended as a form of aid. From one perspective, these operations were a way of compensating for shortfalls in new flows of concessional aid (especially grants). From another perspective, they were a way of reducing debt owed to the IMF, the World Bank, and the other multilateral agencies without compromising the preferred creditor status they have enjoyed since the first days of the Paris Club.

The story of debt reduction for low-income countries is told in chapter 9. In a nutshell, through repeated rescheduling operations with a group of low-income countries, each one extending the scope of payments to be deferred and making the repayment terms for the deferred amounts more favorable to the debtor, the Paris Club exhausted the immediate "cash flow" relief it could provide through rescheduling. The creditor countries had to choose between increasing new commitments of concessional aid to these countries or beginning to engage in debt reduction. At the G-7 summit in Toronto in 1988, they chose the latter course by including a debt-reduction option as one of three ways of providing exceptional debt-relief terms to low-income countries. Over the next eleven years, the debt-reduction option was progressively improved. In particular, when the HIPC Initiative was adopted in September 1996, debt reduction of 80 percent in net present value terms became a standard treatment for HIPCs. In 1999 the reduction ceiling was raised to 90 percent.

To see the nature of these cases as aid operations rather than financial operations, it is necessary to probe under the surface. For example, when the IMF and World Bank participate in a HIPC operation, they do not write down their exposures against their reserves. To protect their preferred creditor status, outstanding loans to the country concerned are paid down by drawing on special funds largely raised from the major creditor countries (that is, the Paris Club's permanent members).[13] Technically, the same result could be achieved by means of grants directly from these creditor countries to each HIPC that would be used exclusively to prepay IMF and World Bank debt.

More fundamentally, the sovereign-debt-restructuring cases that are the subject of this study are precipitated by a payments crisis and are part of a comprehensive effort designed to reorganize the country's external debt to

13. The World Bank's special fund for HIPC operations has also received allocations of net income from World Bank lending activities at the end of each recent fiscal year.

the *minimum* extent consistent with balance-of-payments viability. By contrast HIPCs become eligible for debt reduction by virtue of meeting specific groupwide per capita income and debt criteria, whether or not they are experiencing a crisis. Moreover, the debt relief they receive is designed to yield a target ratio of external debt (in NPV terms) to exports of 150 percent without regard to the economic and financial characteristics (debt-servicing capacity) of each individual country.

In the fifteen-year period from the first "Toronto terms" case in the fall of 1988 to the end of 2002, the Paris Club completed 204 operations, representing almost 60 percent of the total activity over its forty-six-year history. Out of the 204 operations, 118 provided relief on exceptional low-income-country terms (Toronto, London, Naples, Lyon, or Cologne terms, using the terminology from the Paris Club website) to thirty-six countries—an average of more than three per country.[14] Another ten operations to seven of these countries provided relief on "normal" terms (Classic, Houston, or Ad Hoc terms).

Dividing the 1988–2002 period roughly in half helps to highlight the volume of the Paris Club's HIPC-style business. From 1988 to 1994—the peak years for sovereign-debt-restructuring related to the 1980s debt crisis—53 operations provided exceptional low-income-country terms while 57 operations provided normal terms. From 1995 to 2002, the corresponding numbers were 65 and 29. Moreover, almost half of the countries getting normal terms (sixteen out of thirty-four) stayed out of the Paris Club after 1995. In other words, the pace of Paris Club business for the purpose of crisis workouts since 1995 has been on the order of three or four a year, far less than the thirteen or fourteen a year implied by the aggregate numbers that include the HIPC-style, aid-motivated operations.

Regrettably, using the Paris Club machinery for both kinds of operations has obfuscated the public debate in recent years about developing country debt. Functionally, it would be preferable to arrange HIPC-style debt-reduction operations in some other forum, such as aid consortiums or consultative groups. The biggest problem created by this confusion is that taxpayers in the G-7 countries see a certain eagerness by the governments to write down debt for poor countries but great reluctance to write down debt for other countries such as Russia or Nigeria or Indonesia. These positions seem inconsistent.

14. The leader was Senegal with seven operations in this period. The other countries with five or six operations each were Benin, Bolivia, Burkina Faso, Cameroon, Côte d'Ivoire, Guinea, Mauritania, Mali, Madagascar, Mozambique, Niger, Tanzania, and Uganda.

The confusion would be easier to excuse if there were evidence that the recent HIPC-style operations had left countries with sustainable debt burdens, thus obviating the need to return to the Paris Club for more relief. Sadly, the HIPC Initiative has not provided the advertised "exit" from debt relief. An assessment of the HIPC Initiative and alternatives for fixing it is a substantial undertaking, however, and well beyond the scope of this study.[15]

Paris Club Principles

The principles and procedures of the Paris Club were loosely defined during its first twenty years. They were not written down and can only be inferred from the texts of the agreements concluded during this period. The North-South Dialogue in the 1970s forced the Paris Club to codify its rules. That was done in the process of negotiating the "detailed features for future operations relating to the debt problems of interested developing countries," eventually adopted at the twenty-first session of the Trade and Development Board of UNCTAD in September 1980 in Geneva.[16]

By the mid-1980s, following the intensive debate over Paris Club rules in the North-South Dialogue, it was possible to identify three *core principles*: imminent default, conditionality, and burden sharing.[17] Until the Paris Club launched its website in 2001, however, there was no officially approved set of principles and rules.

According to the Paris Club's website, its operations are now guided by five principles: case-by-case approach, consensus, conditionality, solidarity, and comparability of treatment.[18] The selection of principles is admittedly

15. For a critical evaluation at the beginning of 2002, see Birdsall and Williamson (2002). A few of the documents on the HIPC Initiative from the flood produced by the IMF and World Bank are cited in chapter 9.

16. U.S. policy on debt restructuring was also formalized during this period. Congressional committees were concerned about the use of debt restructuring by the executive branch to circumvent the process of appropriating budget funds for foreign loan programs. They sought to require the executive branch to obtain appropriations in advance of participating in Paris Club negotiations. Such a step would have destroyed the Paris Club as a process for speedy sovereign debt workouts. In return for preserving the flexibility to participate in the Paris Club, the executive branch adopted a formal statement of policy in 1978, published for the first time in the report of the National Advisory Council for that year. It has not been changed since then and still limits the terms that the U.S. government can accept in a Paris Club operation.

17. Rieffel (1985, pp. 4–14).

18. IMF (2001d, p. 43) notes that these five principles were spelled out for the first time in 1997, in the process of deciding to accept Russia as a permanent member. Trichet (1989, pp. 110–11), writing while he was serving as Paris Club chairman, highlighted three principles: conditionality, comparable treatment (the same as burden sharing), and consensus. Sevigny (1990) mentions four principles: imminent default, conditionality, burden sharing, and consensus. Kearney (1993,

somewhat arbitrary, but the increase from three to five does not reflect any material change in the operation of the Paris Club. Moreover, the current set of five principles is arguably less clear than the earlier set of three. Nevertheless, the following discussion is organized around the current list because of its "official" character, with the text from the website quoted verbatim at the beginning of each section.

Case-by-Case Approach

"The Paris Club makes decisions on a case by case basis in order to permanently adjust itself to the individuality of each debtor country."

The core principle of imminent default recognized by Paris Club creditors in the 1980s has now been split into two principles: case-by-case approach, and conditionality.

The core principle of imminent default was the Paris Club's first line of defense against two threats: debt restructuring on demand, and generalized debt restructuring. Developing countries frequently experience balance-of-payments strains, and debt restructuring is an obvious way to ease these strains. The principle of imminent default closed the door to all requests except those from countries that had actually defaulted on debt-service payments or were clearly on the verge of defaulting. This door is now shut by the new conditionality principle.

Similarly, since the early days of the Paris Club there have always been some countries burdened with excessive debt and some advocates for restructuring the debt of all of these countries as a group in some consistent and unilateral manner. The principle of imminent default closed the door to generalized restructuring of this kind. The new principle of a case-by-case approach serves the same purpose.[19]

By the 1990s "case-by-case" had become one of the mantras of the debt-restructuring business. Private sector creditors attached particular importance to it, perhaps more than any other feature. The main reason to regard it as a "noncore" principle in the Paris Club context is that only the most extreme advocates of debt reduction for poor countries today argue for across-the-board cancellation. Even in the context of the HIPC Initiative—which is a

pp. 63–64) mentions four principles: imminent default, conditionality, burden sharing, and short-term relief (rescheduling only one year of payments at a time).

19. There was a simple and straightforward test of imminent default: the presence of an ex ante financing gap. Based on the IMF's balance-of-payments projections for the coming year, the debtor country's sources of foreign exchange were compared with its uses of foreign exchange, including scheduled payments of principal and interest on external debt. If the projected uses exceeded the projected sources, this constituted prima facie evidence of imminent default. See illustration in Rieffel (1985, p. 6).

scheme for generalized debt relief—implementation is carried out through a case-by-case approach.[20]

Consensus

"No decision can be taken within the Paris Club if it is not the result of a consensus among the participating creditor countries."

Consensus can be viewed either as a principle or a procedure. As a principle, consensus reflects the policy decision to carry out debt restructuring in an ad hoc framework rather than through a permanent mechanism established by an international treaty. Treaty-based machinery would involve an explicit restriction of sovereign rights of creditor countries in the context of debt workouts. The ad hoc Paris Club machinery involves an implicit restriction of these rights through the consensus principle.

As a procedure, considerable flexibility is seen in achieving consensus in individual negotiations. In setting the terms of rescheduling agreements, for example, there are major decisions (whether or not to include interest payments in the restructuring) and minor decisions (whether the grace period should be four years or five). A single creditor country cannot generally force the others to adopt its position on a minor decision. More importantly, there are big countries and small countries. Japan is the biggest bilateral creditor to developing countries, in part because a smaller share of its aid is in the form of grants, but it generally follows the lead of the United States and the Europeans on international financial issues. The United States is the second biggest bilateral creditor but has the preeminent voice in Paris Club business, as it does in other international forums. It seldom has qualms about maintaining an isolated position until the other creditors agree to it. Small creditor countries, such as Austria or Norway, would encounter unbearable political pressure if they tried the same tactic.

Conditionality

"Debt treatments are applied only for countries that need a rescheduling and that implement reforms to resolve their payment difficulties. In practice conditionality is provided by the existence of an appropriate program supported by the IMF, which demonstrates the need for debt relief."

The principle of conditionality has two distinct elements. One is need, and the other is reform. The need element for many years was addressed by

---

20. The explanations of each principle seem to lose some nuances in the process of being translated from the French. In this first principle, for example, "continuously" would be better than "permanently" and "individual circumstances" would be better than "individuality."

the imminent default principle that opened the door of the Paris Club only to countries that were in default or were about to default.[21] The reform element is a core principle reflecting the only leverage the creditors have over the debtor country. IMF financing can help to cushion the social impact of a program of economic reforms and to accelerate the process of recovery. In most cases the benefit is even greater because an IMF arrangement unlocks financing from other official and private sources. Obviously the Paris Club creditors do not want to restructure repeatedly, and therefore they will not sit down and negotiate until the borrowing country has reached agreement with the IMF on a program of reforms designed to ensure that the country will achieve a viable balance-of-payments position in the near term (notionally three years) and this program has been formally approved by the IMF Executive Board. Viability is defined as a current account deficit that can be financed without IMF credit, debt restructuring, or other forms of "exceptional" financing.[22]

Solidarity

"Creditors agree to implement the terms agreed in the context of the Paris Club."
This feature does not deserve to be called a principle and is awkwardly stated. The Paris Club negotiates a framework agreement that is implemented (given legal validity) by separate agreements between each creditor

21. The Paris Club creditors agreed on several occasions between 1968 and 1976 to reschedule payments owed by India and Pakistan for the purpose of increasing net aid flows, not to help these countries deal with severe payment difficulties. These arrangements were worked out in the aid consortiums for India and Pakistan, not in the Paris Club. They can be seen as policy experiments that convinced the creditor countries not to use debt relief as a form of aid. The creditor country position on this hardened in the North-South dialogue on debt, as discussed in chapter 7. Rieffel (1985, pp. 3–5). The strong attachment of the U.S. government to the principle of imminent default was illustrated in the case of Pakistan in 1981. U.S. aid to Pakistan had been suspended as a result of legislation mandating a cutoff to countries building nuclear weapons. Following the Soviet invasion of Afghanistan, the United States wanted to support Pakistan's economy. After consultations with the Congress, President Jimmy Carter waived the imminent default requirement to allow the United States to participate in a multilateral rescheduling operation (carried out in Pakistan's aid consortium, but following Paris Club rules) as an alternative to changing the legislation. U.S. National Advisory Council (FY1981, p. 66).

22. The Paris Club has concluded several agreements with countries that were not IMF members and therefore were not able to satisfy the Paris Club precondition of having an IMF arrangement in place. These countries include Poland (1981 and 1985), Mozambique (1984), and Angola (1989). In addition Cuba (1983 and 1984) rescheduled debt to Paris Club creditors "outside the Paris Club" (and therefore is not listed on the Paris Club website) but in Paris and following Paris Club principles and procedures. In each case, a task force of Paris Club experts visited the debtor country, analyzed the nature of its debt problem, and assessed the policies adopted by the country to resolve it.

country and the debtor country. The solidarity principle simply commits every Paris Club creditor to respect the terms agreed upon in their joint negotiation when they conclude their individual bilateral agreements.

Pressures to deviate from the multilateral terms come from two sources. One is commercial pressure to restore a country's eligibility for export credit insurance so that export sales can be resumed. As a result, some creditors may implement bilateral agreements even when the debtor country is not respecting its obligations to other Paris Club creditors. Another source is political pressure to extend more generous relief to a debtor country than others are willing to do. In the early decades of the Paris Club, creditors were not bothered by such generosity, recognizing that it would help the debtor country to avoid future payment difficulties. More recently, generosity of this kind has been controversial because it can provide ammunition to domestic critics of the creditor countries taking a hard line in Paris Club negotiations. Bilateral debt-restructuring agreements have been concluded from time to time outside the Paris Club process and not necessarily in connection with a financial crisis. These are viewed as aid operations and are not considered a violation of the solidarity principle.[23]

Comparability of Treatment

"The Paris Club preserves the comparability of treatment between different creditors, as the debtor country cannot grant to another creditor a treatment less favorable for the debtor than the consensus reached in the Paris Club."

Referring back to the assessment of the Paris Club in Rieffel (1985), the phrase *burden sharing* seems to better capture the core principle than the label *comparability of treatment* selected by the Paris Club.[24] Burden sharing clearly conveys the notion that debt restructuring involves costs and that these should not be borne by one group of creditors to the benefit of other creditors. In the language of the current policy debate, no category of creditor should be automatically exempted from sharing the costs of a sovereign workout. Current Paris Club debt experts, however, appear to dislike the connotation that servicing external debt is a burden.[25]

23. Cizauskas (1979) mentions the cases of Egypt and Yugoslavia in the early 1970s. Department of State (1999, tab J) mentions the Jordan case in 1994.

24. It is not clear why the Paris Club prefers "comparability of treatment" to the more straightforward and long-used "comparable treatment."

25. Curious language is found in this principle too. First, debt relief ("treatment") is granted by the creditor countries, not by the debtor country. Second, the phrase "cannot grant" is inconsistent with the boilerplate used in actual agreements that merely commits the debtor country to "seek" comparable treatment from non–Paris Club creditors.

The application of this principle, whichever term is used, is no simple matter in today's international financial system.[26] There are important distinctions among creditor groups that must be reflected in differential treatment to ensure a good workout. The most obvious example is the treatment of multilateral agencies. These have been accorded preferred creditor status for the sound reasons noted in chapter 3. The explanation of comparability on the Paris Club's website and the standard text of its agreements say nothing about debt owed to multilateral agencies. Nevertheless, it is perfectly clear from the record of Paris Club operations that the comparable-treatment principle does not apply to this category of debt. Such fuzziness interferes with efforts by the public to understand the logic behind Paris Club operations.

A further complexity relates to the definition of multilateral creditors. Most Paris Club creditors are comfortable with the preferred creditor status enjoyed by the IMF, the World Bank, and the four main regional development banks, because these institutions are open to universal membership. They are less comfortable when subregional development banks such as the Nordic Investment Bank, the Andean Fund, and the Islamic Development Bank, which are closed to membership from outside their defined region, claim preferred creditor status. Paris Club creditors are even less comfortable with agencies that are multilateral in form only and function like bilateral agencies. The most controversial agencies in this respect are the EU-based agencies, such as the European Investment Bank-European Investment Fund. These function as surrogate bilateral donor agencies, and a strong case can be made for subjecting them to the Paris Club's comparable treatment clause if they choose not to participate in Paris Club negotiations as creditors.[27]

With regard to burden sharing among bilateral official creditors, the arguments for treating them all in exactly the same fashion, whether they participate in the Paris Club negotiations or not, is straightforward. In practice, however, achieving equal treatment can be rather complicated. For example, loans are made in different currencies, incorporate a wide range of maturities and interest rates, and finance an enormous range of activities

26. IMF (2001b, p. 49) observes that "comparability of treatment is more an art than a science."
27. The European Union (EU) only makes loans to the transition countries in Eastern and Central Europe and the former Soviet Union. As some of these countries become EU members, they will become effectively immune from debt crises. By contrast, European Investment Bank–European Investment Fund (EIB-EIF) operations in Africa, Asia, and Latin America have been increasing at a steady pace, so the treatment of EIB-EIF loans is likely to become a bigger issue in the future. The treatment of EU loans was a major issue in one operation in 2001.

from pure budgetary support and procurement of military equipment to infrastructure projects with long payback periods. The Paris Club accommodates some of these differences by setting less demanding repayment terms for debt bearing concessional interest rates than for debt bearing commercial interest rates. The more critical form of flexibility, however, is allowing interest rates on restructured debt to be fixed in the separate bilateral implementing agreements. Another complexity is simply finessed. Some official creditors are committing new money to the debtor country while others are not. As a matter of practice, the Paris Club does not take new money into account in its negotiations, a practice that leads to situations of unequal treatment on a substantial scale.

Burden sharing with private creditors is even trickier in today's world for two reasons. One is the shift during the 1990s in the pattern of capital flows to developing countries. As official flows stagnate, more and more countries are becoming dependent upon private capital flows. Consequently, good workouts take into account the impact on the debtor country's future access to private capital to a far greater degree than in the past. The second reason is an extension of the first. From the first Paris Club operation in 1956 until the mid-1990s, commercial bank loans were the dominant form of private credit to developing country sovereigns. Some debt in the form of bonds existed, but it was on such a small scale that in most (but not all) cases involving commercial bank rescheduling or reduction, bond debt was deemed to be de minimis by both the Paris Club and the London Club and was left alone. The Brady Plan debt-reduction deals in the late 1980s and early 1990s, however, had the effect of sharply scaling back medium-term bank lending to developing countries and creating a large stock of bond debt. Mirroring the pattern seen in the 1970s when commercial banks were recycling "petrodollars," debt problems soon emerged in countries where bond debt was too big to be left alone.

While there were constant disputes between Paris Club creditors and commercial banks about the application of comparable treatment in specific cases in the 1980s and early 1990s, these were generally resolved in a cooperative atmosphere and an orderly fashion. For reasons that are examined in detail in chapters 10, 11, and 12, comparable treatment with respect to bonds became a major international issue after the Mexican peso crisis at the end of 1994. In short, the burning issue at the heart of the current debate about the machinery for sovereign debt workouts is the application of the Paris Club's comparable-treatment principle to bonds held by private investors.

The Paris Club's approach prior to May 2003 was outmoded and was getting in the way of sensible workouts.[28]

Paris Club Negotiations

After concluding 364 separate negotiations involving more than $400 billion of debt with seventy-eight countries over the span of forty-six years, it is hardly surprising that the Paris Club process has acquired a well-defined rhythm.[29] The process can be decomposed into three steps: triggering actions and preparations, the analytical framework of the IMF, and the negotiating session. Each of these steps has been refined to a high degree.

Triggering Actions and Preparations

The first formal step in a Paris Club restructuring is taken when a debtor country submits a written request to negotiate. Several different circumstances can lead a country to take this step:

—An unforeseen shock (earthquake, fall in the world price for a key export commodity, increase in world oil prices, political instability in a neighboring country) that sharply reduces the amount of foreign exchange the government has to meet its debt-service obligations

—A slow deterioration in the country's external position that eventually leads creditors to stop new lending or reduce their exposure

---

28. One technical and one procedural issue merit brief references. The technical issue is the treatment of "securitized" debt such as loans to finance an electric power plant secured by the proceeds of selling electricity. These usually represent a small fraction of the country's external debt and therefore the tendency has been to leave them alone, but there may be cases where such treatment is not practical. The procedural issue involves changes in the text of the standard comparable treatment clause in Paris Club agreements. There has been a puzzling evolution over the past fifteen years in this clause. Until 1996 Paris Club agreements differentiated between "nondiscrimination" applied to nonparticipating official creditors and "comparable treatment" applied to private creditors. These two aspects of burden sharing were addressed in two separate clauses. In 1996, however, these familiar clauses were dropped in favor of two clauses that encompass nonparticipating official creditors and private creditors. The earlier distinction added a valuable element of flexibility to Paris Club agreements. The principle as currently stated appears to reduce the flexibility that debtor countries used to have in negotiating restructuring arrangements with their private creditors. The linguistic confusion associated with the new clauses feeds skepticism about the soundness of Paris Club principles and procedures.

29. Data taken from the Paris Club website (www.clubdeparis.org). The figure for the amount of debt affected exaggerates the role of the Paris Club because it includes a considerable amount of double counting of previously rescheduled debt.

—A political change that brings to power a government less committed to maintaining the country's creditworthiness or less able to mobilize the political support required to do so

Theoretically, new financing could be arranged in every case to maintain the flow of payments to creditors and avoid default. It becomes important then to understand the reasons why such financing does not materialize. They are all variations on a single reason: lack of confidence in the country's ability to adjust. More specifically, external creditors (official and private) no longer believe that the country will be able to reallocate enough resources to meet the additional debt-service payments associated with more lending. In some cases taxpayers in general, or specific interest groups, will not tolerate the diversion of resources required. In other cases the economy cannot grow as rapidly as debt is growing. In short, the invisible trigger for most country defaults is a decision by creditors as a group to stop taking on more exposure. This is not an easy decision because it forces creditors to recognize the likelihood of incurring losses on their outstanding loans.

The preconditions for Paris Club restructuring are now sufficiently well known that countries rarely submit a formal request for negotiations until they have been met. The main one is that the debtor countries reach agreement with the IMF on an adjustment program that will reestablish a viable balance-of-payments position. Debtor countries are also encouraged to work with the Paris Club secretariat in the weeks prior to a negotiation to exchange views on the kind of request likely to be accepted by the creditors and to develop an agreed set of debt data. The initial estimates of the Paris Club members and those of the debtor country always differ about the stock of debt eligible for restructuring and the amount of principal and interest payments associated with this debt. It is also important at this stage to establish a clear picture of debt stocks and flows vis-à-vis other creditors (multilateral agencies, commercial banks, bond investors, suppliers, and so forth). The secretariat is the focal point for the debt reconciliation process, which helps to ensure that negotiations will not fail due to technical issues.

Some countries choose to rely on advice from within their governments on negotiating strategies and tactics, but most seek some outside advice. Both the IMF and the World Bank have frequently been called upon for this purpose and do not charge for their advice. Experienced financial advisors and lawyers also can be hired to help with the negotiations. Some come from well-known international banks, and others work as independent consultants.[30]

30. The "troika" of Lehman Brothers, S. G. Warburg, and Lazard Frères was preeminent in this area from 1975 to 1995. Lawyers have been less visible in Paris Club operations than in London Club

While the debtor country is preparing for negotiations, the Paris Club members begin moving toward a consensus position by exchanging views during *tour d'horizon* sessions that are usually held each time the Paris Club meets. These sessions provide an opportunity for the creditor countries with the largest exposure to stake out positions on upcoming negotiations and for others with specific concerns to rally support from like-minded creditors.

The Analytical Framework Provided by the IMF

The IMF's balance-of-payments projections for each debtor country provide a quantitative framework for the negotiation of specific restructuring terms by the Paris Club. While this framework is objective in character, it has been one of the most contentious aspects of Paris Club negotiations.

The first step in curing a default is for the debtor country to change the behavior of public sector and private sector entities that contributed to its payments crisis. The behavior of businesses, households, and government agencies can be influenced by forceful speeches but is more directly shaped by policies, laws, and regulations. It is the responsibility of the government to change these as necessary to restore the country's creditworthiness. This is by no means a simple process. The current government may know precisely what needs to be done but may not have sufficient support from the country's legislative bodies or its judicial system to implement the required reforms. A new government may be required. Almost always, it is far from obvious exactly how to change fiscal policy, monetary policy, and structural policies, and there are always interest groups that seek to block specific reforms. Theoretically perfect reforms are often political nonstarters, forcing governments to settle for second-best reforms.

The IMF has considerable influence in resolving debt crises because it provides the quickest and purest form of emergency financing and because it is the main repository of the world's knowledge about which reforms work and which do not. Almost all of the external parties in a position to help a country experiencing a debt crisis (multilateral and bilateral donor agencies, private lenders, and investors) wait to act until the IMF has produced forecasts of the country's performance under its recovery program for growth, inflation, employment, balance of payments, and so forth. The key number that pops out of the IMF's analytical work is an ex ante "balance-of-payments financing gap," generally presented one year at a time. This gap represents the shortfall in financing required to meet all payment obligations

---

deals. Three of the most experienced law firms advising debtor countries are Cleary, Gottlieb, Steen & Hamilton in New York, White & Case in New York, and Arnold & Porter in Washington.

without drawing down foreign exchange reserves to an uncomfortable level.[31] In this analytical framework the objective of a workout is to close the financing gap with "exceptional financing" in the form of IMF credit, aid from multilateral and bilateral donor agencies, debt-restructuring arrangements with the Paris Club and London Club, and new sources of private financing (such as direct investment or return of flight capital).[32]

Every source of exceptional financing has its limits. The IMF seeks to avoid lending to any member country in excess of 300 percent of its quota. The World Bank and the regional multilateral development banks are required to avoid excessive exposure in any one country relative to their capital or relative to the exposures of bilateral agencies and commercial creditors. If, after the potential sources of new financing are added on top of "normal" flows of aid, investment, and commercial credit, a residual gap remains, then debt restructuring becomes the only alternative to defaulting and filling this gap by accumulating arrears.

In short the analytical framework of the IMF yields a rather precise amount of loan payments that must be deferred to make the recovery program workable. The process of arriving at this amount, however, is far from straightforward and explains much of the difficulty that countries experience in negotiating with the IMF. Typically, the set of reforms initially proposed by the country is not strong enough. Using its analytical tools, the IMF concludes that this set will not work because the amount of exceptional financing required is simply too big. The IMF and the country then iterate toward a "fully financed" solution. Stronger reforms boost exports and cut imports, attract more foreign capital (aid and investment), and discourage resident outflows (flight capital). Eventually the IMF concludes that there are no further measures that the government can reasonably implement that would reduce the financing gap.

One of the limitations of this analytical approach is its static nature. In countries that have access to international capital markets, there may be links between alternative policies and private capital flows that are not easily captured. As a starting point, however, the IMF framework is useful in showing the balance-of-payments implications of a strong reform program

31. By convention the balance of payments is divided between current account transactions (goods and services, including interest on external debt) and capital account transactions (such as direct investment and loan disbursements). Generally the current account of an emerging market country is in deficit, and the country must run a capital account surplus to finance this deficit. The surplus must be even larger to finance a normal buildup in foreign exchange reserves.

32. The gap will be closed one way or another because the balance of payments always balances, ex post. If exceptional financing in the forms mentioned does not materialize, then the gap is closed by payment arrears. This is in effect involuntary financing by creditors.

and quantifying the shortfall in the country's capacity (ability) to fully meet its payment obligations to foreign creditors. Having reached this conclusion, in effect defining the "size of the pie" (the amount of payments that will have to be deferred), the IMF is careful not to explicitly "divide the pie" among the different creditor categories. It has done this implicitly, however, because it had to be convinced that this residual gap could be filled within the parameters set in previous Paris Club and London Club restructuring operations.[33]

The policy issue arising from this process is that the Paris Club creditors tend to find themselves dealing with a fait accompli. The IMF is telling them rather precisely how much of their payments will have to be deferred during the program period.[34] That leaves only the terms of repayment of the deferred amounts to be negotiated. Much of the tension between the Paris Club and the IMF revolves around this analytical framework. The creditors are suspicious that the IMF is using unduly conservative assumptions to enlarge the financing gap. The IMF is concerned that the Paris Club will be too rigid and not provide enough deferral to ensure the success of the recovery program. This source of tension is inherent in the debt-restructuring process and is probably healthy because it prevents the IMF from spending the Paris Club's money too freely and prevents the Paris Club from applying an unduly short leash on debtor countries.

The Negotiating Session

Since 1983 the Paris Club has reserved one week in every month except for February and August for its business. Only in rare circumstances does the Paris Club engage in negotiations outside this normal cycle. With one day devoted to the *tour d'horizon* and methodology issues, it is generally not feasible to complete more than three negotiations during any one week-long session. Despite the heavy pace of negotiations in recent years, debtor countries have seldom encountered scheduling delays. Every effort is made by the secretariat to complete each negotiation in one day, and its record of success is remarkable.[35]

33. In a few cases the gap has been too large to fill with standard debt-restructuring techniques. Accordingly a special meeting has been organized to obtain pledges of new money (in the form of quick-disbursing nonproject financing) from donor agencies sufficient to close the gap.

34. The arguments on the IMF side are that it has been given the responsibility for determining that the design of a country's program does not leave a financing gap, and it cannot commit its own money without "financing assurances" from the other creditors involved.

35. An early speed record was set in the negotiations with Malawi in 1983, which were concluded in about one hour. Rieffel (1985, p. 17). For countries that owe debt to only a few Paris Club members, agreements have been concluded without a meeting by means of an exchange of letters.

The French finance minister had his office in a wing of the Louvre Palace (Museum) on Rue de Rivoli when the Paris Club was founded, and the secretariat had its offices in the same wing. For most of the 1970s and 1980s, the Paris Club met in an ornate room at the International Conference Center on Avenue Kléber, a few steps from the Arc de Triomphe. A new building constructed for the Finance Ministry 3.5 kilometers up the Seine River at Bercy was opened in 1989. The Paris Club now meets in Bercy in a cavernous and spartan meeting hall.

Negotiations begin with a well-scripted plenary session. The chairman of the Paris Club sits at one end of a hollow square flanked by the secretary general and the observers. The debtor country delegation, usually led by the minister of finance, is seated on the opposing side. Large delegations do not make a good impression but may be necessary in cases where the restructuring is a sensitive political issue domestically. The heads of the creditor delegations fill the other sides, with junior members seated behind them. Traditions vary among countries, with delegations being led variously by an official from the finance ministry, foreign ministry, economic ministry, or export credit agency. Delegation heads sometimes have subministerial rank but more often are senior career officials.[36]

The Paris Club chairman (or a cochairman or vice chairman) opens the negotiation by welcoming the participants and inviting the head of the debtor country delegation to present the request for restructuring. Short presentations are recommended. The observers from the IMF, the World Bank, and UNCTAD are then invited to speak in support of the country's request. Their statements focus on the economic adjustment program approved by the IMF and the operations of the World Bank (along with other multilateral and bilateral donors) that are helping the government implement the program and mitigate its social impact. A question-and-answer period follows the presentations. The creditors listen carefully to get a sense of the strength of the efforts being undertaken by the government to rebuild its debt-service capacity and to reassure themselves that the multilaterals are contributing new money to the full extent possible under the circumstances.

36. The United States has a peculiar arrangement. Its delegations are led by a State Department official, at the deputy assistant secretary level when necessary, but the negotiating position is the responsibility of the Treasury Department. This arrangement was formalized for the Zaire negotiations in the mid-1970s in a compromise reached between Secretary of State Henry Kissinger and Treasury Secretary William Simon. Treasury had the lead, however, in the negotiations with Russia in the early 1990s with respect to Soviet-era debt, because of the special role of the G-7 finance deputies in this case.

When these formalities are concluded, the plenary session is adjourned, the debtor delegation is escorted to a nearby room, the observers are excused, and the creditor delegations reconvene as a closed caucus. Ideally, a consensus is reached within an hour on terms to offer to the debtor country, the chairman leaves the room to communicate the offer to the debtor delegation informally and seek its concurrence. If he succeeds, the plenary session is resumed, the chairman repeats the offer, and the debtor country declares its assent. During a short break, the secretariat prepares the text of the "Agreed Minute," and then the participants reconvene to sign this document, with original copies in French and English.

More often, the process takes longer. The creditor delegations often disagree strongly on the initial offer. Or the initial offer is unacceptable to the debtor delegation, which then formulates a counteroffer. There may be several rounds of offers and counteroffers. The views of the IMF observer are sometimes critical in reaching a creditor consensus. Even after both sides have agreed to the basic terms, problems can surface when the text arrives, resulting in lengthy haggling over details. It is not uncommon for these negotiations to extend far into the night. In the more complex cases, negotiations may continue over three or four days.

A final step involves fine-tuning the press release. As the Paris Club adapted its practices during the late 1990s to become more transparent, it provided progressively more information in its press releases. As of mid-2002, the releases typically included the amount of the debtor country's total debt to official creditors, the amount the country owed to Paris Club creditors and the portion of this amount being restructured, the cutoff date, the consolidation period, the impact on debt-service payments during the consolidation period, and the repayment terms (see definitions below). A few other details are provided in the standard information posted on the Paris Club website for each operation, including a link to the associated IMF arrangement and any special provisions.

Given the current practice of publishing letters of intent to the IMF and detailed country reports prepared by IMF staff, it is curious that the Paris Club has declined so far to publish the text of its Agreed Minutes. Rarely is there any material information in these agreements that is not disclosed in press reports, and debtor countries normally provide the texts to private creditors in the course of negotiations designed to satisfy the Paris Club's comparable-treatment requirement. The main reason for withholding this information, it appears, is that the technical language might be confusing to nonexpert readers. The advantages of disclosure in today's climate of transparency would seem to outweigh the disadvantages. If more user-friendly language were adopted in the process, the advantages would be even greater.

A final point about the negotiating process concerns the expenses involved. One of the remarkable features of the Paris Club is that it routinely completes restructuring accords involving billions of dollars of debt in a single day of negotiations at no cost to the debtor country beyond plane fare to Paris and two nights of hotel accommodations for its delegation. In contrast to negotiations with private creditors, Paris Club creditors have never charged restructuring fees.[37]

Paris Club Terms

Most of the Paris Club's jargon is associated with specific restructuring terms. Some are unique to the Paris Club, a situation that adds an element of opaqueness for private sector analysts and market participants. To help decode the jargon, the discussion of terms is divided into five parts: three policy constraints in the process, six basic parameters, four specific terms, three special features, and four sets of standard treatments.

Policy Constraints

Part of the mystery of the Paris Club arises from three practices found in sovereign restructuring deals with commercial banks that are ruled out in non-HIPC operations: commitments of new money, stock treatment, and debt reduction.

COMMITMENTS OF NEW MONEY. From the beginning the Paris Club followed a policy of never including *new money,* commitments of new lending from bilateral donor agencies, in its debt-restructuring negotiations. This is surprising and arbitrary from a private creditor perspective, which views new money as simply one of the many tools available to resolve a country's debt problems. One basic reason for the Paris Club tradition is that commitments of new lending are made in different forums—aid consortiums and consultative groups—for quite a few developing countries. Another reason is that rescheduling interest payments is financially equivalent to providing new money and Paris Club creditors are generally more willing to do this than banks are. A third and perhaps overriding reason is

---

37. Most debtor countries in recent years have engaged financial advisors and international lawyers to help with their Paris Club negotiations, but the expense associated with such help has varied greatly from case to case. Restructuring fees and spreads have been an issue in the negotiation of bilateral implementing agreements with some creditor countries.

that the IMF and the multilateral development banks normally provide new money to restructuring countries. From the perspective of the G-7 architects, financing from these agencies is just one of the forms of public support in addition to Paris Club debt relief that they can utilize to help a country recover from a debt crisis. In cases where private creditors are not involved, the Paris Club policy of keeping new money off the table has no practical consequences. Where private creditors are also providing debt relief, however, this policy can complicate efforts to achieve appropriate burden sharing.[38]

STOCK-OF-DEBT TREATMENT VERSUS FLOW-OF-PAYMENTS TREATMENT. Instead of replacing a specified stock of outstanding debt with a new stock having different characteristics, the Paris Club selects payments of principal (and sometimes interest) falling due during a narrow time period (the payment window, or *consolidation* period) and replaces them with a new loan contract having an extended repayment schedule. The original loans remain intact. Using Paris Club terminology, this is *flow treatment,* to distinguish it from *stock treatment,* when old loans are entirely replaced by new loans. Some commercial lenders call this approach *window rescheduling.* This is the principal means of keeping debtor countries on a short leash.

The practice of restructuring by means of flow treatments has far-reaching implications for both debtors and creditors. One is that most Paris Club candidates require several years of such relief before they can reestablish a viable balance-of-payments position. As a result the Paris Club tends to slip into a pattern of serial rescheduling in which debtor countries return repeatedly to reschedule the next year's payments. This pattern sometimes contributes to political resistance to reform in these countries. Another concern is that serial rescheduling builds up the stock of outstanding debt when interest repayments are rescheduled, thereby tending to make the country's debt burden appear less sustainable. The Paris Club has been doing stock treatments for HIPCs for several years. Having the same flexibility in non-HIPC cases could make it easier for the Paris Club to tailor its terms to the requirements of each country, especially when private creditors are inclined toward a stock treatment.[39]

---

38. Clark (1986, p. 860) notes that new-money commitments from donor countries were an issue that complicated the Paris Club operation with Poland in 1985.

39. The Paris Club can approximate a stock restructuring by defining the eligible debt broadly, selecting a long consolidation period, and granting a very long deferral. The operation for Jordan in 2002 is an example. This is a second-best approach that tends to confuse taxpayers in the creditor countries without commensurate benefits in the debtor countries.

DEBT REDUCTION. The Paris Club began forgiving debt for low-income countries in the late 1980s. In the same period when commercial banks agreed to debt-reduction deals with middle-income countries under the Brady Plan, the Paris Club stuck to its policy of not engaging in debt reduction. That policy was inconsistent with the practices of commercial banks and remained a source of inflexibility until May 2003.[40]

All lending by commercial banks—to sovereign borrowers as well as private companies—is considered to entail a risk of default and a measurable loss. This view is reflected in a set of commercial practices, including the maintenance of reserves against future losses, which are reinforced by prudential regulation of the banking sector and the tax treatment of reserves and losses. These practices facilitate the use of debt reduction in a flexible, businesslike fashion in any debt workout.

The Paris Club's reluctance to extend debt reduction to middle-income countries until very recently reflected a thorny policy obstacle. Some bilateral donor agencies adopted approaches to potential losses analogous to those of commercial banks and could engage in debt reduction when necessary without any particular complications. Other agencies, however, operate within rather rigid budget parameters. This is especially true of the United States.

Under the Federal Credit Reform Act of 1990, every federal agency making loans is required to estimate probable losses in net present value terms and to obtain budget authority in the congressional appropriations process to cover these losses. In the Paris Club context, as long as U.S. agency debt is rescheduled, no additional budget authority is required. Debt reduction, however, is considered to be a "modification" of the original loan, and lending agencies are required to seek additional budget authority for all modifications. Thus the United States is able to participate in HIPC debt reduction only up to specific limits set by Congress each year. This constraint is tolerable in the HIPC context, where relatively small amounts of debt are involved, but it creates a major problem in the case of non-HIPCs. In effect, without prior congressional approval, the U.S. government cannot participate in any Paris Club negotiation that will grant debt reduction to the debtor country.[41] This budget rule makes it difficult for the U.S. government to participate in meaningful negotiations. Either it must wait until

40. Exceptional politically motivated operations with Egypt and Poland in 1991, which contained substantial debt reduction, are discussed in chapter 6.
41. The process and the complications are neatly summed up in Department of State (1999, tabs H and I).

other creditors decide on the amount of debt reduction to be granted and then seek congressional approval to reduce debt owed to the United States on the same terms, or the other creditors are stuck with the terms approved in advance by the U.S. Congress. The new "staged approach" announced by the G-8 finance ministers in May 2003 offers a possible way out of this dilemma. A better solution would be for the executive branch to reach agreement with the U.S. Congress on a more flexible approach to restructuring debt in cases where private creditors have agreed to debt reduction on the basis of commercial criteria.

Basic Parameters

Four parameters limit the payments to be consolidated and restructured: the original tenor or class of credit, the signature date, the payment window (consolidation period), and the treatment of interest.

ORIGINAL TENOR OR CLASS OF CREDIT. Normally Paris Club restructuring operations exclude short-term loans (original maturity—tenor—of one year or less) and loans extended to private sector borrowers.[42] This practice is designed to protect trade credits that generally roll over, or revolve, every ninety days, rarely reach excessive proportions, and perform a critical function in maintaining a country's trade links with the rest of the world. If trade credits were subject to restructuring, banks would cut them off as soon as signs of debt-servicing difficulties became visible, which would tend to aggravate the country's problems. More precisely, the export credit agencies that are insuring these loans would suspend their "cover" to avoid getting stuck with a big exposure if the country ends up in the Paris Club.

SIGNATURE DATE. A critical step in every negotiation is the choice of a *contract cutoff date*. Loans signed after this date are normally excluded from restructuring. This is done to enable bilateral agencies to extend new loans to a country while it is preparing for negotiations and after negotiations have been completed but before the country has regained its creditworthiness. The cutoff date is usually set eighteen months before the date of

42. The Paris Club website refers to this parameter as "eligible credits." Guaranteed credits have been a source of confusion in some cases. Credits extended by commercial banks and suppliers that are guaranteed by a bilateral donor agency are put into the Paris Club basket, not the London Club's. Borrowing by private companies that is guaranteed by the debtor country government may or may not go into the Paris Club basket. Confusion can arise in part because debtor countries are not always informed about which credits are guaranteed and which are not; they often have poor records of the borrowing they have guaranteed. Private sector debt unguaranteed by the borrowing country and owed to export credit agencies was included in the early years of the Paris Club, but it is now routinely excluded. This fundamental change reflects the trend away from fixed exchange rate regimes and the increasing importance of private sector borrowing.

negotiations. In successive flow restructurings, the practice of the Paris Club is to keep the original cutoff date. This means that over a multiyear period of restructuring, the payments on debt incurred after the cutoff—which are not being restructured—tend to grow relative to the payments on debt incurred before the cutoff. In a number of cases the Paris Club has been forced to move the cutoff date to reduce payments during the recovery period to a sustainable level.

PAYMENT WINDOW. Two other key dates are the beginning and end of the consolidation period. Principal (and sometimes interest) payments falling due during this interval according to the original loan contracts are consolidated and deferred to a later period. Debtor countries generally seek a consolidation period longer than one year because they anticipate they will need help in the form of debt restructuring for a longer period of time and prefer not to make repeated trips to the Paris Club. The length of a country's IMF agreement establishes the maximum length of the consolidation period. Since the IMF does not enter into arrangements longer than three years, neither does the Paris Club. The consolidation period usually begins shortly before the date of restructuring negotiations. As a result, a distinction is created between past payments to be restructured (arrears) and future payments (payments in the consolidation period). This distinction adds an element of flexibility to the negotiations by providing the basis for two separate repayment schedules. Normally the creditors seek more rapid payment of the arrears than the payments falling due in the consolidation period.

TREATMENT OF INTEREST. Paris Club creditors, like all others, resist including interest payments in their restructuring operations. Nevertheless, most of the twenty-nine non-HIPC operations in the 1995–2002 period included interest payments. In at least one case, the Paris Club has started by consolidating principal payments only and has agreed to add interest payments in subsequent agreements. When that happens, it tends to be because the creditors would prefer not to change another parameter such as the cutoff date. Including interest in the restructuring, of course, amounts to capitalizing interest. Each time this is done, the stock of debt owed by the country rises even though the amount it originally borrowed has not changed. This is another feature of Paris Club restructuring that diverges from commercial practice and contributes to a buildup of unsustainable debt in some cases.

Specific Restructuring Terms

The amount of debt deferred, the extent of the deferral, and the cost of deferral are determined by the percentage of payments consolidated, the different treatment of ODA (official development assistance, meaning debt with a concessional interest rate) and non-ODA debt, the length of the grace and repayment periods, and the amount of interest charged on restructured payments.

PERCENTAGE OF PAYMENTS CONSOLIDATED. One of the more impenetrable mysteries of the Paris Club was the distinction between consolidated and nonconsolidated amounts falling due during the consolidation period. To take account of the ability of most countries to pay at a reduced rate, the creditors would set the level of nonconsolidated amounts at 10 percent (or some other percentage). As payments came due under each original loan contract, the debtor country had to pay 10 percent of the scheduled amount, and the remainder was consolidated and restructured. In some cases the nonconsolidated percentage differed between interest payments and principal payments. In other cases even nonconsolidated amounts were deferred but only for a short period of one or two years. In recent years the practice has been to set the percentage of nonconsolidated debt at zero, thereby easing the administrative burden of implementing Paris Club agreements for both debtors and creditors.

ODA VERSUS NON-ODA LOANS. Perhaps the biggest difference between Paris Club and London Club restructuring terms is that the Paris Club creditors make "soft" aid loans on highly concessional terms to low-income countries, and when debt restructuring is necessary, the restructuring terms on concessional loans tend to be different from those for nonconcessional loans. To qualify as official development assistance, a concessional loan must incorporate a "grant element" of 25 percent or more.[43] Normally, ODA loans are restructured on terms more favorable to the debtor country than non-ODA loans, the latter being predominantly export credits that must be extended on quasi-commercial terms to satisfy the rules adopted by the OECD countries to limit export credit competition. For example, rescheduled ODA loan payments might be repaid over twenty years while rescheduled non-ODA loan payments might be repaid over ten years.

GRACE AND REPAYMENT PERIODS. For many years the Paris Club would agree to a grace period (of three to five years) in which no repayments of rescheduled debt were due, followed by a repayment period in which equal payments were made semiannually. In recent years the Paris Club has favored shortening the grace period and establishing a schedule of steadily rising payments (termed graduated or blended payments). Typically the first installment of rescheduled debt is due six months after the midpoint of the

43. See chapter 3 for an explanation of how grant elements are calculated.

consolidation period, with installments continuing at six-month intervals until all the rescheduled debt has been repaid. These installments begin at a low level and rise steadily. For example, the first installment might be 1 percent of the rescheduled debt, and each subsequent installment might rise by 10 percent, with the twenty-fourth installment at the end of twelve years being equivalent to 10 percent of the amount originally rescheduled.

INTEREST CHARGED. One of the most consistent practices of the Paris Club has been to let individual creditor countries set the rate of interest charged on rescheduled amounts in bilateral negotiations with the debtor country. (This rate is sometimes referred to as moratorium interest to distinguish it from the interest rates on the original loans.) The main reason for doing this is the substantial variation in domestic interest rates among the major creditor countries. In May 2003, for example, the government borrowing rate for ten-year funds was 0.57 percent in Japan, 3.50 percent in the United States, and 5.11 percent in Norway. Adopting the same rate for all creditors in the Paris Club agreement would shift the burden of the restructuring from creditors with low interest rates to those with high interest rates. At the same time, the distinction between ODA and non-ODA debt is reinforced in bilateral implementing agreements. The standard Paris Club agreement commits creditor countries to apply interest rates on rescheduled debt that are not higher than "the appropriate market rate" for non-ODA debt or higher than the original concessional rates for ODA debt.

Special Features

Four special features found in most Paris Club agreements are the treatment of de minimis creditors, the option of using debt swaps, multiyear agreements, and the goodwill clause.[44] None of these has a significant cash flow impact.

DE MINIMIS CREDITORS. Minor creditors can escape a restructuring if their claims are de minimis. The standard de minimis level is SDR 1 million of principal and interest payments falling due during the consolidation period.[45] The limit is set lower, however, for countries with very small

44. Some features that were important in earlier years have been discontinued. An example is the use of offshore accounts in cases where the country has repeatedly entered follow-on rescheduling negotiations with arrears on rescheduled debt. To reduce the chances of arrears accumulating, the debtor country agreed to deposit in an offshore account (at the Federal Reserve Bank of New York, for example) monthly installments sufficient to cover all payments due to Paris Club creditors during the consolidation period, on both rescheduled and nonrescheduled debt. Disbursements to creditors were made, after bilateral implementing agreements had been concluded, consistent with the newly agreed payments schedule. This technique was first used in 1983 with Zaire.

45. The SDR is the IMF unit of account. SDR 1 was equivalent to $1.36 on December 31, 2002.

economies where payments of SDR 1 million represent a substantial portion of their debt-service obligations to Paris Club creditors.

SWAPS. In some cases, the debtor country and a particular creditor find it in their mutual interest to extend the restructuring benefit in the form of debt swaps that transfer hard currency liabilities into local currency liabilities.[46] The benefit to the creditor is advancing a particular social objective such as environmental cleanup, nature conservation, or poverty reduction. Swaps have been used to a lesser extent to facilitate the purchase of local equity interests by market investors, especially in privatized state enterprises. There is no limit to the amount of ODA liabilities that can be swapped, but swaps of non-ODA liabilities are commonly capped in Paris Club agreements at a percentage of the creditor country's non-ODA debt (10 percent, for example) or a specific amount (such as SDR 10 million).

MULTIYEAR RESTRUCTURING AGREEMENTS. Debtor countries often ask for a consolidation period that extends over two or three years. Where the country's recovery program is supported by a multiyear (or "phased") arrangement with the IMF, the Paris Club will consider a multiyear arrangement under which the rescheduling of payments falling due in the second (or third) year will go into effect only if the country is in good standing with the IMF. This condition protects the creditors from delivering the benefits of restructuring to a country that is failing to implement the measures required to restore its creditworthiness.[47]

GOODWILL CLAUSE. In cases where the Paris Club has agreed to a consolidation period shorter than the country's arrangement with the IMF, the creditors will readily agree to include a clause that proclaims their positive attitude toward negotiating further Paris Club relief within the period of IMF support. The goodwill clause is not binding on creditors, but it can be helpful to a debtor country government in deflecting pressure from domestic opponents of the government's reform program. In other cases the debtor country is eager to precommit the Paris Club to a subsequent negotiation, but the creditors are not convinced that it will be needed or that the debtor country will be able to meet the conditionality criterion. If pressed they may agree to include a watered-down goodwill clause that simply notes their

46. IMF (2001d, pp. 69, 71) notes that the Paris Club introduced swaps in 1990 for operations with lower-middle-income countries and that a precursor of their use was the Enterprise for the Americas Initiative, launched by the U.S. government in June 1990.

47. The most remarkable multiyear agreement was a two-year rescheduling for Peru at the end of 1978. A sharp improvement in Peru's balance of payments in 1979 made it possible for Peru to give back the relief obtained for 1980. This appears to be the only instance in the Paris Club's history where relief granted has been refunded. Multiyear arrangements have not had good track records, but they have gone out of and come into favor over the past twenty years.

willingness to consider a request from the country for further Paris Club support.

Standard Treatments

Recalling the distinction between exceptional HIPC-style terms for low-income countries and the normal terms of debt relief granted in crisis-driven sovereign workouts, the Paris Club breaks down the latter into three subcategories: Classic terms, Houston terms, and Ad Hoc terms. The Paris Club website defines the first two, but not clearly. No definition of Ad Hoc terms is offered. Based on an examination of the characteristics of the operations that fall into each subcategory, the distinctions appear to be as follows:

CLASSIC TERMS. These are granted to countries that have relatively short-term problems, have achieved higher per capita income levels, or borrow predominantly from commercial sources. Principal payments due on both ODA and non-ODA debt are rescheduled for no more than fifteen years (preferably five to ten years), and interest is charged at nonconcessional rates for both. Interest payments can also be rescheduled if necessary. In the 1988–2002 period, thirteen countries received Classic terms: Algeria, Angola, Argentina, Brazil, Bulgaria, Costa Rica, Croatia, Djibouti, Gabon, Mexico, Panama, Trinidad and Tobago, and Ukraine. This list and those below exclude countries that subsequently received more favorable terms.

HOUSTON TERMS. These have been granted since the G-7 Summit in Houston in 1990 to lower-middle-income countries (by the World Bank's definition. Payments on non-ODA debt are rescheduled over fifteen years or somewhat more. Payments on ODA debt can be rescheduled over twenty years including a ten-year grace period. Moreover, the moratorium interest on ODA debt is at concessional rates. In the 1988–2002 period, thirteen countries received Houston terms: Cameroon, Dominican Republic, Ecuador, El Salvador, Guatemala, Indonesia, Jamaica, Jordan, Kyrgyzstan, Morocco, Nigeria, Peru, and Philippines. (Non-HIPC low-income countries can also get Naples terms.)

AD HOC TERMS. This miscellaneous subcategory is for countries that have been treated as special cases. Generally, this means that extraordinary political circumstances, such as the collapse of the Soviet Union or a peace agreement in the Middle East, justified granting more generous terms than these countries could otherwise expect. In the 1988–2002 period nine countries received Ad Hoc terms: Albania, Egypt, Georgia, Kenya, Macedonia, Pakistan, Poland, Russia, and the former Republic of Yugoslavia. The only cases that involved an element of debt reduction were the Egypt and Poland operations in 1991 and the Yugoslavia operation in 2001.

At this stage in the Paris Club's history, the value of these subcategories is questionable. What is more relevant is that none of them allow for debt reduction. In the years ahead most non-HIPCs seeking Paris Club debt relief are likely to have significant debt owed to private creditors. In those cases where the countries require debt reduction from private creditors to achieve a sustainable debt burden, pressures are likely to intensify on the Paris Club to extend debt reduction too.

Implementing the Agreed Minute

Paris Club agreements are not legally binding on either side. They are signed "ad referendum" by the heads of the participating delegations, who thereby agree to "recommend to their Governments . . . that they provide relief . . . on the following terms." Bilateral agreements that formally change the debtor country's repayment obligations are subsequently negotiated separately with each creditor country.[48] The United States and some other countries furthermore require the negotiation of implementing agreements with each individual creditor agency after a bilateral agreement has been concluded. Others skip the bilateral agreement step and simply conclude an implementing agreement between each of their lending agencies and the debtor country.

The process of concluding bilateral agreements can be extremely easy. The creditor country transmits a text to the debtor country capital, which has terms that are entirely consistent with the Paris Club agreement and proposed interest rates that seem reasonable. The text is signed and sent back to the creditor country. More often, however, at least some features of the proposed text require discussion. For example, a fee may be charged on the rescheduled amount that appears unreasonable, and diplomatic demarches are required to arrive at a compromise. Sometimes the creditor will ask the debtor country to send a delegation to its capital to reconcile differences between the two countries' lists of outstanding loan amounts or resolve other issues. Occasionally a creditor country will agree in bilateral negotiations to extend more favorable terms than provided for in the Paris Club agreement, often reflecting a foreign policy objective or historical relationship.

---

48. Until recently, the U.S. government published its bilateral implementing agreements in the Department of State series of Treaties and Other International Acts (TIAS).

Another quirk is that for many years creditor countries had the option of extending new grants or refinancing loans to the debtor country in lieu of rescheduling. Japan was the only major creditor country to exercise this option consistently, reflecting a deeply ingrained policy of not providing new loans to a country that is unable to meet its contractual payment obligations. In 2002 Japan ended its practice of making grants to implement Paris Club debt relief with respect to ODA loans. This step was taken as part of the process of making the Japanese government's financial statements conform with generally accepted accounting principles.

Finally, the debtor country agrees to keep the Paris Club chairman informed about the status of its bilateral agreements and the payments made pursuant to these agreements. The creditor countries agree to inform the Paris Club chairman of the date of signature of their bilateral agreements, together with the interest rates set and the amounts involved.

Treatment of Debt Owed by Private Sector Borrowers

Some loans from bilateral donor agencies are extended to private sector companies without a guarantee from the borrowing country government. (Loans that carry such a guarantee are rescheduled on the same basis as loans to public sector borrowers.) These are almost exclusively export credit agency loans or commercial bank loans guaranteed or insured under export credit programs. An example would be a loan from the U.S. Export-Import Bank to the Southern Peru Copper Company to finance mining equipment purchased from U.S. suppliers.

The treatment of this debt in the context of a financial crisis varies according to the circumstances. One possibility is that borrowing companies are able to keep up with their scheduled payments, in which case restructuring is unnecessary. A second is that companies are unable to pay because the country's currency depreciated sharply in the crisis, making many companies that borrowed abroad insolvent. In these circumstances, the loans in question would be restructured on a company-by-company basis in the framework of the country's domestic bankruptcy laws. In other words they would be treated in the same manner as an isolated company default unrelated to a country crisis. (Korea and Thailand followed this approach after their crises in 1997.)

A third possibility is that companies are unable to pay because of exchange restrictions imposed by the government to conserve its foreign exchange reserves or defend its fixed exchange rate. In these circumstances, the government in effect assumes the obligation to repay the debt and could include these obligations in its Paris Club negotiations. The current practice, however, is to exclude debt owed by private sector borrowers.

In its 1982 crisis Mexico did not seek Paris Club relief on government debt owed to bilateral agencies. However, it introduced a scheme known as FICORCA to help private companies restructure debts (unguaranteed by the Mexican government) to foreign creditors. Simplifying considerably, the Mexican government committed to provide foreign exchange at favorable rates to companies that were successful in rescheduling debt owed to foreign creditors. The government also specified the terms required to qualify for the scheme.

A major unexpected complication arose because Mexican companies had borrowed substantially from export credit agencies or from commercial banks and suppliers with an export credit agency guarantee. The FICORCA scheme essentially set the rescheduling terms for this debt unilaterally, to which the Paris Club creditors violently objected. Resolving this matter required arduous negotiations that led eventually to the only Paris Club operation that treated exclusively private sector obligations.

This kind of unilateral rescheduling was regarded as one of the major challenges facing the Paris Club in the mid-1980s. It moved off the radar screen because the threat receded.[49]

Summing Up

The Paris Club machinery for restructuring debt owed to bilateral donor agencies functioned with remarkable efficiency in the long parade of sovereign debt workouts from 1956 to the mid-1990s, but with mixed results. Its successes were due in large part to modifications in its practices that were adopted when new challenges arose. By 1988, however, the Paris Club had exhausted the flexibility available within the boundaries of debt rescheduling in responding to the chronic debt problems of a substantial group of low-income countries. As a consequence, it began to undertake debt-reduction operations for these countries. Nevertheless, pressures have inten-

---

49. Indonesia introduced a FICORCA-style scheme in 1998 (INDRA) that provided a government exchange rate guarantee for private sector external debt that was restructured according to specified terms. Very little debt was placed in this scheme because the guarantee was not sufficiently attractive. A related scheme to promote private sector workouts with external creditors (Jakarta Initiative) was successful, and debts owed to bilateral agencies were included in these workouts. Lane (1999, pp. 23, 71).

sified to broaden the group of countries eligible for debt reduction and accelerate implementation.

Another problem surfaced in the late 1990s in dealing with the debt problems of middle-income countries that concluded debt-restructuring agreements with their private creditors in which there was an element of debt reduction. The Paris Club was adamantly opposed to granting debt reduction to these countries or to considering other forms of debt relief commonly used in commercial workouts. At the same time the Paris Club began to use its comparable-treatment principle to force debtor countries (Pakistan, Ukraine, and Ecuador) to restructure their bond debt. This action by the Paris Club was taken in the context of a deliberate effort by the G-7 architects to prove that bonds would not be exempt from sovereign workouts.

Much of the current controversy about the Paris Club results from the sea change in emerging markets finance that took place during the 1990s, when flows of official capital to the emerging market countries stagnated, but flows of private capital surged. The dominance of private flows is expected to prevail indefinitely, which means that workouts in the future are increasingly likely to involve countries that are more dependent on private flows than on official flows. As a consequence workout machinery will be required that is sensitive to the factors enabling countries to regain access to private sources of capital after a crisis. A forward-looking approach to comparable treatment is proposed in chapter 12 that, along with other incremental improvements, could help middle-income countries recover more rapidly from debt crises and reduce the amount of official financing required to support their stabilization and recovery programs.

6

The Bank Advisory Committee
(London Club) Process

Disorderly events tend to appear more orderly as they recede into the past, are analyzed by scholars, and summarized by commentators. The creation of the Bank Advisory Committee, or London Club, process for restructuring sovereign debt owed to commercial banks provides a good example. The impression conveyed in recent discussions is that the commercial bank workout process used in the 1980s with great frequency was a straightforward process from its inception. Most evidence points in the opposite direction.

A close examination of the origins of the Bank Advisory Committee (BAC) process reveals the same pattern of muddling through that was seen after 1994 in the search for an orderly process for restructuring bonds. Indeed, no machinery of any kind existed in 1975 for multibank reorganization of commercial bank debt. It had to be invented. Five years and more than five workout cases were required for the commercial bank process to metamorphose from a series of experiments to a recognizable process. This process was refined over another eight years and more than a hundred rescheduling deals before debt reduction was introduced under the Brady Plan at the end of the 1980s debt crisis.

Chapter 5 explained how the Paris Club grew organically in the 1960s from a series of negotiations to restructure loans extended by bilateral donor agencies to developing countries. Commercial banks also grew the BAC process organically. They were clearly encouraged by G-7 finance officials and the IMF to expedite the process and were even pressured at times to "fish or cut bait," but they were not given a piece of machinery ex ante and directed to use it. The G-7 architects only designed the broad strategy for resolving the debt crisis of the 1980s. The patent on the machinery for restructuring commercial bank debt belongs to the commercial banks.

Significantly, two groups of commercial creditors were not represented on Bank Advisory Committees in the 1975–95 period: bond investors, and suppliers (foreign companies that extended credit directly to importers for the purchase of their products). Readers should bear in mind the growing role of bond investors as bank lending to emerging market countries declined relative to bond financing during the 1990s. As a consequence, the treatment of bonds became a central issue in several prominent financial crises beginning with the Mexican peso crisis in 1994. This shift began to change the nature of the Bank Advisory Committee process. As bondholder representatives were brought into restructuring negotiations, BACs were being relabeled as Advisory Committees or Creditor Committees. Key features of the BAC process described in this chapter were evolving so rapidly that some prominent bankers claimed in the mid-1990s that the London Club was dead.

Origins of the London Club Process

For more than a hundred years before World War II, the bulk of the cross-border long-term lending to developing countries was in the form of bonds. Bank lending was primarily in the form of short-term trade financing or interbank credit lines. Bondholder committees were established to deal with sovereign bond defaults before the war, but nothing analogous existed for commercial banks because there was no need for it. The problems that occurred from time to time with loans to sovereign borrowers were addressed by individual banks on an ad hoc basis.

The first step toward building a workout process for bank debt was a shift in the historic pattern of financial flows. After the war, the amount of bond issuance by developing countries was minimal, but long-term borrowing from commercial banks began growing rapidly. Bank financing exploded in the early 1970s with the development of an active market for long-term syndicated loans, and the challenge of recycling petrodollars from oil-exporting to oil-importing countries. The second step was a rash of debt-servicing problems in the second half of the 1970s, anticipating the epidemic of the 1980s.

The third step was the architectural work of designing and building an effective restructuring mechanism. This could have been done systematically through a public sector initiative or a banking industry one, but it did not happen that way. Instead, the BAC process emerged out of commercial bank negotiations with a handful of debt-distressed countries. Existing procedures for corporate workouts, the practices of the Paris Club, and prewar experience with bond workouts all contributed to the eventual design.[1] Negotiations between 1976 and 1981 with Zaire, Peru, Turkey, Sudan, and Poland were the major milestones in designing the BAC process.

Cross-border lending from private sources to private companies and public sector entities in developing countries grew rapidly in the early 1950s. Some loans were extended by commercial banks in the industrial countries, and others by exporting companies (suppliers). Some loans were guaranteed or insured against inconvertibility and other political risks by export credit agencies in the industrial countries, but many were not. Latin American countries, unscathed by World War II and remote from the hostilities in Korea and Southeast Asia, were prime candidates for this lending. Before long several of these countries encountered payment difficulties. The efforts made to resolve these difficulties appear rather chaotic in hindsight.[2]

The first bank to develop a global lending business was Citibank in New York City. In a leadership succession in 1959, Stillman Rockefeller became chairman, George Moore became president, and Walter Wriston became executive vice president for overseas operations. Under Moore's direction,

1. The design of the BAC process flowed logically from the "custom and usage" of commercial banks in resolving problems that had arisen with syndicated loans over previous decades. (Conversation with John Riggs, January 24, 2003.) The views among practitioners of the BAC process vary systematically depending on their perspective. The perspective here is closest to that of New York–based bankers. Bankers based in Europe place a somewhat different emphasis on specific principles, practices, and country cases. Lawyers as a group have another distinct perspective. Whereas the bankers who chaired BACs tended to see each case as sui generis and had little contact with each other, the lawyers appear to have been constantly searching for relevant precedents and often exchanged information with their professional colleagues. A classic discussion of the legal issues from the perspective of legal advisors to debtor countries can be found in Walker and Buchheit (1984).

2. Bitterman (1973) describes several refinancing operations by the U.S. Export-Import Bank in the 1950s and 1960s for the purpose of clearing arrears on loans from foreign commercial banks to Latin American governments and private companies. Several of these are also mentioned in the quarterly, semiannual, and annual reports of the U.S. National Advisory Council.

Citibank began to establish branches along the major trade routes of the world as part of its business strategy to achieve a dominant position in the U.S. banking industry.[3] Wriston hired Al Costanzo, a senior manager in the IMF, to begin building a cross-border lending business that would be technically sound. Costanzo later hired Irving Friedman, with twenty-five years of senior management experience at the IMF and World Bank, to be his globe-trotting troubleshooter.

Wriston pursued Moore's global vision aggressively, in part as a way to expand business when U.S. banking regulations prohibited interstate banking, and in part to break out of the confines of the Glass-Steagall Act's separation of commercial and investment banking in the United States. An investment bank subsidiary (Citicorp International Banking Ltd., or CIBL) was established in London, and this bank became a leading arranger of cross-border, floating-rate eurodollar loans. Citibank's rigorous approach to country risk assessment was a selling point in syndicating to smaller banks.[4]

In 1967 Moore succeeded Rockefeller as chairman, Wriston moved up to be president (and chief executive officer), and Costanzo became the head of overseas operations. The new team put a high priority on expanding overseas, and by the end of 1976 Citibank had $26 billion in international loans on its books and branches in 103 countries. As an example of the importance of the developing country segment of its business, Citibank's exposure to Brazil at that time was roughly the same as its total consumer (nonbusiness) exposure in the United States.[5] Citibank's success prompted leading banks in the United States and elsewhere to begin competing for developing country clients. Wriston moved up to become chairman in 1970, and quickly announced his intention to increase Citibank earnings per share at a rate of 15 percent annually. Much of this growth was expected to come from international lending. Other banks jumped on the bandwagon to avoid being left in Citibank's dust.

Payment problems appeared quickly in a few countries.[6] Between 1955 and 1970, commercial banks arranged special loans to half a dozen Latin American governments (including Argentina, Brazil, and Chile) to help

3. According to house lore, this vision was inspired by Citibank's experience during the 1930s Depression, when the bank's domestic operations were losing money, and earnings from business in China made it possible to continue dividends to shareholders. (Conversation with Hamilton Meserve, June 2002.)

4. Friedman (1977, p. 1).

5. Lee Lescaze and Don Oberdorfer, "Big Foreign Lender Citibank Hedges Bets in a Risky Business," *Washington Post*, April 24, 1977, p. A1.

6. Cuba's repudiation of external debt following Castro's takeover in 1959, like the Soviet Union's repudiation of Czarist debt following the 1919 revolution and the Chinese repudiation following Mao's victory in 1949, was a familiar example of the risks inherent in cross-border lending.

Box 6-1. The Case of Chile

The case of Chile in 1971–72 illustrates one of the earliest efforts by banks as a group to avoid rescheduling. As the socialist government of Salvador Allende, elected in October 1970, began to nationalize foreign-owned copper mines and other large domestic and foreign businesses, the economy went into a tailspin. Allende declared a debt moratorium in November 1971 and took steps to obtain a generous rescheduling. Despite Chile's refusal to negotiate a standby agreement with the IMF for political reasons, the Paris Club agreed in April 1972 to reschedule 70 percent of principal and interest payment due through 1972 on the basis of IMF monitoring. (This was Chile's second trip to the Paris Club; the first was in February 1965.)

Negotiations with commercial banks for a refinancing loan began early in 1972. Led by Citibank, they were concluded successfully in June. The U.S. government, however, refused to implement the Paris Club rescheduling terms until Chile settled the outstanding expropriation claims of U.S. companies. This issue prevented the Paris Club from concluding a rescheduling agreement for 1973, and relations with creditors deteriorated until September 1973 when Allende was deposed in a coup led by General Augusto Pinochet. The commercial banks concluded a second refinancing loan shortly thereafter, and Chile's Paris Club obligations were rescheduled in March 1974.

them service their external debts during short episodes of balance-of-payments strain. The banks avoided formal rescheduling by extending "refinancing loans."[7] The case of Chile in 1971–72, summarized in box 6-1, illustrates one of the earliest efforts by banks working as a group, rather than individually, to avoid rescheduling developing country debt.[8]

7. Hardy (1982) contains case studies that describe the pre-1980 rescheduling operations of nine countries (Argentina, Brazil, Chile, Ghana, India, Indonesia, Pakistan, Peru, and Turkey) from a debtor country perspective. Bitterman (1973) contains case studies of the same countries for the 1950–70 period and for seven other countries (Colombia, Liberia, Mexico, Philippines, Tunisia, Uruguay, and Yugoslavia) from the perspective of a U.S. Treasury official. Friedman (1983) contains case studies of seven of these countries plus five more (Bolivia, Costa Rica, Jamaica, Nicaragua, and Sudan) from a commercial banker's perspective. In the prehistory of the Paris Club described in chapter 5, official financing was provided to a number of countries to help borrowers—from both the public sector and the private sector—meet payment obligations to commercial banks.

8. An exceptional effort involving the Philippines in 1970 may qualify as the first coordinated attempt by a group of commercial banks from several countries to arrange a refinancing loan for a developing country facing serious balance-of-payments strains.

The oil crisis triggered by the OPEC (Organization of Petroleum Exporting Countries) price increases in 1973 and 1974 (from $2 a barrel of crude to $11 a barrel) set the stage for widespread debt-servicing difficulties among developing countries. These were a precursor of the global debt crisis of the 1980s. Loan demand from oil-importing developing countries mushroomed in the early 1970s from a negligible base. The major international banks were awash in deposits from oil-exporting countries seeking safe places to keep their earnings. Commercial banks outbid each other to attract these new clients, and the low cost made borrowing on commercial terms hard to resist.[9] Both lenders and borrowers expected oil prices to decline over the medium term. Thus it did not appear imprudent for these countries to finance their growing current account deficits rather than adjust macroeconomic policies or enact structural reforms to contain their deficits.

As measured by the IMF, the medium- and long-term external debt of eighty-seven oil-importing developing countries increased from $76 billion at the end of 1972 to $173 billion at the end of 1976, when debt-service problems began spreading. By the end of 1979 this stock of debt had jumped to $299 billion. (Short-term debt was another $80 billion.) The share owed to private creditors (overwhelmingly commercial banks) went from slightly below half ($36 billion) in 1972 to slightly above half ($97 billion) in 1976 to 60 percent ($180 billion) in 1979.[10]

The role of commercial banks in the recycling process was initially welcomed by the G-7 finance ministers in their capacity as managers of the global financial system. By 1977, however, developing country debt had become a major issue on the international agenda.[11] Concerns about excessive bank lending prompted a lively public debate. American bankers testifying before the U.S. Congress in April 1977 pointed out that they had

9. Lending rates even fell below prevailing inflation rates, producing a rare instance of negative real interest rates for borrowers.

10. Nowzad and others (1981, p. 7). Much of the commercial bank debt was guaranteed by export credit agencies or other official programs against inconvertibility and transfer risk, that is, country default. A systemic weakness at the time was the lack of consolidated data on bank lending to developing countries. Each individual bank knew what its own exposure was in a given country but had no reliable means of determining how large a share of total bank lending to the country it represented. The World Bank began collecting and publishing this information from debtor country reporting systems with increasing rigor as the debt crisis unfolded. In the 1970s regulators in the major banking centers collected and analyzed information on cross-border bank lending but used different definitions. In the 1980s the Bank for International Settlements took on the responsibility of harmonizing, collecting, and publishing these data. These are currently published in the BIS quarterly series on Consolidated Banking Statistics.

11. Other relevant developments in the 1970s were the breakdown of the international monetary system based on fixed exchange rates and the maturing of eurocurrency markets.

experienced smaller losses on their foreign loans than on their domestic loans. They also stressed the remarkable capacity of most developing countries to adjust to external shocks.[12] In a speech in New York at the time of the hearings, Federal Reserve Board Chairman Arthur Burns noted the importance of enlarging official sources of balance-of-payments financing for developing countries so that banks would not bear an excessive burden.[13]

Around this time a view of country risk that would come back to haunt the banks gained currency: "countries don't go bankrupt." This mantra is commonly attributed to Citibank's Wriston, who used it in an op-ed piece published by the *New York Times* a month after the Mexican crisis in August 1982. The statement is usually recalled to demonstrate how blind banks were at the time to the potential losses associated with their loans to developing countries.

Unfortunately, constant repetition of this observation has confused the public debate about how to resolve sovereign debt problems. One mistake is that the sentiment did not originate with Wriston in 1982. It was already part of the conventional wisdom in 1977, echoed by highly respected officials such as Federal Reserve Governor Henry Wallich. More importantly, the comment calls attention to the fundamental distinction between lending to national governments and lending to private corporations. This distinction, which is not intuitively obvious, has much to do with why sovereign workouts cannot be carried out under the domestic bankruptcy-insolvency laws used for corporate workouts. (The substantive issues raised by this infamous quip are explored further in appendix A.)

No international law, convention, or treaty governs how a default by a sovereign borrower will be resolved. The process of refinancing, rescheduling, and ultimately (after 1989) reducing the debts owed by many developing countries to commercial banks was a practical alternative to a formal international bankruptcy regime. Several proposals were advanced during the 1975–95 period for creating permanent machinery "to ensure that timely, orderly, and equitable debt relief is provided on a comparable basis by both public and private creditors to countries experiencing difficulty in paying their debt."[14] The same objectives were cited in the North-South Dialogue on debt in the 1970s (see chapter 7).

For twenty years the G-7 finance ministers repeatedly opted to rely on the Paris Club and London Club machinery (with incremental improvements

12. Friedman (1977, p. 1).
13. U.S. House Committee on Banking, Finance and Urban Affairs (1977, p. 861).
14. Hudes (1986, p. 451).

from time to time) rather than put in place a new piece of machinery for sovereign debt workouts. There is more than a little irony in the work carried out by the IMF after 2001, with the support of the G-7 architects, to design permanent machinery in a global environment where market solutions would appear inherently more attractive than before.

Five Milestone Cases

Despite assurances to their shareholders, their regulators, and the public, commercial banks began to feel increasingly uneasy in 1976–77 about the efforts by some borrowing countries to avoid defaulting on their external debt. The banks started to cut back on new commitments and shorten maturities. As a consequence, borrowing spreads for these countries drifted up. This trend coincided with softening commodity prices to aggravate balance-of-payments pressures on many developing countries.[15]

The first major borrowers from commercial banks to be pushed into debt negotiations by rising oil prices (and falling copper prices) were Peru and Zaire in 1976. Turkey and Sudan followed in 1977. Negotiations with Poland that concluded in 1981 were the first with a country that had broader systemic significance. These cases illustrate how commercial banks postponed debt rescheduling for almost four years by arranging special refinancing and new-money loans and by eliciting complementary support from official sources, such as the IMF, World Bank, and aid donors. Collectively these cases gave birth to the BAC, or London Club, process for restructuring commercial bank debt. Appendix B contains short accounts of these five cases, highlighting the contributions made by each one to defining the BAC process used to conclude more than 200 sovereign debt restructuring deals with commercial banks since 1980.

The origins of the London Club label are obscure.[16] Three factors that presumably contributed to the popularity of this label were the meetings that took place in London to deal with the debt problems of Zaire, Turkey, Sudan, and Poland; the choice of English law as the governing law for most eurocurrency loans; and the use of the London Inter-Bank Offer Rate (LIBOR) as a

15. Two shocks that contributed to concerns about the risks of developing country lending among commercial banks were the near default by Indonesia's state oil enterprise, Pertamina, in 1975, and the revolution in Iran in 1978. These surprises saddled the banks with $6 billion of distressed debt. (*Business Week*, January 15, 1979, p. 33.) A moratorium on external debt payments by North Korea in 1975 was a smaller ripple. See Delamaide (1984, p. 71).

16. The earliest use of the term *London Club* in the financial press appears to be in an article published in 1980. See Vivian Lewis, "Inside the Paris Club," *Institutional Investor*, June 1980, pp. 33–37.

benchmark for setting the interest rate on many international loans. The London Club label is also misleading because New York was the venue for a larger number of negotiations between defaulting countries and their commercial bank creditors.[17]

In short, several years of experimentation were required to design the London Club process. It grew out of centuries of commercial bank experience with delinquent borrowers of all kinds. It was not imposed on banks by the IMF or the G-7 finance ministers, although these public sector institutions moved vigorously to apply the principle that private creditors must share the workout burden whenever a country that has borrowed heavily from private sources gets into a position of imminent or outright default. Twenty-five years after the fact, few observers appear aware that the London Club process was not invented to handle a particular country case. The reality is that the birth of the London Club process was a messy affair. As the first major IMF report on developing country debt problems pointed out, "debt restructuring exercises . . . entailed formidable organizational problems."[18]

The Paris Club and the London Club Compared

The Paris Club's membership is easy to describe, but its restructuring practices are full of idiosyncrasies and almost impossible to decode completely. The opposite is true of London Club negotiations with sovereign debtors between 1975 and 1995. Few generalizations can be made about the groups of commercial banks involved; each one had a distinct character. But their agreements were relatively straightforward.

As well as having no fixed membership, there was no secretariat to keep track of London Club deals. That makes it difficult to compile accurate information about the origins and early history of the London Club process. At the core of the process was the formation of ad hoc Bank Advisory Committees, Steering Committees, or Coordinating Committees consisting of representatives from banks with particularly large exposures to the debtor country concerned. In this study the label Bank Advisory Committee is favored, reflecting the preference of New York–based bankers and lawyers.

---

17. All of the negotiations with Latin American countries—the largest regional group by far—in the 1980s and 1990s were held in New York. The advantages of New York were convenience of transportation and access to the main offices (or principal branches) of the creditor banks and legal counsel. Proximity to the IMF, World Bank, and U.S. Treasury in Washington was another attraction.

18. Nowzad and others (1981, p. 34).

The most comprehensive inventories of commercial restructuring deals are found in reports issued by the World Bank and the Institute of International Finance (IIF). The 2002 edition of the World Bank's *Global Development Finance* report lists 221 deals involving sixty countries from the beginning of 1980 to the end of 2001. The latest IIF survey lists 260 deals between 1979 and 2000 involving sixty-two countries.[19] (This compares with 364 Paris Club operations with seventy-eight countries from 1956 through 2002.) Among a variety of differences between these two sources, the World Bank list includes refunding exercises carried out by countries in a strong balance-of-payments position to take advantage of a market opportunity, which are omitted from the IIF list. Another difference is that the IIF list includes the bond exchanges carried out in recent years, which are omitted from the World Bank list. Numerous differences can be found in the descriptions of the same deal, and both lists appear to contain significant errors.

The World Bank report and the IIF survey both provide information about the amounts of debt restructured, but these appear to be more misleading than the Paris Club numbers because they reflect more double counting. Even if eliminating double counting were possible, the figures would be misleading as a measure of the benefit to debtor countries because differences in terms yield large differences in the amounts of cash flow deferral and payment reduction (measured by net present value) for the same amounts of restructured debt.

The role of new money is a further complication. Commercial banks treated new money as an integral part of their deals in the 1970s and 1980s. By providing enough new money to enable the debtor country to keep up with its interest payments during the coming year (or other relevant period), banks were able to count these payments as income and treat their outstanding loans as sound credits. If they had rescheduled these interest payments, they would have lost the income, and banking regulations would have required them to treat the loans as impaired, which would have forced them to allocate income from sound loans to build reserves against possible future losses. Paris Club creditors are not subject to such regulatory requirements, and the Paris Club is consequently more open to rescheduling

---

19. World Bank (2002, appendix 2); Institute of International Finance (2001). Both lists miss the pre-1980 deals with Peru, Jamaica, and Turkey. Other pre-1980 deals do not qualify because they were limited to individual or small groups of banks and were not multilateral in character.

interest payments.[20] At the same time, the Paris Club has consistently refused to negotiate new-money commitments even though its member countries are often committing new money in separate consultative group or aid consortium meetings.

Readers who are confused at this point will find themselves in good company. One reason no one has yet produced a straightforward statistical comparison of Paris Club and commercial bank restructuring operations is that it is devilishly difficult to do so with the information publicly available, especially without an agreed methodology.

Three generalizations may help to regain a sense of direction. First, as detailed earlier, both commercial banks and Paris Club creditors have concluded scores of restructuring agreements with dozens of countries, involving hundreds of billions of dollars. Second, commercial bank restructuring deals are sufficiently different from Paris Club operations to make it nearly impossible to measure the amount of debt relief provided by each creditor group to a particular country over an extended period of time. The inclusion of soft loans in Paris Club operations and the inclusion of new money in BAC deals are two major sources of difficulty.

The third and probably most important generalization is that commercial bank lending and bilateral donor agency lending are functionally quite distinct. The daily business of commercial banks is to make a profit by pricing and managing credit risk effectively. They compete to raise funds and to supply credit in a huge global marketplace. They live with the reality that some measurable percentage of their outstanding loans will go sour and will have to be written down, occasionally to zero. By contrast bilateral donor agencies make loans to developing country borrowers to advance various foreign policy objectives: economic growth, alleviation of poverty, regional stability, civil order, and the like. A substantial volume of this lending is generated by export credit agencies devoted to supporting national suppliers of goods and services in the face of subsidized credit provided by other countries. Bilateral agencies obtain their funds from budgets, not by offering attractive returns to savers. There is no "marketplace" for official financing.

---

20. Some donor country agencies are bound by analogous budgetary requirements, but these do not have the same impact on behavior because public sector agencies are not evaluated on the basis of shareholder value reflected in stock prices.

In short, it is not feasible to assess quantitatively the relative burden of debt restructuring borne by Paris Club and London Club creditors in the past. It is clear, however, that each group has absorbed large-scale losses since the 1970s.

The "Personality" of the Bank Advisory Committee Process

On the creditor side of the table, the main characters in BAC negotiations between 1975 and 1995 were bankers and lawyers.[21] In the beginning the bankers involved were often those responsible for arranging the original loans. Within a few years workout specialists were given responsibility for restructuring negotiations. The lawyers came primarily from a small group of firms that served as the house lawyers for the leading banks selected to chair most of the BACs.

The banks that dominated lending to developing country governments in the 1970s were headquartered in the major industrial countries:[22]

—*United States*: Bank of America, Bankers Trust, Chase Manhattan, Chemical, First National Bank of Chicago, Citibank, Continental Illinois, J. P. Morgan, Manufacturers Hanover

—*United Kingdom*: Barclays, Lloyds, Midland, National Westminster, Standard Chartered

—*Germany*: Deutsche, Dresdner, Commerzbank

—*France*: Banque Nationale de Paris, Banque Paribas, Crédit Lyonnais, Société Générale

—*Japan*: Bank of Tokyo, Dai-Ichi Kangyo, Fuji, Industrial Bank of Japan, Mitsubishi, Sanwa, Sumitomo

All of these banks were interested in building a broad banking relationship with developing country governments. Sovereign loans were just one segment of the business. Some banks were especially interested in trade credit for private sector importers and exporters and other short-term lending activities (such as interbank credit and deposits). Others were more interested in establishing branches or subsidiaries abroad to provide financial services (such as traveler's checks, credit cards, and foreign exchange

21. Citigroup Senior Vice Chairman and Citibank Chairman William R. Rhodes, former Bank of America executive Rick Bloom and former Chase Manhattan executive Harry Tether were important sources for some of the details about BAC operations through written comments and conversations in 2002 and 2003.

22. Wellons (1987, p. 173). Two Canadian banks (Royal Bank of Canada and Bank of Nova Scotia) and two Swiss banks (Swiss Bank Corporation and UBS) arguably belong on this list.

trading) in which they had a comparative advantage over local banks. Still others sought mandates to manage or hold foreign exchange reserves.

Medium-term loans to governments (sovereign loans) generally took three forms: single-bank loans, club loans, or syndicated loans. Single bank loans involved just one lending bank and tended to be for smaller amounts (under $25 million) and to have shorter maturities (five years or less). Club loans involved a small group of banks, usually fewer than five. The amounts could be larger and the tenors somewhat longer. The participants some-times had equal shares but often had different shares.

Syndicated loans became the dominant form of medium-term lending in the 1970s. They had a number of interesting features. Most striking were the number and variety of banks involved. A $100 million loan might easily have twenty-five participating banks. Most of these would be second-tier or even third-tier banks in their respective countries. The attraction of partic-ipating in these loans was the interest rate, typically 100–200 basis points above LIBOR or the prime rate in the United States for highly rated corpo-rate borrowers. By taking small portions of loans to a large group of countries, regional banks were able to raise their interest earnings substan-tially. They tended to discount the risks, in part because of the arguments advanced by syndicate leaders about the creditworthiness of developing country borrowers and in part because of the favorable historical experience.

The marketing of syndicated loans was done in a clubby fashion rather than in an open market. A borrowing country would select a lead bank to arrange a syndicated loan for a specified amount and a specified duration. The lead bank would then find two or three major banks to help "sell down" the loan. They would be coarrangers or co–lead managers, depending on how large a share they took. These leading banks would get a front-end fee, or *praecipium* (such as 1/8 percent), related to the size of their participa-tion.[23] The participation structure was reflected in the "tombstones" placed in the financial press after a syndicated loan was closed. The leaders were listed on the top in larger or bolder fonts.

Most syndicated loans were made in U.S. dollars, and the documentation usually conformed either to New York law or English law. The borrower reimbursed the management group for its expenses, which included docu-ment preparation (by lawyers), marketing (termed "book running"), and post-syndication publicity. One bank was designated as the agent for each

---

23. Lead managers might get a fee of 1 7/8 percent. Small participants might get 1 percent. Co-lead managers and managers would get fees scaled between these two levels.

syndicate and received a fee for this service.[24] Principal and interest payments from the borrower were remitted to the agent bank, which transferred to each syndicate member its appropriate share.

A number of provisions of these loans had an important bearing on the restructuring process. One was the *pari passu* clause that required the borrowing country to treat participants in the loan no less favorably than participants in similar loans. Another was the pro rata sharing clause that bound the agent bank to distribute any payments received from the borrower among the participating banks in proportion to their shares in the initial loan. A third was a clause that required any bank in the syndicate to share any payment received directly from the borrower with all other syndicate members.[25] A fourth was the cross-default clause that allowed the banks in a syndicated loan to declare a default if the borrower defaulted on another syndicated loan (or if any public sector borrower defaulted in the case of loans to government entities).

In London Club negotiations, the commercial banks organized themselves along the lines of a syndicate. Generally the bank with the largest exposure to the defaulting government would be asked by this government to organize and chair a Bank Advisory Committee.

The Principles of Commercial Bank Restructuring

It could be difficult to find two bankers who would agree on the core principles of restructuring in a Bank Advisory Committee context. That leaves ample opportunity for others to identify principles from the 200-odd deals concluded in the past twenty-five years. Three mantras of commercial bank workouts recited with particular frequency and passion are case-by-case, voluntary, and market-based restructuring.

Case-by-Case Restructuring

Case-by-case treatment was, and remains, the starting point for all creditors in debt workouts with sovereign borrowers. Even the most passionate proponents of an international bankruptcy regime would tailor workouts to the circumstances of each case. Even under national bankruptcy regimes,

---

24. Agent fees were normally assessed at $250–400 per participant in the syndicate, representing a negligible cost to the borrower. Bank of America and Citibank dominated this piece of the business in the 1980s and 1990s.

25. The sharing clause was an issue in negotiations with Argentina following the Falklands/Malvinas conflict in 1982. Argentina paid U.S. banks, and a special effort by U.K. banks was required to achieve equitable treatment in the restructuring deal. (Conversation with Alfred Mudge, January 15, 2003.)

where thousands of cases are handled every year, each bankrupt company gets case-by-case treatment.

Voluntary Restructuring

Voluntary in this context meant that the terms of the restructuring were negotiated between the banks and the debtor country until a mutually acceptable outcome was reached. Voluntary did not mean that the creditors decided by themselves when to provide debt relief. In a commercial context, creditors only relinquish their contractual claims when the alternative is not getting paid or when they are able to obtain some advantage such as liquidity or collateral. The opposite of a voluntary restructuring is a workout forced on creditors by some official body such as the IMF or the World Bank or as the result of a take-it-or-leave-it offer by the debtor country.

Here a reference to corporate workouts may be helpful. Two outcomes can be distinguished in the procedure for corporate bankruptcies in the United States. One is a consensual agreement between the debtor company and its creditors without entering a formal bankruptcy process. Another is a restructuring plan prepared by the debtor and accepted by a majority of creditors in each distinct class of creditors. In this outcome, the minority creditors who opposed the plan have no recourse and are forced to accept the result (called a cram down).[26] The first outcome is considered to be "voluntary" in contrast to the second. In the sovereign-restructuring context, commercial banks made a similar distinction. They welcomed restructuring approaches that were "voluntary," in the sense that they were the product of a give-and-take, two-party negotiation, and opposed those that involved a cram down decided by a third party.

Although involuntary approaches are just as unappealing to Paris Club creditors as they are to commercial banks, the Paris Club has never treated this distinction as a principle. Presumably, any international body that had the power to cram down a restructuring on Paris Club creditors would have to be ratified by the governments of the Paris Club members.[27] Involuntary approaches are also unappealing to most borrowing countries because of the potentially adverse impact on their future access to debt financing. The issue that preoccupied the G-7 architects in 2002 was whether a formal framework of international law (permanent machinery) would be necessary to achieve

---

26. Newman (1992, pp. 419–22).

27. The mechanism proposed by the IMF in 2001 (the SDRM) might treat Paris Club creditors as one of the creditor classes coming under its purview. This is one of the unresolved issues in the current debate about the design of the SDRM.

timely and durable workouts in cases where much of the debt to be restructured is in the form of bonds (chapters 10–12).

Market-Based Restructuring

The most treasured restructuring principle for BAC-arranged deals has been a market-based approach. Unfortunately, this is jargon that means little to the general public. Decomposed, a market-based approach has three characteristics. It is flexible, pragmatic, and apolitical.

Relative to the Paris Club, BACs approached individual cases in the 1975–95 period with less baggage from previous operations. There were no standard terms. Commercial banks attached a high value to flexibility because it helped them find solutions acceptable across a large population of participating banks with divergent business objectives. It was easier for BACs to be more flexible because their composition changed from deal to deal more than happens with the Paris Club. Therefore BACs were not hostages to precedent to the extent the Paris Club was.

Commercial banks also had inherently more flexibility than Paris Club creditors because they were not accountable to legislative bodies. Their shareholders expected them to be constantly refining their financial engineering skills. This is not to say that banks were unconcerned about precedents. In the 1980s they were keenly aware that the first restructuring deal involving debt reduction would become a precedent for all other BAC-led negotiations under way or anticipated. Consequently a key strategic objective was to conclude the first deal with the country that required the smallest amount of principal or interest reduction.

A particularly nuanced manifestation of pragmatism was the BAC approach to burden sharing. In corporate workouts, the treatment of different classes of creditors has always been a key issue. In commercial practice all creditors must share in the losses, but not necessarily in the same manner. This differential treatment reflects differences in contractual rights as well as historical commercial practices. The relative treatment has long been a matter of negotiation. In the sovereign restructuring arena, this could be seen in the more favorable treatment of short-term trade and interbank credit. In the 1980s banks usually agreed to let debtor countries stay current on their obligations to bondholders. At the end of the 1990s the banks negotiated a debt exchange that was quite favorable to Russia without pressuring it to obtain comparable relief from Paris Club creditors.[28]

---

28. Clark (1986, p. 863) notes that commercial bank restructuring agreements in the 1980s did not include a comparable treatment clause because of "concern that a provision of this sort might be construed as inducing breach of contractual arrangements." Bank agreements did include, how-

The driving motivation for most banks represented on BACs was the desire to continue doing business with the debtor country. BACs resisted the adoption of overarching principles and procedures so that the restructuring process would remain as pragmatic and ad hoc as possible. When they did take a firm stand, it was usually to avoid actions that would be inconsistent with general business principles or that would compromise their legal rights as creditors.

BACs viewed debt restructuring as a regrettable but normal business activity. The risks in domestic lending operations were generally well known, and workout procedures were highly refined. Most important of all, they were largely insulated from political pressures. Indeed, a good test of the effectiveness of a country's corporate bankruptcy regime was the extent to which it was depoliticized. Laws and regulations provided a legal framework for achieving predictable results, or "legal certainty" in the language of the marketplace. Judgments by bankruptcy courts that allowed partisan considerations to affect their rulings, or gave special consideration to the managers or employees of bankrupt companies and the communities in which they were located, could be reversed by appellate courts. The overriding criterion for workouts was commercial viability. Presiding judges had to approve a restructuring plan acceptable to the creditors as long as it left the company in a position to operate on a profitable basis. Courts could not require that an agreed plan be modified to give a bankrupt company more "breathing space" or a bigger margin for contingencies.

In the arena of sovereign debt workouts, it is impossible to set aside political factors. Most importantly, governments in debtor countries are subject to domestic political resistance to actions—such as cutting budget spending on social programs—that would raise the country's ability to service external debt toward its technical capacity. Another political factor is the financial support debtor countries receive from other friendly governments. The forms and levels of this support are driven by foreign policy objectives more than economic and financial analysis. The greater the official financing received, other things equal, the greater the country's capacity to meet its payment obligations to private creditors. One form of official support is Paris Club debt relief. It is clear from the record that some debtor countries have received especially favorable terms for geopolitical reasons (such as Mideast peace or democratic transition in the Soviet-bloc countries). Despite their efforts to treat all members in a uniform manner, the IMF, the

---

ever, mandatory prepayment clauses that required the debtor country to prepay rescheduled debt if it provided more favorable treatment to other creditors on "comparable indebtedness" and if requested to do so by the rescheduling banks.

World Bank, and the other international financial institutions have also been less demanding of policy reforms by countries in a workout mode when their dominant G-10 shareholders have urged rapid action or supported more than the normal amounts of financing.

Throughout the 1975–95 period, BACs adamantly resisted pressure from official bodies such as the IMF or the Paris Club to go beyond commercially defensible restructuring terms. They fought to ensure that financial support for the purpose of advancing political objectives would be the sole responsibility of official agencies. On rare occasions they were unsuccessful. For example, commercial banks were not able to escape debt reduction in 1991, when the Paris Club reduced the debts of Poland and Egypt as a reward for positive political action—in Poland's case for its role in bringing down the Iron Curtain; in Egypt's case, for its participation in the Camp David peace agreement.[29]

Two devices were used to ensure that a BAC deal would be market-based. The most important device was to set the interest rate on restructured debt above LIBOR, which represented the marginal cost of funds to banks. Any rate below LIBOR was seen as a concessional rate inconsistent with commercial practices. In cases where debt reduction was necessary, banks were able to define a discount consistent with the market's perception of the default risk associated with new lending to each debtor country. Any larger discount would have been seen as incorporating an element of charity incompatible with their responsibilities to their shareholders. The other device was to link the new repayment terms to each country's "capacity to pay." This approach was derived directly from experience with corporate and household borrowers and relied on techniques of quantitative analysis refined over decades if not centuries.

The Principles of the Brazil Advisory Committee, 1990

The principles of case-by-case, voluntary, and market-based debt restructuring have been distilled for this study from the BAC restructurings in the 1975–95 period in the absence of any existing agreed set of principles. An intriguing set of principles was put on paper in the context of the commercial bank negotiations with Brazil in September 1990.[30] When faced with an unrealistic debt-restructuring request from the government of Brazil fol-

29. In cases where banks were asked to agree to maintain short-term credit lines, they usually insisted that export credit agencies in the Paris Club countries keep the debtor country concerned "on cover." These agencies were sometimes reluctant to do so for budgetary or political reasons.

30. Provided by Harry Tether, April 2002.

lowing the announcement of the Brady Plan, the Brazil Advisory Committee outlined six principles that the government would have to accept to conclude an agreement in a timely fashion. These principles were produced through an informal process by a small group of banks, but the banking community in general was given an opportunity to raise objections. None materialized.

The six principles illustrate bank views at a fairly advanced stage in the bank restructuring history of the past twenty-five years. To win a restructuring agreement, the Brazilian government was asked to:

—*Meet four preconditions to negotiations.* (a) Demonstrate progress in implementing Brazil's IMF-supported adjustment program and provide the banks updated statistical information on Brazil's economic situation. (b) Reach agreement in principle with the Paris Club on substantial support from bilateral donor agencies. (c) Repair lapses in Brazil's commitments under the 1988 restructuring agreement with commercial banks, such as the accumulation of interest arrears. (d) Honor the guarantees the government had extended for borrowing by Brazilian public sector agencies.

—*Present the outline of a restructuring plan.* (a) Accept the 1988 deal as a viable basis for further restructuring. (b) Agree not to reschedule again the payments that were restructured in the 1988 deal.[31] (c) Agree to focus the current deal on unrescheduled debt and related interest payments, with a view to lowering the interest rates for a transitory period and reducing principal "by a double-digit billion amount" through debt exchanges, buybacks, and so forth. (d) Obtain funds from multilateral and bilateral donor agencies to support these exchanges.

—*Settle interest arrears.* Eliminate the government's substantial interest arrears commensurate with its overall payment capacity, in which case the banks would consider recapitalizing any remaining interest arrears.

—*Exclude trade and interbank lines.* Agree to continue excluding these short-term credits from the restructuring, with the understanding that banks would continue to roll them over on a voluntary basis.

—*Forgo new money.* Agree not to look to the banks for any new long-term financing, but to obtain such financing as may be required from official sources.

31. The 1988 deal rescheduled principal payments falling due over a multiyear period, with repayment stretched over a relatively long time. Because Brazil had stopped paying interest when it declared a moratorium in 1987, the banks were especially keen in 1988 on resuming a flow of interest payments. They reached agreement on two separate reschedulings of past-due interest before concluding the Brady Plan deal in 1994. The banks yielded on this 1990 principle in their 1994 deal and agreed to restructure the debt associated with the 1988 agreement.

—Attract private capital flows. Take measures to restore confidence to the point of inducing new voluntary lending by banks, reversal of capital flight, and spontaneous flows of direct investment and portfolio investment.

Comparison with Paris Club Principles

The five principles of Paris Club restructuring correspond to some extent to the three BAC principles, but a principle-by-principle comparison reveals some interesting differences.

CASE-BY-CASE APPROACH. This is the "first" principle for both creditor groups, but it had no more practical significance in the BAC context than it did in the Paris Club context. Its main purpose for both was defensive, namely to deflect proposals for generalized debt write-offs and fend off critics who alleged that debt-restructuring operations were insensitive to the special needs of each debtor country.

Apart from politically driven debt forgiveness for the poorest countries in the world, and barring a collapse of the international financial system, it is hard to imagine that any serious consideration of generalized approaches to sovereign workouts will occur in the years ahead.[32] In other words, the case-by-case principle is not an issue in today's world.

CONSENSUS. BACs were somewhat less rigid about unanimity than Paris Club creditors. Typically, syndicated loans contained provisions that required 100 percent agreement of the participants to change payment terms, and unanimous consent was obtained. Practical ways were found to deal with holdouts, sometimes involving arm-twisting at the chairman or CEO level.[33] For new money, however, a high threshold for participation (above 95 percent) would be set, allowing a few exposed banks to escape increasing their exposures. The Paris Club's attachment to consensus should not be exaggerated. The Paris Club, too, had its ways of dealing with dissenting members.

SOLIDARITY. This Paris Club principle had no counterpart in the BAC process because finality for the banks was achieved at closing. There was no

32. The IMF's SDRM proposal—see chapter 11—flirts with becoming a generalized approach because it includes a debt-sustainability test that would be applied in the same fashion for all countries.

33. Another way was an open secret. Banks with small exposures that wanted to exit could sell their loans in a "gray market." Lead banks sometimes purchased these loans and resold them at a loss to eliminate the irritant. Sometimes the debtor country government purchased these loans. The impact of this process can be seen in the Côte d'Ivoire rescheduling at the end of the 1970s, which affected debt held by around 380 banks at the beginning of the negotiations. The deal that was concluded in 1985 involved fewer than 300 banks. (Conversation with John Riggs, January 24, 2003.)

room for individual commercial banks to cut special restructuring deals with the debtor country. If there were business reasons to demonstrate a special relationship, banks had other ways of doing so, such as the extension of new credit.

CONDITIONALITY. Requiring the debtor country to have in place before negotiations an economic program approved and financed by the IMF is perhaps the strongest of all Paris Club principles. IMF conditionality did not appear to be prominent in the BAC process, but appearances were deceiving. Even before the Mexican crisis in 1982, commercial banks adopted the practice of refusing to enter into restructuring negotiations with a country that was unwilling to seek IMF financing to support its recovery program. In several instances, however, BAC negotiations were concluded before the debtor country had reached agreement with the IMF. In negotiating the February 2000 agreement with Russia, for example, the BAC was anxious to convert old obligations of the former Soviet Union to new obligations of the Russian Federation and was relatively unconcerned about weaknesses in Russian policies at the time.[34] The bottom line is that BACs understood the importance of sound policies. They welcomed the role of the IMF in designing and supporting credible programs. However, commercial banks attached roughly the same importance to clearing interest arrears before concluding a negotiation. Although clearing arrears was not always possible, it was seen as a test of whether the debtor country was negotiating in good faith.

COMPARABILITY OF TREATMENT. This study has not given comparable treatment the status of a core principle for commercial banks. Banks were clearly concerned about burden sharing among creditors, but as an objective to be approached pragmatically. In the Brady Plan restructurings, for example, the banks did not press the debtor countries to seek debt and debt-service reduction from their Paris Club creditors. Banks were not putting new money into these countries, and they understood that more new money would flow from bilateral donor agencies if they did not have to accept outright losses. Today, however, the issue of comparable treatment between official and private creditors lies at the heart of the debate about workout techniques. It has become an issue partly because of the role of capital market financing and partly because, until May 2003, the Paris Club approach to comparable treatment did not take into account the growing role of commercial lending to emerging market economies during the 1990s.

---

34. There were also cases where the debtor country was not a member of the IMF (Cuba, North Korea), which ruled out linking the restructuring of bank debt to an IMF arrangement.

The Process of Bank Advisory Committee Negotiations

A typical Bank Advisory Committee deal in the 1975–95 period involved the same three stages identified in this study for the Paris Club process: preparations, negotiations, and implementation. The duration of each stage, however, tended to be quite different. In addition, the BAC process began with an additional stage: establishing the negotiating forum. [35]

Forming a Bank Advisory Committee

The restructuring process for commercial bank debt started with a decision by the debtor country to "mandate" a leading bank to organize a BAC. Initiation by the debtor was almost important enough to be considered a principle. In practice, the authorities in the debtor country were often advised to take this step by commercial bank representatives, or the IMF, or a creditor government official when it became clear that the country's major creditors were unwilling to commit new financing. This step was usually taken before the country had an IMF financing arrangement in place or before a Paris Club operation had been concluded.

For countries that had previous experience with a BAC, the choice of a bank to chair the committee was usually obvious—the same one that chaired the last negotiation.[36] First-time candidates were advised to approach the bank that was the government's largest creditor or had been the most active in arranging syndicated loans. In a few cases, this bank deferred to another bank. The chairmen of some of the most prominent BACs in the 1975–95 period are listed in table 6-1.

Once selected, the chairman of the BAC—in consultation with the chief negotiator for the debtor country—invited other banks to participate on the committee. The number of members was kept as small as practical, rarely exceeding fifteen.[37] Banks resisted forming larger committees to keep the process efficient. The selection of members was governed by nationality as well as exposure. It was important that banks from every major creditor country have at least one seat at the table. The smallest committees had

35. The information in this section draws heavily on conversations with bankers and lawyers involved in BAC negotiations in the 1975–95 period. The primary written sources are IMF (1980), Nowzad and others (1981), Hardy (1982), Friedman (1983), Rhodes (1983 and 1989), Mudge (1984a, 1984b, 1988, 1992), Brau (1983), Clark and Hughes (1984), Mentré (1984), Dillon (1985), Clark (1986), Holley (1987), Dimancescu (1989), and Kearney (1993).

36. Finding a bank to chair a BAC was not always an easy step. Algeria in 1994, for example, had to make a special effort to get the banks involved to recruit a chairman. (Communication from Dominique de Guerre, January 29, 2003.)

37. Brazil's BAC grew to twenty-two banks for the negotiations in the late 1980s.

three to five members. Generally each bank on the BAC would be responsible for obtaining the cooperation of a specific group of small banks not represented on the BAC.

One of the first steps after putting together the committee was the selection of a law firm. This practice contrasted sharply with the Paris Club process where lawyers were almost invisible. One reason for having lawyers was that bankers were accustomed to using lawyers in workouts with corporate borrowers. The more fundamental reason was that the lawyers were responsible for drafting the agreement signed to close the restructuring. In other words BAC agreements were legally binding documents, unlike Paris Club agreements. No other documentation was required to implement restructuring agreements. The chairing bank typically selected the house lawyer. For Citibank, the house lawyer was Shearman & Sterling. It was Milbank, Tweed, Hadley & McCloy for Chase Manhattan Bank, and Simpson, Thatcher & Bartlett for Manufacturers Hanover Bank. Clifford Chance, based in London, was involved in all of the BAC restructurings governed by English law.[38]

Preparations

The preparations stage began with a meeting between the committee and a delegation from the debtor country. These delegations were sometimes headed by a finance minister or central bank governor but more often by a specially appointed debt negotiator. New York, London, and Paris were the most frequent venues for these meetings.

The main purpose of the initial meeting was to receive the debtor country's proposal for the restructuring terms it would like to obtain. This proposal was usually presented in the context of the country's recovery program and included information on how the authorities expected to treat other creditors (such as the Paris Club). The IMF mission chief was usually invited to participate in this meeting to describe the expected IMF support for the country and to answer any questions BAC members had about the assumptions used to arrive at the IMF's balance-of-payments projections for the medium term.

38. Coward Chance became Clifford Chance in a 1987 merger. Faced with high-priced lawyers across the table, debtor governments invariably hired prominent law firms to advise them in their BAC negotiations. These legal advisors helped to design negotiating strategies and examined the fine print to make sure that the debtor country's interests were not compromised. The firms with the most experience advising debtor governments on BAC negotiations were the same as those advising on Paris Club negotiations: Cleary, Gottlieb, Steen & Hamilton, White & Case, and Arnold & Porter.

Table 6-1. Selected Bank Advisory Committee Chairmen and Cochairmen

Country and period	Officeholders
Algeria, 1992–96	Martial Lesay, Société Générale
	Hideshi Komatsu, Sakura Bank (vice chairman)
Argentina, 1983–93	Bill Rhodes/Rima Ayas, Citibank
Brazil, 1983–94	Bill Rhodes/Robert McCormack/Mike de Graffenreid, Citibank
	Leighton Coleman/Alan Lowe, Morgan Guaranty (deputy chairman)
	Guy Huntrods/David Drewery/Michael Hunter, Lloyds Bank (deputy chairman)
Bulgaria, 1994	Peter Tils, Deutsche Bank
Chile, 1983–91	Susan Segal, Manufacturers Hanover
Colombia, 1985–91	Larry Miller/Charles Meissner, Chemical Bank
Costa Rica, 1983–90	Helmut Stromeyer/Ulrich Merton/Peter McPherson/ James Jardine, Bank of America
Côte d'Ivoire, 1985–96	Thierry Desjardins, BNP
Dominican Republic, 1983–94	David Hilton, Bank of Nova Scotia (cochairman)
	Keith Talbot, Royal Bank of Canada (cochairman)
Ecuador, 1983–95	David Drewery/Michael Hunter/Bill Camposano, Lloyds Bank
	David Driscoll/Alan Delsman/Harry Tether, Chase Manhattan (vice chairman)
Mexico, 1983–90	Bill Rhodes/Andrea Bauer/Bob McCormack, Citibank (cochairman)
	Preston Bennett/Rick Bloom, Bank of America (cochairman)
	Eberhardt Von Wangenheim/Tony Spicijaric, Swiss Bank Corporation (cochairman)
Morocco, 1986–90	Christian Peysson, BNP (cochairman)
	Rima Ayas, Citibank (cochairman)
Nigeria, 1987–92	John Champion/Brian Grimmond, Barclays Bank
	Jose de la Ossa/Brooks Frazar, Citibank (vice chairman)
	Christian Peysson/Xavier Deffis, BNP (vice chairman)

Immediately following the introductory session, the BAC would begin meeting, often daily, in a designated "boiler room" to prepare a counteroffer. A key step in this work was the formation of an economic subcommittee responsible for assessing the debtor country's capacity (or ability) to meet its debt-service obligations to external creditors. These subcommittees con-

Table 6-1. Continued

Country and period	Officeholders
Panama, 1983–96	Rick Bloom, Bank of America (1983–88)
	Andrea Bauer/Mitch Hedstrom, Citibank (1989–96)
	Atsushi Watanabe, Bank of Tokyo (vice chairman)
Peru, 1980–96	Bill Rhodes/Susan Bergen/Andrea Bauer, Citibank
Philippines, 1986–92	David Pflug/Susan Segal, Manufacturers Hanover
Poland, 1982–94	Brian Grimmond/John Larkman/Geoff Stokley,
(in rotation)	Barclays Bank
	Gabriel Eichler, Bank of America
	Michael Hunter, Lloyds Bank
	Ernst Moritz-Lipp, Dresdner Bank
Romania, 1982–87	Brian Grimmond, Barclays Bank
Russia, 1991–96	Wolfgang Wendt, Deutsche Bank
Uruguay, 1983–91	Bill Rhodes/Mike de Graffenried, Citibank
Venezuela, 1986–90	Francis Mason/Robert Murphy, Chase Manhattan
	Michael Hunter, Lloyds Bank (cochairman)
	Rick Bloom, Bank of America (cochairman)
	Yorihiko Kojima, Bank of Tokyo (cochairman)
Yugoslavia, 1983–96	Maggie Mudd, Manufacturers Hanover
	Marie-Christine Crosnier, Société Générale
	Robert Gyenge, Chase Manhattan

Source: Based on interviews with bankers and lawyers associated with these committees. Dates primarily from World Bank (2002).

Note: For the period 1980 to 1996 only. The committee for Russia concluded a deal in 1997. The committee for Côte d'Ivoire concluded a Brady Plan deal in 1998. The country went into default, and a new committee was formed in 2000 to negotiate a further restructuring, which was still pending as of mid-2003. Multiple names indicate an initial chairman and his or her successors. Other countries that negotiated restructuring deals with BACs during this period include Bolivia (1980–93), Cuba (1983–85), Gabon (1987–94), Guyana (1982–88), Honduras (1987–89), Iran (1993–94), Jamaica (1981–90), Jordan (1989–93), Liberia (1982–83), Madagascar (1981–90), Malawi (1983–88), Mozambique (1987), Nicaragua (1980–84), Niger (1984–86), Senegal (1984–89), Sierra Leone (1984), South Africa (1985–93), Sudan (1981–85), Togo (1980–88), Trinidad and Tobago (1989), Zaire (1980–89), Zambia (1984). Lomax (1986, p. 152) has a table that lists the advisory committees that were active in the mid-1980s for twenty-five countries. The chairing bank is identified and the number of banks on each committee is given with a breakdown by major creditor country or region.

sisted of four or five economists from the major banks.[39] The following elaboration of the role of economic subcommittees serves to highlight some of the subtle differences between the Paris Club and the BAC approaches to sovereign workouts.[40]

39. Two economists who chaired most of these subcommittees for the Latin American countries in the Brady Plan era were Larry Brainard from Bankers Trust and Jim Nash from Morgan Guaranty.

40. Trade subcommittees and interbank subcommittees were formed for the Brazil and Mexico BACs in the early 1980s. See Rhodes (1983, p. 26).

Unlike the Paris Club, the BACs did not take the IMF's projections as a given. Economic subcommittees looked carefully at each country's adjustment program and arrived at their own judgments of the economic impact of this program. Most subcommittees traveled to the debtor country capital, where they spent several days conferring with policymakers and experts in key ministries to gauge the country's prospects. Occasionally a second trip was necessary. Subcommittees for the Latin American countries usually spent a day in Washington to probe the views of the U.S. Treasury Department and other key agencies. The subcommittees generally had excellent access to data and documents, including IMF staff reports. They worked full time for three to four weeks on their analysis, and when finished they presented their findings to the full BAC. Subcommittee members and IMF staff usually had some informal contact during this period, but the extent and value of this contact varied across cases.

Economic subcommittees usually worked with detailed balance-of-payments models that went out as many as five years. These models gave particular attention to the fiscal position of the government. The budget surplus before payment of interest on debt (primary surplus) was estimated carefully. Sources and uses of funds were analyzed to identify the funds available to meet obligations to the banks. For Brady Plan deals, a critical piece of information was the availability of "enhancements" from the IMF, the World Bank, or the relevant regional development bank to collateralize Brady Bonds or finance buybacks of old debt.

Most Brady Plan deals also included a menu of options. Sometimes technical subcommittees were formed to work on the financial engineering aspects of the menu. Mathematical models were used to ensure that the various menu options would be financially equivalent. In other cases, the full BAC or its economic subcommittee performed this work.

One especially challenging piece of the preparatory work was the reconciliation of data on the country's obligations to foreign banks with the banks' own data. This was generally the responsibility of the BAC chairman and the supporting staff. One of the complications of the reconciliation process was that many bank loans were guaranteed or insured by official agencies in the creditor countries. In countries where the borrowers were primarily private companies, the government usually tracked external borrowing by these companies but often did not know which loans from commercial banks were guaranteed by official agencies and which were not. In a few cases the government's records of its own external borrowing were so poor that they had to be recreated after negotiations commenced. As a result the amount of debt in the BAC's "basket" after reconciliation might turn out to be considerably smaller than initial estimates. Another complication was that some commercial banks sold their loans (or their participations in a syndicated loan) to other banks or investors. In this respect the reconciliation process for commercial bank debt was more complex than for Paris Club debt.[41]

The Mexican rescheduling in 1982 and the workouts with other major borrowers shortly thereafter involved administrative complexities that tend to be glossed over in discussions of the 1980s debt crisis. Box 6-2 illustrates these complexities and serves as a reminder of the practical obstacles to achieving quick workouts regardless of the machinery that exists.

Negotiations

After receiving the report from its economic subcommittee, a BAC would prepare a counteroffer and schedule a meeting to present it to the debtor country delegation. The debtor delegation usually returned to its capital to consider the counteroffer and to produce a revised proposal. Additional negotiating sessions were scheduled as necessary, and the chief of the IMF team negotiating with the debtor country was often invited to these meetings to answer questions.

Because negotiations extended over a considerable period of time (up to two years in some cases), negotiating positions would change as a result of developments in the debtor country or elsewhere. For example, as Brady Plan debt reduction began, the banks gave top priority to concluding deals with the countries that needed the smallest discounts and worked more slowly on less creditworthy countries to avoid precedents that would compromise their negotiating position. The pressure on banks to compromise came largely from the impact of growing arrears on their earnings reports. The pressure on debtor countries came from the desire to normalize relations with creditors so that fresh flows of financing could resume.

Senior finance officials also exerted pressure at key points in the negotiating process. The IMF managing director would contact a BAC chairman on occasion to stress the implications of specific terms for the debtor country's recovery prospects. G-7 finance ministers and their deputies would more often engage in arm-twisting with BAC chairmen or members. The views of certain governors and senior staff members of the Federal Reserve

---

41. In some cases, this work was facilitated by organizing national or regional committees; see Lomax (1986, p. 154–55). In others, leading accounting firms were hired by the BAC to carry out the reconciliation work (conversation with John Riggs, January 24, 2003).

Box 6-2. Administrative Complexities—A Firsthand Account

Rick Bloom, who chaired or cochaired Bank Advisory Committees for Mexico, Panama, and Venezuela, and served as a member of other such committees as a Bank of America executive, provided this account at the author's request. It shows that the complexities of restructuring are not unique to sovereign bond debt. Comparable difficulties were overcome when the London Club machinery for restructuring commercial bank debt was being built in the late 1970s and early 1980s.

"People today seem to think that the commercial bank debt workouts in the 1980s mostly involved syndicated loans to public sector borrowers. While much of the debt we rescheduled was in this form, the body of debt we had to deal with was much bigger. Among the many forms were active lines of trade credit, inactive trade lines, lines of credit from banks in New York and London to the offshore units of debtor country banks, unguaranteed supplier credits, and supplier credits guaranteed either by the debtor country government or export credit agencies in the OECD countries. The borrowers were private companies and commercially viable parastatal enterprises such as oil companies as well as the government, the central bank, and other public sector entities.

"We had to decide which credits could be rescheduled and which should be exempt. If we froze and rescheduled everything, we would choke off the economies of the debtor countries. They would not be able to import medicine, pay leases on offshore drilling rigs and commercial aircraft, remit funds to students abroad, pay landing fees at foreign airports, settle international postal accounts and the credit card balances of individuals, pay the unrescheduled portions of export credits rescheduled in the Paris Club, etc.

"In Brazil's workout at the end of 1982, banks agreed to maintain roughly $6 billion of trade and $9 billion of interbank lines outstanding

Board were conveyed occasionally and were given great weight by banks generally.

Eventually, the two sides converged, and a "term sheet," or "heads of terms," was sent to all participating banks. The deal was considered approved in principle when a critical mass (usually representing more than 95 percent of the outstanding debt) responded positively. Holdouts could be dealt with in several ways. The first was moral suasion exerted by the money center

at the 'standstill date.' By mutual agreement, these lines were maintained by all banks for nine years, and these commitments were actively monitored. The standstill dates were usually the day the country announced its inability to pay, not the end of a normal financial reporting period. As a consequence, exposures had to be manually calculated. As an example, Bank of America had around $670 million of trade lines to 35 banks and 20 major public corporations in the form of hundreds of letters of credit and advances that were booked in various currencies by units in San Francisco, New York, London, Hong Kong, Panama, etc.

"One reason for such a comprehensive reconciliation effort was to arrive at a clear picture of the cash payments the country would have to make during the rescheduling period. Another was to identify holders of medium-term public sector debt who would be asked to provide new money to meet the immediate cash needs of the country.

"Each member of the Steering Committee would manage the reconciliation by a group of banks not on the committee. I focused on regional banks in Indiana, Tennessee, and a number of other states. It was like pulling teeth. Managers had reassigned knowledgeable personnel in their overseas operations. They were keenly aware that the reconciliation of commercial debt would establish the basis upon which new money would be requested and therefore reluctant to cooperate. Ultimately nearly all the banks went along.

"Argentina told its Steering Committee in August 1982 it had approximately $20 billion of foreign debt. We uncovered more than $30 billion. Bankers were surprised, too. The head of international operations at a major bank informed his Board in mid-1982 about the bank's exposure in Argentina. A few months later he had to report that the exposure was twice as large because their offshore subsidiaries, affiliates, consortia banks, etc., were slow to identify defaulted loans covered by their guarantee, unsold loan syndications, etc., all of which were affected."

banks, finance officials in the creditor country, or senior officials from the debtor country. If these efforts failed and the amounts involved were de minimis, the country could service the holdout debt on the original schedule. Alternatively, the country could buy back dissident claims at a mutually agreeable price or take its chances with litigation.

Some BACs, after agreeing on a term sheet, would form a documentation subcommittee to prepare the new instruments for the debt being restructured. As a formal subcommittee or informally, the lawyers for the Bank Advisory Committee prepared drafts of the documentation required to establish new obligations replacing or supplementing the original contracts.[42] The debtor country's legal advisors carefully reviewed the documentation, and haggling between the two sides over the precise text could become quite intense and time consuming. Naturally this refinement of terms tended to take longer in a country's first BAC deal and was completed relatively swiftly in subsequent deals. The introduction of a menu of options in the Brady Plan debt reduction deals after 1988 also required extra work and prolonged negotiations with the early candidates.

Implementation

For the landmark rescheduling deal with Mexico following its 1982 crisis, the BAC negotiated a framework agreement that was not signed by either side. Instead, a thirty-foot-long telex was sent to the banks involved describing the entire deal ("restructuring principles") and requesting each one to commit a specific amount of new money. Each bank's formal agreement to the deal came in the form of a return telex acknowledging receipt of the restructuring principles and repeating the amount of new money being committed. It took the lawyers two years to conclude bilateral implementing agreements with the individual banks involved.[43]

Most of the subsequent deals in the 1980s and 1990s were handled differently because the debt being treated had already been consolidated in previous rescheduling deals. In these cases, when the definitive legal text of the restructuring agreement was reached, the closing agent sent a package of final documents to all affected banks, and they confirmed their agreement with a telex message.

Restructuring agreements generally designated a "servicing bank" to receive payments from the debtor country, distribute them among the participating banks or the nonbank holders of the restructured debt, and perform other clerical functions.[44] In this fashion, thousands of loans with

42. Mudge (1984b, p. 72) notes that in some cases an Operations Subcommittee was formed to focus on the "mechanical and clerical complexity" of preparing a restructuring agreement.

43. Mudge (1988) notes that between 1982 and 1986 the Mexican government, the central bank, and fifty-one distinct public sector borrowers signed eighty-nine restructuring agreements covering $52 billion of debt. Furthermore, fifty-three of these agreements were amended once, and one was amended twice. He concludes that the process "demonstrated remarkable good will, ingenuity, and cooperation on all sides." (Also, conversation with Alfred Mudge, February 13, 2003.)

44. Mudge (1984b) explains in detail how the functions of an "agent bank" for a syndicated loan differ from the functions of a "servicing bank" for a restructuring agreement.

hundreds of banks would be consolidated into a single loan or a small number of new debt instruments (such as par bonds and discount bonds). The agent bank was also responsible for advising holders of restructured debt if any conditions of the agreement were not met or if an event of default had occurred.

One of the components of most closing packages was a "comfort letter" from the managing director of the IMF or another senior IMF manager. The typical comfort letter provided assurances that the debtor country's recovery program would lead to a viable balance-of-payments position, that the IMF would monitor closely the progress made under the program, and that the IMF would keep the banks informed about the results.

Typical Commercial Bank Restructuring Terms

The terms of "plain vanilla" BAC rescheduling deals were simpler than the terms of a typical Paris Club operation because there was no commercial bank counterpart to the concessional (ODA) debt that was present in most Paris Club operations. The debt- and debt-service reduction deals concluded under the Brady Plan, however, were considerably more complex than Paris Club operations.

Plain Vanilla versus Complex Deals

Plain vanilla BAC deals were limited to rescheduling principal payments falling due in a specified period of time (and sometimes principal in arrears). Complexity in the BAC context was associated with new money, menu options, and enhancements, none of which had genuine counterparts in Paris Club terms.[45]

New money was an especially important difference. Paris Club operations have been backward looking in the sense that they treated exclusively outstanding debt even though the bilateral donor agencies involved have usually committed to making new loans to the debtor country. Paris Club procedures have precluded incorporating commitments about the amount, form, and timing of these loans in its debt-restructuring agreements.

45. Another complexity was value recovery. The deals with Mexico and Venezuela, for example, included an increase in payments (value recovery) triggered by a rise in oil prices above a precise level. Value recovery was the final sticking point in the 1989 Brady Plan negotiation with Mexico. Value recovery in the case of Uruguay was linked to export earnings from a package of wool products and meat products (nicknamed "wool and bull"), offset by an oil import cost factor.

The commercial world had long-standing precedents for including new money in workout packages, and this practice was carried into BAC negotiations with sovereign borrowers. Deals including new money, however, implied an increase in exposure to a borrower in distress, and such deals had a complex character.[46] Similarly deals that allowed participating banks to select among a number of options (mostly seen as exit options) and deals that included collateral or guarantees or some other support provided by official agencies fell into the category of complex deals. Complex deals began to appear in the mid-1980s and were characteristic of the debt-reduction deals concluded under the Brady Plan.

The role of new money in BAC agreements had several technical dimensions. The regulatory considerations that made new money more appealing to banks than rescheduling interest have already been noted. New money was also treated as senior to old debt and thus exempt from future restructuring arrangements. In this sense new money was analogous to "debtor-in-possession" (DIP) financing in corporate workouts. Finally, previous new-money commitments were usually left out of the base amount of each bank's exposure when calculating shares of any subsequent concerted lending.

Eligible Debt

In payment crises, countries were inclined to exempt payments relating to short-term trade credit and interbank lines of credit from the exchange controls that blocked the use of scarce foreign exchange to pay external creditors.[47] These two kinds of short-term debt were often treated preferentially because they constituted the lifeblood of a debtor country's economy. Trade credit is self-liquidating because funds are debited as export and import commitments are made and then credit balances are restored when goods are received and paid for. Interbank lines of credit are an essential feature of an efficient and reliable international payments system.

---

46. Bridge loans were a particular form of new money that was important in a few BAC deals. These were short-term loans that disbursed while the terms of the restructuring were being negotiated to enable debtor countries to avoid arrears. Bridge loans were usually accorded senior status over outstanding loans and were "taken out" (repaid) when deals were closed using the proceeds of the new money component of the deal or drawing down the country's foreign exchange reserves.

47. Mudge (1984a, p. 89) provides a partial list of the range of obligations that could be treated in a sovereign debt restructuring deal with commercial banks. These are short-term, medium-term, long-term, current past-due amounts, amounts to become due in a specified period, single bank, syndicated, trade-related, letters of credit, acceptances, leases, publicly offered securities, bonds, floating-rate notes, overdrafts, foreign exchange obligations, supplier credits, and a forfeit paper.

Including any portion of these in a restructuring tends to push the economy toward operating on a more costly cash-and-carry or barter basis. In a number of cases, however, banks interested in maintaining a long-term business in the country preferred to convert short-term debt into medium-term debt rather than let other banks cut their exposure by letting short-term credits expire.

As noted above, commercial bank loans guaranteed by official export credit agencies (or other agencies) were moved into the Paris Club basket, but often a small portion of these (5–10 percent) was unguaranteed, and sometimes these unguaranteed portions were included in BAC deals. Commercial bank loans to private sector borrowers also went into the BAC basket when the debtor country authorities had guaranteed them and these guarantees had been invoked by the borrowers.

Stock-of-Debt versus Flow-of-Payments Restructuring

Commercial banks were more receptive than Paris Club creditors to restructuring the stock of eligible debt when the debtor country's problem appeared to be an unsustainable amount of debt rather than a short-term liquidity problem.

When commercial banks started to restructure developing country debt through the BAC process in the late 1970s, they rescheduled payments of principal falling due during a specified "capture period" of a year or so (equivalent to the Paris Club's consolidation period).[48] For countries unable to resume normal debt servicing at the end of the period, follow-on rescheduling deals were negotiated. Commercial pressures favored keeping debtors on a short leash in this fashion and minimizing the debt eligible for restructuring.

As negotiating fatigue spread during the 1980s, banks were more willing to contemplate stock-of-debt treatments. One factor contributing to this attitude was the short tenor of bank loans (five to ten years) compared with bilateral donor agency loans (ten to fifty years). Another was a desire to avoid diverting the attention of bank officers and managers from originating new business to working out problems with old debt. The Brady Plan deals beginning in 1989 were all stock deals designed to enable the debtor country and the banks to exit the debt-restructuring process.

---

48. These payments could be rescheduled through an unconditional "lift out" or through a "serial pick-up" that could be suspended if certain measures of performance by the debtor country were not met.

Grace and Repayment Periods

Grace and repayment periods tended to be shorter in BAC deals than in Paris Club operations. One reason was the shorter tenor of commercial bank loans. In noncomplex BAC deals, the longest grace period was nine years (Jamaica, 1987). Morocco (1990) got just less than nine years, and Mozambique (1991) got eight years. Russia (1995) got seven years, but this was an exceptional case. The average grace period in the deals concluded between 1975 and 1995 was four or five years. The longest repayment period was twenty-five years for Russia (1995), the same exceptional case. Brazil (1988) got twenty years in special circumstances, and so did Nigeria (1989). Yugoslavia (1988) and Morocco (1990) got eighteen years, while the Philippines (1987) and Uruguay (1990) got seventeen years. The average repayment period was eight to ten years.[49]

The complex deals under the Brady Plan typically included conversion options into bonds with thirty-year tenors. Most of these were "defeased" (collateralized) with U.S. Treasury securities purchased with funds obtained from the IMF, the World Bank, and the Inter-American Development Bank.

Interest and Fees

Perhaps the biggest difference between BAC and Paris Club terms was that the plain vanilla BAC deals attached a single (but floating) interest rate to all of the restructured debt, regardless of the rate charged on the underlying instruments.[50] This was a welcome simplification for the debtor countries relative to Paris Club practices. It was possible because the major banks in the main creditor countries were accustomed to lending in dollars and funding their operations in dollars. By contrast, the bilateral donor agencies were generally required to lend in their home currencies.

Interest on rescheduled commercial bank debt was generally a market rate set with reference to LIBOR and adjusted every six months. The highest reported spread was 250 basis points (2.5 percent), accepted by Guyana in a series of four deals in the mid-1980s and Jamaica in 1984. The lowest spread was 13/16ths of a percent, for thirteen different countries during the 1986–95 period.[51]

---

49. World Bank (2002, appendix 2).

50. In most cases the bulk of the debt being restructured was originally denominated in dollars, which facilitated the choice of a single, dollar-based interest rate. Restructured debt that was originally denominated in other currencies (such as yen, pounds, or marks) would be converted into dollar debt at some negotiated rate.

51. IIF (2001). It is important to understand the distinction between market rates and market-based rates. Commercial banks would not have extended new credit to these countries, with similar

In the complex Brady Plan deals beginning in 1989, outstanding bank loans could be exchanged for bonds with different features. Par bonds had the same face value but a below market, fixed interest rate. Discount bonds had a heavily discounted face amount and a market-based spread above LIBOR. These variations are discussed further in chapter 8.

Fees were charged in many of the pre-1989 deals. These were variously called front-end, restructuring, or management fees. The lowest fees reported were 1/8th of a percent for Chile in 1985 and Jordan in 1989. The highest fees were 2 1/8 percent for Malawi in 1983 and Senegal in 1984.[52] The general practice in the Brady Plan deals from 1989 onward was not to charge any fees.

Finally, out-of-pocket restructuring costs were higher for BAC deals than for Paris Club operations. Debtor countries were not asked to reimburse any Paris Club costs, but following standard commercial practice, they were responsible for paying the expenses of a BAC organized at their request. These costs included travel and communications costs incurred by BAC members as well as services provided by the BAC's legal counsel.[53] Debtor countries usually engaged legal advisors for both their Paris Club and their BAC negotiations. The advisors could be more expensive for Paris Club negotiations or for the BAC negotiations depending on the relative size of the debt stocks involved and the complexity of the documentation required.

Summing Up

The BAC process for restructuring commercial bank loans caught in a country debt crisis grew out of a rash of crises in the 1970s. Five years of experience with more than five countries was required to refine the process to the point that it was predictable and familiar. The architects of the process were the commercial banks themselves, not the IMF or any other public

tenors, at the spreads accepted in BAC restructuring deals. The market rates at the time would have been higher by as much as several hundred basis points. The rates in the BAC deals were market-based, however, because they were set above the banks' basic cost of funds, not below, and moved up and down as market rates fluctuated. A spread of 13/16 became a standard during the 1980s. It was well below the market rate for most debtor countries and therefore contained an element of concessionality (loss of net present value). This fraction emerged as a compromise put forward by U.S. Treasury Secretary James Baker during the IMF/World Bank annual meetings in Seoul, Korea, in 1985. (Communication from Harry Tether, January 3, 2003.)

52. World Bank (2002, appendix 2).

53. Normally, the chairing bank periodically billed the debtor country for costs to be reimbursed, and these were settled by cash payments. In some cases these costs were incorporated in new-money loans. (Conversation with John Riggs, January 24, 2003.)

sector body. The design drew heavily on commercial experience with corporate workouts under national bankruptcy regimes. Unlike the corporate process, however, the BAC process involved close collaboration or coordination with public sector institutions such as the IMF and the Paris Club, reflecting the political factors inherent in sovereign workouts.

The BAC process was heavily used in the 1980s and early 1990s as countries in every developing region of the world—but especially in Latin America—defaulted on their external debt or slid to the edge of default. A hallmark of the process was its pragmatism, demonstrated in the range of cases treated and the innovations introduced, such as the menu of options.

Critics of the process tended to focus on three aspects: the protracted nature of BAC negotiations, their cost, and their terms. Paris Club negotiations, generally completed in a single day, provided a sharp contrast to BAC negotiations that extended over months and sometimes for more than a year. But when a BAC deal was signed, that was the final step. Signing a Paris Club agreement was an early step in an equally long process; months of negotiations with each creditor country were required to conclude bilateral implementing agreements. BAC negotiations were clearly more expensive than Paris Club negotiations, because debtor countries had to reimburse banks for their costs. But banks are commercial lenders and were only following well-established commercial practices. The repayment terms for the BAC restructurings were market-based and therefore appeared less generous to the debtor countries. The banks, however, did adopt a below-market standard for restructurings under the Brady Plan (13/16 percent over LIBOR for discount bonds) and agreed to debt reduction for middle-income countries despite the Paris Club's refusal to do so.

In a sense the BAC process must have been too generous to debtor countries because bank lending to developing countries dropped sharply in the 1990s. Many developing countries still sought commercial financing, however, and compensated by issuing bonds at an unprecedented pace. Mirroring the pattern with the surge of bank lending in the early 1970s, problems with bond debt soon surfaced, and new workout techniques had to be developed. That happened in a politically charged atmosphere where the G-7 architects were under heavy pressure to demonstrate that private creditors were not being "bailed out" with official financing. The effort to achieve private sector involvement after 1995 called into question the BAC process and prompted a major debate about the machinery for sovereign workouts. One side favored improvements in the BAC process to reflect the prominence of bond debt (held largely by asset managers and institutional investors such as fund management companies and insurance companies, but also by banks). The other side favored the creation of an international bankruptcy regime formalized in a treaty or an amendment of the IMF's charter. That debate is the subject of the last three chapters of this book.

7

The North-South Dialogue in the 1970s

The first great debate in the Bretton Woods era about sovereign debt workouts took place in the 1970s in the context of the North-South Dialogue. The developing countries of the South pleaded for generalized debt relief to alleviate widespread balance-of-payments strains and for permanent machinery to replace the Paris Club and London Club machinery. In the end the industrial countries of the North agreed to negotiate "features" to guide Paris Club negotiations and to convert loans to grants for the least-developed countries. There are intriguing parallels between this debate and the current debate about the machinery for restructuring bond debt.[1]

The UN's Second Development Decade

The seeds of the North-South Dialogue on debt were planted in late 1961 when U.S. President John F. Kennedy proposed that the United Nations General Assembly declare the 1960s to be the First Development Decade.

---

1. The material in this chapter is drawn largely from Rieffel (1985), U.S. National Advisory Council (annual reports from FY 1975 to FY 1980), and McDonald (1982).

The founding resolution set two specific goals: an economic growth rate of 5 percent a year for the developing countries by 1970, and an annual transfer of capital (official and private) to these countries equivalent to 1 percent of the gross national product of the high-income countries.

Preparations for setting the goals of the Second Development Decade began in 1966 under the direction of the General Assembly. World Bank President Robert McNamara convened a Commission on International Development in 1968 to "undertake a study of the consequences of twenty years of development assistance and . . . to offer solid proposals for a global strategy in the 1970s and beyond."[2] The commission, chaired by Canadian prime minister Lester Pearson, included prominent political leaders from around the world and had an impact on the UN debate on development goals.

One of the principal issues investigated by the Pearson Commission was "the problem of mounting debts."[3] The commission's report noted "a sequence of debt crises in the late 1950s and throughout the 1960s." It concluded that "the procedures and principles for providing debt relief have often been inadequate."[4] The commission made two recommendations of note in this area. The first was to move away from the short-leash approach and provide relief over a sufficiently long period to avoid the need for repeated rescheduling operations. The second was to "consider debt relief a legitimate form of aid and permit the use of new loans to refinance debt payments, in order to reduce the need for full-scale debt relief negotiations."[5]

The General Assembly resolution on the International Development Strategy for the Second UN Development Decade, adopted by consensus in 1970, set a growth target of 6 percent for the developing countries. It also included the still controversial target of delivering annually official devel-

---

2. Commission on International Development (1969, cover note).

3. Commission on International Development (1969, p. 18).

4. Commission on International Development (1969, p. 156).

5. Commission on International Development (1969, p. 158). Less than a year later, in March 1970, a high-level task force convened by President Richard Nixon to examine the economic assistance programs of the United States produced a report covering many of the same issues. The task force was chaired by Bank of America president Rudolph Peterson and included a mix of business, academic, and civil society leaders. Its most significant recommendations were to give priority to delivering development assistance through multilateral institutions over bilateral agencies, to raise the level of funding for development assistance but not to embrace any specific target, and to take steps to improve coordination among U.S. government agencies and donor countries. The task force's views on debt are buried in its report. In brief, it concluded that the short-leash approach to rescheduling was not adequate, recommended joint action by all parties concerned to devise a "comprehensive strategy" for preventing debt crises, and suggested that the World Bank and IMF play key roles in implementing such a strategy. See Peterson Commission (1970, pp. 33–34).

opment assistance equivalent to 0.7 percent of donor country gross national product.[6] No specific targets or objectives in the area of debt were adopted.

Exceptional Debt Operations in the Late 1960s

Fuel was added to the debate over debt by the experiences of India, Indonesia, Ghana, and Pakistan in the late 1960s:[7]

—India found its development spending plans squeezed in the mid-1960s by an uptick in debt-service payments, while the growth in new aid commitments slowed. In the context of its World Bank–led aid consortium, India obtained commitments from major donors to reschedule some payments falling due in every year except two during the 1968–74 period. India's case can be seen as an experiment in using debt rescheduling as a form of development assistance (a particularly desirable form because it was untied to procurement in the donor country).

—Following the collapse of the Sukarno regime in 1965, a new anticommunist government came to power in Indonesia. Debt-rescheduling operations in the Paris Club were concluded in 1968 and 1969 to support the promising economic program of the Suharto regime. In 1970 a unique and exceptionally generous rescheduling operation was carried out in the Paris Club. The terms of this operation extended to a much larger stock of debt owed to Soviet bloc creditors through the principle of nondiscrimination.[8] This operation undoubtedly whetted the appetite of many third world countries for debt relief.

—The Nkrumah regime in Ghana came to an abrupt end in 1966, leaving the new government with a large stock of debt owed to suppliers that it was unable to service. Ghana's OECD creditors disappointed the government, however, by refusing to reschedule on the generous terms offered to Indonesia. After negotiating three rescheduling agreements in London (under Paris Club rules) in the late 1960s, a new military government in

6. The United States and several other countries explicitly opted out of the ODA commitment.

7. Much of the material here is drawn from Cizauskas (1979). It may be relevant that the leaders of two of these countries, India and Indonesia, were the conveners of the Nonaligned Movement, which helped developing countries coalesce into a voting bloc in the United Nations. (The third convener was Yugoslavia.)

8. The entire stock of "Sukarno era" debt was restructured. The principal was to be repaid in thirty equal annual installments with no interest charged. Scheduled and unpaid interest due under the original loans was to be repaid over thirty years including a fifteen-year grace period with no interest charged. Drawing on a feature of the Anglo-American Financial Agreement of 1946 to settle World War II debt, Indonesia also had the option to defer half of the principal payments falling due in the early years ("bisque clause").

1972 announced its intention to disavow these agreements, repudiate certain debts tainted by corruption, and unilaterally reschedule its remaining obligations. Counterproposals were made by the creditors, and after protracted (sometimes bitter) negotiations, Ghana agreed in 1974 to generous terms, although they were still far from those that Indonesia had obtained. This case served to underscore the political dimension of debt rescheduling and provided ammunition for developing country advocates of generalized debt relief.

—A cyclone and tidal wave in 1970 triggered a series of events that led Bangladesh to declare independence from Pakistan in March 1971. A civil war broke out that ended in late 1971, shortly after India entered the conflict on the side of Bangladesh. Facing severe balance-of-payments pressures related to these developments, Pakistan declared a moratorium on debt service to aid donors. The donors responded by committing to emergency rescheduling operations in Pakistan's World Bank–led aid consortium. In subsequent negotiations, Pakistan's preconflict debt was divided between Pakistan and Bangladesh, and a long-term restructuring of Pakistan's share was carried out in 1974 in its aid consortium as part of a donor package to keep Pakistan's development program on track. The Pakistan experience broadened the use of debt restructuring as a form of aid, but it also contributed to a decision by the U.S. government in October 1974 to rule out further use of debt rescheduling as a form of aid.[9]

UNCTAD and the G-77

The United Nations was the developing countries' forum of choice for advancing their demands because, unlike the IMF and the World Bank, it operated on the basis of one country, one vote. The main organizational vehicle for advancing the developing country cause was the Group of Seventy-Seven. The counterpart for the industrial countries, essentially the first world members of the OECD, was known as Group B.[10] Although some of the North-South debate took place in the UN General Assembly, the sharpest exchanges took place—over the firm opposition of the industrial coun-

9. U.S. National Advisory Council (annual reports).

10. The group system originated in the General Assembly resolution passed in 1962 to convene the first UNCTAD conference. Countries in Asia and Africa were put in Group A and Latin American countries in Group C. Groups A and C, totaling 77 countries, joined together shortly thereafter to form the G-77. Although the number of countries in the group grew to exceed 125, the G-77 label remained. The Soviet bloc countries of the "second world" were members of Group D.

tries—in a specialized agency established in 1964 to promote third world development: the United Nations Conference on Trade and Development.[11]

At the first UNCTAD conference in 1964 in Geneva, the G-77 rammed through several dozen resolutions calling for changes in the international system. The resolution dealing with the debt problems of developing countries recommended that the relevant international financial institutions "stand ready, at the request of any developing country, to review . . . [its] external indebtedness . . . with a view to securing agreement, or consolidation of debt, with appropriate periods of grace and amortization and reasonable rates of interest."[12]

The second conference, dubbed UNCTAD II, in 1968 in New Delhi was less confrontational because Group B largely ignored the resolutions passed at UNCTAD I. Although no action was taken on debt, documents produced by the UNCTAD secretariat emphasized shortcomings in the existing procedures for rescheduling developing country debt, especially its ad hoc and time-consuming nature. The secretariat suggested that procedures be adopted to avoid disrupting the development process, especially in countries where debt problems were "more of a structural than of a short-term character."[13]

Confrontation in the Debt Area

The atmosphere of North-South confrontation intensified sharply at UNCTAD III in Santiago, Chile, in 1972. At a preparatory meeting in late 1971 in Lima, Peru, the G-77 adopted "The Declaration and Principles of the Action Programme of Lima." On debt the two key paragraphs in the declaration stated that:

> The criteria and procedures of rescheduling . . . should be reviewed and revised so as to ensure that the rescheduling of debts does not interfere with the orderly process of development planning in debtor countries and should be systematically designed to prevent both disruption of long-term development plans and need for repeated rescheduling.
>
> A special body should be created within the machinery of UNCTAD to find practical solutions to the debt servicing problems of developing countries. Consultations should be held within such a body

11. McDonald (1982) provides a short summary of the North-South Dialogue in the 1960s and 1970s.

12. UNCTAD (1985, p. 94).

13. UNCTAD (1985, p. 95).

between representatives of debtor and creditor countries and international experts serving in their personal capacity.[14]

While the theme of using debt relief as a form of development assistance can be found in the Pearson Commission report, the Lima Declaration appears to contain the earliest reference to a second theme that ebbed and flowed over the next thirty years: the creation of a new mechanism (permanent machinery in the language of the debate) to arrange debt workouts.[15] The design of the mechanism took a distinctly debtor-friendly form because it was attached to UNCTAD and because it was mandated to address broad development-financing requirements as well as debt-servicing crises. At UNCTAD III, Group B rejected the G-77's proposed resolution on debt based on the Lima Declaration. Group B stoutly defended the view that debt negotiations should continue to be carried out through ad hoc forums (meetings of the Paris Club) on a case-by-case basis.

The oil crisis that began in 1973 at the end of an Arab-Israeli conflict stoked the flames of North-South confrontation. Advocates of generalized debt relief—automatic rescheduling or reduction for low-income countries as a group without regard to their individual ability to service outstanding debt and without country-specific policy conditionality—gained ground. Extremists in this camp proposed that the developing countries as a group declare a unilateral payment moratorium on their external debts until economic growth resumed at a satisfactory pace or aid flows achieved the target level of 0.7 percent of donor country gross national product.[16] They also proposed generalized debt rescheduling for the poorest countries.

The high point of the period of confrontation (and its final act) was the Sixth Special Session of the UN General Assembly in May 1974. A Declaration and Program of Action on the Establishment of a New International Economic Order (NIEO) were adopted, and the NIEO became a powerful rallying cry for developing country activists.[17]

14. UNCTAD, TD/143, November 12, 1971.
15. At this stage the distinctions between sovereign borrowers and private sector borrowers, and between official creditors and private creditors, were not so important. The bulk of the external debt of developing countries consisted of sovereign obligations to official lending agencies.
16. Harvey Shapiro, "The Search for Solutions to the LDCs' Problems," *Institutional Investor,* October 1976, p. 42.
17. The New International Economic Order Declaration was reinforced at the end of the year by the adoption of a Charter of Economic Rights and Duties of States at the twenty-ninth General Assembly. This charter formalized a global consensus for giving developing countries preferential treatment in the operation of the international economic system. The declaration and the charter were both adopted with strong reservations entered into the record by the Group B countries.

Over the course of the next year, the demands of the South in the debt area crystallized around a proposal, advanced in a series of UNCTAD meetings, to cancel the debts of the "least developed, land-locked and island developing countries" owed to bilateral donor agencies on concessional terms (ODA debt), to declare a moratorium on ODA debt payments to these agencies owed by the countries "most seriously affected" by the oil crisis, and to reschedule over at least twenty-five years the payments due on commercial (non-ODA) debt owed by other "interested" developing countries.[18]

Meanwhile, an Ad Hoc Group of Governmental Experts, convened by UNCTAD in 1973, met three times to discuss the problem of developing country debt. The experts produced a final report in March 1975 that contained an agreed set of "common elements for consideration in future debt negotiations" and addressed several institutional questions.[19] The common elements presumed a case-by-case approach and accepted the "customary multilateral framework" for negotiation (meaning the Paris Club)—two points the G-77 later contested. Other elements were repeated in most of the subsequent consensus language: (a) debt reorganization would take into account "the development prospects of the debtor country"; (b) "equality and non-discrimination among creditors" is an essential principle; and (c) the terms of debt relief would take into account the "long term debt servicing capacity of the debtor country and the legitimate interests of the creditors."[20]

Remarkably, the agreed text on institutional questions held out the prospect of convening special meetings of creditor countries and developing countries to examine a debtor country's debt problem—in advance of Paris Club negotiations. These special meetings, organized with the assistance of UNCTAD, would be chaired by a developing country, would follow their own rules and procedures, and would produce a report for consideration by the Paris Club without making specific recommendations. The experts' report also suggested that UNCTAD participate in Paris Club nego-

18. Press reports later indicated that Peru had given serious consideration to declaring an UNCTAD-style moratorium in late 1974 (see *Latin America Economic Report*, December 23, 1977). The Group B countries, however, opposed these and other proposals for debt moratoriums or generalized debt rescheduling on the grounds that they would lead to inequitable treatment of debtor countries, penalize countries that were implementing effective adjustment programs, and discourage new flows of aid to developing countries across the board.

19. UNCTAD (1975, p. 9).

20. A fifth element, which disappeared subsequently, was the possibility of adjusting terms at the end of the consolidation period for rescheduled payments to reflect deterioration or improvement in the debtor country's economic situation. This was presumably inspired by the "bisque clause" in Indonesia's 1970 Paris Club operation.

tiations on the same basis as the IMF and the World Bank. The report was considered at the fifteenth session of the UNCTAD Trade and Development Board in 1975. Resolution 132(XV), adopted by the board, authorized UNCTAD to provide assistance to developing countries in preparing for debt-rescheduling negotiations and to participate in Paris Club meetings on the same basis as the IMF and World Bank.[21]

The period of confrontation ended later in 1975 when several key events occurred. These included a special session of the UN General Assembly in September focusing on the concerns of developing countries, the first Economic Summit (at Rambouillet, France) in November, and the opening of the Conference on International Economic Cooperation (CIEC) in December.

It should be borne in mind that momentous changes were taking place in the international system in the early 1970s:

—The fourfold increase in oil prices implemented by the OPEC cartel after the Yom Kippur War in October 1973 threw the global economy into a recession and created a flood of petrodollars.

—The Tokyo Round of multilateral trade negotiations was launched in 1973 and concluded in 1979.

—The United States entered a period of détente with the Soviet Union in 1969, reopened diplomatic contact with China in 1971, and withdrew from Vietnam in 1975.

—The fixed exchange rate system established in 1945 collapsed when the United States broke the dollar's link with gold in August 1971. The European currencies abandoned their link to the dollar in March 1973. A new international monetary system based on flexible exchange rates was codified in the Second Amendment of the Articles of Agreement of the IMF. (Agreement in principle was reached in 1976; the amendment was formally ratified in 1978.)

Developing country support was essential to the reform of the international monetary system, and the leaders of the North made exceptional efforts to prevent issues of concern to developing countries from derailing it. In addition to convening the temporary CIEC, a permanent forum to address development issues was also created: "the Joint Committee of the Boards of Governors on the IMF and the World Bank on the Transfer of Real Resources to Developing Countries," otherwise known as the Development Committee. Another step was selling a portion of the IMF's gold holdings to fund balance-of-payments loans to low-income countries on concessional terms.

21. UNCTAD (1985, p. 95).

From Confrontation to Dialogue

The Seventh Special Session of the UN General Assembly in September 1975 marked the shift from confrontation to dialogue. On this occasion, U.S. Secretary of State Henry Kissinger announced a package of initiatives for improving relations with the South.

The strategy of the North was to preserve the architecture of the post–World War II trade and payments system by identifying and implementing several initiatives in areas of interest to the South that would defuse the radical proposals emanating from the G-77 camp. The initial agenda for the North-South Dialogue was broad, but it centered on commodities, transfer of technology, and trade policy. Debt emerged as a major issue at UNCTAD IV held in Nairobi in 1976. Over the next four years, as North-South negotiations reached a crescendo and then faded, debt was continuously among the top three or four issues, but never at the very top. Ultimately no agreements of major significance were concluded in this area.

With the world economy in turmoil, the heads of state and government of France, Germany, Italy, Japan, the United Kingdom, and the United States met for three days in mid-November 1975 in the Chateau de Rambouillet outside of Paris. This was the first of the summits that have been held every year since then.[22] The leading economies were struggling to overcome inflationary pressures and rising unemployment. The developing countries were suffering from unprecedented current account deficits and ballooning levels of external debt. The purpose of the Rambouillet summit was to demonstrate that the political leadership of the world was actively and cooperatively working to stabilize the global economy and restore the conditions required for sustainable growth. The key accomplishment was a delicate compromise between the United States and France that set the stage for completing the reform of the international monetary system and turning to the challenges facing developing countries.[23]

The Conference on International Economic Cooperation, based on a U.S. proposal, began in December 1975 expressly for the purpose of North-South Dialogue. The object of the exercise was to reach a consensus on a package of improvements in the existing international economic order as an alternative to creating a new order. The first six months of the CIEC were devoted

22. French president Valéry Giscard d'Estaing proposed the meeting four months earlier. He and the leaders of the United States (Gerald R. Ford), the United Kingdom (Harold Wilson), and Germany (Helmut Schmidt) were all relatively new to their offices, which made the moment especially favorable for collective leadership. The original G-6 became the G-7 when Canada joined in 1976.

23. See Putnam and Bayne (1984) for a detailed account of the early summit meetings.

to analyzing the various issues and the remaining twelve months were spent negotiating agreed conclusions. Participation was limited to twenty-seven countries: eight from the OECD (the European Commission represented the nine members of the European Economic Community), seven oil-exporting countries, and twelve oil-importing countries. Discussion took place in four commissions, Energy, Raw Materials, Development, and Financial Affairs. Debt was discussed both in the Financial Affairs Commission (where finance ministries took the lead) and in the Development Commission (where aid agencies took the lead).

In May 1976, in the middle of the CIEC, the fourth UNCTAD conference was held in Nairobi. The main topic of discussion was an "integrated program for commodities," and a resolution was adopted by consensus on this topic as well as on transfer of technology. Inspired by a declaration adopted at a preparatory meeting of G-77 ministers in February in Manila, debt was also vigorously debated at UNCTAD IV. The Manila Declaration called for cancellation of debt owed by the least-developed countries to bilateral aid agencies, indefinite deferral of payments owed to these agencies by the countries "most seriously affected" by the oil crisis, and rescheduling over twenty-five years of debt on commercial terms owed by "interested" developing countries to bilateral export credit agencies.[24]

To deflect this proposal for generalized debt relief, the OECD countries succeeded in winning G-77 agreement on a resolution opening the door to possible improvements in the existing (Paris Club) approach to debt rescheduling. Specifically, UNCTAD Resolution 94(IV) invited:

> appropriate existing international forums to determine, before the end of 1976, what features might usefully be discerned from past [debt relief] operations, together with others that might be identified in the light of the present situation of the least developed countries, the most seriously affected developing countries and other countries in need, which could provide guidance in future operations relating to debt problems as a basis for dealing flexibly with individual cases.[25]

This invitation was pursued in the CIEC. The developing countries tabled a hard-line position modeled on the Manila Declaration. The OECD countries countered with a paper drafted by the United States and European Commission outlining "features" to guide future debt-rescheduling operations. In a major concession to the developing countries, the donor countries

24. United Nations (1977, pp. 116–17).
25. United Nations (1977, pp. 16–17).

accepted the notion that some debt problems were associated with "acute balance-of-payments difficulties requiring immediate action," while others were associated with "longer term situations relating to structural, financial and transfer-of-resources problems." Progress was made in many areas (especially toward the establishment of the Common Fund to promote stability in commodity prices), but the two sides did not converge significantly in the debt area. The final CIEC communiqué adopted by consensus at a ministerial meeting in June 1977 was inconclusive on the subject of debt.[26]

The International Debt Commission

Resolution 94(IV) also instructed the UNCTAD secretary general to convene an Intergovernmental Group of Experts on Debt and Development Problems of Developing Countries. It was chaired by a Canadian official and met in July and December 1977 but was unable to narrow the differences between the G-77 and Group B.

The debate on debt intensified at the ninth special session of the UNCTAD Trade and Development Board in Geneva in March 1978. In the course of negotiating the language of TDB Resolution 165(S-IX), the industrial countries made substantial concessions on generalized debt relief, but only cosmetic ones on the machinery for debt-relief operations. Pressure to yield came both from the preponderance of UN members that were not members of the OECD and from a few OECD members (the Netherlands and Sweden, for example) that had a tradition of strong support for poverty alleviation in the developing world.[27]

In the area of generalized debt relief, the Group B countries committed themselves to "seek to adopt" certain measures for the benefit of a group of thirty "least developed countries." A few years earlier, the OECD donor countries had agreed to extend new aid to these countries exclusively in the form of grants to help them avoid debt-servicing difficulties. Now the OECD countries agreed to extend this policy to old debt. The euphemism for this

26. Discussions at the economic summit in London in May 1977—the third in the series that began at Rambouillet in 1975—helped the OECD countries go into the final CIEC negotiations with enough to offer the developing countries to make it a success. In an effort to advance its objectives in a more accommodating forum, the G-77 arranged in December 1977 to constitute the UN General Assembly as a Committee of the Whole to prepare for the UN Special Session on Development in 1980. Acting as a Committee of the Whole, the General Assembly held a series of meetings in 1978 and 1979 but did not produce any noteworthy results.

27. For a World Bank perspective on the early stages of the debt debate, see Klein (1973). For a somewhat later academic perspective, see Kenen (1977).

procedure was retroactive terms adjustment, or simply RTA. A number of qualifications were incorporated into the text, however, to make it clear that RTA would be carried out as an aid operation, not as a debt operation.[28] In particular, donor countries were allowed to implement RTA in different ways. At one extreme countries could simply write off old debt, and some actually extended this relief to countries beyond those on the official United Nations list of least-developed countries. Other countries could provide additional amounts of fast-disbursing grant assistance—one year at a time—to offset payments due on old debt.[29]

In the area of debt relief machinery, the resolution laid out four "agreed concepts" to be used in further negotiations to refine a set of features to guide future operations. The four concepts were common denominators from the divergent approaches of the G-77 and Group B countries. The intergovernmental group of debt experts met again in October 1978 to hammer out the features, but the two sides were headed in different directions. Group B stood by the position that improvements in the existing ad hoc machinery (the Paris Club) could be made to address the concerns of developing countries; no new machinery was required. The G-77 waged a determined campaign for new and permanent machinery.[30]

The main features of the G-77's new machinery were foreshadowed in a note prepared by the UNCTAD Secretariat for the October meeting of the experts group.[31] The note suggested that "an independent forum—which does not consist only of creditors—could be given responsibility for supervising the negotiations concerning the debt reorganization." The note argued that attaching creditor clubs (like the Paris Club) to a permanent implementing institution (such as UNCTAD) would ensure continuity and

28. The retroactive terms adjustment (RTA) approach to the debt problems of the poorest developing countries was a precursor of the HIPC Initiative in the mid-1990s that is discussed in chapter 9.

29. The United States never implemented RTA. Legislation was proposed by the Carter administration and passed by the Senate, but rejected by the House. Even though the cost of RTA was estimated to be only about $15 million a year, the opponents argued that at the margin scarce aid funds could be better used in other countries for specific projects that would yield tangible results.

30. As an illustration of how fluid Paris Club procedures were before the North-South negotiations on debt, there was a debate about the venue and chairmanship of the negotiations with Zaire in 1976. Belgium proposed holding the negotiations in Kinshasa. The French chairman of the Paris Club suggested a compromise involving a meeting in Kinshasa cochaired by France and the IMF. The eventual consensus was to conduct substantive negotiations in Paris in the usual fashion but to finalize the details and sign the agreement at a later meeting in Kinshasa, which in the end was not done. (Based on a report cabled from the U.S. Embassy in Paris to the Department of State on April 28, 1976.)

31. UNCTAD (1978a, p. 7).

technical expertise from one negotiation to the next, which it suggested would be a distinct improvement over the ad hoc character of the existing machinery.[32]

The October meeting of the intergovernmental group of experts was unable to bridge the differences in approach. Indeed the two sides appeared to drift further apart. The report of the group of experts highlighted four elements of the G-77 position that were unacceptable to Group B:

— ... the need for ... institutional arrangements to have independence, permanence, authority and technical competence. (Paragraph 3)

— ... comprehensive treatment would ... require that, within the same multilateral framework, the problems arising from official debt, as well as those arising from private debt, were considered so that it would no longer be necessary for a debtor country to go to a succession of meetings each dealing with individual aspects of its debt problem in ways which were not necessarily mutually consistent and were sometimes off-setting. (Paragraph 6)

—The institutional arrangements must also be independent of any particular country or group of countries and must enjoy impartiality and the confidence of all for both its expertise and its reliability and its inclination to support the development of developing countries. Furthermore, they must ensure equitable and consistent results. (Paragraph 8)

—The adjustment package must be carefully designed so that within a given time the package of measures properly implemented would lead the debtor developing countries back to a development path consistent with the minimum rates of growth endorsed by the international community. (Paragraph 3)[33]

The North-South Dialogue on debt reached its crescendo at UNCTAD V in Manila in May 1979. The G-77 arrived with a concrete version of the permanent machinery foreshadowed in the work of the group of experts. The machinery acquired a label—the International Debt Commission (IDC)—at the G-77 Ministerial Meeting to prepare for UNCTAD V, which was held

---

32. The note also raised the issue of the treatment of private creditors "in view of the growing importance of private banks as creditors." UNCTAD (1978a, pp. 9–10). It suggested that banks could be brought into debt negotiations through "a bank consortium, which would be chaired by the implementing institution in parallel with the intergovernmental exercise." The Group B stance was that "governments were not competent to discuss such loans precisely because they were private." UNCTAD (1978b, p. 6).

33. UNCTAD (1978b, pp. 3–5).

in Arusha, Tanzania, in February 1979. The vision of the G-77 was spelled out in the Arusha Programme for Collective Self-Reliance and Framework for Negotiations:

> The establishment of an international debt commission, comprising eminent public figures with recognized knowledge and experience of debt problems and economic development. Any interested developing country which believes it has, or may have a debt problem could address itself to the commission;
>
> The commission will: (i) Examine the debt and development problems of the requesting country; (ii) In the light of such examination and in accordance with the modalities of the detailed features, make recommendations on the measures required to deal with the debt problem in the broader context of development including measures of debt reorganization and additional bilateral and multilateral finance; (iii) Convene a meeting of all parties concerned with a view to implementing the recommendations under (ii) above.
>
> In carrying out its work, the commission will be assisted throughout by relevant international organizations including UNCTAD. This procedure and the detailed features drawn up in terms of resolution 165 (S-IX) will assure a global approach in which countries in similar situations will be treated similarly.[34]

These terms of reference were repeated in the draft resolution on debt submitted by the G-77 at UNCTAD V in Manila. In addition, the draft resolution urged "concerned developing countries and relevant international institutions to co-operate fully with the working of the International Debt Commission and so ensure that the objectives defined in the detailed features are realized in each case." Finally it requested the secretary general of UNCTAD "to bring into operation as soon as possible the International Debt Commission and the detailed features."[35]

The G-77 campaign ran into the brick wall of Group B's united stand in defense of the Paris Club. No substantive concessions on machinery were made. With a few cosmetic gestures, the U.S.-EC paper on "features to guide future negotiations" was formally submitted by Group B, and an exhausting discussion of the two approaches ensued.[36] In the end the G-77 and Group

---

34. United Nations (1981, p. 157).

35. United Nations (1981, p. 108).

36. The chairman of the Paris Club at the time, Michel Camdessus, led Group B with consummate charm and skill throughout the UNCTAD debt negotiations.

B texts were forwarded without comment to the Trade and Development Board.

Agreed Features for Addressing Acute and Longer-Term Debt Problems

The North-South debate on debt effectively ended in October 1980 when TDB Resolution 222(XXI) was adopted by consensus at the twenty-first meeting of the UNCTAD Trade and Development Board in Geneva.[37] Part B of this resolution contained "Detailed Features for Future Operations Relating to the Debt Problems of Interested Developing Countries." Every word was fought over, and in the end Group B accepted a number of ambiguities to avoid prolonging the controversy. Still the result was a clear victory for the status quo in the form of the existing Paris Club process.[38]

It is hard to say what convinced the G-77 to abandon its campaign. Other issues were being negotiated, and trade-offs were made at the very end of the meeting late at night in a small contact group. Perhaps Group B made concessions in areas such as commodities or technology transfer to protect its interests in the debt area. Another factor may have been the position of the more advanced developing countries, which appeared to move away from the more radical G-77 positions as the debate intensified. This split is reflected in the addition of the word "interested" in the title of Resolution 222(XXI) and in earlier resolutions.[39]

The features contained in the resolution look quite different from those contained in the U.S.-EC proposal tabled at the CIEC, but the changes are superficial. Instead of presenting one set of features for countries with "acute" debt-servicing problems and another set for countries with problems of a "longer-term nature," the agreed resolution addressed both types of situations under the common headings of "objectives," "operational framework," and "action."

The Group B countries did make one notable institutional concession to obtain G-77 support for a benign version of features. They agreed to invite an UNCTAD observer to attend all Paris Club negotiations. The negotiations

37. United Nations (1980, pp. 155–59).

38. Paris Club chairman Camdessus described the resolution as "a codification of previous practices . . . which until now have been deemed confidential and, above all, establishes their international legitimacy." Camdessus (1984, p. 127).

39. Some of the G-77 countries were concerned that steps in the direction of debt relief on demand could affect them adversely by cutting off their access to new flows of capital from private as well as official sources.

THE NORTH-SOUTH DIALOGUE 147

with Togo in 1979 were the first in which an UNCTAD observer participated. Other steps taken to defuse G-77 pressure in this area were changing the venue for negotiations from the offices of the French Treasury (in a wing of the Louvre Palace) to the International Conference Center on Avenue Kléber, and more hand-holding by the Paris Club secretariat with potential Paris Club clients.

The thirty-fourth UN General Assembly in 1979 and the assembly's Eleventh Special Session on Development in August-September 1980 contributed to and overshadowed the end of the debt debate. These sessions focused on the adoption of a new International Development Strategy for the Third UN Development Decade. An attempt was made by the G-77 to launch a round of "global negotiations" addressing five areas simultaneously: trade, money and finance, raw materials, development, and energy. This effort ran out of steam before producing any significant results despite a second initiative by World Bank president McNamara in early 1977 to add political weight to the process by means of a high-level commission. Former German chancellor Willy Brandt announced the formation of the Independent Commission on International Development Issues in September 1977.

The report of the Brandt Commission, delivered to UN Secretary General Kurt Waldheim in 1980, was remarkably silent on the issue of debt. Particular emphasis was given to increasing new aid flows to the poorest countries, tackling hunger and population growth, cutting back military expenditures and encouraging sound policies in developing countries, stabilizing commodity prices, increasing energy efficiency, reducing trade barriers, and sharing technology. In the area of money and finance, the commission called for creating special drawing rights by the IMF and distributing them in favor of developing countries, developing a system of global taxation to finance development, and establishing a World Development Fund that would give developing countries a leading role in the allocation of these global revenues. The only specific debt recommendation was that "middle-income countries need special measures to lengthen the maturity of their debt structures and poorer developing countries should be enabled to borrow more easily in the market [with the help of various cofinancing techniques]."[40]

Neither the Third Development Decade targets, nor the global negotiations campaign, nor the Brandt Commission report had a measurable impact on developing countries during the 1980s. The Brandt Commission

40. Independent Commission on International Development Issues (1980, p. 292).

report did, however, lead to the Cancun Summit, in October 1981, which brought together twenty-two heads of state and government to exchange views on food security, agricultural development, commodities, trade, industrialization, energy, and monetary and financial issues. To encourage free discussion, the participants agreed not to take any decisions or issue a communiqué. These ground rules presumably contributed to the success of the Cancun Summit from the perspective of the leaders, and the cochairmen from Mexico and Canada reported a consensus on launching global negotiations. But larger forces soon overwhelmed these sentiments and global negotiations never got off the ground.[41]

Less than a year later, a payment crisis in Mexico ushered in the debt crisis of the 1980s and a very different debate began about the machinery for debt restructuring. This second debate, focused on the unsustainable amounts of debt owed to commercial banks by fifteen to twenty relatively advanced developing countries, is the subject of the next chapter.

Summing Up

The first global debate about sovereign debt workouts featured a proposal from the developing countries of the South to replace the ad hoc Paris Club machinery with permanent machinery that would deal with debt problems "in the broader context of development." The creditor countries of the North were not moved by the arguments for establishing an International Debt Commission. They successfully defended the existing ad hoc approach, in part by formally spelling out the "features" (principles) used in the Paris Club process.

Since 1994 the policy choice between ad hoc machinery and permanent machinery has been at the core of the debate about the workout machinery for debt in the form of bonds. Unless the nature of bonds makes it impossible to restructure them in ad hoc machinery, the experience of the North-South debt debate suggests that the proponents of creating permanent machinery are unlikely to prevail.

41. UNCTAD VI was held in Belgrade, Yugoslavia, in 1983. The G-77 arrived with another laundry list of proposals, but "did not achieve, or even significantly advance its objectives of securing substantial new resource transfers or restructure the international economic system." U.S. National Advisory Council (FY 1983, p. 16). Not much later the G-77 gave up on global negotiations. A UN-sponsored guide to international debt restructuring noted that an agreement was reached in an UNCTAD forum in July 1987 to "provide greater flexibility in debt restructuring and to coordinate debt-rescheduling terms with a country's medium-term development policy." United Nations Center on Transnational Corporations (1989, p. 55).

8

The Debt Crisis of the 1980s
and the Brady Plan Solution

The North-South Dialogue was a five-year effort to improve the architecture of the international financial system to deal with a problem stemming from unsustainable debt owed to bilateral donor agencies. The problem was not a threat to the international financial system, however, because of the political origins of much of this debt, and because the debtor countries had borrowed relatively little from private creditors. The North-South Dialogue yielded no changes of consequence in the international system, but it did focus attention on the debt dimension of the disappointing performance of the poorest developing countries. That performance remained a challenge for the global community in 2003.

The North-South Dialogue also forced policymakers to assess with some thoroughness the pros and cons of the existing machinery for debt restructuring (specifically the Paris Club) and a range of alternative approaches. This exercise helped to solidify the foundations of the system in advance of the 1980s debt crisis. On the eve of the Mexico's crisis in 1982, developing countries grudgingly accepted that the Paris Club process could reschedule debt with reasonable speed and efficiency even though it might not always yield durable solutions.

Box 8-1. Main Features of the Brady Plan

The debt crisis of the 1980s centered on debt owed to commercial banks by about twenty relatively advanced developing countries. The crisis began in August 1982, when Mexico announced that it would not be able to continue servicing this debt and requested a rescheduling of principal payments. Other countries reached the same critical point in quick succession. The G-7 architects adopted a step-by-step strategy for overcoming the crisis. The early steps emphasized rescheduling near-term payments and extending new loans. The final steps emphasized debt and debt-service reduction.

The Brady Plan, announced in March 1989 by U.S. Treasury secretary Nicholas Brady, was designed to help these debtor countries exit from repeated rescheduling negotiations and restore their access to new financing from commercial sources. The hallmark of the Brady Plan was its cooperative approach in which each of the parties involved—debtor countries, commercial banks, the IMF, and other official agencies—made a significant contribution.

Strong adjustment programs by debtor countries. Over the preceding seven years, the economic reform programs of most rescheduling countries were not particularly ambitious and were implemented inconsistently. To qualify for Brady Plan support, debtor countries had to adopt comprehensive reform

---

By contrast, the second debt debate in the Bretton Woods era addressed a fundamental threat to the international financial system: the unsustainable level of commercial bank lending to developing countries in the 1980s. The threat was eventually resolved through the Brady Plan, a workout strategy that succeeded beyond most expectations at the time it was announced and that provided lessons likely to remain valid for decades to come. In the narrow policy area of international debt, the design and implementation of the Brady Plan stands out as the most significant accomplishment of the G-7 architects since the Bretton Woods system was put in place in the mid-1940s.[1] Box 8-1 describes the main features of the Brady Plan.

The G-7 finance ministers and central bank governors acted promptly to mitigate the shock to the system of the Mexican crisis and the others that fol-

---

1. The number one success in all areas was probably the reform of the international monetary system in the mid-1970s. The G-7 architects would have been even more deserving of praise, of course, if they had managed to avoid the breakdown of the fixed exchange rate system in the 1970s or prevent the debt crisis in the 1980s.

programs and commit to accelerated implementation schedules. Reforms that would encourage a spontaneous reversal of capital flight were stressed.

Debt and debt-service reduction by commercial banks. Using a variety of financial engineering techniques, outstanding commercial bank debt was exchanged for marketable bonds with a substantially lower net present value or for other assets such as cash (buybacks) or equity in privatized state enterprises (swaps). Each debtor country negotiated a unique menu of options with its Bank Advisory Committee. The core options were par bonds and discount bonds. Par bonds had the same face value as the loans tendered in exchange but paid interest at a fixed, below-market rate. Discount bonds had a lower face value but paid interest at the market rate (adjusted regularly to reflect current conditions).

Enhancements from the IMF and other official agencies. The IMF, World Bank, regional development banks, and some bilateral donor agencies provided financing for buybacks and for purchasing bond collateral. Most of the bonds were fully collateralized with thirty-year, zero-coupon U.S. Treasury bonds. Funds were also placed in escrow accounts to cover one or two interest obligations on par and discount bonds, if necessary.

For the seventeen countries that concluded Brady Plan deals between 1990 and 1997, roughly $210 billion of commercial bank debt was reduced by around $85 billion (40 percent).

lowed on its heels. These actions included measures to sustain noninflationary growth in the industrial countries, promote far-reaching policy adjustments in the developing countries, provide financial support for these countries to prevent a vicious cycle of import compression and economic contraction around the world, and require banks to strengthen their capital positions.

The G-7 effort also entailed a significant policy reversal by the U.S. government. The administration of Ronald Reagan, which took office in January 1981, started off with an international economic program that had a distinctly laissez-faire orientation. It was disinclined to increase the resources of the IMF and World Bank or to take any steps that might encourage more risky private lending to developing countries, especially ones that might expose the administration to charges of "bailing out" commercial banks. The financial rescue operation for Mexico, orchestrated by the U.S. government in August 1982, was the first in a series of increasingly bold initiatives to use budget resources and international institutions to resolve the debt crisis of the 1980s.[2] By 1988 the circumstances were favorable for recognizing the losses being carried on bank balance sheets with forbearance from the regulators.

The Brady Plan was a cooperative strategy for persuading banks to move beyond debt rescheduling to debt reduction. Typically commercial banks negotiated with each country a menu of exit options, some of which were "enhanced" by official support. Most of the outstanding bank debt was exchanged for tradable par bonds or discount bonds. The first Brady Plan deal was signed with Mexico in February 1990. By 1994 most of the countries that had begun rescheduling bank debt in the late 1970s or early 1980s had completed similar deals. These deals were instrumental in helping these countries reestablish their creditworthiness and attract the large-scale flows of private capital that materialized in the mid-1990s.

Nevertheless, assessments of the Brady Plan have not been universally positive. Some observers have suggested that the debt-reduction arrangements carried out between 1988 and 1994 should have been completed instead at the beginning of the 1980s, thereby restoring the momentum of growth in the major borrowing countries at an earlier stage, to the benefit of the entire world economy. Scholars are likely to debate this matter for decades to come without being able to reach a definitive conclusion one way or the other.[3] The belief inherent in this study is that it was necessary to "bump down the stairs" before beginning broad-based debt reduction. Leaping from the top to the bottom would have risked systemic consequences that could be avoided by taking more time.[4] One of these risks related to how the legal systems in the United States and the United Kingdom would react to actions by governments to force banks to write down their claims on borrowing countries. This uncertainty provided a powerful argument for finding voluntary solutions at each step along the way.

Among the assessments of the 1980s debt crisis, one of the more analytically solid was undertaken by William R. Cline, a senior fellow at the Institute for International Economics, and published in 1995. Cline argued

2. Cline (1995, p. 205).

3. Bowe and Dean (1997) provide a technical analysis that points to the superiority of the Brady Plan approach over other approaches, but they conclude that more distance will be required to determine the magnitude of the benefit.

4. In theory the industrial country governments could have purchased the banks' developing country debt with special government securities at some discount that would have left most banks solvent. Then these governments could have negotiated new long-term payment terms at favorable interest rates with the developing country borrowers. An approach of this kind was ruled out both because of the scale and the precedent it would set.

that viewing the problems of the major borrowing countries in the early 1980s as liquidity problems rather than insolvency problems was the right "contingent strategy" for the G-7 architects to pursue. In particular, this approach bought time "for the eventual process of triage that separated the countries that needed debt forgiveness from those that did not."[5]

Cline was making here the often-overlooked point that a number of major borrowing countries—especially in Asia, but also Chile and Colombia—were able to adjust to the shocks of high oil prices, high interest rates, and weak demand for their exports. These countries successfully avoided having recourse to debt forgiveness and came out of the 1980s with good access to international capital markets. A strategy of reducing the debt burdens of the more advanced developing countries across the board (along the lines of the HIPC Initiative in the 1990s for the poorest countries) could not have been implemented in all likelihood without risking a deeper and longer global recession and grave political risks.

The G-7 strategy for managing the debt crisis of the 1980s was thus close to the best that was politically feasible at the time and may have been the best for advancing global welfare in the long term. Furthermore the commercial bank debt-reduction deals negotiated in the Brady Plan framework at the end of the decade represented a major advance in the art of sovereign workouts.

Step One: The Recession at the Beginning of the 1980s

After the relatively benign fifties and sixties, the turbulent 1970s set the stage for the debt crisis of the 1980s. Severe balance-of-payments strains prompted the United States in 1971 to break the dollar's convertibility to gold at a fixed rate. The move from an international monetary system based on par values to a floating-rate system had several implications for developing countries. One immediate impact was the uncertainty it introduced in the management of their external obligations; exchange rates could move adversely from the time of borrowing to the time of repayment. In addition, the removal of capital controls that often accompanied the adoption of floating rates contributed to rapid growth in external borrowing by private

5. Cline (1995, p. 204). Chapter 4 in this volume contains a critical review of the literature focusing on academic theory and empirical research relating to the occurrence of debt problems and the behavior of debtors and creditors. A detailed and comprehensive account of the 1980s debt crisis from the perspective of the International Monetary Fund can be found in Boughton (2001), the official history of the IMF between 1979 and 1989.

companies. At the same time, the eurocurrency market, created in the 1960s, experienced a boom, providing an eager and convenient source of funds for both public and private sector borrowers in developing countries. Unprecedented oil price increases in 1973 and 1974 sparked a recession in the industrial countries, thereby dampening demand for financing from this part of the world.

By the end of 1978, it was clear that the severe debt-servicing problems being experienced by a number of developing countries (such as Peru, Sudan, and Zaire) that had borrowed heavily from commercial banks could not be resolved with new money and refinancing alone. Banks began to conclude rescheduling agreements with these countries, but they still had confidence in the heaviest borrowers such as Argentina, Brazil, Mexico, and Venezuela, which were more advanced economically. Two unanticipated events shattered this confidence: the OPEC oil price increases in 1979–80; and the tight monetary policy adopted by the Federal Reserve to beat down inflationary pressures in the U.S. economy.

The price of Saudi crude, which had been under $3 a barrel at the end of 1973, was close to $11 at the end of 1975. Two more rounds of increases pushed the price above $17 a barrel at the end of 1979 and above $28 at the end of 1980. The price peaked in 1982 at more than $33 a barrel. In the summer of 1979 Paul Volcker succeeded William Miller as the chairman of the Board of Governors of the Federal Reserve System. Committed to bringing double-digit inflation under control, Volcker began pushing interest rates up. The Federal Funds rate, which stood at 4 percent at the end of 1976, rose above 6 percent at the end of 1977 and to almost 11 percent at the end of 1978. A year later it was close to 15 percent, and at the end of 1980 it was at 22 percent and still climbing. The rate peaked at 22.36 in July 1981 and ended the year at just above 13 percent. The rate did not drop back into single digits until mid-1983. Real interest rates, which had averaged a negative 10 percent in the 1973–78 period, were a positive 8 percent in the 1979–82 period.[6] The world economy gradually slid back into recession. Global GDP growth as measured by the IMF went from 4.8 percent in 1976 to 0.2 percent in 1982 before recovering to 2.2 percent in 1983 and 4.9 percent in 1984.

6. Watson and Regling (1992, p. 67). The prime rate for U.S. banks was 6.25 percent at the end of 1976. It stepped up to 7.75 percent at the end of 1977, 11.75 percent at the end of 1978, and 15.25 percent at the end of 1979. It peaked at 21.5 percent on December 19, 1980. It had fallen back to 15.75 percent by the end of 1981 but did not drop to single digits until it was set at 9.5 percent on June 18, 1985. The Federal Funds rate and the bank prime rate are from the Federal Reserve Board website www.federalreserve.gov, under "Statistics: Releases and Historical Data."

The impact of these two variables on developing countries, oil-exporting as well as oil-importing, was devastating. As happened in the Depression of the 1930s, commodity prices fell and export growth slowed.[7] A few countries, especially in Asia, were able to implement bold adjustment programs and resume growing relatively quickly. Many more countries, especially those in Latin America, were plunged into a decade-long period of economic stagnation.

The impact of these circumstances on the balance sheets of the leading globally active commercial banks was potentially disastrous. In a nutshell, commercial bank lending to a group of about twenty relatively advanced developing countries expanded rapidly in the 1970s to a point where it represented a multiple of the banks' capital. The exposure of all U.S. banks at this moment, for example, was so great that writing off 30 percent of their developing country loans would have wiped out most of their capital. That course of action would have disrupted the international trade and payment system, thereby risking a deep contraction of the world economy. The improvement in the ratios of developing country exposure to capital for U.S. banks between 1982 and 1988 is summed up in table 8-1.

The G-7 architects responded to these strains in the system in several ways. They encouraged the IMF to play a more active role in designing adjustment programs that would catalyze new financing from official and private sources. They directed the World Bank and the regional development banks to cut back on project loans in favor of fast-disbursing structural adjustment or policy-based loans. The Paris Club started meeting on a monthly basis to provide debt relief to a growing queue of candidates. The list of countries negotiating rescheduling agreements with commercial banks quickly lengthened.

The hallmark of the international strategy to overcome the debt crisis of the 1980s was cooperation among four parties with divergent financial interests but a common interest in the stability of the international financial system: debtor countries, commercial banks, the IMF and multilateral development banks, and the creditor countries in the OECD (which were also Paris Club creditors). The IMF's mandate made it the obvious party to be at the center of the process. It was fortunate to have a seasoned and highly regarded managing director, Jacques de Larosière, when Mexico crashed. Until he returned to France in 1987 to become the governor of the central bank, he worked tirelessly with the U.S. Treasury secretaries in the Reagan

---

7. As measured by the IMF, the drop in nonfuel commodity prices in the 1980s was the largest ever recorded. Boughton (2001, p. 24).

Table 8-1. Exposure of U.S. Banks to Developing Countries, 1982–88
Percentage of bank capital

Year-end	All U.S. banks	Nine major banks	All others
1982			
Exposure (percent)	186	288	116
Capital ($ billions)	71	29	42
1986			
Exposure (percent)	95	154	55
Capital ($ billions)	116	47	69
1988			
Exposure (percent)	63	108	32
Capital ($ billions)	136	56	80

Source: Adapted from Bowe and Dean (1997, table 1, p. 6).

administration (Donald Regan and James Baker), with Federal Reserve
Board Chairman Volcker, and with the other G-7 finance ministers and central bank governors and their deputies. The approach was above all
pragmatic. Rigid rules were shunned in favor of three broad principles:
approaching each case on its merits, sharing the burden among all four parties, and modifying the strategy as circumstances changed.

Step Two: The Mexican Crisis in 1982

The 1980s debt crisis began on August 12, 1982, when Mexican finance minister Jesus Silva Herzog phoned Regan, Volcker, and de Larosière to say that
his government had insufficient foreign exchange to meet its imminent obligations to external creditors. Silva Herzog made the crisis public in a press
conference from his office on August 17, and he briefed the commercial
banking community at a meeting in the Federal Reserve Bank of New York
on August 20. Specifically, he asked banks to extend for ninety days all payments of principal falling due within the next ninety days, and he committed
to meeting all interest payments on their due dates. He also indicated that
some new money would be required.[8]

The crisis was dramatic because Mexico was the single largest developing
country borrower from commercial banks. Out of a total external debt of

8. These and other details can be found in Kraft (1984), a blow-by-blow account of the Mexican workout in 1982.

$78 billion at the end of 1981, Mexico owed more than $32 billion to commercial banks.[9] Jean-Claude Trichet, a French finance official involved in the workout process throughout the decade, called the Mexican crisis "a brutal turning point."[10]

Yet Mexico's crisis did not come out of the blue. The Mexican economy, like those of other oil-exporting countries, had been bouncing between expansion and contraction as oil prices shot up or plummeted. The strains in 1981 were so severe that the government had to arrange $20 billion of financing from commercial banks to avoid default. In February 1982 the government was forced to devalue the peso.[11]

The Argentine invasion of the Falkland Islands/Malvinas in April also called attention to the vulnerability of the Latin American countries. When U.K. banks refused to clear Argentine financial transactions, other international banks deferred new lending.[12] Without fresh infusions of funds, Argentina could not avoid default for long. Banks also began cutting back on new lending to other countries in the region, which the borrowers needed to pay off maturing loans and meet rising interest obligations.

Overlaying the global economic cycle was an election cycle in Mexico that acquired exceptional significance over the next two decades. Presidential elections are held every six years, during the summer, and the inauguration of the new president takes place in December.[13] Fiscal and monetary discipline have tended to weaken during election campaigns, and implementation of credible stabilization measures has tended to be delayed during the long transition periods. Miguel de la Madrid was elected to succeed Jose Lopez Portillo on July 4, 1982. A payment crisis occurred barely five weeks later, and the job of crisis management fell to the lame-duck team headed by Silva Herzog.[14]

9. World Bank (2002).

10. Trichet (1989, p. 117).

11. Delamaide (1984, p. 102).

12. This episode provided a test of the sharing provisions in syndicated loan agreements. Argentina withheld payments to U.K. banks but paid other banks. The U.K. banks than invoked the sharing provision.

13. Even though the dominant party (PRI) had an unbroken string of election victories going back to the beginning of the 1920s, each of the transitions between 1976 and 1994 was difficult and associated with an economic crisis. The pattern was broken in 2000, which is part of the story in chapter 10.

14. On September 1 outgoing president Lopez Portillo nationalized the Mexican banking system and imposed sweeping exchange controls, which dealt another blow to investor confidence in the country's economic prospects.

The immediate challenge for the G-7 in the face of the Mexican payment suspension was to provide sufficient liquidity to meet Mexico's cash requirements while the authorities (outgoing and incoming) negotiated a recovery program with the IMF and related support from other creditors and donors. The cash gap was filled through various forms of bridge financing. The U.S. government and the Bank for International Settlements provided parallel bridge loans totaling $1.85 billion. In addition the U.S. government prepaid $1 billion for oil to be purchased from Mexico and guaranteed $1 billion of commercial financing for agricultural commodities imported from the United States.[15]

The centerpiece of the Mexican rescue package was a three-year extended arrangement with the IMF for $3.7 billion negotiated by Silva Herzog, who was kept on as finance minister by incoming president de la Madrid. After the Mexican stabilization program was nailed down in November, IMF managing director de Larosière called a meeting of creditor banks to outline the nature of the support they would be expected to provide. This consisted of rescheduling principal payments falling due during the program (about $20 billion) and extending $5 billion of new loans (increasing exposure by 7 percent).[16] Without this support, de Larosière made clear, he would be unable to recommend to his executive board the amount of IMF financing assumed in the program, which Mexico would need to meet the interest payments due on its bank debt.

The intervention by de Larosière at this point, clearly supported by the G-7 architects, crossed an important psychological line. In previous cases the commercial banks had been allowed to conclude workouts on their own terms. Now for the first time an explicit benchmark for bank participation was established at the beginning of the workout process. By some accounts, de Larosière's intervention meant that bank lending to restructuring countries changed from being voluntary to involuntary. Yet the G-7 and the IMF stood back from the negotiations between banks and debtor countries as they iterated toward mutually agreeable terms. In this sense the banks considered the deals with individual countries to be voluntary. Moral suasion, arm-twisting, and concerted action organized by the public sector were regarded as legitimate actions. By contrast, actions by the G-7 to force banks to negotiate with a borrower that was not implementing serious reforms or to absorb a disproportionate share of the workout burden would make par-

15. U.S. National Advisory Council (FY 1982, p. 65).
16. Kraft (1984, p. 51).

ticipation involuntary. This subtle difference remains important in the process of sovereign debt workouts today.

While the Bank Advisory Committee process for rescheduling commercial bank debt was well tested by mid-1982, the scale of the Mexican deal far exceeded the previous record holder (Poland in 1981). The number of banks with Mexican exposure was on the order of six hundred.[17] A ten-meter-long telex spelling out the details of the Mexican proposal was transmitted to the banks on December 8, and by December 22 the committee was able to report that a "critical mass" of banks had responded positively. The IMF Executive Board approved a three-year extended arrangement with Mexico the following day.

From the end of 1982 through 1984, commercial banks concluded forty-two debt-rescheduling deals with thirty-two countries.[18] Many more were negotiated before the final stage of the 1980s debt crisis that began in 1989 and involved officially supported debt reduction under the Brady Plan. Some deals were concluded within a few months. Others took years to go into effect. Argentina's deal, for example, took almost three years to wrap up. More than a dozen banks chaired Bank Advisory Committees formed in the first half of the 1980s, and each contained from four to seventeen banks. Citibank, as expected, chaired more committees than any other bank, but Bank of America was a close second. U.S. banks naturally dominated the Bank Advisory Committees for the Latin American debtors.

Virtually all of the deals concluded after the Mexican crisis were closely linked to IMF-supported adjustment programs.[19] Serious negotiations on rescheduling terms were not possible until the main elements of an adjustment program had been spelled out, and disbursements of new money from banks were usually phased and conditioned on meeting the quarterly performance targets specified in the country's IMF arrangement. This was a

17. A large fraction of the banks involved were not participants in syndicated loans but had extended single-bank loans. These banks consequently were not subject to sharing clauses and faced few legal obstacles or other disincentives to holding out and litigating. Nevertheless, none of the BAC-led workouts in the 1980s were disrupted by litigation. Banks weighed the low odds of recovering more money against the costs of litigation, taking into account their varying tax and regulatory regimes. The attractions of negotiated solutions were apparently far superior to the attractions of litigation.

18. World Bank (2002).

19. Venezuela said it did not need new money and therefore did not need an IMF arrangement. The banks eventually agreed to reschedule on the basis of "enhanced surveillance" by the IMF, but various issues delayed closing until early 1986. Enhanced IMF surveillance was also used in the cases of Colombia and Yugoslavia; see Holley (1987, p. 28). Cuba was not an IMF member, and therefore its debt was rescheduled without an IMF arrangement.

Box 8-2. The Institute of International Finance

Bank lending to developing countries exploded in the 1970s, largely driven by the process of recycling petrodollars. Debt-servicing difficulties spread toward the end of the 1970s and approached epidemic proportions in the early 1980s. At that point no effective statistical system existed for monitoring bank exposure in individual countries. Furthermore the wealth of information about borrowing country policies and performance generated by the IMF and World Bank was not available to the public. As a consequence banks were handicapped in managing their exposures in developing countries. The largest money center banks had highly trained staff to carry out sovereign risk analysis, but few of the regional banks, which supplied much of the financing, had comparable talent.

The Institute of International Finance was established to fill this vacuum. In May 1982, three months before the Mexican default, the Washington-based National Planning Association organized a meeting at the Ditchley Park conference center outside of London to exchange views on the role of banks in helping to restore international financial stability in a shaky world economy. In addition to senior executives from the leading industrial country banks, the meeting was attended by Jacques de Larosière, managing director of the IMF, and senior officials from the World Bank, the U.S. Treasury Department, and the Bank of England. William McDonough, from the First National Bank of

---

Faustian bargain, and it remains a sensitive issue in the current debate about sovereign workouts. The IMF would push the debtor country to undertake the maximum amount of adjustment that was politically feasible over the period of the program. When it judged that the country could do no more, the IMF would calculate the external financing gap associated with this set of reforms. Financing from the IMF filled part of this gap, and new loans from other official agencies (such as the World Bank, regional development bank, export credit agencies, and aid agencies) were penciled in based on relevant precedents or consultations. That process left a residual gap to be filled by the commercial banks. While the banks avoided the messy business of negotiating a credible adjustment program, they ended up in a weak position to argue for a smaller contribution.

G-7 concerns over burden sharing by commercial banks had surfaced in the late 1970s and were a constant policy issue during the long string of workouts in the 1980s. Banks also had concerns. First, they had little say in

Chicago, presented a paper that suggested terms of reference for an international banking association that would address the critical information deficiencies that existed.

The IIF began operations in January 1983. Its principal product was a series of regular reports on the main borrowing countries, based on visits to discuss policies and prospects with the financial authorities. The objective was to provide member banks with information on a par with that contained in IMF and World Bank reports. IIF reports aspired to provide even better analyses of bank lending (and other private capital flows) based on information gleaned from member firms. For the past twenty years, IIF country reports have been a highly valued risk management tool for the banking industry. As equity and bond flows picked up in the 1990s, the IIF opened its membership to nonbank financial firms (insurance companies, mutual funds, and other asset managers). It also initiated work on policy issues of concern to the industry, especially the international standards for regulatory capital, which were developed by the Basel Committee on Banking Supervision. After the Mexican peso crisis in 1997, the IIF played an active role in the policy debate about the architecture of the international financial system, especially private sector involvement in crisis prevention and resolution.

The IIF, headquartered in Washington, D.C., had more than 320 member firms and organizations from more than sixty countries at the end of 2002. Its staff numbered sixty people.

the design of debtor country adjustment programs. More often than not, the analytical work carried out in Bank Advisory Committees gave these programs barely passing marks. Stronger programs would have reduced the amount of new money or other support required from the banks. Second, the levels of financing from official sources seemed on the low side, in effect treating the banks as lenders of last resort and putting banks in the position of "bailing out" official creditors.

A noteworthy step to improve cooperation between the private sector and the public sector was the formation of the Institute of International Finance. The concept was floated at a meeting in Ditchley Park, England, in May 1982, and it began operations a year later with thirty-seven banks as founding members (box 8-2). The two core functions of the IIF were to generate accurate and timely data on bank exposures in the major borrowing countries and to produce reports on the economic outlook for these countries. The reports were intended to be as thorough as those produced by the IMF and World Bank, which were available at that time only to the governments of their member countries.[20]

Step Three: Multiyear Rescheduling Agreements, 1984

Industrial country growth picked up from a negative 0.3 percent in 1982 to 2.5 percent in 1983 and 5.1 percent in 1984. The aggregate trade balance of oil-importing developing countries swung from a $65 billion deficit in 1981 to a $15 billion surplus in 1984. Developing country growth remained weak, however, hovering around 1.5 percent in 1982 and 1983 before picking up to around 4 percent in 1984 and 1985. The strains in Latin America were reflected in consumer price inflation, close to 120 percent a year in 1983 and 1984 and topping out at 127 percent in 1985. Political pressures pushed policymakers toward more debtor-friendly restructuring arrangements. The next step down the stairs toward debt reduction was the introduction of multiyear rescheduling agreements, or MYRAs.

The move to MYRAs was motivated by hopes among the banks that improved prospects for growth would permit these agreements to be exit deals and by the banks' desire to avoid the management time and legal expense associated with annual reschedulings. Mexico was the first country to obtain a MYRA, in September 1984. It covered principal payments over six years, 1984–89. This deal also contained a debt-equity conversion clause, which was the first hint of the menu approach that became formalized under the Brady Plan in the final stage of the 1980s debt strategy. The Argentina agreement later in 1984 included on-lending and trade facility options for new-money commitments.[21] Other countries that negotiated MYRAs during this period were Chile, Dominican Republic, Ecuador, Jamaica, Uruguay, Venezuela, and Yugoslavia.

In addition to consolidating payments falling due over several years, commercial banks made a number of other significant concessions in the MYRA period. These included lengthening repayment periods to as long as twenty years, reducing the spread over LIBOR on both rescheduled debt and new money, and eliminating the 1 percent restructuring fee that was included in

---

20. Surrey and Nash (1984) contains a detailed account of the launching of the Institute of International Finance. The Japan Center for International Finance was established at the same time with a similar mandate. By 1997 the IIF had grown to represent all segments and regions of the global financial industry and had become an important vehicle for communicating the views of the industry to the G-7 architects and the IMF on preventing and resolving crises in emerging market countries.

21. Rhodes (1989, p. 21).

earlier deals.[22] The flexibility shown by banks contributed to a decision by the Paris Club to experiment with MYRAs, although in a more restrictive form.[23]

Step Four: The Baker Plan, 1985

When James Baker became the U.S. Treasury secretary in January 1985, the debt crisis was one of the biggest problems he inherited. As the year progressed the odds that the major debtors would not be able to grow out of their problems lengthened. The bellwether country, Mexico, fell out of compliance with its IMF-supported program at the beginning of the year and was having trouble getting back on track. In September a pair of deadly earthquakes on successive days struck Mexico City, compounding the country's already severe fiscal strains.

The pros and cons of taking another step down the stairs toward debt reduction had been examined during the summer. The annual meetings of the IMF and World Bank at the beginning of October in Seoul, Korea, served to force a decision. On October 1, Baker and Volcker met with the chairmen of the lead U.S. banks to outline a new approach. A week later in Seoul, Baker publicly unveiled his Program for Sustained Economic Growth.[24] The strategic bargain embedded in the Baker Plan was to mobilize more financing from official and private sources in return for reforms in three areas deemed critical to achieving higher rates of growth: import barriers, restrictions on foreign investment, and money-losing state enterprises.[25]

The Baker Plan focused on fifteen major borrowing countries.[26] To help these countries achieve minimally acceptable growth rates, the banks would have to provide $20 billion of net new financing over the next three years (an increase in exposure of roughly 3 percent a year). The World Bank and the Inter-American Development Bank would increase their net financing to these countries by $10 billion over the same period. (Baker announced at the same time U.S. support for creating a trust fund in the IMF with $2.7 billion of concessional financing for low-income countries.)

22. Holley (1987, p. 32).
23. Harrison (1989, p. 6).
24. Bogdanowicz-Bindert (1985, p. 267).
25. Cline (1995, p. 209).
26. Argentina, Bolivia, Brazil, Chile, Colombia, Ecuador, Mexico, Peru, Uruguay, Venezuela; the Philippines; Yugoslavia; Morocco, Nigeria, and Côte d'Ivoire. Costa Rica and Jamaica were added to the group a year later.

The debt-rescheduling deals negotiated with commercial banks in the context of the Baker Plan did not fall into place any more easily than had the deals in the 1982–85 period. The deal with Mexico was not signed until March 1987, the one with Argentina the following August, and the one with Brazil only in November 1988. The approach to "concerted lending" at this point also brought to the surface tensions among banks in different countries due to variations in the regulatory and tax treatment of their losses. For example, the regulatory regime for U.S. banks made capitalization of interest quite costly, while the regimes in Europe tended to favor interest capitalization.[27] These kinds of differences became more relevant as time went by and continue to be an important factor in the design of sovereign workouts.

The results of the Baker Plan were unclear, partly because experts have reached different conclusions about the amount of financing actually delivered against the initial targets. What is clear is that growth did not resume. Therefore the main contribution of the plan may have been to buy time for countries to introduce essential policy reforms and for banks to build up their reserves against eventual losses.

Debt problems were by no means limited to the Baker Plan countries during this stage. A larger number of smaller countries were in arrears to external creditors of one type or another by this time. One measure of the difficulties is that nineteen small debtor countries were in arrears to IMF in August 1985. Workouts for these countries were given low priority because their role in the global economy was negligible.[28] Any effort by the G-7 architects to design special approaches for these countries could have created precedents that might undermine the strategy for restoring the creditworthiness of the larger debtors.

Step 5: Ad Hoc Innovation, 1987

By early 1987 the Baker Plan seemed to be running out of steam. Developing country growth had not picked up as much as hoped, adjustment fatigue was setting in, and the money center banks were having increasing difficulty mobilizing new money to meet the targets contained in the plan. During the course of 1987, the Baker Plan was effectively abandoned as banks began to experiment with a variety of debt-restructuring techniques that included elements of debt reduction.

27. Bogdanowicz-Bindert (1985, p. 271).
28. Bogdanowicz-Bindert (1985, p. 272).

The collapse of oil prices in 1986 pushed banks to take the next step toward debt reduction by adding a number of oil exporters to the list of large debt-distressed borrowing countries. Another factor was the politically motivated decision by Brazilian President José Sarney in early 1987 to declare a moratorium on payments to external creditors. (Peru made a similar move a few months earlier.)

Both of these events apparently contributed to the surprise announcement by Citibank in May 1987 that it was setting aside provisions for losses equivalent to 25 percent of its exposure in restructuring countries.[29] Other major U.S. banks quickly followed suit, and a second round of provisioning was announced later in the year. Banks in other countries joined the parade in 1987 and 1988, and provisioning levels gradually rose toward 50 percent of developing country exposures.

The first significant experiment with debt reduction was carried out in mid-1987. Mexico offered commercial banks twenty-year bonds backed by zero-coupon U.S. Treasury securities in exchange for a higher face value of old debt. The transaction was designed by J. P. Morgan, which saw the potential for reducing debt by offering a better asset. An uptick in Mexico's foreign exchange reserves created the opportunity to purchase collateral with the country's own funds. The exchange went to market in January 1988, was closed in March, and yielded $1 billion of debt reduction. Although this was only a third of the target amount, it demonstrated the feasibility of market-based debt reduction. Another lesson was that exchanges of this kind would be more attractive with some backing for interest payments.[30]

More menu options appeared in Argentina's August 1987 restructuring package. These included cofinancing with the World Bank, a trade credit and deposit facility, new-money bonds, and an exit bond with a below-market interest rate. The exit bond was not successful because, according to market reports, it was mispriced and had no "enhancements" (collateral).[31]

A 1988 deal with Brazil showed that new money and debt reduction could be combined in a single voluntary package. The package included $5 billion of new money and the most innovative menu to date. In particular, some bank loans could be exchanged into exit bonds convertible into government bonds denominated in Brazil's currency, which could in turn be traded or

29. Bowe and Dean (1997, p. 8). The announcement came shortly after John Reed succeeded Walter Wriston as chairman of Citicorp. It may also have been prompted by Reed's desire to give Citicorp a new look and a competitive advantage over other U.S. banks.
30. Wagner (1989, pp. 37–38).
31. Rhodes (1989, p. 21).

sold for domestic purposes. This deal had the potential of reducing bank debt by $18 billion over five years, one-third of the starting amount.[32] The debt-reduction champion in 1988 was Chile, which launched several debt-conversion programs and a major buyback operation.[33]

A scorecard on the debt strategy at this point would have shown a fairly even division of positives and negatives. On the positive side, some key reforms that skeptics predicted would be long in coming had been implemented successfully. These included Mexico's decisions to join the GATT and to undertake a hemisphere-leading privatization program. Among the creditors, greater flexibility was evident, and some remarkable feats of financial engineering were being performed. Most important for the banks, their balance sheets were much stronger, and there were signs that the G-7 architects were edging toward a more aggressive approach.

On the negative side, the political will to implement macroeconomic and structural reforms necessary for sustainable growth remained weak in several key countries. The industrial countries were succumbing to protectionist pressures that were constraining the growth of developing country exports. Most distressing for the bankers was timidity in wielding the carrot of official financing. Capital increases for the multilateral development banks were being delayed, objections were raised to more cofinancing from these banks, export credit agencies were slow in restoring cover for countries launching credible adjustment programs, and the Paris Club was taking an inflexible attitude toward debt reduction for middle-income countries.

An important systemic improvement in this period was the adoption of the first capital adequacy standards for internationally active banks. These were developed in the Basel Committee on Banking Supervision, an informal group of banking regulators from the G-10 countries formed in 1974 and supported by the Bank for International Settlements. The Basel standard announced in 1988 required banks engaged in substantial cross-border lending to maintain shareholder capital equivalent to 8 percent of their assets (adjusted to reflect the different degrees of risk associated with various asset classes). Adopting the Basel standard was a bit like closing the barn door after the cows had escaped, but it represented another incentive for banks to develop more sophisticated risk management tools.[34]

32. Côte d'Ivoire and Yugoslavia also used exit bonds at this stage. According to Bowe and Dean (1997, p. 8), around $40 billion of debt was reduced, before Brady Plan negotiations, through debt-for-equity and debt-for-local-currency conversion.

33. The U.S. Treasury encouraged banks to donate debt to nongovernmental organizations for environmental or social programs, but not much was donated (Robinson and Bartels 1989, p. 184).

34. At the same time, the Basel standard contributed to financial innovations such as derivatives and a considerable amount of "regulatory arbitrage" that began to erode the prudential value of the

Apart from the pull of successful debt-reduction transactions, the next step in the debt strategy was propelled by secondary market trends and mounting arrears. The provisioning initiated by banks in May 1987 had an immediate impact on secondary market prices of distressed debt owed to commercial banks. From an average of sixty-seven cents on the dollar at the beginning of 1987, the price dropped to forty-five to fifty cents in the middle of the year. (The bottom on a weighted average basis was thirty-two cents, reached in late 1989.) This price decline had the effect of lowering the cost of debt reduction by establishing a cheaper benchmark for cash buy-backs.[35] Simultaneously, the rising level of arrears to external creditors among the fifteen Baker Plan countries was becoming alarming, doubling by some estimates from $4.5 billion in 1985 to more than $10 billion at the end of 1988. More than half of the end-1988 amount was owed to commercial banks.[36]

At this point in the implementation of the G-7 debt strategy, two factors seemed to militate against a broader debt-reduction program. First, the banks were reluctant to conclude deals involving substantial reductions that might compromise their negotiating position with countries requiring smaller reductions. Efficient tailoring of the reductions to each country's circumstances argued for concluding the first deal with the country that could handle the smallest write-down and then working through the other cases in progression toward larger and larger write-downs.[37] Second, the moment did not seem to be politically ripe. Before putting the weight of the public sector behind a broad debt-reduction program, the G-7 needed to find a debtor country able to meet performance standards that would justify a "reward." There was an exceptional coincidence of elections in the major Latin American countries in 1988–89, and it was risky to take the next step before the outcomes were known.[38] The G-7 also needed a creditor-country leader with enough political capital to make a debt-reduction program palatable to critics of any government intervention.

As frustrations among both debtors and creditors built up during this period, proposals for quick or generalized solutions began to proliferate.[39] A number of them were variations on the theme of creating an interna-

---

standard. Consequently, a major effort to update the standard was launched in 1999 that is expected to culminate in global implementation in 2006.

35. Cline (1995, p. 214).

36. Wertman (1989a, p. 15).

37. Costa Rica made a strong case for debt reduction in 1986, but the banks held off because of the precedent it would create.

38. Rhodes (1989, p. 26).

39. These are noted in Rogoff and Zettelmeyer (2002).

tional facility to purchase developing country debt at a discount (box 8-3). Support for this approach advanced to the point of being incorporated in the Omnibus Trade and Competitiveness Act (P.L. 100-418) passed by the U.S. Congress in August 1987.[40] This legislation required the Treasury Department to report to Congress on the advisability and feasibility of establishing an International Debt Management Authority to buy bank loans at well below face value and assume the risks of collecting the remaining value from the borrowing countries in due course. The Treasury Department was also directed to initiate discussions with other countries with a view to establishing the authority.[41] French president François Mitterand and Japanese finance minister Kiichi Miyazawa advanced proposals in the same direction.

Step Six: The Brady Plan, 1989

Presidential elections in the United States as well as Mexico made major initiatives in the debt area difficult to undertake during 1988. Carlos Salinas was elected president of Mexico in August by a narrow and allegedly fraudulent margin, beginning a perilous four-month transition period reminiscent of the troubled successions in 1976 and 1982. Salinas stressed the importance of debt reduction as part of his economic program both publicly and privately in conversations with U.S. leaders. To help stabilize the Mexican economy during the transition and allow the new administration time to adopt a fresh program supported by the IMF without accumulating arrears, the U.S. Treasury provided a $3.5 billion bridge loan to Mexico.[42] In the U.S. election campaign the leading candidates were not inclined to promote a major debt-reduction initiative for the benefit of developing countries because of domestic considerations. Farmers and other groups were clamoring for government action to alleviate their debt burdens, which would be difficult to accommodate within a responsible budget policy.

After his election in November 1988 and before his inauguration in January 1989, President-elect George H. W. Bush announced that a thorough review of the international debt strategy would be a high priority of his new administration. The result came quickly, in part because much of the necessary analytical work had been carried out by Treasury Department staff at the end of the previous administration. Deadly riots in Venezuela in Febru-

40. Among the political pressures in this direction in the United States was a desire to support the democratic governments that had replaced military regimes in a number of Latin American countries since the Mexican default in 1982.

41. For the perspective of the Congressional Research Service, see Wertman (1989a, 1989b).

42. Robinson and Bartels (1989, p. 184).

Box 8-3. Reform Proposals in the 1980s

In the 1970s the most daring proposals for new workout machinery came out of the North-South Dialogue, especially from the foreign ministry–oriented officials who led the UN Conference on Trade and Development and the G-77. In the 1980s the most prominent advocates for fundamental reform were academics. Peter Kenen at Princeton University was one of the earliest. Jeffrey Sachs was the most visible.

In 1983, barely six months after the Mexican payment moratorium, Kenen proposed the establishment of an International Debt Discount Corporation to buy commercial bank loans at a discount.[1]

Sachs, who joined the Harvard faculty in 1980 immediately after receiving his Ph.D., had done work on hyperinflation that led to his engagement by the Bolivian government to help develop a strategy for stopping inflation that had reached 24,000 percent in 1985. The strategy adopted included a freeze on payments of debt owed to foreign banks, followed by negotiations that resulted in a series of buybacks at eleven cents on the dollar.[2] Sachs became a passionate advocate of reducing bank debt owed by developing countries suffering from substantial debt "overhangs." In 1986, he proposed a new approach to the 1980s debt crisis that put debt reduction at the center of the process.[3] For the remainder of the decade, in speeches, op-ed articles, television interviews, conferences, and other occasions, Sachs waged a public campaign for debt reduction, becoming the "enfant terrible" of the banks in the process. These efforts contributed to the initiative taken by New Jersey senator Bill Bradley to push banks (and the U.S. government) toward debt reduction, and the action taken by the Congress in the Omnibus Trade and Competitiveness Act of 1988 directing the executive branch to take steps toward establishing an International Debt Management Authority.

The number of proposals from academic and even financial industry sources grew exponentially toward the end of the 1980s. One was from Benjamin Cohen, at Tufts University, for the establishment of an International Debt Restructuring Agency.[4] Another was from James D. Robinson III, Chairman of the American Express Company, for the establishment of an "Institute of International Debt and Development."[5]

1. Peter B. Kenen, "A Bailout Plan for the Banks," *New York Times*, March 6, 1983, p. 3-3.
2. Sachs (1988).
3. Sachs (1986).
4. Cohen (1989).
5. Robinson and Bartels (1989).

ary protesting austerity measures added to the urgency of taking the last step down the stairs toward debt reduction.

On March 10, 1989, U.S. Treasury secretary Nicholas Brady outlined an "exit strategy" in a speech delivered at the Brookings Institution.[43] In one sense, the Brady Plan contained nothing new. Virtually all of the elements could be found in one or more of the rescheduling deals completed in the 1987–88 period. The U.S. political commitment to the Brady Plan was strong, however, and it succeeded in helping most middle-income rescheduling countries to regain their creditworthiness.

Within three years the largest debtor countries were receiving substantial net inflows of private capital, and their economies were expanding at a brisk pace. By the end of 1995 Brady Plan deals had been concluded with thirteen countries. As measured by Cline, these involved write-downs totaling about $60 billion, or one-third of the $190 billion of bank claims treated in these deals.[44] The write-downs reduced the total external debt of the countries concerned by only about 15 percent once the amount owed to nonbank creditors is factored in. It is hard to argue with Cline's conclusion that the psychological impact of this forgiveness—in the debtor countries and in global markets—was bigger than its financial impact. Four more Brady Plan deals were done in 1996 and 1997, bringing the total to seventeen. All are listed in table 8-2 along with the face value of the old debt and a rough estimate of the total reduction.[45]

Perhaps the most important feature of the Brady Plan deals is that they were implemented without resort to generalized or coercive methods. Consistent with the principles developed for the London Club machinery over the preceding fifteen years (see chapter 3), the Brady Plan workouts were case-by-case, voluntary, and market-based. The new features of the Brady Plan were stronger adjustment programs, menus of debt-restructuring

43. Numerous descriptions and assessments of the Brady Plan have been published. Three of the better ones are Cline (1995), Bowe and Dean (1997), and Boughton (2001).

44. Cline (1995, p. 235).

45. There is no agreed methodology on how to calculate the amount of debt reduction in Brady Plan deals. Cline's estimates, for example, are quite different from estimates published by the IMF in 1995, which are cited by Allen and Peirce (1997, p. 150). One source of the difference is that the IMF calculations ignore past-due interest, which was capitalized in some cases and represented a substantial fraction of the debt being restructured. Another complication is that the amount of net present value reduction is determined by the yield curve selected, and yield curves change over time. As a consequence, a deal involving NPV reduction of 50 percent based on the yield curve on the day the term sheet was initialed could become a deal with NPV reduction of only 40 percent based on the yield curve on the formal closing date six months later (communication from Peter Allen, May 22, 2002).

Table 8-2. Brady Plan Debt Reduction

Billions of U.S. dollars unless otherwise specified

Country	Date of agreement	Debt treated[a]	Approximate discount (percent)[b]	Approximate amount reduced[c]
Mexico	March 1990	48.2	35	16.9
Costa Rica	May 1990	1.6	84	1.3
Venezuela	December 1990	20.6	30	6.2
Uruguay	February 1991	1.6	44	0.7
Nigeria	January 1992	5.3	60	3.2
Philippines	December 1992	5.7	50	2.8
Argentina	April 1993	28.6	35	10.0
Jordan	December 1993	0.9	35	0.3
Brazil	April 1994	48.0	35	16.8
Bulgaria	July 1994	8.3	62	5.1
Dominican Republic	August 1994	1.2	35	0.4
Poland	October 1994	14.4	52	7.5
Ecuador	February 1995	7.8	45	3.5
Panama	May 1996	3.9	45	1.8
Peru	November 1996	8.0	45	3.6
Côte d'Ivoire	May 1997	6.5	76	4.9
Vietnam	December 1997	0.8	53	0.4
Total		211.4	40	85.4

Source: Adapted from World Bank (2002, app. 2).

a. Including past-due interest.

b. Arrived at by averaging the discount reflected in any discount bond component and the discount reflected in any buyback component. The amounts shown tend to be significantly higher than the amounts that would emerge from a more technical analysis because of the weight and characteristics of the menu option in each case.

c. The product of the debt treated and the approximate discount.

options, enhancements for these options from official agencies, and new money from official sources.

Strong Adjustment Programs

The economic programs adopted by debtor countries had to be strong enough to elicit relatively large funding commitments by the IMF, the World Bank, and the regional development banks, and to justify debt reduction by commercial banks. Beyond prudent macroeconomic policies, the Brady Plan programs generally stressed structural reforms (especially privatization) essential to sustainable growth.

Restructuring Menus

The Bank Advisory Committee for each Brady Plan negotiation developed a unique menu of options for debt and debt-service reduction. These were negotiated with the debtor county concerned and the relevant official institutions. The options were carefully designed to fit the varying regulatory and tax regimes of the banks involved, while remaining financially equivalent. The basic choices were:

—a *par bond,* exchanged for the same principal amount of old loans but bearing a fixed, below-market interest rate;

—a *discount bond,* exchanged at a substantial discount from the principal amount of old loans but paying interest based on the current market rate;

—a *debt-equity swap* program yielding a local-currency claim that could be exchanged for shares of an enterprise being privatized; and

—a *cash buyback* at a discount.[46]

Official Enhancements

Multilateral and bilateral agencies agreed to enhance the new bonds received in exchange for outstanding bank loans. The most popular enhancements were zero-coupon, thirty-year U.S. Treasury bonds purchased with a combination of debtor country reserves, IMF credit, and World Bank-IDB loans. These were used to collateralize (defease) the new Brady bonds by ensuring full payment upon maturity. Another form of enhancement was money placed in escrow to be used to pay interest on Brady bonds in the event that the debtor country missed one or more scheduled payments. Financing for cash buybacks was also provided. As a guideline to limit this form of support, the IMF and the World Bank agreed to set aside up to 25 percent of their new commitments of balance-of-payments financing to enhance principal reduction and up to 40 percent of the country's IMF quota or World Bank capital subscription to enhance interest obligations.[47]

46. The interest rate on discount bonds was a market rate, normally expressed as a spread over LIBOR and reset every six months. In the Baker Plan rescheduling with Mexico concluded in March 1987, the spread was set at 13/16 of a percent. This became a standard spread for subsequent deals with countries considered to have good economic prospects and a cooperative attitude. The fixed interest rate on par bonds was set at a below-market level calculated to make investors indifferent between purchasing one or the other on the day of issue.

47. The enhancements had symbolic as well as financial importance. By shifting a small amount of risk from banks to official institutions, they contributed to the appearance of burden sharing. But

Some subtle "sticks" were also incorporated into the Brady Plan. The one with the most relevance to the current debate was the threat of *lending into arrears* by the IMF. Up to this point the IMF had taken care to reinforce respect for contractual obligations by requiring debtor countries to clear up arrears to official and private creditors before the IMF would disburse fresh credit. Under the Brady Plan, a formal change in the IMF's policies was adopted to permit IMF lending in situations where the debtor country was implementing a credible adjustment program and was negotiating in good faith with its commercial bank creditors but had not yet concluded these negotiations. The IMF funds in such a case helped the country maintain an adequate level of foreign exchange reserves while negotiating a debt-reduction deal.[48]

New Money

Complementary support was provided by a variety of official sources, including new loans from bilateral aid agencies and export credit agencies, as well as Paris Club rescheduling when appropriate. In this context, countries experiencing large balance-of-payments surpluses were invited to make special commitments. Japan, for example, came forward with $2 billion of cofinancing earmarked for Mexico and $4.5 billion of untied trade financing for other Brady Plan countries.[49]

The most important form of new money, however, was the spontaneous return of flight capital, catalyzed by accelerated reforms in the debtor countries and strong public sector support for these reforms. Although it was not possible to predict with precision the magnitude of these capital flows, the amounts assumed served to cut back on the debt reduction by commercial banks and the

---

almost all of the enhancements were financed from debtor country reserves or from IMF and multilateral development bank loans that these countries would have to repay. (The preferred creditor status of the multilateral agencies made their risk minimal.) Except for small amounts provided to finance buybacks for several low-income countries, no new budget resources (taxpayer monies) from the creditor countries were used in the process of reducing commercial bank debt at this time. More important, the collateral made it possible for banks to convert high-risk exposures to developing countries into low-risk exposures on their balance sheets. Tactically, the enhancements also helped close the gap between the debt-reduction requests by debtor countries and the offers from commercial banks.

48. The United States in particular was uneasy about this change in policy and went on record against any interpretation of this action that might interfere with the legal enforcement of the contractual rights of creditors. It also stressed that the IMF should have recourse to this policy only when there was evidence that most banks involved were satisfied that the country was negotiating in good faith.

49. Wertman (1989a, pp. 4–5).

financial support from the IMF and other official agencies required by the debtor countries to achieve viable balance-of-payments positions.

Brady Plan Negotiations

The first Brady Plan deal was with Mexico because it was the biggest debtor, had the best track record of adjustment, and had the greatest amount of political support from the U.S. government. Still, the negotiations were difficult; agreement in principle was not reached until July 1989 (the deal was closed in March 1990). The banks started by offering a haircut of 15 percent, and the Mexicans started by asking for 55 percent. The final deal, covering $48 billion of outstanding long-term bank debt, included a discount bond with a 35 percent discount. The other menu options were an equivalent par bond and new money. The discount and par bonds were both secured with thirty-year zero-coupon U.S. Treasury bonds and further enhanced with eighteen months of collateral for interest payments.[50]

Both the U.S. Treasury Department and the Federal Reserve played critical roles in bringing the two sides together. When the negotiations bogged down in New York, Brady invited the Mexican team and the three lead banks (Citibank, Bank of America, and Swiss Bank Corporation) to Washington to discuss the status of the negotiations.[51] Negotiations proceeded in a Treasury Department conference room for two days virtually nonstop, with Under Secretary David Mulford nearby to help refine the amounts and forms of official support required to close the deal. Angel Gurria, the lead Mexican negotiator, and Bill Rhodes from Citibank, the chairman of the Bank Advisory Committee, were highly regarded for their negotiating skills and ably supported by their legal advisors. They provided models for others who assumed responsibility for shepherding deals with other countries to a successful conclusion.[52]

Another eighteen countries reduced their debt to commercial banks during the 1990s and in 2001 using a different process. These were low-income

50. According to Cline (1995, pp. 220–21), the value of the enhancements totaled $7.2 billion ($2 billion from the World Bank, $1.3 billion from the IMF, $1.4 billion from the Export-Import Bank of Japan (JEXIM), a $1.1 billion bridge loan from the banks partially taken out by more JEXIM financing, and $1.4 billion from Mexico's own foreign exchange reserves.

51. Citibank chairman John Reed and Bank of America chairman Tom Clausen participated in these final negotiations. Rhodes's counterpart from Bank of America was Rick Bloom. Gerald Corrigan and Terrence Checki were the key people from the Federal Reserve Bank of New York supporting Fed chairman Paul Volcker.

52. Gurria and Rhodes were debt-restructuring veterans. Both had been involved in Nicaragua's negotiations with banks in the late 1970s and had played key roles in Mexico's 1982 rescheduling deal. Gurria in 1989 was the director of external credit in the Mexican Ministry of Finance.

Table 8-3. Donor-Financed Buybacks

Millions of U.S. dollars, unless otherwise specified

Country	Date completed	Principal extinguished	Buyback price (cents per dollar)	Cost of forgiveness
Albania	July 1995	371	26.0	97
Bolivia	May 1993	170	16.0	27
Ethiopia	January 1996	226	8.0	19
Guinea	April 2000	63	13.0	9
Guyana	November 1992 and August 1999	104	12.3	14
Honduras	August 2001	13	18.0	2
Mauritania	August 1996	53	10.0	6
Mozambique	December 1991	124	10.0	13
Nicaragua	December 1995	1,100	8.0	89
Niger	March 1991	107	18.0	19
Sao Tome and Principe	August 1994	10	10.0	1
Senegal	December 1996	71	20.0	15
Sierra Leone	September 1995	235	13.0	32
Tanzania	April 2001	77	12.0	10
Togo	December 1997	45	12.5	6
Uganda	February 1993	153	12.0	23
Yemen	February 2001	362	2.9	11
Zambia	September 1994	200	11.0	25
Total/average		3,484	12.0	418

Source: World Bank (2002, table A2.1). Excludes associated interest that was cancelled in the cases of Tanzania and Yemen. All of the buybacks were funded in part by the IDA Debt Reduction Facility, except Nicaragua. Cost of forgiveness includes technical assistance grants. Buybacks for Côte d'Ivoire (March 1998) and Vietnam (March 1998) were part of Brady Plan packages and are included in table 8-2.

countries with dubious economic prospects whose bank debt was trading at deep discounts. With concessional financing from the World Bank's IDA Debt Reduction Facility and a number of bilateral donor agencies, these countries bought back $3.5 billion of bank debt at an average of twelve cents on the dollar (table 8-3).[53] The banks involved did not appreciate these deals

53. The facility, created in 1989, was funded with allocations from the World Bank's net income totaling $300 million. www.worldbank.org/html/fpd/guarantees/html/ida_facility.html (February 1, 2003).

because most were carried out by means of unilateral offers rather than negotiations (see chapter 6).[54]

The Legacy of the Brady Plan

The second great debt debate in the Bretton Woods era was about how to prevent a breakdown in the international financial system from being triggered by defaults among a group of twenty large developing countries on debt owed to commercial banks. The G-7 architects adopted a cautious step-by-step strategy to resolve the debt crisis of the 1980s. Ten years were required to reestablish conditions conducive to strong flows of private capital to these debtor countries. Throughout the period concerned citizens clamored for quicker solutions, and politicians, academics, and bankers advanced proposals for bold fixes, including new workout machinery. The results of the G-7 strategy will remain contentious for years to come. The social costs of the decade-long crisis were high, and no one wants to repeat the experience. At the same time, it will be difficult to prove that any alternative strategy would have yielded greater global welfare or higher living standards in the debtor countries.

Three legacies of the Brady Plan solution are relevant to the current debate about workouts involving bond debt. Perhaps the most important legacy is the emphasis the plan placed on policy reforms in the process of resolving financial crises in developing countries. Over the course of the 1980s, most of the Latin American countries abandoned growth strategies that were inward looking and oriented to the public sector and built more open and market driven economies. The return of capital flight was a critical measure of this progress, signaling a restoration of confidence in future economic growth among the citizens of these countries.

A second legacy is the set of tools created for reducing sovereign debt that has become unsustainable. By offering a menu of options to lenders with different objectives and constraints, the Brady Plan deals matched debt reduction to the circumstances of each case in a manner that left remarkably few scars to interfere with new borrowing from market sources by well-managed countries.

A third legacy is the cooperative approach in which debtor countries, multilateral agencies, bilateral donor agencies, and private lenders worked

---

54. In the case of Senegal in 1996, the banks refused to tender their debt at the offer price, and additional donor funds had to be mobilized to support a higher price.

closely together to craft durable workouts, with each one shouldering a substantial share of the burden. The G-7 architects and the IMF deserve credit for adopting this modus operandi. Curiously they did not build on this legacy of cooperation in designing a strategy for resolving the post-1995 crises. They opted instead for a relatively confrontational approach to burden sharing by private creditors.

9

The HIPC Initiative in the 1990s

The G-7 strategy for overcoming the debt crisis of the 1980s focused on the developing countries that had borrowed heavily from private sources of financing, mainly commercial banks. These tended to be the countries with larger and more advanced economies. Problems with excessive debt owed to official creditors were also endemic at that time among the smaller and less advanced countries, but a solution was not found until the major borrowing countries had completed Brady Plan debt-reduction deals and restored their creditworthiness. The G-7 architects finally mustered enough political will in the mid-1990s to tackle the debt problems of the poorest countries.

The approach adopted took the form of a special program for heavily indebted poor countries, or HIPCs. Sadly, the HIPC Initiative—formally launched in September 1996—has been as clumsy and ineffective as the Brady Plan was clever and successful. Senior finance officials in the HIPCs, the donor countries, and the international financial institutions have spent a prodigious amount of time and energy on this exercise over the past seven years—conceivably more time than was spent in implementing the Brady Plan. Most of the complexities of the HIPC Initiative derived from efforts to defend the preferred creditor status of the IMF and the multilateral development banks. As a matter of policy, outright debt reduction by these agencies was ruled out, and indirect means had to be found.

The net present value of the public debt of the thirty-three countries considered by the World Bank likely to qualify for the HIPC program (out of forty-two eligible countries) is roughly $90 billion, less than half the face value of the $190 billion of commercial bank debt treated under the Brady Plan.[1] The fraction of debt of these thirty-three countries eventually to be reduced under the HIPC Initiative is projected to be about one-half, compared with the 40 percent reduction under the Brady Plan. After six years of implementation, only six countries had reached the point in the process of actually having their "excessive" debt canceled (table 9-1). The G-7 architects had labored for more than six years to remove a smaller mountain and had less to show for it.[2] Moreover, the method of implementing debt forgiveness continues to breed resentment within the HIPCs and cynicism among poverty-oriented NGOs around the world.

The HIPC Initiative is more directly related to the machinery for delivering development assistance (aid) than the machinery for sovereign debt workouts. It was, in effect, a second-best solution. Most HIPCs were not experiencing financial crises or facing imminent default. Their debts were gradually becoming unsustainable because the burden of debt service on their budgets was at or approaching the limit of what was politically tolerable. The simplest and most direct fix would have been to increase the amount of grant financing provided to HIPCs capable of maintaining sound policies until economic growth made their debt burdens sustainable. This approach was ruled out, however, because of political constraints in the donor countries. Voters were experiencing "aid fatigue," and parliaments were reluctant to support major increases. Debt forgiveness was an easier sell than committing new aid to enable poor countries to pay their existing debts in full.

Thus a discussion of the HIPC Initiative does not fit comfortably in this study. There are two reasons for including it. First, it is a product of the third global debt debate in the Bretton Woods era, the roots of which can be

1. The HIPC figure comes from the World Bank's HIPC website: www.worldbank.org/hipc. It is not precisely comparable to the Brady Plan figure for several technical reasons. Moreover, the HIPC total may be exaggerated by large amounts of interest charged on overdue interest payments, and penalty interest, owed by a few countries. Only twenty-six countries had qualified for HIPC debt reduction by mid-2002.

2. The total cost of implementing the HIPC Initiative for the thirty-three countries expected to qualify was estimated to be around $30 billion in 2000 net present value terms. The cost borne by the public sector for implementing the Brady Plan was negligible.

Table 9-1. Groupings of Countries under the Enhanced HIPC Initiative, July 2002

Decision point countries			
Benin	Ghana	Madagascar	Rwanda*
Cameroon	Guinea	Malawi	Sao Tome and Principe
Chad	Guinea-Bissau*	Mali	Senegal
Ethiopia	Guyana	Nicaragua	Sierra Leone*
The Gambia	Honduras	Niger	Zambia

Completion point countries	*Predecision point countries*		*Potentially sustainable cases*
Bolivia	Burundi*	Lao P.D.R.	Angola*
Burkina Faso	Central African Rep.*	Liberia*	Kenya
Mauritania	Comoros[a]	Myanmar*	Vietnam
Mozambique	Congo, Dem. Rep.*	Somalia*	Yemen[b]
Tanzania	Congo, Rep. of	Sudan*	
Uganda	Côte d'Ivoire	Togo	

Source: World Bank, "Financial Impact of the HIPC Initiative: First 26 Country Cases." HIPC Unit. July 2002. www.worldbank.org/hipc.

* Conflict-affected countries.

a. Comoros has been added to the group because a preliminary assessment of its debt situation showed a potential need for HIPC debt relief. (See Comoros: External Debt Sustainability Analysis, IDA/SecM2001-0461, July 6, 2001, and EBS/01/110, July 3, 2001.)

b. Yemen reached a decision point in June 2000. Its debt sustainability analysis indicated that the country has a sustainable debt burden after the application of traditional debt relief mechanisms. (See SM/00/138 and IDA/SecM2000-359, June 28, 2000.) The Paris Club provided a stock-of-debt operation on Naples terms in July 2001.

found in the first debate during the 1970s in the context of the North-South Dialogue. Furthermore, the practices of the Paris Club were a major factor pushing the debt of the poorest countries to unsustainable levels. Second, the HIPC Initiative has confused the latest debate, which is about the machinery for reducing the unsustainable debts of middle-income developing countries when a substantial portion of those debts is in the form of bonds.

The techniques used to forgive the debts of the HIPCs are inherently ill suited for debt workouts involving the advanced, middle-income developing countries that depend more on financing from private sources (the global capital market) than from official sources. HIPC-style debt forgiveness for the advanced developing countries would not only require much larger amounts of new aid, but would also tend to shift the costs of workouts from commercial creditors to the public sector.

Developing countries that are neither poor nor advanced, however, face a troublesome dilemma. The debt forgiveness available under the HIPC Initiative is tempting, but the route to qualification lies in the direction of economic stagnation or worse. The alternative of capital market financing entails significant risks, and access to these markets generally requires reforms that are fiercely opposed by vested interests. As a consequence countries beginning the process of weaning themselves from development assistance face a perverse incentive structure. Creating incentives to encourage these countries to choose the capital markets route instead of the HIPC route could be a fruitful exercise for the G-7 architects.

Basket Cases and More Basket Cases

The debt problems of the poorest developing countries first became a global issue in the mid-1960s, after the wave of decolonization that took place at the beginning of the 1960s. The recommendations of the Commission on International Development, known as the Pearson Commission (1969), and the campaign by the G-77 in the 1970s to win generalized debt relief for the "least-developed" developing countries were examined in chapter 7. The G-7 architects responded by committing to retroactive terms adjustment at a meeting of the UNCTAD Trade and Development Board in 1978: converting old aid loans to grants for low-income countries that were getting new aid only in the form of grants.

Relatively few arguments occurred at the time about which countries fell into the category of the least-developed countries, and a number of donor countries went beyond the UNCTAD commitment to lighten the burden of outstanding export credit debt and to extend retroactive terms adjustment to countries with per capita incomes above the agreed cutoff point.[3] Nevertheless, the growth prospects of these countries remained bleak, and their debt problems became progressively more severe during the 1980s. More of the poorest countries started accumulating arrears. Worst of all, arrears to the IMF and the multilateral development banks began to pile up.

At least two reasons lay behind this trend. The more fundamental one, without question, was poor governance in the countries concerned. Many factors contributed to this phenomenon, including ethnic rivalries unleashed when countries became independent, the cold war struggle for

3. Bowe and Dean (1997, p. 14) note that between 1975 and 1987, bilateral donors unilaterally converted $1.9 billion of ODA loans to grants, representing about 6 percent of outstanding ODA debt.

influence between the Western Alliance and the Soviet Bloc, and the absence of institutional frameworks that helped other countries maintain political stability and sustain economic growth over long periods of time. At the same time, a number of countries with low per capita incomes in 1960 were able to make impressive progress over the next forty years despite similar handicaps, especially countries in Asia from India to South Korea.

The second reason was the volume and quality of the aid provided to these countries by foreign donors—from both the East and the West. Some advocates of greater efforts to reduce global poverty have argued that too little financial support was provided to these countries. They have suggested that financing on the scale of Marshall Plan aid for Europe's post–World War II reconstruction is required.[4] In contrast, others have argued that too much aid is being given to the poor countries, or the wrong kind of aid, and that further aid should be withheld until critical internal reforms are undertaken.

Arguments that the wrong kind of aid had been delivered to the poorest countries became hard to refute by the mid-1980s. After years of rescheduling operations for the benefit of these countries, the Paris Club had backed itself into a corner. As noted in chapter 5, the Paris Club would start rescheduling principal payments and then reschedule interest payments if more cash flow relief was required. When principal and interest relief were not sufficient, the Paris Club would also reschedule payments on previously rescheduled debt and perhaps short-term debt. As a last resort the Paris Club would move forward the original contract cutoff date and sweep "new loans" into the rescheduling operation. Each time the Paris Club cut more deeply into the payment stream to provide cash flow relief, the country's debt stock would increase (because of the capitalization of interest payments) without a commensurate increase in the country's capacity to service debt. This pattern of serial rescheduling had a snowball effect on the external debt of these countries.

After exhausting the relief available through rescheduling, the Paris Club creditors had to choose between forgiving debt or making cash grants that the countries could use to retire debt. They chose to do the latter.[5] Even after the Paris Club began to include a debt-reduction option in its opera-

4. This is not to suggest that aid flows to the poorest countries were ungenerous. The World Bank has calculated that net resource flows (gross flows less principal repayments) averaged 8 percent of the gross national product of the HIPC countries during the 1990–94 period (Boote and Thugge 1997).

5. The Paris Club chairman at this time cited "aid fatigue" as a major factor in the Paris Club's decision to take the route of debt reduction (Trichet 1989, p. 117).

tions with the poorest countries, however, the debt burdens of these countries remained unsustainable due in part to the responses of the multilateral agencies and the treatment of private creditors.

As the Paris Club was rescheduling more and more of each year's payments, the multilateral lending institutions were continuing to make loans, albeit on increasingly favorable terms. Because they never rescheduled, the share of multilateral debt in the total stock of poor country debt grew larger. Debt to commercial banks shrank, but in a way that made matters worse. Most of these countries were not viewed as creditworthy by commercial banks, so few of them owed significant amounts of debt to banks. The Paris Club principle of comparable treatment forced the few countries that did have some bank debt to pursue heavy-handed if not entirely involuntary methods of restructuring it. The World Bank provided a framework for this process. Its IDA Debt Reduction Facility was created in 1989 to finance buybacks of bank debt at very deep discounts, with the World Bank deciding on the appropriate discount.[6] This may have exacerbated the debt-servicing problems of some countries by discouraging new flows of private finance, including to private sector companies.[7]

Frustrations within the Paris Club over the pattern of serial rescheduling for low-income countries reached the point by 1987 that specific proposals to fix the problem were advanced informally. One of these came from Canada and involved deferring repayment of rescheduled debt over twenty years or more, considerably longer than normal. U.S. Treasury secretary Baker unveiled a proposal along these lines at the African Development Bank annual meeting in the spring of 1988. To preserve France's leadership image on what was seen as a largely African issue, President François Mitterand shortly thereafter proposed special debt-relief terms for low-income countries, including outright debt reduction.[8] These competitive pressures, in the context of tentative steps toward debt reduction for the major Latin American debtors, contributed to a consensus at the G-7 Summit in Toronto in mid-1988 to accelerate implementation of exceptional Paris Club treatment for low-income countries.

6. More information can be found in "Debt Reduction Facility" (www.worldbank.org/rmc/recdrf.htm [August 1, 2002]).

7. The case of Ghana is particularly troublesome in this regard. The Ghanaian authorities made a valiant effort to differentiate their country by opting out of the HIPC Initiative but were ultimately forced by their major donors to join the parade of HIPC supplicants.

8. Based on a June 13, 2002, conversation with Michael Monderer, the U.S. Treasury Department's Paris Club representative in 1988.

A menu approach had been adopted in the course of restructuring commercial bank debt in the late 1980s because banks operated in the context of different tax and regulatory regimes. Similarly, to accommodate the different statutory and budgetary regimes in their countries, the Paris Club adopted a menu approach for reducing the debt of the poorest countries. Paris Club creditors could choose any one of three roughly equivalent options:

—Forgiving one-third of the payments due in the consolidation period, with the remaining payments rescheduled over fourteen years.

—Rescheduling all payments over twenty-five years, with interest charged on the basis of market rates of interest.

—Rescheduling all payments over fourteen years, with interest charged at concessional rates of interest.

These so-called "Toronto terms" were extended for the first time in October 1988 to Madagascar and Mali. By the time of the G-7 Summit in London in 1991, however, it was clear that Toronto terms were not sufficient, and the Paris Club was directed to find a more generous formula. "London terms" formalized the net present value calculation as the measure of forgiveness and raised the level of NPV reduction for eligible countries to 50 percent.[9] In addition, the Paris Club indicated that it was prepared to reduce the outstanding *stock* of debt eligible for forgiveness after successful implementation of a three-year, IMF-supported adjustment program. The expectation was that a stock reduction of this kind would permit countries to exit from repeated Paris Club negotiations. Three years later, in 1994, the NPV level of forgiveness on consolidated payments was boosted to 67 percent under "Naples terms."

The 90 Percent Solution

Even with these big steps to reduce poor country debt, the remaining debt for quite a few countries appeared to be unsustainable, because of the level of debt owed to the IMF, the World Bank, and the regional banks. The G-7 architects were faced with a serious dilemma. They either would have to change the policy of never writing off multilateral debt or would have to invent some scheme for alleviating the burden of multilateral debt on the poorest countries without write-offs. They opted for the latter. Presumably, one reason for the choice was to avoid the precedent that forgiveness of

9. These NPV percentages were applied to non-ODA debt. The NPV reduction percentages for ODA debt were somewhat different.

multinational debt would create for the debt-restructuring arrangements being negotiated at that time by middle-income countries. The G-7 Summit in Lyon, France, in mid-1996, produced a political consensus to tackle the debt of the poorest countries owed to multilateral agencies. The HIPC Initiative was adopted in September. At the end of the year, as one element of the initiative, the Paris Club agreed to make available NPV debt forgiveness up to 80 percent for HIPCs ("Lyon terms"). At the Cologne Summit in 1999, the G-7 agreed to "enhance" the HIPC program, and the following November the Paris Club adopted "Cologne terms" allowing for NPV reduction up to 90 percent.

This is not the place to explain the intricacies of the HIPC Initiative or assess its results. A major complication is that it keeps changing. Significant improvements in the program have been adopted in virtually every year since 1996. The basic features at the end of 2002 were the following:

—To be eligible for HIPC forgiveness, a country must have a per capita income that qualifies it for borrowing only from IDA, the World Bank's soft-loan window.

—To qualify for HIPC forgiveness, an eligible country must have a stock of external debt that is unsustainable based on a sustainability analysis performed jointly by the IMF and World Bank, assuming debt forgiveness on Naples terms from Paris Club creditors.

—To obtain HIPC forgiveness, a qualifying country must adopt a three-year adjustment program developed through an elaborate and participatory process. This process involves the preparation of a Poverty Reduction Strategy Paper (PRSP) that reflects a high degree of country "ownership." The PRSP sets out development goals, the policies and resources required to reach these goals, and the responsibilities of the parties involved. It is prepared in consultation with the IMF, the World Bank, the relevant regional development bank, interested donor agencies, concerned NGOs, and domestic parties ("civil society").

—Upon approval of a country's PRSP by the executive boards of the IMF and World Bank ("the decision point"), a number of actions become possible:

—Funding on highly concessional terms from the IMF's Poverty Reduction and Growth Facility (the new name given to the Enhanced Structural Adjustment Facility when it was retooled in September 1999) and from the World Bank in the form of quick-disbursing Poverty Reduction Support Credits from IDA.[10]

10. Some IDA financing in the form of grants was to become available beginning in 2003.

—The most generous debt reduction terms available from the Paris Club ("Cologne terms" allowing for 90 percent NPV reduction), as long as these are required to reduce the country's debt to a sustainable level, on payments falling due before the "completion point."

—After at least one year of successful performance as measured by the country's PRSP ("the completion point"), additional actions are taken to reduce the country's debt to a sustainable level, deemed to be a ratio of debt (measured on an NPV basis) to exports no greater than 150 percent.[11]

—Debt owed to multilateral agencies is repaid by drawing on a variety of sources, including net income of the World Bank, and income earned by the IMF from investing the proceeds from sales of a portion of its gold holdings. Roughly half of the resources will be grants from donor countries to the HIPC Trust Fund administered by the World Bank. The donor countries and the non-HIPC borrowers from the multilateral agencies are in effect buying back multilateral debt at face value with grants.

—The outstanding stock of debt owed to Paris Club creditors is reduced by up to 90 percent as required to bring the country's debt down to the sustainability threshold.

—HIPCs are required to seek comparable reduction of debt they owe to commercial banks and other private creditors. This feature has led to some complications, including litigation. Among other implementation issues that have arisen is the treatment of debt owed by one HIPC to another HIPC.

The Legacy of the HIPC Initiative

The HIPC Initiative is a work in progress.[12] Like the Brady Plan for the most advanced developing countries, it can be seen as an effort to help countries exit from repeated debt-restructuring arrangements. As of mid- 2003, it was hard to be optimistic that this initiative would be successful, but that may simply be because the end was not clearly in sight. In further refinements of the program, the write-offs may come more quickly and be more definitive.[13]

11. A loophole sets the ratio at 250 percent of government revenues for "very open economies" such as Côte d'Ivoire.

12. The latest six-monthly statistical update on the HIPC initiative, issued in April 2003, can be found at www.worldbank.org/hipc/StatUpdate_April03.pdf.

13. As an example of the endless discussions of the minutiae of the HIPC Initiative, the Paris Club creditors had divergent views in mid-2002 about the form of HIPC debt reduction. Countries

Success in addressing the debt problems of the HIPCs could come in either of two forms. One would be improved economic management that produces greater macroeconomic stability (especially price stability) and faster GDP growth. As their capacity to service debt increases, the HIPCs will be able to resume borrowing from official sources.

The second form of success would be access to the global capital market. But here a paradox would have to be resolved. The HIPC Initiative requires that eligible countries forgo borrowing from commercial sources. Even though the donor countries say that building a credit culture is one of the objectives of the program, it looks as though the HIPCs will have to pass through an extended period without commercial financing before they will be permitted to take advantage of this source of capital. It is unfortunate that the HIPC Initiative does not include a component that helps build the capacity to manage commercial borrowing responsibly.

Meanwhile, the HIPC Initiative will remain a source of confusion for the citizens of non-HIPCs that are experiencing debt problems and for people in the rest of the world who are working to alleviate poverty in the world's poorest countries. In countries like Indonesia and Nigeria (and even Argentina), politicians and civic leaders are putting pressure on their governments to get external debt written off as has been done for HIPCs such as Bolivia and Uganda.[14] The quick route to achieving this objective is to pursue policies that will produce economic stagnation, hardly a healthy approach. The better objective, of course, is to adopt policies that will increase the country's capacity to service external debt. The G-7 strategy seems to involve perverse incentives. Countries that make greater efforts to establish the conditions for sustainable growth should be rewarded with more aid, not less. As noted earlier, however, this is a development challenge, not a debt challenge, and therefore falls outside the scope of this study.

---

committed to ODA debt reduction beyond the HIPC requirement and with substantial amounts of non-ODA debt preferred to meet their HIPC requirement with ODA debt to minimize the amount of additional debt reduction provided. Debtor countries, and other Paris Club creditors, preferred to have the HIPC requirement met first with non-ODA debt to maximize the additional amount of debt reduction they would receive.

14. In April 2002 the Center for Global Development released a nine-point program for improving the HIPC Initiative that included expanding eligibility to all low-income countries, specifically citing Indonesia, Nigeria, and Pakistan. See Birdsall and Deese (2002).

10

The Post-1994 Crises and the Role of Bonds

The Brady Plan resolved the debt crisis of the 1980s. Putting the plan in place earlier might have moved the global economy to a higher growth path sooner, but the political conditions were not favorable until early 1989. The success of the Brady Plan had much to do with its cooperative nature. Debtor country governments, creditor country governments, commercial banks, and the multilateral agencies were full partners in every workout. The G-7 architects were unable to prevent some flooding in the basement, but they managed to keep the roof on during a hurricane.

In the 1990s the international financial scene was dominated by three big stories. First was the muscular, but ultimately unsustainable, performance of the U.S. economy. Second was the birth of Euroland. Third was the stomach-churning roller-coaster ride that carried the emerging market countries to new highs and new lows. An unprecedented surge of private capital flowed into emerging market equities and bonds in 1992–93, creating the emerging markets asset class. Two years later a financial crisis in Mexico sent a shock wave through the system. Subsequent crises in Asia in 1997 and Russia in 1998 severely dampened investor interest in emerging market assets. Heavy-handed efforts by the G-7 and the IMF to restructure the bond debt of some small emerging market borrowers in 1999 cut private flows further. Argentina's default at the end of 2001 hammered what little interest remained. This string of crises is examined here against the backdrop of a changing pattern of capital flows.

The Mexican peso crisis at the end of 1994 triggered the latest debate about sovereign debt workouts. In contrast to the tone of the debate in the 1980s about commercial bank debt restructuring, the tone of the current debate about bank restructuring has been confrontational. Antagonism on this scale was last seen in the arena of international finance in the 1970s when the countries of the South demanded support from the countries of the North for major systemic reforms. This time the confrontation was between the private sector and the official sector, with the official sector pushing for radical change.

The narrow issue at the core of the current policy debate is the treatment of sovereign debt in the form of bonds. One objective of the G-7 architects has been to involve bondholders in rescue operations at an early stage to help countries in crisis avoid default. A second objective has been to develop suitable machinery for restructuring sovereign bonds when a default cannot be avoided. Sovereigns, however, owe debt to private creditors in other forms, notably bank loans. Moreover, direct and portfolio investment are important sources of private capital for some countries, and private sector borrowers can be seriously affected by a sovereign default. Thus the broader issue, explored in depth in chapter 11, is private sector involvement (PSI), or burden sharing between the public sector and the private sector.

One of the mysteries of the current policy debate is the hypersensitivity of the G-7 architects to charges of "bailing out" private investors. Mexico's crisis in 1994 was resolved without a default or any debt restructuring by means of a large package of official financing from the IMF, the United States, and other sources. Clearly, holders of short-term peso-denominated but dollar-linked bonds were able to sell out without taking a loss. However, private investors and lenders more generally absorbed multibillion-dollar losses from falling secondary market prices on long-term debt, and from debt workouts with Mexican companies that became insolvent after the peso was floated. Not a single penny of official financing was lost in this operation. Nevertheless, the U.S. government and the IMF were tarred with the brush of "bailing out" private investors. They have been struggling ever since to design a workout process that would protect them from this false accusation.

Recent Trends in Emerging Markets Finance

Capital flows to developing countries from the 1950s to the early 1990s were discussed under the rubric of "development finance." The phrase emphasized their purpose: to help low-income countries raise their standards of living. The flows came primarily from official agencies with a mandate to promote economic development in the third world.

A new phrase became popular in the 1990s: "emerging markets finance." To this day, no universally accepted definition exists to determine which countries are emerging and which are not, but the origin of the term suggests a direct link to private capital flows. The International Finance Corporation—the World Bank affiliate for financing private sector growth—worked actively in the 1970s and 1980s to encourage developing countries to establish domestic capital markets and to encourage global investors to take an interest in these markets. One device used by the IFC was the formation of country or regional stock funds (unit trusts). By the end of the 1980s enough developing countries had equity markets open to foreign investors to make it possible for the IFC to create an index of their performance. The IFC coined the phrase "emerging markets" to distinguish the countries in this index from other developing countries. The phrase caught on to become a synonym for developing countries in many contexts. At the heart of the phrase is the notion that the emerging market countries are the subset of developing countries able to attract private capital flows.

Paralleling the shift in terminology, a remarkable shift in capital flows to developing countries occurred during the 1990s. Flows from private sources surged while official flows stagnated. Foreign direct investment became the largest form of financing. Bonds replaced bank loans as the main form of private debt flows.

The Institute of International Finance tracks capital flows to 29 emerging market countries, which together account for more than 90 percent of the private capital flows to all 130–40 developing countries.[1] The other developing countries, largely ignored in this study, fall into two groups: 40-odd poor countries (HIPCs), and 60–70 small but more prosperous countries.

Net *official* flows to the twenty-nine emerging market countries declined steadily after 1990, except for an uptick in 1997 and 1998 reflecting the lender-of-last-resort function of the IMF and to a lesser extent the multi-

1. The main analytical breakdown currently used by the IMF is advanced countries (mostly members of the OECD), developing countries, and countries in transition. In several reports, the IMF discusses "emerging market countries" as a group, but the definition of this group is elusive and appears to vary over time.

Table 10-1. Capital Flows to Twenty-Nine Emerging Market Countries, 1990–2002

Billions of U.S. dollars

Capital flows	1990	1992	1994	1996	1998	2000	2002e
External financing, net	75	160	201	338	191	187	112
Private flows, net	35	121	175	334	139	194	110
Direct investment	14	31	65	92	121	138	111
Portfolio investment	3	16	34	35	12	14	-3
Commercial banks	9	29	43	123	-55	0	-10
Nonbanks, net (including bonds)	8	45	33	84	61	42	12
Official flows, net	40	39	26	4	52	-7	2
International financial institutions	10	9	5	7	38	3	13
Bilateral creditors	30	29	22	-3	14	-10	-11

Source: Institute of International Finance. These figures are for twenty-nine countries that together account for well over 90 percent of net private flows to developing countries.

e = estimate.

lateral development banks (table 10-1). Net bilateral flows to these countries plummeted from $25 billion a year in the first half of the decade to $12 billion in the second half.

In contrast, net *private* flows increased almost tenfold, from $35 billion in 1990 to $334 billion in 1996, fell back to $186 billion by 2000, and dropped sharply to $112 billion in 2002. Disaggregating the private flows, net *direct investment* during the decade was large and steady, with China alone receiving 30–40 percent of it. These direct investment flows were arguably the best form because they generally financed productive activities and did not saddle countries with additional debt-service obligations. They were clearly responding to improvements in macroeconomic management and structural policies in previous years.

Portfolio equity flows—the purchase of emerging market equity shares by foreigners and the issuance of equity shares by emerging market companies in foreign markets—began the decade at a negligible level and rose modestly over the course of the 1990s. They were not a major component of emerging markets finance but have the potential of becoming one.

Reflecting the large-scale write-offs that took place after 1988, net *commercial bank* flows were modest at the beginning of the decade. They soared in 1995 and 1996 in the aftermath of the Mexican crisis. They have been negative (reflecting net repayment) since 1998, largely driven by reductions in exposure to Argentina and Turkey.

The appearance of *bonds* as a major component of emerging markets finance was the key change that fueled the current policy debate about workout machinery. Bond flows were negligible before the Brady Plan. As countries issued bond debt in exchange for restructured bank loans, the bond numbers rose quickly. They remained strong, despite several periods when markets were effectively closed to new emerging market issues, until the onset of the Argentina crisis in 2001.[2]

The various forms of debt financing from official and private creditors have different characteristics, a situation that produces a profile of the outstanding debt stock different from the profile of flows. For forty-two emerging market countries followed by the IIF, the aggregate stock of debt at the end of 1995 was just under $2 trillion. Unfortunately, more recent data for this group of countries are not available. The World Bank's annual reports on Global Development Finance, however, provide detailed data for the much larger universe of developing countries. At the end of 2000, the total outstanding external debt of these 136 countries amounted to almost $2.4 trillion. Table 10-2 shows a breakdown of this amount among the various forms of debt.

Historical Experience with Sovereign Bond Defaults

The emerging market bond defaults and forced exchanges that began in 1999 shocked bond investors for five reasons:

—For roughly fifty years, from the 1940s to the 1990s, developing countries issued few bonds, and no significant defaults occurred.

—With a few exceptions, bond debt escaped restructuring during the workouts in the 1980s. This exclusion was justified at the time by the small scale of the bond debt outstanding and by concerns that restructuring this debt would inhibit new borrowing on international capital markets.

2. Emerging market bonds can be divided into two categories: bonds issued by *governments* in their domestic capital market (that foreigners are allowed to purchase), and bonds issued by governments in foreign capital markets (overwhelmingly in the United States or the United Kingdom). In many cases foreigners are not permitted to purchase government bonds issued domestically. But the trend is in the direction of greater openness, and future workouts (including the pending case of Argentina) are likely to entail exceptional challenges to share the burden of losses equitably between domestic bondholders and foreign bondholders. Bonds are also issued by emerging market *companies* in their domestic markets and in foreign capital markets. The foreign bonds of these companies can be forced into default in the context of a financial crisis. As discussed in chapter 2, the risk of this happening is a standard commercial risk, and such defaults are normally worked out in the framework of the debtor country's bankruptcy regime.

Table 10-2. External Debt of Developing Countries, 2002
Billions of U.S. dollars

Type of debt	Amount
Long-term debt	1,976
Owed and guaranteed by public sector entities	1,419
To official creditors	800
(Multilateral agencies)	(345)
(Bilateral agencies)	(455)
To private creditors	619
(Bondholders)[a]	(392)
(Commercial banks)	(158)
(Others)	(69)
Owed by private sector entities, nonguaranteed	557
To bondholders	124
To commercial banks	433
Short-term debt, owed by both private and public sector entities	347
Use of IMF credit	64
Total external debt	2,387

Source: World Bank (2002).

Note: These numbers cover 136 countries that report public and publicly guaranteed debt under the World Bank's Debtor Reporting System.

a. According to the IMF's International Capital Markets report published in November 1997 (pp. 74–75), the stock of Brady bonds peaked at $156 billion following the Peru deal in March 1997. Later deals with Côte d'Ivoire and Vietnam were more than offset by buyback and exchanges for uncollateralized bonds. For example, the International Capital Markets report published in September 1996 (p. 96) mentions that Mexico announced an exchange in April 1996 that extinguished $2.3 billion of par bonds and discount bonds (by face value) in an exchange for thirty-year uncollateralized global bonds.

—The heart of the emerging market bond market consisted of Brady bonds. One of the selling points for Brady bonds was the notion that they would be treated as senior debt or "previously rescheduled" debt and therefore would be exempted, or given preferential status, in any future restructuring. The defeasance and other enhancements provided by official agencies for these bonds helped to reinforce this notion.

—In the Mexican peso crisis at the end of 1994, a large package of official financing was provided to help Mexico avoid defaulting on its substantial *tesobono* debt (short-term, dollar-linked, peso-denominated government notes). This package was seen as a precedent for other countries facing similar crises.

—Marketing pitches for new bonds sometimes implied that the sovereign issuers would accord these instruments seniority in the event of future debt-servicing difficulties.

For all of these reasons, many investors in emerging market bonds in the mid-1990s were inclined to discount the risks associated with these instruments. More prudent investors recognized that the U.S. and other creditor-country governments would be unwilling to assume the risks associated with an open-ended commitment to provide emergency financing to countries experiencing a debt crisis. Therefore, a country with an unsustainable debt burden would not be able to exempt bonds from a workout. These investors were also mindful of the checkered history of sovereign bonds. The bond defaults in the nineteenth and twentieth centuries have been well documented, and this experience is briefly summarized here.[3]

Sovereign bond defaults came in four waves between 1820 and 1930. Three occurred before World War I, when British merchant banks and a variety of London-based issuing houses dominated international lending. The first began with a burst of issues after 1817 for sovereign borrowers such as Austria, France, Prussia, and Spain.[4] Argentina, Brazil, Chile, Guatemala, Mexico, and Peru launched issues in the early 1820s. Unable to raise new money to service these bonds when they began to mature, most of these countries defaulted in 1826–27.[5]

The second wave of defaults followed a deluge of 150 international issues between 1860 and 1876 (including funds raised for the Confederate States of America). In addition to the same Latin American countries involved in the first wave, the major borrowers included Egypt, Russia, and Turkey. After the overthrow of Mexican emperor Maximilian in 1867, the new regime repudiated the previous regime's debts. Venezuela stopped paying interest on its bonds in the same year, but other Latin American countries continued to

3. This account draws on a presentation by Anthony B. Greayer at a conference sponsored by *Euromoney* and AMR International in October 1977 in London on "Financing the LDCs: The Role of the Euromarket." The presentation is summarized in the November 1977 issue of *Euromoney* (pp. 76–83). Another overview of the early history can be found in Dammers (1984). Dammers draws on a 1933 work by Winkler and the two-volume opus produced by Borchard and Wynne (1951). More anecdotes can be found in chapter 2 of Makin (1984). A more recent legal perspective on past defaults is in Macmillan (1995). Standard and Poors maintains a survey of sovereign defaults on foreign currency bonds and bank loans that goes back to 1824. The latest update was issued on September 24, 2002 ("Sovereign Defaults: Moving Higher Again in 2003?"), available upon request to Standard and Poors.

4. The first international bond was for 100 million French francs, raised by Barings in 1817.

5. In 1839 the states of Louisiana and Mississippi defaulted, followed in 1842 by the states of Maryland and Pennsylvania (Dammers 1984, p. 78).

raise funds in London. Defaults became more widespread in the 1870s, and by 1876 half of Latin America's bond debt was in default. Egypt, Spain, and Turkey also defaulted in this period.

The third wave followed with a spurt of issues after the turn of the century. Argentina and Brazil together were able to raise £1 billion. Other major borrowers included Australia, Canada, India, Japan, Russia, and the United States. Defaults became widespread after the outbreak of World War I in 1914.

Some of these defaults prompted collection efforts using military force. Navies blockaded ports until unpaid debts were settled. Customs houses were taken over, even though the creditors were not governments but private parties. Following Egypt's default in 1875–76, Great Britain took control of the country. A few years later an international debt administration was established in Turkey to collect the revenue required to service Turkey's bond debt. In 1902 Germany, Italy, and the United Kingdom blockaded Venezuela to force a settlement of its defaulted debt. The blockade prompted the enunciation of the Drago Principle by the Argentine minister of foreign affairs, which ruled out armed intervention in the Americas by European powers. The Roosevelt Corollary by U.S. president Theodore Roosevelt established that the United States would assume responsibility for making the American republics fulfill their financial obligations. In 1905 the U.S. government collected the customs receipts in the Dominican Republic to cure a default on bonds mostly held by European investors. As late as 1915 the U.S. Marines were sent into Haiti to ensure that the country would honor its foreign debts.[6]

The United States emerged during World War I as a source of bond financing to rival Europe, and a torrent of New York bonds flooded the market after the end of the war. Forty-three countries raised $7 billion during the 1920s. The fourth wave of defaults began shortly thereafter. Fifty percent of the bonds issued in the second half of the 1920s went into default, including issues from seventeen Latin American countries. Barry Eichengreen neatly summed up the workout process during this period in a short paper published in 1988.[7] Findings relevant to this study include the following:

—The defaults in the 1930s had multiple causes including plummeting commodity prices, increased protectionism in the creditor countries, and inappropriate policy responses in the debtor countries.

6. Delamaide (1984, p. 100).
7. Eichengreen (1988). See also Eichengreen and Portes (1989).

—The workout process was far from straightforward. A bondholder council (the Corporation of Foreign Bondholders) had been formed in 1868 to represent holders of bonds issued in London in negotiations with defaulting issuers. A U.S. counterpart, the Foreign Bondholders Protective Council (FBPC), was established in 1933, at the initiative of the Department of State and with the support of the Securities and Exchange Commission.[8] Negotiations were generally protracted, and the losses absorbed by bondholders did not follow any predictable pattern. (The negotiations with Bolivia, which began in 1931, were not concluded until 1955.)

—Broader debt issues, especially the reparations imposed on Germany at the end of World War I, had a major impact on the workouts with developing countries. Germany's inability to keep up with its reparations prompted France and Belgium to occupy the Ruhr in 1923. German obligations were sharply reduced under the Dawes Plan (1924) and were reduced again under the Young Plan (1930). Large debts owed to the United States by the Allies at the end of World War I went through a parallel set of workouts because the capacity of the borrowers to repay depended in part on the amount of reparations they received from Germany. President Hoover announced a one-year moratorium on war debt in 1931, but the moratorium was not extended. France defaulted in 1932, and other defaults followed shortly thereafter. (As Eichengreen put it, "War debts and reparations sputtered out like a candle in the rain.")[9] Meanwhile, the U.S. government declared a moratorium on farm foreclosure as one measure to address domestic debt stress. Under these circumstances, holders of developing country bonds were seriously handicapped in pursuing their claims against issuers.

—At the outset of most workouts, the positions of debtors and creditors were far apart. Pressure from the U.S. and other creditor governments contributed to the process of convergence. (The defaulting countries had no outstanding debt to the U.S. government or other creditor governments, and there was no multilateral agency or other "preferred creditor" debt to complicate the negotiations.)

—A number of global solutions were proposed. One was to have the Bank for International Settlements, founded in 1930 as part of the Young Plan, issue international certificates that could be used to settle any cross-border claim, including principal and interest payments. Another involved creating a new institution to make loans to countries and corporations

---

8. Both of these bondholder organizations produced annual reports, which are rich sources of information.

9. Eichengreen (1988, p. 26).

unable to find liquidity financing elsewhere; it would be capitalized with contributions from governments and funded by issuing bonds. A third was to convert short-term credits into loans repayable over twenty years. A fourth would allow debtors to repay hard-currency loans with local currency. Other proposals were advanced at the World Economic Conference convened in London in 1933 to address the issues of debt, deflation, exchange rate volatility, and trade warfare simultaneously. Policymakers in the United States and the other creditor countries opted instead to "muddle through."

—Despite the complications, a reasonable degree of burden sharing between creditors and debtors was achieved.

World War II delayed the workouts of the bond defaults in the 1930s, and the victory of the Allies in 1945 gave a renewed impetus to settlement efforts. The attitude of the U.S. government toward war debt in the meantime changed 180 degrees. Reparations were not imposed on Germany and Japan, and World War II debts owed to the United States by its Allies (including Russia) were written down on quite favorable terms.

The Crises after 1994

The present debate about the machinery for sovereign debt workouts was fueled by a series of financial crises that began in Mexico at the end of 1994.[10] This was a drama in four acts.

The first act featured a large package of emergency financing from the IMF and other official sources that was mobilized to help Mexico avoid default. The second act revolved around three crises in Asia in 1997, starting with Thailand and followed by Indonesia and South Korea. The third act began with the partial debt moratorium declared by Russia in August 1998. Unilateral bond exchanges by Pakistan, Ukraine, and Ecuador followed in 1999. The fourth act involved the default of the emerging market borrower with by far the largest outstanding amount of bond debt: Argentina.

The impact of each crisis on the economy of the stricken country was severe. The losses absorbed by private investors and lenders dwarfed the losses absorbed by commercial banks in the 1980s debt crisis. In response, the G-7 finance ministers launched a major initiative to improve the "architecture" of the financial system, both to prevent future crises and to facilitate debt workouts when restructuring could not be avoided. The IMF surprised

10. The primary sources for the descriptions of these cases were the IMF annual reports and *World Economic Outlook* reports from 1994 to 2002.

many observers by putting forward a proposal for creating permanent machinery to restructure unsustainable sovereign debt, including bonds.

The Mexican Peso Crisis in 1994

The Mexican presidential election campaign during the first half of 1994 set the stage for the financial crisis that erupted at the end of the year. The campaign was rocked by two tragedies: the Zapatista rebellion in the state of Chiapas in January, and the assassination of the anointed successor to President Carlos Salinas in March. The substitute PRI candidate, Ernesto Zedillo, won by a slim majority of the vote in August accompanied by credible allegations of voting fraud. A burst of government spending during the campaign left the economy in a precarious position after the election, with stabilization measures delayed by the long transition period preceding the inauguration in December.

Mexico's current account deficit in 1994 was running on the order of 8 percent of GDP, more than twice the level considered to be sustainable. A portion of this deficit was financed by issuing *tesobono*.[11] About $30 billion of *tesobono* were due to mature in 1995. Mexico's foreign exchange reserves in late 1994 were only around $6 billion. When a run on the peso began in November, these reserves quickly evaporated as the Mexican government attempted to defend the peso's link to the dollar.[12] The government was forced to float the peso and implement a strong stabilization program. The U.S. government responded, as it had in 1982, by arranging a large package of emergency financing from the IMF and other official sources. This time, however, rescheduling debt owed to banks was not part of the package. There was not enough of this form of debt to make a difference.

IMF managing director Michel Camdessus famously described the Mexican crisis as the first of the twenty-first century.[13] The point is that the crises in the 1970s and 1980s sprang from current account imbalances. When current account deficits became so large that they could not be financed by external borrowing, countries ran out of foreign exchange to service their outstanding debt and had to restructure it. By contrast, the Mexican crisis sprang from capital account imbalances.[14] From a forensic perspective, how-

11. *Tesobono* are often described as bonds, but they were fundamentally different from the long-term bonds floated in international capital markets that are the main issue in this study. *Tesobono* were more like the Convertible Turkish Lira Deposits restructured in Turkey's 1978 crisis.

12. Institute of International Finance (1996, p. 12).

13. The remark was made in a speech on May 22, 1995, on "Drawing Lessons from the Mexican Crisis: Preventing and Resolving Crises—The Role of the IMF."

14. In standard balance-of-payments accounting, the current account includes trade in goods and services that either earns foreign exchange (such as exports) or uses foreign exchange (such as

ever, the crisis in the European Monetary System (EMS) in September 1992 preceded the Mexican crisis.

In the EMS crisis, domestic and foreign investors lost confidence in the ability of the United Kingdom to change policies enough to preserve the value of the pound. They started moving assets out of the United Kingdom, putting severe pressure on the pound. At the height of the EMS crisis, the U.K. authorities had to choose between tightening their monetary and fiscal policies, which would push the economy further into recession, or breaking the fixed link between the pound and the other major EU currencies. They chose the latter. Box 10-1 contains a thumbnail description of the EMS crisis.[15]

In the case of Mexico, residents as well as foreign lenders and investors sensed that a new government would have to implement exceptionally strong measures to maintain the recent pace of capital inflows. They doubted the capacity of the Zedillo government to take such measures because it had weak popular support; those doubts prompted them to move out of pesos and into dollars. Without enough reserves to accommodate this movement, the Mexican government was forced once again to appeal for help from Washington.

Once again the U.S. government had to make a fateful policy choice. It could withhold support, making it impossible for Mexico to avoid default and difficult to attract capital market financing for several years, if not a decade. A default would also shake confidence in other large emerging market borrowers and possibly induce financial crises elsewhere (contagion). Alternatively, the United States could construct a financial rescue package of such large proportions that investors would be foolish to bet against Mexico. There was a chance, however, that this strategy would not be successful and the United States would be stuck with the bill. A middle option was to back a smaller financial package in combination with some restructuring of *tesobono* debt. This alternative was perhaps the riskiest approach, however. U.S. Treasury secretary Robert Rubin chose the big rescue package.[16]

---

imports). The capital account includes inflows and outflows of financial assets, such as direct investment by foreign companies and repayments on loans from foreign creditors. The current account and the capital account must sum to zero, after accounting for changes in the country's foreign exchange reserves. A surplus of foreign exchange earnings and capital inflows increases reserves; a deficit decreases reserves.

15. The summary is drawn primarily from Eichengreen (2000a), which is a succinct, nontechnical analysis. Other sources were the *World Economic Outlook* and *International Capital Markets* reports produced by the IMF during the year following the crisis.

16. Kenen (2001, p. 2) notes that the U.S. Congress rebuffed inquiries from the U.S. Treasury about the possibility of exceptional bilateral loans to Mexico. These loans could have kept IMF financing within normal limits and would have put more of the risk on the United States, which was the main non-Mexican beneficiary of the rescue effort.

Box 10-1. The European Monetary Crisis in 1992

The September 1992 crisis was arguably the biggest setback Europe suffered since launching the process of economic integration in the 1950s. The customs union created by the original six members of the European Economic Community (EEC) was a brilliant success. It was enlarged in the 1970s and 1980s and transformed into the European Community. Monetary integration began in 1972, with the creation of a "snake" linking member currencies, and advanced substantially in 1979, when the European Monetary System (EMS) was put in place. Within the EMS, the exchange rate mechanism (ERM) created firm pegs for a core group of member currencies to the European currency unit (ECU), a basket of these currencies. The United Kingdom entered the ERM in October 1990.

The twelve members of the European Community reached agreement in 1986 on forming a single market, and this culminated in the remarkable Maastricht Treaty signed in December 1991 to form the European Union (EU). Maastricht set in motion both an enlargement process (quickly adding three Scandinavian members and then beginning lengthy accession negotiations with the transition countries of Central and Eastern Europe) and more rapid structural integration.

With a goal of introducing a single currency in the near term, Maastricht committed the EU members to an ambitious timetable for harmonizing their monetary and fiscal policies. As usual the crisis in 1992 combined economic and political factors. The main economic factors were divergent budget bal-

---

The package was stunning in size, totaling $50 billion. The IMF committed $18 billion, other multilateral agencies committed $10 billion, and bilateral agencies committed $22 billion. The U.S. government provided bridge financing from the Exchange Stabilization Fund (ESF). The criticism that followed the announcement of the package was also stunning. Charges of favoritism came immediately from the Europeans and the Japanese, who suspected that the United States would not be as generous in addressing crises in their backyards. The conservative press accused the Clinton administration of "bailing out" private investors in *tesobono*. The U.S. Congress called hearings and placed new restrictions on the use of the ESF.[17] The

---

17. The ESF was created when the United States joined the IMF. It has been used to finance intervention to stabilize the dollar and to make short-term bridge loans to other countries facing temporary balance-of-payments problems.

ances and inflation rates among the members. These had to converge between 1991 and 2001 to make full monetary integration possible. The main political factor was the differing abilities of the member countries to adjust their policies or the market's perception of these abilities. The anticipated strains were exacerbated by German reunification, which saddled this anchor economy with a large budget deficit.

The first sign of trouble was Finland's decision to adjust its peg to the ECU in late 1991, after the collapse of its exports to the disintegrating Soviet Union. The precipitating event was the vote in Denmark on June 2, 1992, against ratification of the Maastricht Treaty. With ratification votes coming up in other countries, especially France in September, Denmark's vote called into question the feasibility of Maastricht. Investors had already been engaging in a "convergence play" by borrowing in countries with low interest rates and investing them in EU countries with high interest rates, betting that the convergence process would bring these rates down and produce a nice return with little risk because the ECU peg would be defended. After the Danish vote the betting went in the other direction, with pressure directed especially at the United Kingdom and Italy. An attempt to arrange a coordinated defense of the ERM at the beginning of September failed. A few days later Finland floated the markka. Sweden raised its central bank rate to an astronomical level to defend the krone. Norway intervened massively. Italy did also, but was forced to devalue on September 13. The United Kingdom pulled out of the ERM on September 16. With these exchange rate moves, the strains eased and the process of convergence resumed with an emphasis on fiscal policy.

"bailout" charges were not new; every Treasury secretary for the past twenty years had faced similar charges. But they came with a new intensity.[18]

The results of the Mexican stabilization program were stunning as well. To the astonishment of many observers, the new Zedillo government acted decisively and boldly. The results were clearly visible in a sharp reduction of its current account deficit in the second quarter of 1995. Access to the international capital market was regained later in the year. By 1997 Mexico's economy was booming.

18. The chairman of Manufacturers Hanover Bank, Gabriel Hauge, alluded to this issue twenty years earlier when he wrote in an opinion piece for *Euromoney* in October 1977 (page 59): "It would be unfortunate, indeed, if assistance to member countries from the [IMF] is shipwrecked on the rock of bail-out allegations." Hauge also quoted U.S. Treasury secretary Michael Blumenthal as saying: "Legislatures are not prepared to vote the massive amounts of official funds, or guarantees, required for a basic shift from reliance on private financing to reliance on official financing."

Not a single penny was lost by the official agencies that participated in the rescue operation. All the emergency loans were repaid on schedule or prepaid. The U.S. government actually made money on its ESF financing because it charged a spread over the cost of borrowing by the Treasury.

Some private investors made money, but more lost money. The losers were primarily investors in Mexican companies that had too much unhedged dollar debt and became insolvent. Money center banks around the world announced large provisions for anticipated losses on loans to Mexican companies.

In short, the notion that taxpayer resources were used to protect private investors from losses was a fiction. The rescue effort mounted on Mexico's behalf produced large benefits for Mexico and also for the rest of the world. Without it, the contraction of the Mexican economy would have been much deeper. More Mexican workers would have lost their jobs. Imports from the United States and elsewhere would have shrunk further, contributing to unemployment elsewhere. These are just a few of the negative repercussions associated with alternative approaches. Despite the evidence, the sting of the "bailout" charge left a deep scar that affected the choices made by the G-7 architects in subsequent crises.

On a more positive note, the 1994 crisis appears to have catalyzed a transformation within Mexico that may help to make the Mexican economy as immune to financial crises as are countries such as Finland, Ireland, and Spain that were regarded as developing countries at the end of World War II. To its immense credit, the Mexican leadership took two steps beyond implementing diligently a strong stabilization program.

First, with the support of the cabinet, the Ministry of Finance put in place an investor-relations program as a tool to prevent future crises. Second, a critical mass of officials and political leaders committed themselves to maintaining market confidence through the presidential election and transition in 2000. These efforts were successful despite the first election loss by the party (PRI) that had been in power since 1928.

Countries anxious to avoid financial crises would be well advised to study the Mexican approach. It is not easy, and it is not a panacea. It requires a commitment to transparency that goes beyond what most developing country governments are prepared to embrace. It also requires a degree of political consensus about the goals and instruments of economic policy that few developing countries have achieved.

The Asian Crises in 1997

The Mexican peso crisis seemed to feed, more than dampen, investor optimism about the economic prospects of the emerging market countries. Net private capital flows to the major borrowing countries reached a new peak of $334 billion in 1996. The euphoria ended abruptly the following year when three countries in Asia experienced financial crises: Thailand, Indonesia, and South Korea.[19]

THAILAND. Thailand's crisis began in May 1997 when its currency—pegged to the U.S. dollar for some years—came under increasing pressure. Market concerns at the time related primarily to the country's large current account deficit and signs that its investment boom was unsustainable. Forced to float the baht on July 2, the Thai government immediately turned to the United States, Japan, and their G-7 partners for the kind of financial support that Mexico had received in 1994–95. While Japan was eager to help, the United States and other G-7 countries hesitated, still smarting from the widespread misperception that they had "bailed out" private investors with the package of official financing they arranged for Mexico. They were determined to avoid actions that might be perceived as protecting private creditors from losses. As a consequence, the rescue package for Thailand was modest, necessitating an adjustment program that was close to draconian.[20]

The Thai government had borrowed lightly from private sources before the crisis, and its debts to official creditors were relatively small. With the sharp depreciation of the baht, the current account quickly moved into surplus. The government was able to meet its obligations to all creditors without any debt restructuring, although it did obtain some fast-disbursing loans from the World Bank and the Asian Development Bank. Domestic banks and private companies, by contrast, had borrowed heavily from foreign creditors, and little of this borrowing was hedged. The devaluation made many banks and many leading Thai companies insolvent. The government shored up the banks with bonds, guaranteed bank depositors and creditors, and undertook a sweeping reform program for the banking sector. Private investors and lenders absorbed large losses as numerous nonbank finance

---

19. An IMF postmortem of these crises can be found in Lane (1999).

20. The Thai rescue package was just over $17 billion, with $4 billion committed by the IMF. Actual disbursements from the package totaled $13 billion. The figures for commitments and disbursements for the three Asian crisis countries are taken from Kenen (2001, p. 8).

companies were liquidated and corporate debt was written down in workouts governed by Thailand's domestic bankruptcy law.

In short, the burden of adjustment fell more heavily on the Thai population than it did on the Mexican population following the 1994 crisis, in part because of the limited amount of official financing provided. Private investors and lenders shared fully in the losses. Sovereign default was not an issue because the government had relatively little external debt. The government's stabilization program was well implemented, and the economy recovered rapidly. In 2002 the government announced its intention to prepay the financing provided by the IMF.

INDONESIA. The Indonesian crisis broke out in October when the government announced it would seek IMF support in the face of a rapidly depreciating currency. Indonesia's growth rate going into 1997 was distinctly higher than Thailand's, but the Thai crisis had broken the complacency of investors in the Asian region, and capital began leaving Indonesia as confidence fell in the ability of the Suharto government to implement reforms. The government party emerged from parliamentary elections in May 1997 with a large majority of the seats, but there were numerous voting irregularities. The parliamentary victory assured Suharto's reelection to another five-year term as president in early 1998, but he was having health problems, and speculation that he would anoint a successor was rife. The political uncertainty, combined with growing investor concerns about growth prospects in Asia generally, produced a sell-off of Indonesian assets.[21]

Like the Thai government, the Indonesian government sought a generous package of emergency financing. It was rewarded with a package that included a substantial amount of window dressing, because it was tied to reforms that the government seemed unlikely to implement.[22] The Indonesian rupiah depreciated by 85 percent from mid-1997 to mid-1998, much more than the Thai baht. Output also contracted more sharply, reflecting the weaker policy response.

Like the Thai government, the Indonesian government had borrowed lightly from private sources, but its debt to Paris Club creditors was more than twice as large. The Paris Club agreed to reschedule principal payments falling due in the 1998–2003 period, and interest payments for the last two of these six years. The relatively small amount of debt owed to banks by the

---

21. A contributing factor in all three Asian crises was the weak Japanese economy, which limped through the 1990s with growth averaging less than 1.5 percent a year.

22. The Indonesian rescue package totaled $36 billion, with $10 billion committed by the IMF. The amount actually disbursed was only $14 billion.

government was rescheduled through a Bank Advisory Committee agreement to meet the Paris Club requirement for comparable treatment, but the Paris Club agreed to waive comparable treatment with respect to a $400 million eurobond issue maturing in 2006.

Mirroring the situation in Thailand, private creditors had fallen over themselves to make loans to Indonesian banks and companies in the precrisis boom years. Most of these loans went into default following the slide of the rupiah. The government moved quickly to prevent a total collapse of the banking system by guaranteeing bank deposits and replacing nonperforming loans with government bonds. This operation instantly transformed the Indonesian government from one of the least indebted domestically to one of the most. Bankruptcies in the corporate sector were on a larger scale than those in Thailand, partly because funds borrowed abroad had been used less efficiently and partly because the depreciation of the Indonesian rupiah had been larger. An agency was established to restructure and reprivatize the banking system and to dispose of nonperforming loans. A government scheme was introduced to facilitate company-by-company workouts with foreign creditors. Both of these efforts were frustrated by uncooperative owners, a largely dysfunctional judicial system, meddling by the parliament and other government entities, and powerful interest groups. The pace of workouts was glacial.

The burden of adjustment on Indonesia's population was enormous, but more from the government's inability to implement reforms required to put the economy back on a high-growth path than from a lack of burden sharing on the part of multilateral and bilateral creditor agencies or private creditors. Again, as in Thailand, private investors and lenders—domestic as well as foreign—absorbed billions of dollars of losses. By contrast, not a penny of the emergency financing from the IMF and other official sources was lost through 2002, although some risk of future losses remained.

SOUTH KOREA. South Korea's crisis followed closely on the heels of Indonesia's crisis. The stakes were much larger: South Korea's economy was three times the size of the Thai and Indonesian economies (but only two-thirds the size of Mexico's). Other strategic factors were the acceptance of South Korea in 1996 into the OECD, the "club" of advanced industrial countries, and the unresolved conflict with North Korea. The crisis began in the same manner as those of Thailand and Indonesia. Years of rapid growth had masked a number of underlying weaknesses, including a fragile banking system and a corporate sector dominated by large conglomerates with historical links to the government. Bad economic news accumulated during

1997, and a potentially destabilizing presidential election at the end of the year heightened investor concerns. A tipping point was reached in November when residents and nonresidents alike rushed to unload assets denominated in won. The government had insufficient reserves to defend the won and actually took some early steps that aggravated the situation instead of stabilizing it. To protect the global economy from the impact of a meltdown, the G-7 mobilized a $58 billion rescue package, even bigger than Mexico's.[23]

As a consequence of the more aggressive adjustment effort, the contraction of the Korean economy was relatively mild and short. The Korean authorities rewarded their rescuers by prepaying much of the emergency financing. Three months after the crisis, Korea was able to return to the capital markets with a eurobond issue by the Korean Development Bank.[24]

Another similarity with the Thai and Indonesian crises was the small amount of foreign debt owed by the government going into the crisis and the large amount owed by Korean banks and companies. No restructuring of sovereign debt was required, but the government was stuck with a sizable bill for overhauling the insolvent banking system, and an enormous amount of corporate debt had to be restructured. Private investors in and lenders to Korean companies experienced large-scale losses as stock prices plummeted and company-by-company workouts were concluded.

A special feature of South Korea's recovery program was some exceptional support from commercial banks. As the crisis approached, foreign banks began cutting their exposures to Korean banks. That could only continue by greatly increasing the magnitude of the emergency financing package, which would represent a blatant departure from the G-7 objective of obtaining burden sharing from the private sector. There were two alternatives: impose exchange controls that would prevent creditors from cashing out, or arrange some kind of voluntary standstill and rollover agreement. The Korean government opted for the more cooperative approach, and a deal was arranged. The banks agreed to restructure $22 billion of short-term claims on Korean banks into bonds guaranteed by the government maturing in one to three years.[25]

The South Korean case was the first experiment in orchestrating private sector involvement following the Mexican peso crisis. It was successful for at

23. The package included $21 billion from the IMF. Only $19 billion from the total package was actually disbursed. Because Korea's reforms were front-loaded, its need for emergency financing diminished rapidly.

24. Institute of International Finance (1999b, p. 10).

25. Institute of International Finance (1999a, p. 65).

least five reasons. The Korean adjustment program was more than credible, which gave banks confidence in an early return to normalcy. The support committed by the IMF and other official agencies was massive. The commercial banks were not asked to bear a disproportionate burden. The form of support sought from the banks was moderate and market-based; they were not asked to put up new money, restructure, or accept losses. Finally, the banks were treated as partners in the rescue effort, as they had been with the Brady Plan workouts, not as villains.

In short, South Korea's adjustment program entailed substantial social costs, but the relatively rapid recovery helped to contain these costs. Every penny of emergency financing from official agencies was repaid, with interest, and much was prepaid as Korea regained access to international capital markets. At the same time, the losses absorbed by private investors and lenders were a multiple of the official financing provided.

POSTSCRIPT. Two factors help to explain why so many analysts and investors were surprised by the Asian crises. First, there was a lot of hype about the Asian economies from the mid-1980s up to the moment of crisis. They earned the sobriquet of "tigers" by virtue of their pace-setting economic growth and their ability to avoid default in the 1980s. A World Bank report on "the Asian Miracle" published in 1993 fed the hype. The Mexican peso crisis at the end of 1994 reinforced the image of strong economic policies in Asia in contrast to weak policies in Latin America. Analytical talent was allocated away from the boring Asian countries to focus on the exciting transition countries in Eastern Europe and the former Soviet Union. People just were not paying close enough attention.

Second, a subtle political change had occurred in the three crisis countries that escaped the attention of most analysts and investors but represented a key factor in all of them. Following the first oil crisis in the early 1970s and several subsequent shocks, the Asian countries had exhibited a remarkable capacity to adjust far surpassing that of other countries. In hindsight, this exceptional capacity to adjust was related in part to the authoritarian traditions of government prevailing in Asia. When governments became convinced that policy changes were necessary, they were able to resist opposition efforts to water down far-reaching reforms and to implement them without being undercut by vested interests. Over the same period, however, steps were taken in Thailand, Indonesia, and Korea to develop or tolerate democratic institutions and movements. In the years immediately preceding the crises, democratic forces gained influence rapidly. By 1997 the governments in these countries needed to mobilize popular support to implement bold economic reforms, but they lacked mechanisms for doing so.[26] Over the same twenty-five years, the cronies of the authoritarian regimes in these three countries became ever more deeply entrenched. By 1997 they were sufficiently strong to block critical economic reforms. Caught between the old cronies and the new democratic forces, the governments were unable to avert a crisis as they had done repeatedly in the past. The lesson for global investors and lenders as well as governments in countries becoming more dependent on private capital flows is to pay close attention to potential political obstacles to implementing economic reforms when a crisis is brewing.

The Russian Crisis in August 1998

In the world of international finance, August has been the cruelest month for practitioners who are still active today. The Mexican crisis in August 1982 was a body blow to commercial banks, signaling unprecedented losses to come in their developing country loan portfolios. Russia's default in August 1998, on the heels of the three Asian crises, brought the boom in emerging market bonds to a screeching halt.[27]

After the breakup of the Soviet Union, the G-7 architects made Russia's transition from a centrally planned to a market economy a top priority. They used all the instruments at their disposal, in particular the IMF, the World Bank, the EBRD (the European Bank for Reconstruction and Development), and the OECD.[28] These institutions took on with relish the task of promoting reform in Russia and all the other transition countries.

Proponents of the "shock therapy" approach to economic transition in Russia won out over proponents of gradualism, putting pressure on the G-7 to commit generous financial and other support to ensure success. The IMF wasted no time in lending billions of dollars, but Russia's ability to implement reforms turned out to be no greater than the average emerging market country and distinctly inferior to the ability of the leading reformers in Central Europe: the Czech Republic, Hungary, and Poland.

26. The most advanced country in this respect was Korea, which was preparing for its most democratic election ever in late 1997. Indonesia was less advanced than Thailand, but the population was chafing over the imminent anointment of President Suharto for a seventh successive five-year term.

27. The collapse of the hedge fund Long-Term Capital Management in mid-September added an extra layer of anxiety about the stability of the international financial system.

28. The Russian Federation joined the IMF in 1992. With twenty-three other countries from the former Soviet bloc joining, all as borrowers, the IMF was able to conclude the first quota increase in a decade, a 50 percent increase that became effective in November 1992. The staff increased by roughly 25 percent between 1991 and 1994, although part of this increase was for an expansion of its work in sub-Saharan Africa.

Performance targets adopted by the Russian government were frequently readjusted to compensate for weak implementation. Year after year capital flight from Russia exceeded the support provided by the multilateral institutions, exposing them to criticism for financing these outflows.

In the breakup of the Soviet Union, the Russian Federation agreed to assume all outstanding Soviet debt to external creditors, leaving the other former republics virtually debt free. Russia negotiated four generous reschedulings of these obligations with Paris Club creditors between 1993 and 1996. Beginning in 1991 Russia was also in continuous negotiations with commercial banks to reschedule Soviet-era debt. Under an agreement signed at the end of 1997, $32 billion of outstanding Soviet-era debt to commercial banks was converted into tradable twenty- and twenty-five-year notes. Over the years that the Russian government was rescheduling Soviet debt, it was also contracting new loans at a rapid clip. Its new debt, almost all on commercial terms, soon began to look unsustainable as economic indicators pointed to subpar performance.

Ignoring disastrous experiences elsewhere (Turkey in 1978, Mexico in 1994), Russia began issuing short-term ruble-denominated treasury bills (GKO) in large volumes while fixing the ruble-dollar exchange rate. By July 1998 Russia was offering rates of 130 percent at GKO auctions, which many investors found irresistible. Foreigners, who held as much as 30 percent of the GKO, were clearly aware of the risks but seemed to be gambling on an eventual rescue by the G-7. That hope was not entirely foolish because of Russia's strategic importance, reflected in the IMF's decision in mid-July to commit another $11 billion of financial support for an "anticrisis" program on top of $8 billion previously advanced.[29]

A few weeks later the Russian parliament voted down key parts of the emergency program supported by the IMF, and selling pressure on the ruble intensified. In mid-August the government let the ruble float, suspended payments on GKO and other domestic debt instruments, and announced a ninety-day moratorium on principal payments due to external creditors. Shortly thereafter, around $6 billion of GKO obligations were exchanged on a unilateral basis for $4.4 billion of eurobonds. Another $15 billion of GKO held by banks were restructured unilaterally in November 1998 into three-year and five-year bonds with large losses in net present value terms.

The Russian government was scrupulous in making payments on its new external debt, but initiated negotiations with a reconstituted Bank Advisory

29. Significantly, the IMF commitment was funded in part by activating the GAB, the first time ever for a non-G-10 country.

Committee to restructure the Soviet-era debt previously rescheduled in 1997.[30] In the deal signed in September 2000, Soviet-era debt was exchanged for Russian Federation eurobonds with a face value reduction on the order of 38 percent. Russia also went back to the Paris Club in 1999 to reschedule its Soviet-era debt for the fifth time.

The Russian crisis again forced the G-7 architects to choose between committing public funds to mitigate the social costs of adjustment in the crisis country, which would have the inescapable effect of also reducing the losses that private lenders and investors would otherwise bear, or holding back and letting the country and its private creditors take the consequences. In July the G-7 tested the feasibility of the former course with the $11 billion injection of IMF financing, but the Russian government was not able to implement an emergency program in a credible fashion. A month later, rather than throw more money at the problem, the G-7 pulled the plug.

To some degree the G-7 was caught in a trap of its own making. In the G-22 "architecture" exercise (see chapter 11), and in the IMF's soul-searching after the Asian crisis, the G-7 had drawn a line in the sand: it would not repeat the kind of massive rescue package arranged for Mexico in 1994–95. The responses to the Asian crises in 1997 flirted with this line but did not cross it because sovereign debt was not the problem; domestic private company and bank debt was the problem. In the case of Russia, GKO were a bit too much like Mexico's *tesobono*. The G-7 could not do any more to help Russia without crossing the arbitrary line reflected in its new policy on burden sharing or private sector involvement. Perhaps more accurately, the G-7 had gambled that Russia's capacity to maintain sound macroeconomic policies would be on a par with Mexico's or Korea's and was disappointed.

The losses absorbed by private investors and lenders in the Russian crisis were large and highly visible. The losses they absorbed in the Asian crises in 1997 were considerably larger but less visible because they materialized through secondary market trading and hundreds of individual corporate workouts. The Institute of International Finance estimated that private sector losses related to all four crises were $350 billion in round numbers. The bulk of this—$240 billion—represented the drop in market value of Asian securities (plus those of Brazil and Russia) held by foreigners from precrisis levels to the depth of the crisis. Commercial bank losses were about

---

30. Because the restructured debt included tradable securities, the Bank Advisory Committee was amenable to including bondholder representatives, but the Russian authorities objected. Nevertheless, the committee consulted with bondholders (institutional investors), and their views had an impact on the terms eventually agreed.

$60 billion, based on publicly announced provisions. Two-thirds of this amount related to Russian GKO. The losses absorbed by nonbank bond-holders and investors in GKO were about $50 billion. The losses related to the Asian crises were on the order of $250 billion (80 percent equity losses), while the losses related to Russia were $100 billion (80 percent debt losses).[31]

Forced Bond Restructuring in 1999

The G-7's hard-line policy on private sector involvement, adopted in 1998, was applied in 1999 through the Paris Club and the IMF.[32] It targeted bond debt. The first test case was Pakistan; Ukraine and Ecuador became guinea pigs later in the year.

PAKISTAN. To help overcome balance-of-payments strains, the government of Pakistan adopted a comprehensive adjustment program in late 1997 that was supported by multiyear arrangements with the IMF. In early 1998 the country experienced a payments crisis when a series of nuclear weapons tests prompted a suspension of foreign assistance from multilateral agencies and bilateral donor agencies and an outflow of private capital. Arrears to Paris Club creditors began to pile up. Toward the end of 1998 Pakistan reworked its adjustment program sufficiently to qualify for the second year of financing under its IMF arrangements and a larger amount of financing. Continued IMF support reopened the door for aid flows and for a Paris Club operation. Pakistan was not eligible for the HIPC Initiative because of its relatively light debt burden, so the Paris Club granted Pakistan "Classic" rescheduling terms in January 1999. The agreement included the standard comparable treatment clause targeting commercial bank debt, but it also included a new provision explicitly extending comparable treatment to three eurobond issues with about $600 million outstanding.

The Pakistan authorities had never had recourse to restructuring debt owed to private creditors and resisted doing so now to avoid the adverse impact on their creditworthiness. From the government's point of view, it had not borrowed excessively from commercial banks or the bond markets, and the debt service requirements associated with this borrowing were manageable. Moreover, the debt difficulties it faced were directly linked to the political decision of its donors to suspend aid, which of course the commercial lenders had not been part of in any way.

Commercial banks were disappointed by the application of comparable treatment in this case but not totally surprised. In any case they were only

31. Institute of International Finance (1999a, pp. 57–61).
32. Some of the material in this section is drawn from IMF (2001a).

being asked to reschedule, not to take a haircut.[33] Bond investors were out-raged. The forced restructuring of Pakistan's bonds may have been foreshadowed in various communiqués and speeches, but the G-7 and the Paris Club had not carried out any prior consultations with bondholders. Moreover, instead of openly announcing what was being done and making the case for it, information about the Paris Club action seeped into the marketplace when rumors about the content of the agreement began circulating. On top of this the Pakistan authorities chose to restructure the bonds by means of a unilateral exchange offer rather than a negotiated deal.[34]

UKRAINE. In mid-1999 Ukraine got into a jam with a different flavor. Ukraine emerged from the Soviet Union debt free and quickly began exploring all the possible forms of international borrowing, including bonds. Because of Ukraine's status as an untested borrower, the yields on these bonds were quite attractive, and a large volume was sold to retail investors in Europe, especially in Germany. By 1995 Ukraine was experiencing balance-of-payments strains and obtained its first standby arrangement with the IMF. This was followed by two more, and in 1998 Ukraine negotiated a three-year extended arrangement with the IMF. One of the conditions of the 1998 arrangement was that Ukraine would seek new commercial financing sufficient to cover its bond payments and therefore avoid using IMF resources to reduce the claims of private lenders. Ukraine attempted some piecemeal restructuring at first but had to adopt a more aggressive approach in 1999 to ensure continued IMF support. (The Paris Club rescheduled Ukraine's debt in July 2001.)

As Pakistan had done, Ukraine decided to restructure its bond debt through a unilateral exchange rather than a negotiated settlement. Ukraine's exchange was technically much more complex than the Pakistan exchange and was carried out successfully at the beginning of 2000.

ECUADOR. Balance-of-payments strains in Ecuador reached crisis proportions in 1999.[35] The government had issued a relatively small amount of

33. About $900 million of bank debt was restructured. This included more than $500 million of trade finance facilities that were rolled over for three years (a sore point because the Paris Club did not restructure short-term debt), rescheduling of principal payments on medium-term debt, and some other relief. The deal was negotiated bilaterally with the lending banks and syndicate leaders, not with a BAC.

34. The outstanding eurobond issues were exchanged for a new six-year bond with principal payments beginning after two years.

35. The 1999 crisis was only the latest in a series stretching back to the early 1960s, reflecting political turmoil of fictional proportions. President Jamil Mahuad Witt, who narrowly won election in May 1998, introduced a bold economic reform program later in 1998 that prompted a general strike, riots, and the resignation of the finance minister. A new economic emergency plan announced

eurobonds but had a substantial amount of Brady bonds outstanding. The Ecuador case became a major test of the G-7's new policy on private sector burden sharing. As in the case of Ukraine, the IMF, rather than the Paris Club, was the G-7's instrument for enforcing its policy. The IMF arrangement obtained by the government to support its stabilization program was predicated on a restructuring of Ecuador's Brady bonds as well as its post-Brady eurobonds.[36] To make sure no one overlooked the point, the IMF disbursed its first tranche of financing shortly after Ecuador missed a payment on its discount Brady bonds, thereby "lending into arrears." (See chapter 11 for further discussion of the IMF's policy on lending into arrears.)

The forced restructuring of Ecuador's bonds was a double knife-stroke at the heart of the market for emerging market bonds. First was the impact on Brady bonds, which had never before been restructured. Second was the restructuring technique: a unilateral exchange as opposed to a negotiated deal. The aggressive use of "exit consents" (a legal device to make old bonds difficult to trade after the exchange) made this exchange appear even more involuntary than the Ukraine exchange.[37] A deeper concern among bond-holders was that the new bonds might contribute to another debt crisis in the medium term.

Successful Cooperation (Brazil, Turkey)

Backtracking from the three forced bond restructurings in 1999, none of which involved crises in the sense of a sudden loss of market access, the next country after Russia in the parade of financial crises was Brazil. The Brazilian crisis at the end of 1998 and beginning of 1999 began as almost a pure case of contagion. Four years earlier, Brazil had adopted a bold stabilization program (the "Real Plan") to restore price stability after seeing inflation approach 3,000 percent a year. The Real Plan was successful in reducing inflation to single digits and generating annual GDP growth of 3–4 percent, but Brazil's fiscal and current account deficits remained at worrisome levels.

---

in April 1999 was greeted with more protests, especially by indigenous Indian groups. To help stabilize the economy, President Mahuad announced in January 2000 the replacement of Ecuador's currency with the U.S. dollar, but another wave of unrest forced him to flee the country less than two weeks later. The military command appointed the former vice president as president.

36. Ecuador was one of the last countries to conclude a Brady bond deal. It was signed in February 1995 and involved one of the biggest haircuts. Old debt was exchanged for discount bonds at fifty-five cents on the dollar. After this deal, no new medium-term bank loans were extended to the Ecuador government up to the time of the Brady bond default in 1999. However, Ecuador's government was able to issue some new bonds.

37. The most authoritative discussion of exit consents is found in Buchheit and Gulati (2000).

When Russia defaulted in August 1998, access to capital market financing for most emerging market borrowers dried up, and Brazil found itself against the ropes in the midst of an election campaign. President Fernando Henrique Cardoso was reelected at the beginning of October and immediately announced some measures to regain investor confidence. In November the government adopted a comprehensive adjustment program supported by an emergency financing package totaling almost $41 billion ($18 billion from the IMF). Resistance to elements of the program in the Brazilian Congress and a move by several states to restructure their debt owed to the federal government put renewed pressure on the real shortly after President Cardoso's second inauguration on January 1, 1999. In mid-January Brazil was forced to abandon its crawling peg exchange rate regime and float the real, which quickly depreciated by about 40 percent against the dollar. Cardoso appointed a new governor of the central bank (Arminio Fraga) to reinforce the credibility of the government's reform program.

Brazil has arguably one of the most systemically significant emerging market economies—in the same league as Russia, Korea, and Mexico. The G-7 architects could not let Brazil default without risking a domino effect in other countries such as Argentina. Nor could they commit more money without getting some burden sharing from private creditors. Fortunately the Brazilian government acted promptly and effectively to conclude an arrangement in March 1999 with its commercial bank creditors to roll over maturing short-term debt. That was enough burden sharing to enable the IMF (and the World Bank and IDB) to commit additional funds. Altogether, the package of official assistance and commercial bank support gave Brazil enough breathing space to stay current on all of its external debt obligations (especially bonds) without having to borrow at the huge spreads the market was demanding. More important, the reforms were effective in restoring investor confidence in Brazil. In March, Bradesco, one of Brazil's leading private banks, was able to issue a $200 million eurobond. By mid-2000, the government was able to retire another chunk of its Brady bond debt with the proceeds of a $2 billion eurobond issue at a comfortable spreads.[38]

The March 1999 bank deal was a kind of burden sharing that market participants viewed positively. First, the government acted effectively to implement reforms. Second, the government initiated negotiations with its commercial bank creditors before arrears began to accumulate, made clear that it was seeking a voluntary solution, and reached agreement in a busi-

38. Institute of International Finance (1999c, p.10).

THE POST-1994 CRISES AND BONDS   215

nesslike fashion on a limited restructuring tailored to its circumstances. This episode, along with the similar arrangement made by South Korea at the end of 1997, underscored the capacity of commercial creditors to play a constructive role in helping countries overcome a crisis before the point of default.

Similar action was taken in addressing Turkey's crisis at the beginning of 2001. Turkey had earned the title of "the sick man of Europe" in the 1960s and 1970s, when it was repeatedly rescued from economic collapse by its NATO allies and West European neighbors (appendix B). After 1980 Turkey was able to steer clear of serious debt difficulties for almost twenty years. Balance-of-payments strains began to erode confidence in Turkey after 1995, as a succession of fragile governments failed to keep budget deficits within prudent limits and inflation moved up above 50 percent a year. Determined to join the European Union among the first wave of accession candidates, Turkey introduced a draconian "disinflation" program at the end of 1999 with the primary goal of bringing inflation down to EU norms. Progress under the program was reasonably good, but the political coalition supporting the program was extremely fragile.

In February 2001 an argument between the president and the prime minister became public, triggering a rush to unload Turkish lira for euros and dollars and forcing the government to devalue. If Turkey had been located at the tip of South America, the G-7 response no doubt would have been different. Because of Turkey's strategic role in the Middle East, and because of the importance of bringing Turkey into the European Union, the G-7 architects pulled out all the stops. In particular, they supported an unprecedented level of financing by the IMF without insisting on a corresponding degree of burden sharing by private creditors.

Argentina's Default in 2001

The biggest sovereign default ever as of mid-2003 occurred in 2001. Unlike the Mexican crises in 1982 and 1994 or the Russian crisis in 1998, Argentina's default at the end of 2001 was not a surprise. The handwriting was on the wall by the middle of the year at least. The terrorist attacks in New York and Washington on September 11 demolished the last hope that Argentina's recovery would be sparked by a rebound in the U.S. economy.

The depths to which Argentina has sunk over the past 100 years are hard to fathom and may be unmatched by any other country. Argentina was one of the wealthiest countries in the world at the beginning of the 1900s. Every generation of political leaders since then has dragged the country through a crisis that has dropped the country several notches down the ranks as measured by per capita income. A recurring malady has been inflation engendered by bursts of public sector spending that the landed aristocracy was unwilling to finance with income or property taxes.

Periodic debt crises were part of the pattern, but not always. One of the curious chapters in this tragedy is that during the 1930s the United Kingdom helped Argentina meet its bond payments when most of its neighbors were defaulting. However, trade concessions and other advantages that the United Kingdom extracted in this period produced a deep well of resentment that contributed to the election of the populist regime of Juan Peron in 1943. Peron presided over Argentina's worst hyperinflation.[39]

Argentina was the Paris Club's first debt-relief candidate, in 1956, and joined with most of the other Latin American countries seeking debt reduction under the Brady Plan at the end of the 1980s. The crises experienced by Mexico in 1994 and Brazil and Ecuador in 1999 reinforced concerns about endemic debt problems in Latin America, but Argentina distinguished itself as one of the strongest performers in the region during the first half of the 1990s. Regrettably, it was unable to sustain this performance. Argentina's default at the end of 2001 was spectacular by any standard. It could only be eclipsed by a default of one of the industrial countries or of Brazil, Korea, or Mexico.[40]

Argentina's 2001 crisis had its roots in an episode of hyperinflation in the early 1990s. The "convertibility plan" implemented by Economy Minister Domingo Cavallo in 1991 was successful in wringing inflation out of the Argentine economy in part by creating a hard link between the peso and U.S. dollar. After a few years of strong growth, the pressures of large budget deficits combined with high interest rates required to maintain convertibility tipped the economy into recession. In the meantime Argentina borrowed heavily in international capital markets from investors who were impressed with the government's commitment to the peso-dollar link and attracted by the high yields being offered. Borrowing from commercial banks was limited, although leading Spanish banks and a number of others invested heavily in Argentine branches and subsidiaries in this period. The bulk of the government's new borrowing was in bond markets, both domestic and abroad. The ratio of its debt to GDP rose from 35 percent at the end of 1994

39. Sachs (1986, p. 422).
40. The bankruptcy of Enron, the large U.S. energy company, occurred at roughly the same time and was more or less on the same scale. Six months later, WorldCom's bankruptcy overshadowed both the Argentina and Enron defaults.

to 64 percent at the end of 2001.[41] The country's total external debt at the end of 2002 was $140 billion. Broken down by borrower, $90 billion was owed by the public sector and $50 billion by the private sector. Broken down by creditor, $34 billion was owed to multilateral agencies, $9 billion to bilateral donor agencies, $14 billion to commercial banks, $71 billion to holders of bonds and notes, and $12 billion to other private creditors (including suppliers).[42]

Argentina's prospects took a distinct turn for the worse after the Russian crisis in August 1998 and the Brazilian crisis a few months later. The strains reached a critical point in late 2000, when Argentina adopted a tough adjustment program and obtained a $40 billion package of financing to support it (including $14 billion from the IMF). Domestic support for the program was weak, however, and market investors did not respond as hoped. Cavallo was brought back as economy minister in March 2001 in the hope that he could once again save the country from disaster. To succeed, however, he needed support from two sources that never materialized: the citizens of Argentina, and the external environment.

Other countries survived the same external shocks, so it is probably accurate to attribute Argentina's 2001 default to a failure of adjustment. In this case, as in almost all, the timing of the crisis was largely determined by when creditors lost confidence in the government. Bondholders began voting with their feet in the summer of 2001. With the bursting of the high-tech bubble in the U.S. equity market and the U.S. economy headed toward a recession, and with signs of weakening domestic support for Cavallo's program, Argentina's bond spreads began moving out of junk bond territory into default territory. As measured by JPMorgan Chase for its emerging markets bond index, the spread on Argentina's sovereign bonds went from around 1,100 basis points in June to 1,430 basis points at the end of August, almost 2,200 at the end of October, and more than 3,300 at the end of November.

Despite these signs of trouble ahead, the IMF continued to pump money into Argentina, urged on by the G-7 architects who were hoping to avoid another default. In an action reminiscent of the support it provided shortly before the Russian default in August 1998, the IMF committed an additional $8 billion to Argentina in August 2001.[43] The market response was not

41. Speech by Anne Krueger entitled "Crisis Prevention and Resolution: Lessons from Argentina," www.imf.org/external/np/speeches/2002/071702.htm (August 4, 2002).

42. Institute of International Finance, unpublished country report issued on December 20, 2002.

43. Support for this additional commitment within the IMF and among the G-7 was precarious. The decision hung on a knife-edge.

encouraging. Following the terrorist attacks in the United States in September, sentiment soured. In response the IMF began to signal that it would not provide additional funds without a restructuring of Argentina's debt to private creditors.[44]

The default came in December 2001, when street riots forced the government to resign. A short-lived successor government floated the peso and stopped payments of interest and principal on all external debt, except debt owed to the multilateral agencies. This narrative is of course a gross oversimplification of what happened and why, but by mid-2002 Argentina's default was well on the way to becoming one of the messiest as well as being the largest.

Postscript

Turkey's situation remained precarious throughout 2002, in part because of uncertainties surrounding the change in government at the end of the year. The IMF continued to disburse exceptionally large amounts of financing without any visible requirements for private sector involvement. In mid-2003 Turkey's prospects were particularly hard to assess because of developments related to the military action led by the United States to bring about regime change in Iraq.

Brazil's situation also became very tense during 2002 as it headed toward presidential elections in October with a socialist candidate in the lead. The IMF approved an exceptional $30 billion standby arrangement in September to support the outgoing government's efforts to avoid a crisis. A series of statements by the incoming president, Luiz Inácio Lula da Silva, before and after the elections, were helpful in calming market anxieties. At the beginning of 2003 the prospects for avoiding a debt crisis had improved, but the country remained vulnerable to new shocks.

At the beginning of 2003 the IMF approved a controversial "interim" standby arrangement for Argentina that appeared to be a weakly disguised means of avoiding the emergence of arrears to the IMF before elections in May. Bondholders in the meantime organized themselves into a number of committees and called on the government to begin good-faith negotiations. Some bondholders initiated litigation when they became frustrated by the government's procrastination. The new president, Néstor Carlos Kirchner, took office at the end of May without a clear electoral mandate but with an economy that seemed to be on the mend. Reports in the financial press indi-

44. Mussa (2002) tells the story of Argentina's ups and downs in the 1990s, focusing on its relations with the IMF.

cated that debt reduction on the order of 60–70 percent would be required to make Argentina's debt burden sustainable.

The case of Argentina is at the heart of this policy study. When the government of Argentina is ready to adopt a credible recovery program and negotiate with its bondholders, will there be workout machinery in place to ensure a satisfactory workout? If not, should the G-7 architects establish some new and permanent machinery—such as the Sovereign Debt Restructuring Mechanism proposed by the IMF—to facilitate sovereign debt workouts in the future?

11

The Debate over Private
Sector Involvement, 1995–2002

The steps taken by the G-7 architects to manage the Mexican peso crisis at the end of 1994 initiated a debate about the role of private investors and lenders in preventing and resolving financial crises that was still bubbling in mid-2003. The debate spawned new official forums, special working groups of officials and private sector representatives, and a bookshelf full of reports and proposals. A new set of acronyms came into use, especially PSI—private sector involvement. This study focuses on only one aspect of PSI, namely, the machinery used for sovereign debt workouts when all attempts to avoid a default have failed. The inherently more important aspect of crisis prevention is outside the scope of this study. Nevertheless readers are reminded from time to time that prevention should be the top priority. Passing references are also made to the middle ground between prevention and workout, where opportunities exist to defuse a crisis before it reaches the stage of outright default.

The workout part of the PSI debate both responded to and contributed to the crises that occurred following the Mexican peso crisis (see chapter 10). In this chapter four phases of the PSI debate are examined, each linked to specific proposals for improving the machinery for sovereign debt workouts. The first phase centered on a report prepared by the G-10 deputies addressing policy issues raised in the context of the Mexican peso crisis (1995–96). The second centered on a set of reports produced by three working groups organized under a new forum, the G-22, to improve the architecture of the international financial system (1997–99). The third centered on a "framework for PSI" developed by the G-7 finance ministers and presented in their report for the economic summit in June 1999 in Cologne (1999–2001). The fourth centered on a proposal unveiled in November 2001 by the IMF to establish a piece of permanent machinery for sovereign workouts (2002–03).

In each phase, the position of the G-7 architects, the actions taken by the IMF, and the views of the global financial industry are explained and linked to the post-1994 crises.[1] The period as a whole was a veritable whirlwind of activity, verging on frenzy at times. The results in terms of better workouts were unimpressive.

Phase One: The G-10 Report on the Resolution of Sovereign Liquidity Crises

The Mexican situation was sufficiently under control by the middle of 1995 to allow the G-7 architects to initiate an in-depth policy review. The G-7 leaders, at their summit meeting in Halifax, Canada, in June 1995, mandated the task to the G-10 finance ministers and central bank governors. The G-10 officials were directed to carry out a review of procedures for the "orderly resolution" of debt crises, "recognizing the complex legal and other issues posed" and "the wide variety of sources of international finance involved."[2] The phrase "orderly resolution" in the Halifax communiqué is significant because it drove much of the activity by the G-7 architects and the IMF over the next seven years. The thrust of the G-10 exercise was to

1. Principal sources on the G-7 initiatives were the report of a G-10 working party on "The Resolution of Sovereign Liquidity Crises" (1996) and the "Report of the Working Group on International Financial Crises" (1998) from the G-22. Principal sources on the IMF's work were the IMF annual reports for the years 1995 through 2002, a series of IMF policy papers included in the reference list, and the text of speeches by Anne Krueger and other officials from the relevant websites. Principal sources on the IIF's work were the report of its Working Group on Crisis Resolution (1996), three reports produced under the auspices of the IIF's Steering Committee on Emerging Markets Finance (1999), and the Action Plan of the IIF Special Committee on Crisis Prevention and Resolution in Emerging Markets (2002). Kenen (2001) and Eichengreen (2002) provide excellent overviews of the architecture exercise since 1995. Rogoff and Zettelmeyer (2002) inventory and categorize the various proposals made since 1976 for improving the process of restructuring sovereign debt.
2. Communiqué issued at the G-7 Summit in Halifax, Canada, June 17, 1995.

find alternatives to the kind of massive packages of official financing used in the Mexican peso crisis. On a parallel track with the G-10 exercise, the IMF undertook its usual careful and comprehensive assessment of the causes of the Mexican crisis, the implications for other countries, and possible steps to avoid a repetition of the experience. These public sector policy initiatives prompted the Institute of International Finance to form a working group to produce a report presenting a financial industry perspective on crisis resolution.

The G-10 Track

The G-10 finance ministers and central bank governors followed up on the Halifax Summit mandate by forming a working party of their deputies chaired by Jean-Jacques Rey, the Belgian Central Bank deputy. The report of the working party entitled "The Resolution of Sovereign Liquidity Crises," issued in May 1996, was a remarkable document and is still a good primer on the issues covered in this chapter. The first paragraph of the executive summary invoked the objective of orderly resolution of crises and noted that the working party had focused on bonds ("internationally traded securities") that "have increased in importance . . . but that in the past have usually been shielded from payments suspensions or restructurings."

A notable feature of the G-10 exercise was a survey of market participants presented in annex III of the working party's report. The conclusions of the G-10 report were remarkably consistent with the views expressed in the survey.

The heart of the G-10 report was a framework for developing a "flexible, case-by-case approach" to crisis resolution consisting of eleven steps to be taken by the parties involved. Six of these were familiar and uncontroversial steps such as fostering sound policies in borrowing countries. Five were especially relevant to the PSI debate:

—Work "with the grain of the market."

—Ensure that the burdens of exceptional financing are allocated fairly within and across classes of creditors.

—Be cooperative and nonconfrontational.

—Build on contractual arrangements (such as collective action clauses).

—Make use of existing practices and institutions (specifically the Paris Club and the London Club).

Six years after they were enunciated, these features remain a sound basis for an effective workout approach. In the next two phases of the PSI debate, however, more aggressive approaches were considered and in some instances applied. These did not gain broad support from market participants, and in early 2003 the debate was drifting back toward the cooperative framework spelled out in the G-10 report.

To make sure private investors and lenders would not miss the point, the G-10 report stressed in several places that bond debt would not be given preferential treatment in future workouts. For example, the report said that "given the limitations on the availability of official finance, the need to contain moral hazard and the desirability of equitable burden sharing, there can be no presumption that any form of debt will be excluded from workout arrangements in the future."

Operationally, the most significant conclusion in the G-10 report was that collective action clauses—provisions in bond covenants to facilitate restructuring—should be developed in a "market-led process" and be included as a normal feature of all sovereign bonds. The report included a detailed analysis of "forms of collective action" in international debt contracts. The findings provide an excellent starting point for exploring the topic of collective action clauses.[3]

The G-10 report arrived at three conclusions that troubled market participants. One was the view that the London Club would continue to play an important role in restructuring sovereign debts owed to commercial banks. Commercial bankers were skeptical about the future of the London Club because they did not anticipate having large exposures in defaulting countries. As a corollary, since bonds did not fit into the London Club process, the G-10 suggested that the best approach to restructuring bond debt was to introduce collective action clauses in bond contracts. Institutional investors saw more negatives than positives associated with collective action clauses.

A second troubling point was the G-10's attitude toward "standstills," meaning temporary suspensions of debt-service payments by a crisis country. Although noting that these could be justified only in exceptional circumstances, the working party's report went on to discuss a number of technical features of standstills. Furthermore, by rejecting as infeasible the establishment of an international bankruptcy court or other formal arrangements to resolve crises, the report implied that more active use of standstills could be an effective substitute. Market participants were bothered by the inference that standstills might be needed to force creditors to respond constructively. They were even more concerned that granting some

3. According to the Group of Thirty (2002, p.10), the study by Eichengreen and Portes (1995) was instrumental in focusing the attention of the G-10 working party on bond clauses.

kind of official approval to standstills (by the IMF, for example) would tilt the burden-sharing balance in favor of debtor countries.

The third troubling point was the G-10's unqualified recommendation that the IMF extend its policy of "lending into arrears" to include bonds. From its inception the IMF had declined to provide financing to countries in arrears to other creditors or without a reasonable plan for eliminating these arrears (including through debt relief). An exception to this practice was formally adopted in 1989 in the context of the 1980s debt crisis to allow IMF lending to countries with arrears to commercial banks, but only when the banks had decided for strategic reasons to delay the conclusion of negotiations under way. Market participants saw the extension of the IMF's policy to bonds as another step away from maintaining a level playing field for debtors and creditors in the context of any sovereign debt workouts.[4]

The IMF Track

The focus of the IMF's work in the wake of the Mexican peso crisis was on crisis prevention. To this end the IMF's Special Data Dissemination Standard (SDDS) went into effect in April 1996. Since then there have been marked improvements in the timeliness, accuracy, and coverage of vital statistics on economic policies and performance provided by emerging market countries. Huge leaps were also made in IMF transparency, including the public release of staff papers on countries and on policy issues that were previously available only to member governments.

In the area of crisis resolution, the PSI issue first surfaced at the IMF in an executive board discussion of private market financing in September 1995 that noted the important changes in the composition of emerging markets financing taking place at the time. This discussion was the springboard to a more policy-oriented discussion in February 1996 of proposals for "orderly workouts." According to the summary of this discussion in the IMF's 1996 annual report, most executive directors reacted negatively to the concept of establishing a "formal debt adjustment mechanism," marking the introduction of the word "mechanism" into the vocabulary of PSI.[5]

4. The policy was formally changed in mid-1999 (IMF 1999a). The related criterion for good-faith negotiations with creditors was clarified in 2002 (IMF 2002e).

5. Throughout this chapter, the executive board should be understood to include the senior management of the IMF and the staff. Great skill is required to detect differences in view between these three parts of the IMF. The decisionmaking process on policy issues begins with a work program reflecting the priorities articulated in the latest Interim Committee (International Monetary and Financial Committee) meeting. Issues are analyzed by the staff and forwarded with a policy recommendation to senior management, meaning the managing director and his three deputies. The recommendation is refined as appropriate and presented to the board. The board's discussion leads to either a formal decision or general guidance for the staff.

In a move mirrored in the post-2001 campaign to establish the Sovereign Debt Restructuring Mechanism, the IMF launched an ultimately unsuccessful campaign to amend its charter to establish clear jurisdiction over capital movements. For historical reasons, the original IMF charter obligated members to remove controls on current account transactions (trade in goods and services) but allowed them a free hand with respect to capital account transactions (especially investment and lending). After the shift to a floating exchange rate system in the 1970s, capital movements became a more critical element of the balance of payments, but net private flows to developing countries remained low during the 1980s (reflecting the debt crisis), and there was little interest in the IMF's role in this area. Nevertheless, the trend among developing countries was to remove capital controls, and this liberalization contributed to the surge in private capital flows in the years immediately preceding the Mexican peso crisis in 1994. As the IMF focused on this phenomenon, it saw an opportunity to rectify the historical anomaly and gain formal responsibility for establishing rules of good behavior relating to capital flows.

The issue of capital account liberalization featured prominently on the agenda of the October 1994 meeting of the IMF's ministerial-level, policy-setting interim committee. The committee directed the fund's executive board to consider the implications for the IMF. This led to a decision in July 1995 to focus more on capital account issues in its annual Article IV consultations with member countries. At the same time, the IMF staff began intensive work on an amendment of the IMF's charter that would give it formal jurisdiction over capital movements.

At its April 1997 meeting the interim committee directed the board to seek agreement on specific elements of an amendment. Three months later the crisis in Thailand raised serious questions about the benefits of capital account liberalization. Nevertheless the interim committee adopted at its fall 1997 meeting a six-paragraph statement on the amendment that began: "It is time to add a new chapter to the Bretton Woods agreement."[6] The statement specifically called for an amendment that would make the liberalization of capital movements one of the purposes of the IMF. It also directed the executive board to give "a high priority" to completing the amendment.

The fall 1997 meeting represented the high-water mark of the amendment campaign. As the reality of the Asian crises and the risks of premature liberalization sank in, the campaign began to lose steam. At its spring 1998

6. Statement attached to the Communiqué of the Interim Committee, September 21, 1997. See www.imf.org.

meeting the interim committee noted the provisional agreement reached in the board on the text of an amendment adding capital account liberalization to the purposes of the IMF. The interim committee's fall 1998 communiqué did not mention the amendment at all. The spring 1999 communiqué called on the staff to "further refine its analysis of the experience of countries with the use of capital controls." This signaled the end of the amendment campaign and highlighted the difficulty for the IMF of spearheading a major change in the system that does not command broad support from the public and the financial industry.

The Financial Industry's Response

An exceptional policy exercise by the financial industry was carried out over the same period as the G-10 exercise under the auspices of the Institute of International Finance led by Charles Dallara. A working group was organized at the beginning of 1996 to present the viewpoint of industry practitioners on the issues raised in the process of resolving the Mexican crisis. The report of the working group was issued in September 1996.[7] One departure from the G-10 working group was the greater emphasis placed on crisis prevention in the IIF report. From this point on, the industry perspective reflected in the work of the IIF stressed repeatedly that efforts to prevent crises should take priority over efforts to resolve crises. On this occasion the IIF working group made two contributions to the debate. First, it anticipated the architecture exercises that followed the Asian crises by underscoring the benefits of strengthening weak banking systems. Second, it urged the IMF to expand its dialogue with the private financial community.[8]

In the area of crisis resolution, the IIF working group was in full agreement with the G-10 report on the primacy of prompt and effective policy reforms by crisis countries. Contrary to press reports that persisted for years, the IIF report was perfectly clear about not protecting the private sector ("market participants") from losses. It firmly ruled out "massive official sector financing along the lines of the action taken to contain the Mexican peso crisis," noting, however, the important role for traditional support from the

7. The contrast between "liquidity" crises in the title of the G-10 report and "financial" crises in the IIF title is noteworthy. The G-10 was making a distinction between liquidity crises and solvency crises, as discussed in chapter 2. The IIF found this distinction unhelpful in crafting a market-based approach to crises. The word "financial" was chosen because it encompassed nondebt flows, such as direct investment, which were playing a key stabilizing role in capital flows to emerging market countries.

8. This step was eventually taken in September 2000 when the IMF established the Capital Markets Coordinating Group, and was reinforced by the creation of a new International Capital Markets Department in the IMF in March 2001.

official sector such as IMF standby arrangements. The IIF working group welcomed the G-10's dismissal of formal bankruptcy mechanisms in favor of a market-based approach to crisis resolution.

The working group suggested three elements of an effective market-based approach. One was to build on the ability of asset price movements "to serve as both signals and shock absorbers" in a crisis situation. Another was to avoid actions that might impair the functioning of secondary markets for debt instruments. A third was to organize new ad hoc creditor groups. The working group noted here that "the London Club may no longer have the same role as it did in the 1980s" due to the growing importance of bond debt relative to commercial bank debt.

At the same time the IIF working group took exception to the main thrust of the G-10 report, which was to include "collective action clauses" in most bond contracts to facilitate the restructuring of bonds in a crisis. Again, contrary to persistent press reports and some academic treatments of the subject, the IIF did not object to these clauses per se. Rather it cautioned that the G-10 report exaggerated the benefits of these clauses and advised against forcing their adoption by means of regulatory changes.

The IIF working group reserved its sharpest criticism for the G-10 proposal to extend informal official approval for "standstills" imposed by crisis countries on payments to foreign creditors in certain circumstances.[9]

Phase Two: The G-22 Work on Crisis Prevention and Crisis Resolution

No significant changes in the approach to resolving financial crises in emerging market countries were introduced during the year following the publication of the G-10 and IIF reports in 1996. The Thai crisis that broke out in July 1997 diverted the attention of the G-7 architects toward the specific steps that could be taken to restore stability there and shortly thereafter in Indonesia and Korea. By the end of 1997, the architects were dealing with a different world.[10]

9. Proposals for improving on the approach used to resolve Mexico's crisis were also advanced at this time by academic experts and others. Two received particular attention. Jeffrey Sachs (1995) revived the notion of establishing an international bankruptcy process modeled on bankruptcy regimes of the United States and other countries for resolving corporate (or municipal) defaults. Barry Eichengreen and Richard Portes (1995) presented a rigorous case for officially sanctioned standstills on debt payments.

10. None of the three Asian crises involved unsustainable amounts of sovereign debt. That helped to shift the attention of the G-7 architects toward crisis prevention and away from crisis resolution.

At a meeting of APEC (Asia-Pacific Economic Cooperation) leaders in Vancouver in November 1997—between the Indonesian and South Korean crises—U.S. President Bill Clinton announced plans to organize a special forum of finance ministers and central bank governors to accelerate work on crisis prevention and resolution. Instead of forming another G-10 working party, the G-7 created a brand new North-South forum—the G-22—in some ways reminiscent of the Conference on International Economic Cooperation in 1975–76 (chapter 7). This new forum, however, was led by finance ministers rather than foreign ministers, and its focus was on the more advanced "systemically significant" emerging market countries rather than the least-developed countries.[11]

The G-22 Track

The U.S. Treasury Department was both the originator of the phrase "international financial architecture" and the architect of the new forum. Treasury Secretary Robert Rubin delivered a seminal speech on the subject on January 21, 1998, at Georgetown University.[12] It was arguably the most significant speech about developing countries (emerging market economies) since Secretary Brady's speech in 1989 unveiling the cooperative strategy for commercial bank debt reduction. Several excerpts that convey the scope of his initiative and the terms of reference for the new forum are presented in box 11-1.

The G-22 held its first meeting at the level of finance ministers and central bank governors in April 1998 at the Willard Hotel in Washington immediately before the IMF-World Bank spring meetings. The eight industrial countries invited by the United States were its G-7 partners plus Australia.[13] The fourteen others were leading emerging market and transi-

---

11. The Financial Stability Forum (FSF) was also created by the G-7 architects at this time. At a meeting in October 1998, they commissioned Hans Tietmeyer, president of the German central bank, to design machinery that would help to promote stability in the international financial system by enhancing cooperation among the various national and international bodies engaged in supervising financial institutions and markets. The first meeting of the FSF was in April 1999. It focused initially on the role of hedge funds, the role of offshore financial centers, and problems associated with short-term capital flows. It has stayed out of the PSI debate.

12. The first reference to "architecture" seems to be in testimony by Deputy Treasury Secretary Lawrence H. Summers before the House Committee on Banking and Financial Services on November 13, 1997: "As the world's largest economy, with the world's largest capital market, the United States has had a strong interest in promoting these efforts, which have included a major review of the international financial architecture initiated by President Clinton at the Halifax Summit [in June 1995]."

13. The fourteen nonindustrial countries were Argentina, Brazil, China, Hong Kong SAR, India, Indonesia, Korea, Malaysia, Mexico, Poland, Russia, Singapore, South Africa, and Thailand. The G-22 was enlarged at the beginning of 1999 to accommodate the four missing G-10 members and Spain plus six more developing countries (Chile, Côte d'Ivoire, Egypt, Morocco, Saudi Arabia, and Turkey), bringing the total to thirty-three countries.

Box 11-1. Reforming the International Financial Architecture

Excerpts from a speech by U.S. Treasury secretary Robert Rubin on January 21, 1998:

"The global economy needs architecture as modern as the markets. That is why, even as we have tried to confront the immediate crisis in the Asian region, we have also begun an intensive effort to improve the global financial system to both better prevent crises from occurring and better deal with them if they do occur."

"To make the most of the opportunities and limit the risks of the new global financial system . . . we must also modernize the architecture of the international financial markets that we helped create and that has served us so well for the last fifty years. This will be a long and complex process . . . yet it is imperative for the strength of our economy and the prosperity of our citizens as we enter a new century."

"It is critically important that . . . creditors and investors bear the consequences of their decisions as fully as possible, while minimizing adverse consequences. . . ."

"To build on these efforts, we have begun an intensive internal effort . . . to identify and analyze possible mechanisms for dealing with new challenges to the international financial system. . . . At President Clinton's initiative, we will convene a meeting later this spring with finance ministers from around the world to share our views on this subject and to begin to develop a consensus on further steps."

"This initiative will focus on four objectives: improving transparency and disclosure; strengthening the role of the international financial institutions in helping to continue to deal with the challenges of today's global markets; developing the role of the private sector in bearing an appropriate share of the burden in times of crisis; and strengthening the regulation of financial institutions in emerging economies."

tion countries. Three working groups, cochaired by deputies, were formed to focus on transparency and accountability, strengthening financial systems, and international financial crises. Priority was given to crisis prevention over crisis resolution.

Reports from the three working groups were issued in October 1998 in connection with the second ministerial meeting of the G-22. The recommendations from the transparency and financial systems working groups were significant and far-reaching, but they related exclusively to crisis prevention and therefore fall outside the scope of this study. The recommendations from the Working Group on International Financial Crises included both crisis prevention and crisis resolution measures.[14] The key crisis resolution recommendations and subsequent implementation were as follows.

—*Encouraging the adoption of collective action clauses.* Recognizing that no meaningful progress had been made in the use of such clauses since they had been recommended in the post-Mexico G-10 report, the G-22 advocated educational efforts to promote their acceptance in major capital markets, identifying specific emerging market countries that might adopt them without undue risks, and adding them to international bonds issued by all G-22 countries. Over the following two years, the educational efforts were low key and had no perceptible effect. No emerging market country offered to be the "guinea pig," and several major borrowers expressed strong opposition. The United Kingdom and Canada both introduced collective action clauses in new sovereign issues, and a few other industrial countries followed suit somewhat later.

—*Increasing the resources of the IMF and encouraging countries encountering difficulties to seek IMF assistance at an early stage.* While building the IMF's capacity to provide emergency financing conflicted with the objective of minimizing the potential for creditor moral hazard, the case for augmenting multilateral resources available for emergency financing was more compelling to G-7 parliaments than the case for expanding the capacity of bilateral lending agencies. The New Arrangements to Borrow (NAB) went into effect in November 1998, and a 45 percent quota increase became effective in January 1999. The IMF strengthened the surveillance process to signal more clearly to governments and to the public its concerns about unsus-

---

14. Group of Twenty-Two (1998). The crisis prevention measures highlighted were limiting the scope of government guarantees, making arrangements for "contingency financing," maintaining appropriate exchange rate regimes, and strengthening domestic bankruptcy regimes.

tainable trends, but the tendency of countries to procrastinate in the face of balance-of-payments strains remained.[15]

—*Innovation by the private sector to modernize the existing procedures and institutions for orderly and cooperative workouts.* The working group noted that workout procedures developed in the 1980s for commercial bank debt might not be so relevant in future cases because of the growing importance of bond debt. The group suggested that bondholders find a solution to this problem, drawing on the impressive capacity of the financial industry to design new instruments and financing techniques. The private sector did not heed this call and continued with business as usual.[16]

—*In cases where an interruption in debt payments is unavoidable, seeking a voluntary, cooperative, and orderly debt restructuring.* This recommendation seemed intended to defuse concerns in the private sector about coercive approaches to PSI, but it was undercut by the next two recommendations.

—*In extreme cases where a temporary suspension of payments cannot be avoided, devising a framework for official financing in the context of such a suspension.* This recommendation was heavily qualified, reflecting the reservations of some G-22 countries about an approach explicitly designed to help debtor countries that lacked "the bargaining power to obtain sustainable terms for the restructured instruments." Nevertheless this recommendation was viewed by the financial industry as a more forceful and therefore objectionable version of the standstill recommendation in the 1996 G-10 report.

—*Supporting IMF lending into arrears, including arrears on bond debt.* This recommendation was taken by the private sector as a hardening of the G-7 position on burden sharing with private creditors since the publication of the G-10 report in 1996. In hindsight it is possible to read between the lines a warning to bondholders that they would soon be put to the test of participating in voluntary restructuring arrangements in the case of Pakistan and that they would face some form of involuntary restructuring if they failed this test.

In contrast to the G-10 exercise, which had no discernible impact on the sovereign workout process, the G-22 exercise was a watershed event. Three

15. The IMF has a highly refined process for signaling its concerns to the governments of its member countries through confidential papers, discussions, and communications. In this phase of the PSI debate, it began experimenting with ways of signaling concerns to financial market participants, but there is room for improvement in this area.

16. The working group also noted the possibility of creating a privately funded mechanism to provide new money in a workout, which would have seniority over other claims. Group of Twenty-Two (1998, p. 33).

months after the G-22 reports were issued, the Paris Club forced Pakistan to restructure its bond debt. In June 1999 the IMF formally amended its policy of lending into arrears to encompass bonds. Before the end of 1999 two more experiments in restructuring bond debt were initiated (Ukraine and Ecuador).

The IMF Track

The IMF was active on the PSI front and many others while the G-22 exercise was under way. The Asian crises were a major wake-up call for the IMF, initiating a process of soul-searching well beyond the capacity of most public sector institutions. The reforms carried out in the policies and operations of the IMF were far-reaching and substantial, and in some cases went further than the recommendations in the G-22 reports. The most important included the following:

—*Transparency.* The IMF began to disclose much more information about country performance, country programs, financial operations, policy analysis, and policy discussions. An external evaluation office was established in 2001.

—*Financial sector reform.* Jointly with the World Bank, the IMF launched a financial sector assessment program to identify and repair vulnerabilities in the financial sectors of the most important emerging market countries.

—*Standards and codes.* Various standards and codes were adopted for policy areas relevant to building the resilience of economies becoming increasingly integrated into the global economy. To promote compliance the IMF began to produce regular Reports on the Observance of Standards and Codes (ROSCs).

—*Surveillance, program design, and conditionality.* Steps were taken to focus surveillance on critical areas of vulnerability such as exchange rate regimes and domestic banking systems. Conditionality was revamped to target a narrower range of economic objectives and to enhance "country ownership."

—*Capital market relations.* A Capital Markets Consultative Group was established in September 2000 to provide a forum for frank exchanges of views between the senior management of the IMF and leading financial industry executives.[17] An International Capital Markets Department was

17. The G-22 report discussed the pros and cons of creating new channels to enhance communications between the IMF and private sector representatives but stopped short of recommending any action. The discussion appeared to be a response to calls from the private sector to restore the spirit of cooperation that was a hallmark of the debt strategy of the 1980s. The IIF proposed a forum along the lines of the Capital Markets Consultative Group in a letter to the ministerial policy committees of the IMF and World Bank in April 1998.

created in 2001 to monitor developments in capital markets, and to integrate capital market factors into country surveillance and the design of adjustment programs.

—*IMF facilities.* The Contingent Credit Lines facility was established in April 1999 to pre-position IMF financing for countries with sound policies that could be mobilized quickly to ward off financial market contagion.[18]

In the area of crisis resolution, the IMF became the main instrument for implementing the recommendations contained in the report of the G-22's Working Group on Financial Crises. In particular, along with the Paris Club, the IMF played a key role in implementing the G-7's tougher policy on the treatment of bond debt in sovereign workouts.

Echoing the language of the U.S. initiative to launch the G-22 process, the spring 1998 communiqué of the IMF Interim Committee included a section on "Strengthening the Architecture of the International Monetary System— Prevention, Management, and Resolution of Crises." One element of this strategy was "More Effective Procedures to Involve the Private Sector in Forestalling or Resolving Financial Crises." The committee directed the IMF Executive Board to undertake further work on collective action clauses, lending into arrears, and other elements of the "framework for crisis management" identified in the G-22 exercise. The committee also directed the board to intensify work on steps to strengthen "private sector involvement"— a good example of the IMF's consummate skill in coining euphemisms. Thus the acronym PSI entered the lexicon of international finance.[19]

The Interim Committee adopted a relatively soft line on PSI in its fall 1998 communiqué. It noted the complexity of the issues in this area and asked the executive board to "study further the use of market-based mechanisms to cope with the risk of sudden changes in investor sentiment leading to financial crises." The executive board held its first in-depth discussion of PSI in the spring of 1999, but no policies were changed.[20] In particular, the board considered measures that might be required, when voluntary debt restructuring failed, to ensure an "orderly" restructuring. The board noted the scarcity of "modern experience with restructuring sovereign bonds" and

18. No arrangements under this facility had been approved as of early 2003, despite several refinements to make it more attractive. It remains to be seen if this facility can become an effective tool for crisis prevention.

19. One objection to the term private sector involvement is the implication that the private sector would be uninvolved (bear none of the burden) in sovereign workouts in the absence of measures by official bodies to make them involved. In fact private investors and lenders absorbed substantial losses in every sovereign debt or financial crisis in the past and are likely to absorb more in every future crisis, regardless of what official bodies do.

20. IMF (1999b).

the "possibility that creditor litigation could block progress toward orderly debt restructuring and challenge the IMF's ability to provide effective support for a member's adjustment efforts." In this context, the board considered a staff proposal for "a mechanism to allow the official community to endorse a temporary stay on creditor litigation, possibly through an amendment of Article VIII, Section 2(b) of the IMF's Articles of Agreement."[21]

Article VIII, Section 2(b), is an obscure provision that remains unchanged since the founding of the IMF in 1944. It allows the IMF to block the enforcement of claims pursued in the courts of member countries when such enforcement might undermine a member's efforts to maintain the par value of its currency.[22] The provision became controversial on two previous occasions. One was at the end of the 1980s, when the IMF adopted its policy of lending into arrears to commercial banks. The other was during the mid-1990s, when the IMF launched its campaign to gain formal jurisdiction over capital movements. Extending the IMF's jurisdiction without changing Article VIII, Section 2(b), could extend the fund's purview over loan contracts that have always fallen outside its jurisdiction. Lawyers with long experience advising the financial industry believed that such a step could upset the delicate balance that exists between creditor and debtor rights and responsibilities. The spring 1999 discussion of Article VIII, Section 2(b), was a red flag for the financial industry that may have contributed to negative market sentiment toward lending and investing in emerging market countries after 1998.

The Financial Industry's Response

As it had done following the Mexican peso crisis, the Institute of International Finance organized a set of working groups in mid-1998 to develop crisis prevention and crisis resolution proposals paralleling those emanating from the G-22 working groups. This time the IIF work was carried out under the direction of the Steering Committee on Emerging Market Finance, composed of senior executives from leading commercial banks and investment banks from New York, Europe, and Japan, plus banks from Mexico and Poland. Experts from more than 100 member firms representing all segments of the industry and all regions of the world were involved in five

21. All quotes are from the IMF Annual Report for 1999, pp. 49–50.

22. The provision was intended to resolve a conflict of law where a private party was prevented by the laws of one country (for example, exchange controls in the country of an obligor) from respecting the laws of another country (contract enforcement in the claimant's country).

working groups formed to produce recommendations in the areas of financial crises in emerging markets, risk assessment, transparency, loan quality, and liberalization of capital movements. Four working group reports were issued between January and July 1999.[23] The steering committee, cochaired by William Rhodes and Joseph Ackermann, issued a *Preliminary Report* in October 1998 and a *Summary Report* in June 1999.

The *Preliminary Report*, issued on the eve of the IMF-World Bank annual meetings in October 1998 (shortly before the G-22 reports were issued), contained two noteworthy comments. First, the steering committee observed that: "Speedy resolution of future crises with minimal contagion effects will require a breakthrough by financial officials in working cooperatively with the private financial community." Second, the committee suggested that: "The losses absorbed by private investors over the past year . . . have reduced the potential for moral hazard in emerging markets generally. The balance of risk in the system has now shifted from potentially excessive private lending . . . to potentially excessive reductions in such lending." This statement was intended as a warning that heavy-handed or unilateral attempts to secure PSI could further depress private capital flows to emerging market countries below desirable levels.

In its *Summary Report*, the steering committee outlined a "country-focused, market-friendly approach" to PSI consisting of five elements:[24]

—*Confidence-restoring programs.* The speedy recoveries in Mexico, Korea, and Brazil were attributed to the high quality of their adjustment programs. The slow recoveries in Indonesia and Russia were linked to their weak programs. The views of the financial industry and the G-7 architects were congruent on this element.

—*Official support.* IMF and World Bank conditionalities lend credibility to adjustment programs. Moreover, their financing reduces pressure on countries to impose harmful capital controls or accumulate arrears and can help to catalyze new flow of private capital. The IIF stressed the benefits of official support, while the G-7 and IMF stressed the risks.

—*Spontaneous flows of private capital.* The growing diversity of market participants and instruments enhanced the opportunities for an early resumption of spontaneous financing from private sources after a crisis and would thus facilitate prepayment of official financing by crisis countries.

23. The Working Group on the Liberalization of Capital Movements did not complete a report because of dwindling interest among IMF members in amending the IMF's charter to grant it formal jurisdiction over capital movements.

24. IIF (1999c).

The implications for the design of adjustment programs and related official support were underscored. The G-7 and IMF seemed sensitive to the pre-payment point, but unsure how to design and support programs that would encourage flows of private capital.

—*Tailored approaches.* The benefits of voluntary approaches to PSI, tailored to the circumstances of each case, were stressed. The G-7 and IMF were willing to contemplate involuntary approaches to PSI when voluntary approaches were not working, while the IIF steering committee was not convinced that such circumstances were any more than a theoretical possibility.

—*Public-private cooperation.* "Cooperation between the public sector and the private sector can accelerate the recovery process through the sharing of information and the adoption of mutually reinforcing actions," the committee said. The committee proposed that countries in crisis initiate meetings at an early stage with a "group of key investors and lenders." After a government loses access to market financing, consultations "with a broader range of market participants can help identify policy reforms most likely to bring forth spontaneous market financing."

A large gulf between the views of the financial industry and those of the G-7 architects on the issue of cooperation existed after 1994. For reasons that remain obscure, the G-7 finance deputies and the IMF appeared to shy away from the kind of cooperation that was a hallmark of the strategy for resolving the debt crisis of the 1980s. One stated reason was the potential for compromising the confidentiality of the dialogue among public sector authorities (debtor country government, IMF, G-7 finance officials). Another was the potential for releasing information to private parties that would create opportunities for making money. Strong rebuttals to these arguments had been advanced over the years, however.[25]

The IIF steering committee's *Summary Report* raised specific objections to three elements in the G-22 approach to PSI. One was forced bond renegotiation of the kind carried out by Pakistan at the beginning of 1999. In the clearer language of the special report issued in April: "The principal problem with the approach reportedly being suggested by the Paris Club to Pakistan . . . is that it would mandate the rescheduling of bonds rather than

---

25. Some observers speculated that personalities or politics got in the way. Others guessed that the 1980s experience was seen by officials as a model to be avoided rather than emulated. Some of the reluctance to engage in dialogue may have reflected the sensitivity of the G-7 architects to constant warnings about "bailing out" the private sector. "Bailouts" were a theme of editorials in the *Wall Street Journal* as far back as the 1970s. Carvounis (1984, p. 78) mentions that the *Wall Street Journal* at that time dubbed the U.S. legislation for participation in an IMF quota increase the "Bankers Relief Act of 1978."

leave it up to the country to decide the best way to alleviate the cash flow burden posed by bonds coming due." Three months after the Paris Club action there were still no clear statements from the Paris Club or the IMF or the G-7 architects about what Pakistan had been asked to do and why. This incident contrasted sharply with G-7 statements about the need for greater clarity about official actions in crisis cases.

A second objection related to the IMF's plan to extend its policy of lending into arrears to target bonds. The IIF acknowledged that lending into arrears would be appropriate "in those cases in which a broad spectrum of private creditors involved supports such lending to deal with rogue creditors or other exceptional impediments." Despite this clear statement, repeated in other IIF reports and statements, finance officials continued to portray the financial industry as opposed to lending into arrears under any circumstances.

The third objection was to blocking creditor litigation in the context of a suspension of payments to creditors (a standstill) imposed by a crisis country. The steering committee pointed out that "the right to litigate is a basic factor in preserving the respect for contractual obligations that underpins all cross-border flows of private finance. Further consideration of stays [of litigation] is likely to have a significant dampening effect on the willingness of private creditors to provide cross-border financing and could thereby introduce an element of disorder." Despite this argument and the absence of cases where litigation had been a problem, the G-7 and the IMF continued to give great weight to the threat of litigation.

The steering committee also adopted a slightly more positive stance on collective action clauses. Its *Summary Report* said: "When entered into freely by borrowers and lenders, collective action clauses could be useful. Mandatory approaches that treat emerging market borrowers as 'second class citizens' would create disincentives for countries committed to global standards for market access and may well inhibit new flows." Despite this statement, G-7 and IMF officials and the financial press continued to portray the industry as adamantly opposed to such clauses.[26]

---

26. A comment in the IMF Annual Report for 2001 (p. 31) provides another illustration of the communication problem: "Directors noted that financial markets *now* generally recognize that international sovereign bonds are not immune from debt restructuring" (emphasis added). The *Summary Report* of the IIF steering committee, issued two years earlier, said: "Investors and lenders recognize that Eurobonds constitute a growing proportion of the external obligations of certain emerging market economies. Consequently, it may be necessary for bond restructuring to take place in some exceptional cases."

Finally, the steering committee called attention to the lack of transparency in Paris Club operations. It suggested that "releasing the basic terms of Paris Club negotiations—in detail similar to IMF letters of intent, for example—could help official creditors achieve the goal of comparable treatment." This argument fell on fertile ground. Two years later the Paris Club took a giant leap toward transparency by opening a website.

During the eighteen months that its steering committee was active, the IIF arranged a number of meetings with G-7 and IMF officials to exchange views on both crisis prevention and crisis resolution. These included separate meetings with several G-7 finance deputies and G-7 central bank governors, as well as the managing director and first deputy managing director of the IMF. With some notable exceptions the officials appeared reluctant to attend these meetings or to engage in a collegial debate. Until August 2000 there was not a single occasion where a group of finance officials invited a multinational group of industry representatives, affiliated with the IIF or not, to join in an informal discussion of these issues. The point is that the private financial industry mounted an exceptional effort to contribute constructively to identifying and implementing measures to improve the sovereign workout process. For reasons hard to fathom, these efforts were not reciprocated.[27]

The space devoted here to the views of the financial industry presented through the IIF could leave the impression that the G-7 and the IMF were dealing with only one protagonist on the issue of PSI. In fact other views were advanced during this and other phases from several other sources. For example, the Council on Foreign Relations sponsored an independent task force chaired by Carla Hills and Peter Peterson. The task force published a report in 1999, largely written by Morris Goldstein as project director, that included seven key recommendations.[28] On PSI the task force advocated the inclusion of collective action clauses in all sovereign bond contracts and offered qualified support for IMF lending into arrears and IMF-supported payment standstills. A more influential initiative was the report issued in 2000 by the International Financial Institution Advisory Commission chaired by Alan Meltzer, which stressed the dangers of using public sector

27. One major contribution by the steering committee to improving the architecture of the international financial system that was accepted by the G-7 was pointing out the potential value of "investor relations programs" as a tool of crisis prevention. These programs involve systematic efforts by governments in countries seeking to maintain access to private sources of capital to provide material information about their policies and performance to the global investment community and to constantly monitor and respond to evolving market sentiment.

28. Council on Foreign Relations (1999).

resources to mitigate the effects of crises.[29] Other financial industry groups also weighed in, notably EMTA (formerly the Emerging Markets Traders Association) in New York and the International Primary Markets Association in London.

Phase Three: The G-7 Framework for PSI and the G-20

The ink was barely dry on the IIF's contribution to the PSI debate when the G-7 finance ministers raised the ante. In a report for the economic summit in June 1999 in Cologne, the ministers included a "Framework for PSI." Their report came out while Ukraine was groping for an acceptable PSI formula and two months before Ecuador defaulted on its Brady bonds. A few months later the G-7 architects shut down the G-22 forum and created a new one: the G-20. The IMF stepped up the pace of its work on PSI, focusing on the implementation of the G-7 framework. The IIF replaced its steering committee with a special committee.

The G-7 Framework

Ideally an agreed international framework for PSI would come out of a forum in which emerging market borrowers were represented, such as the IMF or even the G-22. Instead, the G-7 architects produced a framework that was born with the handicap of being fathered by a strictly industrial-country body. Perhaps the G-7 finance ministers calculated that broader consultations would delay policy guidance that was needed immediately or would water down the result. Or they may simply have been looking for a policy initiative to unveil at the G-7 Summit. Whatever the reasons, the G-7 finance ministers appended a "framework for private sector involvement in crisis resolution" to their report for the Cologne Summit. Three months later, they were successful in persuading the other members of the IMF's interim committee to broadly endorse the framework when it met in Prague in September. It was labeled the Cologne Framework by the G-7, and the Prague Framework by the IMF.

The Cologne framework consisted of a set of principles, considerations, and tools.[30] Five principles for PSI were put forward, and the IMF was called on to sort out any issues related to implementation. First, workouts "must not undermine the obligation of countries to meet their debts in full and on time." Second, "market discipline will work only if creditors bear the conse-

29. International Financial Institution Advisory Commission (2000).
30. Group of Seven Finance Ministers (1999, paragraphs 44–52).

quences of the risks they take." Third, reducing net debt payments in a crisis has some benefits, but these must be balanced against the impact on the crisis country's ability to attract new flows of private capital and on other countries through contagion. Fourth, "no one category of private creditors should be regarded as inherently privileged relative to others in a similar position." Moreover, "when both are material, claims of bondholders should not be viewed as senior to those of banks." Fifth, "the aim of crisis management . . . should be to achieve cooperative solutions . . . building on effective dialogues established in advance."

Four considerations were listed. The first pointed out the advantages of making clear in advance the factors that would guide action by the G-7. In particular, this transparency would "help provide a degree of predictability for investors, without sacrificing the flexibility required." The second stressed the variety of circumstances that might exist in a crisis. At the two extremes were cases amenable to "market-based, voluntary solutions" and cases "where more comprehensive approaches may be appropriate." Between these two extremes would be "a spectrum of cases." The third noted that "the feasibility of different policy approaches will depend on the nature of outstanding debt instruments." That, in turn, would have an impact on "the scope for voluntary versus more coercive solutions." The fourth called for "incentives that would encourage a country to take strong steps at the early stages of its financial difficulties."

One of the "tools" identified was the possibility of linking official support to one or more of four actions by the country and its private creditors: initiation of discussions, voluntary commitments of support, specific commitments to maintain exposure levels, or agreement on restructuring or refinancing of outstanding obligations. Another tool would impose a floor on foreign exchange reserves to ensure that the private sector would make "an adequate contribution." In exceptional cases the G-7 finance ministers noted the possibility of IMF lending into arrears or the imposition of capital or exchange controls "as part of payments suspensions or standstills, in conjunction with IMF support for [debtor country] policies and programs, to provide time for an orderly debt restructuring."

The tools section also included an intriguing reference to cases involving the restructuring of debt owed to Paris Club creditors: "The Paris Club principle of comparability of treatment applies to all categories of creditors other than the international financial institutions. The Paris Club should adopt a flexible approach to comparability, taking into account factors including the relative size and importance of different categories of claims."

In hindsight, the reference in the fourth principle to bonds looks like an attempt to signal the intention of the G-7 architects to let Ecuador default on its bonds. If so, the signal was either missed or discounted by market participants.

The G-20 Track

The decision to establish the G-20 was taken when the G-7 finance ministers met in September 1999. The first meeting of the new group was held in December 1999 in Berlin. The G-22 had turned out to be too Asia-oriented initially and too unwieldy after being expanded to include thirty-three countries. U.S. officials remained concerned that the major emerging market countries were not adequately represented on the IMF's ministerial-level Interim Committee. Therefore another forum was needed to ensure more ownership by these countries in the systemic reforms required to enhance global financial stability.[31]

One of the distinctive features of the G-20 was a work program designed to respond to growing public concerns about globalization. A second feature was an implicit commitment by its members to set and meet the highest international standards for financial policies and performance. A third was its mandate to engage the private financial community in dialogue.

The first meeting of the G-20 focused on its work program. The communiqué issued at the conclusion of the meeting noted the commitment by all members to cooperate with the IMF and World Bank in completing Reports on the Observance of Standards and Codes and Financial Sector Assessments for their countries.[32]

At their second meeting, held in October 2000 in Quebec, Canada, the G-20 adopted a statement of best practices that could help countries reduce their vulnerability to crises in four areas: exchange rate arrangements, liability (debt) management, international standards and codes, and PSI. The best practices for PSI did not go significantly beyond the views articulated in earlier IMF communiqués and reports and the work of the G-22.

The October 2000 statement also "welcomed the results of the Round-table held by our Deputies with senior members of the private financial sector in Toronto on August 25." The August 25 meeting was the first time that financial industry representatives as a group were invited by senior

31. The G-20 members are listed in chapter 3. Five countries in the original G-22 were not included in the G-20: Hong Kong, Malaysia, Poland, Singapore, and Thailand.
32. All G-20 documents are available on or from the G-20 website: www.hacienda.gob.mx/g20-2003.

finance officials to exchange views on PSI. Regrettably, the format of the meeting was not conducive to a productive discussion, and there was no meaningful follow-up.

The third meeting of the G-20 was held in November 2001 in Ottawa, Canada, squeezed into the morning of the day the IMF's ministerial-level policy-setting committee held its fall meeting (postponed by the terrorist attacks on September 11 in New York and Washington). The Ottawa meeting was understandably dominated by the international campaign to combat terrorism. A second meeting with private sector representatives in 2001 was no more fruitful than the first, and was not even mentioned in the communiqué.[33]

The IMF Track

With the wind from the G-7 framework at its back, the IMF moved ahead briskly on the PSI front.[34] The Ecuador case was tailor-made as an object lesson for bondholders. The IMF made no visible effort to encourage Ecuador to pursue a negotiated workout with its private creditors and did not hesitate to put its weight on the debtor side of the table by lending into arrears. Nor did the IMF appear to offer any resistance to the bond exchange technique that Ecuador opted to pursue.

Without mentioning Ecuador by name, the Interim Committee communiqué for the September 1999 meeting took a somewhat confrontational stance by citing "the progress achieved in securing the involvement of the private sector in individual cases."[35] The committee also endorsed the framework for PSI developed by the G-7 finance ministers. This was advertised as

33. The chairmanship of the G-20 shifted from Canada to India at the end of the Ottawa meeting, and the fourth meeting was held in New Delhi in late 2002. At the beginning of 2003, the chairmanship moved to Mexico because of a cabinet change in India, and a system of annual rotations began. The prospects for the G-20 in mid-2003 were dim. It lacked strong leadership, a solid secretariat, political support from the G-7, and an agenda—distinct from those of other forums—focused on issues of compelling interest.

34. While the IMF was working on ways to get the private sector to bear more of the workout burden, it was also taking steps to augment the resources available to help members in crisis circumstances. In addition to the quota increase that became effective in January 1999, the Supplemental Reserve Facility (SRF) was established in April 1999. The SRF was designed to top up ordinary financing from the IMF with emergency financing for a shorter duration and bearing a higher rate of interest.

35. Curiously, the communiqué for the spring 1999 meeting of the Interim Committee ignored the experiment with forced bond restructuring in the case of Pakistan at the beginning of the year. Instead, it focused on the IMF's response to the crises in Asia and subsequently in Russia and Brazil. The section of the communiqué on "Forestalling and Resolving Financial Crises" did not go significantly beyond the sentiments in its previous communiqué.

a developing country endorsement of the G-7 framework, but it looked as much like a case of the developing countries trying to avoid a fight in a period of global instability.

The executive board immediately scheduled a number of discussions to make the G-7 framework "operational." The results of the IMF's work on a "framework of principles and tools" for achieving PSI in specific cases were reflected in the communiqué for the April 2000 meeting of the Interim Committee, newly renamed the International Monetary and Financial Committee (IMFC).[36] The framework contained five controversial points:

—The IMF should be in the driver's seat at the beginning of the process (the approach should be "based on the IMF's assessment of a country's underlying payment capacity and prospects of regaining market access") and at the end ("the IMF should consider whether private sector involvement is appropriate in programs supported by the Fund"). This feature was a bit like making the IMF both the prosecutor and the jury.

—A distinction was made between three kinds of cases. In the easiest cases, a "combination of catalytic official financing and policy adjustment should allow the country to regain full market access quickly." In the somewhat more difficult cases, "emphasis should be placed on encouraging voluntary approaches . . . to overcome creditor coordination problems." By implication, some kind of deal with private creditors would have to be negotiated. In the most difficult cases: "early restoration of full market access on terms consistent with medium-term external sustainability may be judged to be unrealistic, and a broader spectrum of actions by private creditors, including comprehensive debt restructuring, may be warranted." Implicitly, the IMF would decide the category to which a country in crisis would be assigned.

—Elaborating on the most difficult cases, the communiqué stated that adjustment programs supported by the IMF should "strike an appropriate balance between the contributions of the private external creditors and the official external creditors, in light of financing provided by international financial institutions." This feature could be seen as a restatement of the classic burden-sharing principle, but implicitly the IMF would be the judge of what was appropriate.

—"No class of creditors should be considered inherently privileged." This feature was hard to argue with, but a more helpful statement might have noted that some differentiation in the treatment of different forms of credit

36. The April 2000 communiqué was the first since April 1998 without the word "architecture." The new rubric was "strengthening the IMF's role in the global economy."

(such as short-term trade lines) or classes of creditor (such as multilateral agencies) would be appropriate.

—"The international financial community should not micromanage the details of any debt restructuring or debt reduction negotiation." These words seemed designed to allay some of the concerns of market participants, but the real test of the G-7 framework would be the way the IMF acted in the next crisis.

No new crises occurred between Ecuador's default in August 1999 and the end of 2000, when balance-of-payments strains in Argentina and Turkey reached crisis levels. The IMF was, however, diverted by antiglobalization demonstrations and the appointment of a new managing director. Both had an impact on the PSI debate

A broad coalition of social activists began to mount increasingly large demonstrations against globalization at major international meetings in the late 1990s. The narrow concerns of these activists ranged from global warming to animal rights. Debt cancellation for heavily indebted countries was one of the more popular causes. The demonstrations arrived on the doorstep of the G-7 architects during the spring meetings of the IMF and World Bank in April 2000 in Washington. Demonstrations at the IMF-World Bank annual meetings in Prague the following September were even bigger and more vicious. The G-7 architects and the IMF responded to the concerns reflected in these events largely through increased transparency and public education initiatives. While the demonstrations did not result in any specific responses in the debt area, they provided political ammunition to officials inclined toward more coercive forms of PSI.

After serving as managing director of the IMF for thirteen years, Michel Camdessus stepped down in 2000. Unfortunately, the process of appointing a successor was mishandled. Germany put forward a candidate who was not acceptable to the membership and had to withdraw. After consulting more carefully with the various IMF constituencies, Germany nominated Horst Köhler. To his credit Köhler got off to a fast start at the IMF. At the annual meeting in Prague in September he outlined his vision of an IMF that would focus on "promoting international financial stability as a global public good" and "making globalization work for the benefit of all." This statement was clearly aimed at calming the antiglobalization protests directed at the IMF. In the area of PSI, Köhler's attitude toward the private financial community was a refreshing change in the direction of dialogue.

Without more crises, the work in the IMF on making the G-7 framework for PSI operational took on a somewhat academic character. The effort was also hampered by a stratospheric debate in the back rooms of G-7 finance ministries and central banks that had been papered over when the framework was adopted at the Cologne Summit in mid-1999. On one side of the debate were the Europeans (especially U.K. officials) who favored a "rules-based" approach. Their idea was to establish a clear limit on the amount of IMF financing that would be provided to a country in crisis (say, 300 percent of the member's IMF quota), which would force the country and its private creditors to find a mutually acceptable workout arrangement. The proponents of this approach were also inclined to favor IMF approval of payment standstills to protect the country from litigation by creditors while it put in place an economic adjustment program and initiated negotiations with its creditors. The United States was on the other side, favoring a "case-by-case" or "discretionary" approach to crises.[37]

In September the executive board had discussed a staff paper on standstills without reaching any firm conclusions.[38] The communiqué issued at the close of the IMFC meeting at the end of September included nothing new on PSI. At the end of 2000, when the difficulties of Argentina and Turkey reached crisis proportions, work on making PSI operational picked up steam. The executive board discussed a staff paper on "Involving the Private Sector in the Resolution of Financial Crises—Restructuring International Sovereign Bonds" in January 2001.[39] The paper analyzed the bond restructuring by Ecuador, Pakistan, and Ukraine in 1999 and assessed the principles for debtor-creditor negotiations developed by the Council on Foreign Relations's Roundtable on Country Risk.[40] The board concluded that the experience with bond restructuring was too limited to draw clear lessons. At the same time the directors took note of the concerns among private investors about these cases and stressed the importance for debtor countries of engaging in constructive dialogues with their creditors. The communiqué for the April 2001 meeting took a tougher line, signaling that high levels of access to IMF resources "must presume substantial justification," implying visible PSI. It went on to note that "there may be cases requiring more concerted approaches," implying approaches where private

37. A veiled reference to this controversy was included in the summing up of the September 2000 executive board discussion of standstills. Another appeared in the IMF's annual report for 2001: "Differences remained on the question of a formal link between the level of access to IMF resources and concerted private sector involvement." A good dissection of the debate at this point can be found in Eichengreen (2000b).

38. IMF (2000).

39. IMF (2001a).

40. Council on Foreign Relations (2000).

creditors would be compelled to conclude refinancing or restructuring arrangements with crisis countries.

Intriguingly, the April 2001 communiqué also encouraged progress on practical issues such as "the comparability of treatment between official and private creditors." The staff responded by producing a paper on the Paris Club's approach to comparable treatment that was considered by the executive board in the summer. The paper provided a remarkably frank examination of the subject, but the board discussion was inconclusive.[41] The paper pointed toward a number of possible improvements in Paris Club procedures, but the G-7 architects clearly preferred not to delegate responsibility to the IMF for reforming the Paris Club.

The Financial Industry's Response

The period from mid-1999 to the end of 2000 saw no new initiatives by the IIF on PSI for several reasons. There was a certain amount of burnout from the steering committee exercise. In the spring of 2000 Camdessus's departure from the IMF and the arrival of a new managing director offered the prospect of a different approach to PSI. The election campaign in the United States in 2000 discouraged new initiatives by the G-7. Most important, no major new crises occurred.

Following the U.S. election in November, and with concerns about Argentina and Turkey intensifying, the IIF announced in January 2001 the formation of a high-level Special Committee on Crisis Prevention and Resolution in Emerging Markets, cochaired by William Rhodes and Josef Ackermann. Its purpose was to "guide the Institute's work on operationalizing crisis prevention and bridging the gap between public and private sector views on crisis resolution."[42] Two working groups of the committee were organized, one focusing on crisis prevention and the other on crisis resolution.

At the same time, the IIF issued a set of "Principles for Private Sector Involvement in Crisis Prevention and Resolution" to serve as a foundation for the work of the special committee.[43] Because the industry position on "bailouts" was still being misrepresented, the first paragraph of the principles included the statement, underlined, that: "private investors and creditors expect to bear the consequences of their decisions and do not seek to be 'bailed out' by the official sector." This position was amplified under the last principle: "No category of private credit should be exempted a priori from

41. IMF (2001b).
42. From the IIF's annual report for 2001.
43. Available on the IIF website: www.iif.com.

restructuring. Where bond obligations form a considerable portion of total debt, market participants should expect that these obligations will be restructured."

Consistent with IIF's long-standing position, the first four principles emphasized crisis prevention. The next two principles, under the heading "Responding to Signs of Eroding Market Confidence," stressed the benefits of prompt and bold action by emerging market countries when investor sentiment appeared to be weakening and of initiating intensive consultations with key investors and creditors if strains worsened.

The last three principles were presented under the heading "More Difficult Situations." These principles called for continuing to follow "country-centered approaches," tailoring official support to each country's circumstances, and relying on cooperative approaches to restructuring debt owed to private creditors. The IIF special committee highlighted the scope for voluntary arrangements with banks to maintain credit lines as well as other steps that could help to diminish reliance on official financing in country workouts.[44] The necessity for countries to impose payment standstills in extreme cases was recognized, but the committee warned that actions by the IMF or other official bodies to impose or endorse standstills could have adverse consequences for emerging market financing in general. Some suggestions were offered for ensuring that official financing would help to unlock the private flows that countries would need to repay the official agencies. Guidelines were proposed for cases where comprehensive debt restructuring or reduction was unavoidable.

The main differences between the IIF approach to PSI and the G-7–IMF approach were in four areas:

—The G-7–IMF framework appeared to depend critically on inherently arbitrary judgments by the IMF or other official bodies. The IIF advocated a "country-centered" workout process that put the debtor country in the driver's seat for the purpose of assessing the trade-offs between alternative forms of PSI.

—The G-7–IMF framework seemed prone to moving quickly into the comprehensive workout mode. The IIF approach stressed the possibilities for constructive involvement by private investors and creditors as a way of avoiding recourse to comprehensive workouts.

—The G-7–IMF framework was biased against exceptional commitments of official financing. From the IIF perspective, this bias would shift to private

44. This could be seen as a harbinger of the action taken by banks to help Brazil in August 2002.

creditors some of the burden of support that the public sector could reasonably be expected to shoulder.

—The G-7–IMF framework seemed to bring external politics into decisions on the timing and form of a standstill on payments. The IIF opposed the formal or informal approval of standstills by the IMF and objected to IMF lending into arrears, unless such action was broadly supported by the private creditors involved.

The IIF position on the role of the London Club changed at this stage, reflecting an intense debate within the financial industry. On one side were proponents of unilateral bond exchanges, such as Ecuador's exchange in 1999. On the other side were proponents of an "enhanced" London Club that would include bondholder representatives, along the lines of Russia's successful negotiations in 1999 to restructure and reduce its Soviet-era commercial debt. The IIF principles statement took a distinctly more positive position on creditor groups: "Recent experience demonstrates that the London Club process need not be restricted to commercial banks but can be adapted to a broader group of creditors."

Following the publication of the principles and the formation of the special committee, the IIF organized several meetings with finance officials in an effort to build support for a pragmatic middle ground. Among these was the first publicized meeting of the Paris Club with representatives from the private sector, in April 2001.[45] The Paris Club unveiled its new website on this occasion and presented an analysis of comparable treatment in the cases of Ecuador and Pakistan.

Other Responses

Among the numerous proposals for improving the machinery for sovereign debt workouts that appeared during this phase, the following five illustrate the range of ideas.

University of Cambridge professor Willem Buiter and University of London professor Ann Sibert suggested a simple device to achieve PSI: the inclusion in foreign currency contracts of an option to extend maturing debt for ninety days (for example) with a penalty in the form of a higher spread. They called this Universal Debt Rollover with a Penalty (UDROP)

---

45. The private sector participants included representatives of firms affiliated with EMTA (formerly the Emerging Markets Traders Association), EMCA (Emerging Markets Creditors Association), and IPMA (International Primary Markets Association) as well as the IIF. EMCA's participation was significant because it had only recently been formed as an association to represent the "buy side" of the market for emerging market bonds.

and suggested that UDROP clauses be mandated through legislation in each borrowing country.[46]

Princeton University professor Peter Kenen, in an assessment of the architecture debate in mid-2001, characterized the G-7 approach as "deeply flawed, because it relies much too heavily on voluntary cooperation by the private sector."[47] He recommended an approach centered on "prequalification" by countries for large-scale official financing in the event of a payments crisis. Among the conditions for prequalification would be the inclusion of collective action clauses in sovereign bonds issued by the country and "ninety-day rollover options in all foreign currency obligations, public and private."[48]

Following up on its earlier task force, the Council on Foreign Relations sponsored a Roundtable on Country Risk in the Post–Asian Crisis Era.[49] A Sovereign Debt Restructuring Working Group formulated a set of eight principles for restructuring bonds. These addressed, among other topics, the role of professional advisors, the organization of creditor committees at the initiative of creditors, coordination with the Paris Club, and collective action clauses.

Rory Macmillan laid out a compelling legal case against a formal bankruptcy mechanism and offered an alternative designed to facilitate a negotiated restructuring.[50] This alternative involved the formation of strong bondholder councils, reinforced by several changes in U.S. legislation that would strengthen their position vis-à-vis both the debtor country and dissident bondholders.

Bartholomew, Stern, and Liuzzi at J. P. Morgan suggested a way of aggregating a diverse set of bonds to facilitate restructuring through a two-step process.[51] In the first step bonds would be exchanged at different discounts or premiums into a homogeneous class of claims. In the second step this class of claims would be exchanged for new bonds at whatever discount was required to achieved debt sustainability.

---

46. Buiter and Sibert (1999). The UDROP concept can be seen as a reincarnation of the "bisque clause" advocated by UNCTAD and the G-77 in the 1970s as part of the machinery they proposed for sovereign workouts.

47. Kenen (2001, p. 138).

48. Kenen (2001, p. 154). Kenen (2002) elaborates on this proposal.

49. The roundtable was chaired by Robert Hormats and Roger Kubarych and directed by Albert Fishlow and Barbara Samuels.

50. Macmillan (1995).

51. Bartholomew, Stern, and Liuzzi (2002).

September 11 and the Fight against Terrorism

Other activities to operationalize PSI scheduled in the fall of 2001 by the IMF and the IIF were interrupted by the terrorist attacks in New York and Washington on September 11. The annual meetings of the IMF and World Bank, scheduled for the end of September, were put off to mid-November. The communiqué from the delayed IMFC meeting was one of the shortest for many years and made only passing references to PSI.

Shortly before the IMF meeting, the IIF's Special Committee on Crisis Prevention and Resolution in Emerging Markets issued a policy statement setting forth an "integrated approach to developing proposals for action." The newest wrinkle in this statement was the idea that a "sounding board," composed of experienced industry executives, could be helpful to governments in crisis countries and the IMF "to review the intellectual foundations for the IMF's assessment of the balance of payments, to enhance the understanding of potential financing possibilities, and to exchange views on market conditions." The committee also called for "trilateral consultations" by the Paris Club with the IMF and the private financial community before adopting a particular rescheduling approach. Finally the committee noted that it was "seeking ways to strengthen the debt-restructuring process traditionally carried out within the London Club by involving a group of private creditors that reflects the larger diversity of creditors today."[52]

At the same time, a thoughtful paper on PSI was circulated by a senior economist at the Bank of England and his counterpart at the Bank of Canada.[53] This was an attempt to find middle ground between the rules-based approach and the case-by-case approach by articulating a set of principles spelling out the "respective roles and responsibilities of the public and private sectors." These included a presumption about the scale of official financing and a range of tools for achieving PSI, including a relatively benign form of standstill.

The Bank of England–Bank of Canada framework was soon overshadowed by a much bolder proposal. Nine days after the November IMF-World Bank meetings, Anne Krueger, IMF first deputy managing director, dropped a bombshell: a piece of new machinery for sovereign workouts soon to be called the Sovereign Debt Restructuring Mechanism, or SDRM.

---

52. IIF, "Policy Statement of the Special Committee on Crisis Prevention and Resolution in Emerging Markets, November 7, 2001." Available at www.iif.com/press/pressrelease.quagga?id=28 (August 29, 2002).

53. Haldane and Kruger (2001).

Phase Four: The IMF and the Sovereign
Debt Restructuring Mechanism

Krueger succeeded Stanley Fischer as first deputy managing director at the beginning of September 2001. Nothing at the time suggested that she would dramatically rekindle and sharpen the workout debate.

Krueger's appointment was momentous because the position had become enormously influential under Fischer.[54] Krueger's arrival coincided with two immense challenges for the IMF. One was reorienting the IMF to support the G-7 effort to shut down international sources of financing for terrorism in the aftermath of the September 11 attacks on New York and Washington. The other was managing the looming crisis in Argentina.

Given these priorities and the more pressing business of crisis prevention, it is surprising that Krueger chose to unveil a radical proposal for PSI when she did. Anecdotal evidence suggests that she took a comment by U.S. Treasury secretary Paul H. O'Neill in a congressional hearing as evidence that the U.S. government would support such a move. It must also be assumed that she found sufficient support within the IMF to proceed, including from IMF managing director Köhler.

The IMF–G-7 Track

Krueger's proposal to create permanent machinery for sovereign workouts was contained in a speech presented at the annual members' dinner of the National Economists' Club on November 26 in Washington.[55] She began by identifying a "gaping hole" in the architecture of the international financial system: "we lack incentives to help countries with unsustainable debts resolve them promptly and in an orderly way. At present the only available mechanism requires the international community to bail out the private creditors."

To fill this gap she proposed a framework that would offer a debtor country "legal protection from creditors that stand in the way of a necessary restructuring." Her explicit model was a domestic bankruptcy court.[56] After

54. Since the beginning in the 1940s, the IMF's managing director was a European national and the World Bank's president was a U.S. national. To balance these appointments, the deputy managing director in the IMF was an American and Europeans held top positions at the World Bank. Two subordinate deputy managing director positions were created in 1994 in response to the IMF's increased workload related to the transition in Eastern Europe and the former Soviet Union, and to the poorest countries that were mostly in Africa.

55. All quotations are from speeches and documents found on the IMF website: www.imf.org.

56. She cautioned that it would take some time to establish such a framework, and therefore it could not apply to current crises such as those of Argentina and Turkey.

touching on steps the IMF was taking to help prevent crises, she elaborated on the current obstacles to achieving orderly workouts. She contrasted the tidier world of the 1980s, in which commercial bank debt was restructured through a "protracted but generally orderly process," with the world at the turn of the century, when private creditors were "increasingly numerous, anonymous, and difficult to coordinate." She noted that fears of litigation in the recent bond-restructuring deals for Pakistan, Ukraine, and Ecuador were not realized but suggested that a suit recently pursued successfully against Peru by a holdout creditor could be a sign of more serious litigation problems in future cases.[57]

Krueger cited the IMF's policies on supporting temporary standstills and lending into arrears as useful tools in cases where voluntary restructuring by private creditors was not forthcoming, but she argued that the current approach "does not provide an adequate incentive for debtors and creditors to reach agreement of their own accord." The solution she offered was "a formal mechanism for sovereign debt restructuring [that] would allow a country to come to the Fund and request a temporary standstill on the repayment of its debts" and be protected from possible legal complications. She spelled out four key features of the proposed mechanism: it would prevent creditors from "disrupting negotiations" by taking the country to court; it would provide creditors with "some guarantee that the debtor country would act responsibly during the course of any standstill"; it would offer providers of new money senior status over old claims; and it would "bind minority creditors to a restructuring . . . agreed to by a large enough majority."

Addressing six practical questions raised by her proposal, Krueger declared that the IMF would be the proper place to "reach a judgment on the sustainability of a country's debt" and the policies it is pursuing to avoid future problems. Some other body, however, would be needed to "adjudicate disputes among creditors and between the creditors and the debtor . . . to verify creditor claims and confirm the integrity of voting on a potential restructuring." The body, subsequently labeled the "dispute resolution forum," would be activated when the IMF acted on a request from the debtor country.

To ensure satisfactory performance by the debtor country, the IMF would endorse a standstill only for a limited time. IMF financing in such cases

57. The suit was initiated by Elliott Associates, a U.S.-based hedge fund, and related to pre-Brady Peruvian debt owed to commercial banks. Faced with a judgment in favor of Elliott and an attachment order directed at interest about to be paid on its Brady Bonds, Peru paid off Elliott in June 2000.

would be limited to amounts necessary "to help rebuild reserves and pay for essential services and imports." The scope of the mechanism might have to extend to debt owed by the government to domestic residents and to debt owed by domestic companies to foreign creditors. The mere existence of the mechanism, she suggested, could induce creditors to reach agreement with the debtor country without having recourse to the mechanism. To have a firm legal basis, she mentioned that "the mechanism must have the force of law universally."

Krueger concluded by noting the potential benefits for debtors and creditors. For debtors, she stressed reducing the cost of restructuring. For creditors, she suggested that "the guarantee of an orderly restructuring is much to be preferred to the threat of a disorderly one."

Contrary to convention, the Krueger initiative was announced before the IMF executive board had a chance to consider it. The board quickly scheduled a discussion of the proposal, and it began changing shape in response to various political forces.[58] By the end of January it had acquired a formal IMF label: the Sovereign Debt Restructuring Mechanism. Krueger also undertook a remarkable public relations campaign to promote the proposal. Early speeches in New Delhi and Melbourne fleshed out the proposal. Later speeches in Washington and São Paolo responded to criticisms.

Despite the interest shown by Treasury Secretary O'Neill in some kind of international bankruptcy mechanism, an alternative approach, which can be viewed as a high-octane version of the approach recommended in the G-10 report in 1996 on sovereign liquidity crises, was advanced by the Treasury Department early in 2002. In testimony before a congressional committee in February, Under Secretary John Taylor described the problem as follows: "when countries get close to a situation where debt is unsustainable, it is like approaching a black hole; no one knows exactly what will happen next." He went on to observe that "a more predictable sovereign debt restructuring mechanism—a workout strategy—for countries that reach an unsustainable position would therefore be useful." The most practical and promising proposal, he suggested, was a decentralized approach that would create

58. The summary of the executive board's first discussion narrowly focused on PSI, in March 1999, noted that "Directors agreed that there is no silver bullet to ensure that private creditors will participate fully in the resolution of financial crises and that improvements in this area are likely to be evolutionary rather than revolutionary." Krueger's SDRM proposal rolled out two and a half years later clearly fell in the revolutionary category, and the subsequent modifications were apparently insufficient to move it into the evolutionary category.

"debtor and creditor ownership of, and participation in, the process." He noted the IMF's proposal without commenting on it.[59]

Two months later, at a conference organized by the Institute for International Economics in Washington, Krueger and Taylor delivered speeches on consecutive days elaborating on their views. Krueger summarized the arguments in favor of the SDRM. Taylor outlined the three elements of a "workable, decentralized, market-oriented approach to reform." These were a package of new collective action clauses, guidelines for borrowers and lenders as they decided on the detailed terms of these clauses, and incentives to encourage countries to adopt them.

IMF staff work on the SDRM proposal reached a fever pitch as the April 2002 meetings of the IMF and World Bank approached, yielding a revised version of the proposal quickly dubbed "SDRM-light." This version was presented in a forty-page pamphlet issued in April under Krueger's name entitled "A New Approach to Sovereign Debt Restructuring."[60]

The modified version of the SDRM addressed two concerns in particular. It stepped back from the notion that domestic bankruptcy procedures were a good model, and it sought to recast the mechanism as creditor-centered rather than IMF-centered. Two controversial features of the proposal remained, however, and one was reinforced. First Krueger reiterated that to be effective the mechanism would have to be formalized by means of an international treaty, or more simply an amendment of the IMF's Articles of Agreement. Second she began to spell out the role to be played by a "dispute resolution forum" in administering creditor claims and resolving disputes (among creditors and between creditors and the debtor) relating to the verification of claims and the voting process.

In its inimitable fashion, the IMF created labels for the alternative approaches: Taylor's was dubbed the "contractual approach," and Krueger's became the "statutory approach." In addressing the issue of crisis resolution at its late-April 2002 meeting, the IMFC directed the IMF to pursue both approaches. In the words of its communiqué:

> The Committee welcomes the consideration of innovative proposals to improve the process of sovereign debt restructuring to help close a gap in the current framework. It encourages the Fund to examine the legal, institutional, and procedural aspects of two approaches, which

59. The text can be found on the U.S. Treasury website at www.treas.gov/press/releases/po1016.htm.
60. Krueger (2002).

could be complementary and self-reinforcing: a statutory approach . . . and an approach, . . . which would incorporate comprehensive restructuring clauses in debt instruments.

Follow-up on the contractual approach centered in a G-10 working group, chaired by a senior U.S. Treasury official, which was directed to produce the desired clauses by the time of the annual meetings of the IMF and World Bank in September. In June the IMF staff produced two detailed papers on collective action clauses, one on encouraging greater use of them and the other on their design and effectiveness.[61] The staff also produced another paper on the SDRM, focusing on the scope of sovereign debt that might be treated and on the powers and composition of the dispute resolution forum.[62]

Measured by the communiqué issued by the IMFC at its September 2002 meeting, neither side was able to solve the weaknesses inherent in its approach or to make a compelling case for choosing one over the other: "The Committee strongly welcomes the progress made with the contractual and statutory approaches to restructuring unsustainable sovereign debts," the communiqué said. Nevertheless the SDRM seemed to have the upper hand. The committee directed the IMF "to develop, for consideration at its next meeting, a concrete proposal for a statutory sovereign debt restructuring mechanism. . . ."

At the end of 2002 the IMF staff produced a lengthy paper containing "recommended design features" of the SDRM, together with eleven "principles guiding the design of the mechanism."[63] The summing up of the executive board's discussion of this paper highlighted numerous areas of agreement, but also noted that "on some important aspects of the mechanism Directors insisted that, at this stage, all options under consideration should remain on the table." On January 22, 2003, the IMF held a conference and public forum designed to address concerns about the SDRM and rally support for it. The mood of the SDRM advocates at the conference was subdued, however.[64] A new U.S. Treasury secretary was waiting to be confirmed,

61. IMF (2002b, 2002c). A third paper was sent to the executive board in March 2003 (IMF 2003c).
62. IMF (2002f).
63. IMF (2002d).
64. U.S. Treasury assistant secretary Randal Quarles pointed out on this occasion that the pressure to create a corporate bankruptcy regime in the United States came from creditors who were dissatisfied with the procedures for dealing with defaulted railroad bonds in the late 1800s, not from the debtors or from public sector institutions.

and the U.S. government was preoccupied with Iraq and domestic budget issues. Support for the SDRM seemed to be fading. Other factors contributing to the sentiment were the strong and persistent opposition of the financial industry, the progress the industry was making in drafting model collective action clauses, and positive developments in Argentina and Brazil. In addition, a proposal by French central bank governor Jean-Claude Trichet to find common ground in a code of good conduct seemed to be attracting growing interest.

A revised staff paper on the features of the SDRM was issued in February and discussed by the executive board in March.[65] Finally, on the eve of the April 2003 IMF meeting, IMF managing director Köhler delivered a report to the IMFC on the SDRM, attaching a statement noting the features on which there was a broad consensus and highlighting two features where differences remained.[66]

At the April meeting of the IMFC, the newly appointed U.S. Treasury secretary, John Snow, brought the eighteen-month debate over a statutory approach versus a contractual approach to a halt by announcing that "it is neither necessary nor feasible to continue working on the SDRM."[67] Snow cited opposition from financial markets and emerging market issuers as reasons for putting the SDRM proposal on the back burner.

Academic and other experts will now begin to explore this curious chapter in the IMF's history. What prompted the IMF to propose the SDRM in 2001? Why was the proposal moved to a back burner in 2003? From the perspective of this study, the IMF initiative reflected an inherent tendency by the IMF to discount the political factors contributing to most crises and shaping the recovery process. The SDRM seemed designed for a world in which technicians decide issues such as the amount of debt that is "sustainable" for a given country.

65. IMF (2003c). A staff paper on broader policy aspects of sovereign debt restructuring was issued in January and discussed by the board in February; see IMF (2003b).

66. IMF (2003d).

67. The IMFC communiqué issued later the same day put a positive spin on the matter: "The Committee, while recognizing that it is not feasible now to move forward to establish the SDRM, agrees that work should continue on issues raised in its development that are of general relevance to the orderly resolution of financial crises. These issues include inter-creditor equity considerations, enhancing transparency, and aggregation issues." The new U.S. stance can be seen as a return to the long-standing U.S. aversion to creating new mechanisms and a rejection of the surprising support for the SDRM concept provided by Snow's predecessor, Paul O'Neill. Snow's position can also be seen as much easier to reconcile with the broad foreign policy objectives of the Bush administration as it was basking in the success of its military action in Iraq.

The Financial Industry Response

The Krueger proposal precipitated a monsoon of commentary from supporters and opponents, reinforced by Argentina's historic default on December 20.[68] The IIF responded in early December with a letter from its managing director to IMF's Köhler expressing several concerns about the proposal and reiterating the financial industry's preference for market-based mechanisms to address sovereign debt problems. Dialogue and collaboration with the IMF was proposed to encourage more active use of collective action clauses and to develop cooperative legal strategies to limit the ability of rogue creditors to disrupt a workout.[69]

At its April 2002 membership meeting in New York immediately following the IMF-World Bank meetings in Washington, the IIF put forward an alternative to the statutory and contractual approaches being pursued by the G-7 deputies and the IMF. This alternative was spelled out in considerable detail in an action plan developed by the IIF's Special Committee on Crisis Prevention and Resolution in Emerging Markets.[70] Sharing the skepticism of most G-7 finance officials that an approach focused narrowly on collective action clauses would be sufficient, and stressing the adverse impact of the SDRM approach on investor sentiment toward emerging markets, the special committee proposed a collaborative effort by finance officials and the financial industry to frame an international code of conduct to be applied on a case-by-case basis. As a step toward the adoption of such a code, the action plan sketched out a three-pronged approach consisting of a new consultative process, a range of market incentives to encourage broader use of collective action clauses, and a legal strategy to prevent vulture funds from disrupting good-faith negotiations. The new consultative process involved the creation of a Private Sector Advisory Group composed of "a small group of senior executives representing a broad spectrum of private sector investors and creditors, including bondholders" to consult with individual countries "when investor confidence begins to wane." This group would give way to a

68. In a private conversation in December 2002, a rating agency analyst said the impact of the SDRM proposal on spreads paid by emerging market borrowers was significant and labeled it "Anne Krueger risk." The terms "PSI risk" and "burden-sharing risk" were also used by market participants in the 1999–2003 period to describe this new element of the country risk premium associated with emerging market debt. A sharp and early legal critique of the SDRM proposal can be found in Gianni (2002).

69. James Smalhout captured well the range of early reactions in his article "Critics Attack IMF's Standstill Proposal," in the January 2001 issue of *Euromoney* (pp. 110–11).

70. IIF (2002).

group of interested creditors for the purpose of negotiating debt-restructuring arrangements, if this step could not be avoided.

After taking stock of the statements emanating from the April IMF and World Bank meetings, the financial industry began to accelerate the pace of work on a set of collective action clauses that would be broadly acceptable to market participants. Six separate industry associations joined in this initiative, which was announced at the beginning of June in a joint letter to the G-7 finance ministers and central bank governors.[71] The work on collective action clauses continued at a steady pace through the remainder of 2002. The objective was to draft model clauses addressing four issues: amending or waiving key terms with the approval of a supermajority of bondholders (majority action), appointing a committee to represent bondholders in restructuring discussions with the sovereign issuer (engagement), accelerating principal after an event of default or rescinding acceleration (initiation), and committing the sovereign issuer to disclose data publicly and to provide bondholders with forecasts and relevant information about relations with other creditors such as the Paris Club (transparency).

At the time of the IMF-World Bank annual meetings (and the IIF annual meeting) at the end of September, a meeting took place between representatives of the six industry groups, officials from several issuing countries, and G-7 officials. The private sector participants on this occasion took the position that the IMF's continuing work on the SDRM would make it impossible to reach agreement on a set of marketable bond clauses, and they urged the officials to suspend work on the SDRM. By the end of 2002 there appeared to be a remarkable degree of solidarity within the financial industry on how to improve the machinery for sovereign debt workouts.[72]

71. The six were the Emerging Markets Creditors Association, EMTA, the Securities Industry Association, the Bond Market Association—all based in New York, the Institute of International Finance based in Washington, and the International Primary Market Association based in London. See IIF press release on June 11, 2002. Available at www.iif.com/press/pressrelease.quagga?id=49 (August 4, 2002).

72. During 2002 there was considerable kibitzing on the statutory and contractual approaches to PSI by academics, officials, and market participants, but few distinctly new approaches were proposed. One proposal that appeared at the beginning of 2002 came from a group of poverty-oriented NGOs based in Europe, building on a proposal advanced by University of Vienna professor Kunibert Raffer (Raffer 1990). Described as an effort to "internationalize chapter 9 of the U.S. Bankruptcy Code" in the form of a "fair and transparent arbitration process" or "Independent Debt Commission," the NGO proposal featured an arbitration panel similar in a number of respects to the "dispute resolution forum" that was part of the SDRM. It was also evocative of UNCTAD's International Debt Commission proposal in the 1970s. The NGO proposal is available at www.erlassjahr.de/15_pub-likationen/15_ftap_englisch.htm (August 29, 2002). Another proposal, from a prominent international lawyer, involved the establishment of a "sovereign debt forum." (Gitlin 2002).

Summing Up

Phase four of the PSI debate drew to a close when the U.S. government made clear its opposition to the SDRM at the IMFC meeting in mid-April 2003. The introduction of collective action clauses in new bonds issued by Mexico on the eve of this meeting provided a practical basis for moving forward with the contractual approach.[73] Perhaps more important, the election of a new president in Argentina held out the prospect of serious negotiations by mid-2003 to restructure that country's defaulted debt. The success or failure of this workout was likely to have more of an impact on the shape of workout machinery in the future than any further debate among the G-7 architects about alternative approaches to PSI.

73. Bulgaria and Egypt issued bonds under New York law in 2002 with collective clauses, but these were largely ignored in the policy debate.

12

What Is Broken? What Fixes Make Sense?

Financial crises in emerging market countries impose terrible costs on innocent citizens. These crises occur primarily as a result of failures by the governments of these countries. To some extent, however, they represent a failure of the global economic system that has brought impressive increases in standards of living to people throughout the world over the past sixty years.

The G-7 finance ministers and central bank governors have accepted responsibility for managing the global system. During the 1994–2002 period they gave a high priority to improving the architecture of the system to prevent crisis and to reduce the costs associated with those that occur despite their efforts.

In the area of crisis prevention, the G-7 architects cast their net widely and identified many useful steps that could be taken. Already by 2000 numerous international agencies and bodies were engaged in the process of implementing tangible improvements. Crisis prevention is unglamorous work, but much remains to be done and it deserves the highest priority. The benefits of avoiding a crisis are large and extend well beyond the crisis country.

In the area of crisis resolution, an inherently narrower one, the G-7 architects set out to adapt the machinery for sovereign debt workouts to a world in which private flows of capital to developing countries dwarf official flows and where bonds represent a major component of the private flows. After six years of labor, they had little to show for their efforts. It was not even clear whether they were trying to produce a mouse or an elephant. To give the impression of progress, they directed their draftsmen to work on designs for both a contractual approach (the mouse) and a statutory approach (the elephant).

Private investors and lenders, the target of the G-7 exercise, raised strong objections to a number of principles, proposals, and actions for crisis resolution endorsed by the G-7. Led by the Institute of International Finance, the financial industry produced a series of reports and statements outlining alternative "market-based" approaches. In addition, a remarkable coalition of six financial industry associations, formed in mid-2002, issued a sharp critique of the statutory approach and began to draft a set of model clauses for bonds designed to strengthen investor protections as well as facilitate future workouts. At the beginning of 2003 there were signs that the debate was moving out of a polemical phase into a more collaborative one. By mid-April, reflecting a shift in policy by the U.S. government, the statutory approach was set aside in favor of the gradualist and market-friendly contractual approach.

The thesis of this chapter is consistent with the policy drift in mid-2003. Specifically, the chapter argues that broadly satisfactory workouts in the future can be achieved with a package of incremental improvements in the existing ad hoc machinery and the same spirit of public sector–private sector collaboration that helped in managing the 1980s debt crisis.[1]

The workout machinery in place at the beginning of 2003 had two deficiencies. The more visible deficiency was the absence of a clear procedure for consensual restructuring of bond debt. The policy choice, in its crudest form, was between a formal process (permanent machinery) imposed by the G-7 architects and an ad hoc process that would evolve organically from a series of workout experiences, as the London Club process did in the late 1970s. This chapter concludes that the ad hoc approach is likely to yield viable bond workouts with fewer systemic risks.

---

1. The work undertaken since 1996 by the Basel Committee on Banking Supervision to update the regulatory capital standards for banks suggests that fruitful cooperation between finance officials and the financial industry remains possible.

The less visible deficiency was the Paris Club's approach to burden sharing (private sector involvement) in cases where a substantial amount of the debtor country's external debt is owed to private creditors. Although the comparable-treatment principle worked reasonably well for more than thirty years, two modifications would contribute to better burden sharing in the future. One is to add to the Paris Club toolkit three forms of debt restructuring that have been used for decades by private creditors but have been rejected until now by the Paris Club: new money, stock treatment, and debt reduction. The second modification is to adopt a more forward-looking technique for determining whether or not the burden sharing by private creditors in a particular case is adequate.

More generally, the approach to sovereign debt workouts recommended here is a tools-based approach. The G-7 architects appear to be handicapped by the limited number of policy tools available for use in specific debt crises. With more tools they could help countries initiate workouts at an earlier stage, and they could more easily tailor the public sector component of workouts to the circumstances of each case.

The Problem with Bonds

There is nothing new about defaults on sovereign bonds and nothing new about restructuring them. The four waves of sovereign bonds defaults and workouts between 1820 and 1940 were recalled in chapter 10. Many officials seem to believe that bonds were exempted from restructuring in the workouts of the 1980s, contrary to the facts. In the case of Costa Rica, for example, bonds held by banks were included in an initial "European-African-style" restructuring on the same terms as bank loans.[2] It is true that bonds were given preferential treatment in a number of workouts. In each of these cases, however, the outstanding volume was small and the interest burden was not significant. The restructuring banks decided to exclude bond debt from these workouts for a variety of strategic, administrative, and regulatory reasons.

The situation changed in the 1990s. From 1990 through 2001, cumulative net flows of nonbank lending (mostly bonds) to the major emerging market countries were more than $500 billion, while cumulative bank lending was around $260 billion.[3] After the Asian crises in 1997 net commercial

2. Costa Rica subsequently carried out a bond exchange to ensure across-the-board burden sharing; Clark (1986, p. 861). The treatment of bonds in Poland's 1981 restructuring is described in appendix B.

3. From the regular reports of the IIF on *Capital Flows to Emerging Market Economies*.

bank flows turned negative, leaving bond investors increasingly vulnerable to restructuring in sovereign debt workouts. The relatively favorable treatment enjoyed by bondholders during the preceding forty years could not continue. The question was when and how it would end. Under increasing pressure to avoid actions that might be perceived as protecting private investors and lenders from losses at taxpayer expense, the G-7 drew a line in the sand at the beginning of 1999. When severe balance-of-payments strains developed in Pakistan, Ukraine, and Ecuador, official support for their recovery programs was conditioned on restructuring bond debt to obtain PSI from bondholders. Although senior finance officials gave verbal signals that bond debt would have to be restructured, market participants were shocked. The shock was not about the principle of restructuring bonds, however, but about restructuring when it was not obviously necessary, or with countries that were pursuing weak reform programs, or without negotiations to find mutually agreeable terms.

Bond Restructuring by Pakistan, Ukraine, and Ecuador

An obvious difficulty for the G-7 in applying PSI to bonds in Pakistan, Ukraine, and Ecuador was the absence of a familiar procedure for a consensual restructuring. No experts were still active (or alive) who had participated in the restructurings of the 1920s and 1930s. The institutions (bondholder committees) created to facilitate these arrangements no longer existed.

Compelled to restructure without an obvious roadmap, these three "guinea pig" countries opted to use a seductively simple device: the unilateral exchange offer. Given the abundant financial engineering skills in the world of investment banking, structuring a successful exchange was a relatively straightforward process. This technique had two attractions to the G-7 and IMF from a PSI perspective. One was giving the job to the private sector. If the bondholders disliked the exchange, then the investment bankers who structured the deal could be blamed for the result. The other attraction was being able to claim that the deals were market based and voluntary.

Unfortunately, the medium-term impact of these deals seemed to be a secondary consideration. The primary purpose was to solve the short-term cash flow problem faced by each country. Unlike most Brady era restructurings, the creditworthiness of the three countries did not improve after the exchanges were completed. That may simply have been a consequence of the weak adjustment programs they adopted, and even weaker implementation, but the repayment terms were relatively heavy. All three deals were poorly received by market participants in general. Asset managers in particular were dissatisfied with the lack of negotiations.

The object lesson administered by the G-7 through the IMF and the Paris Club prompted several attempts to develop alternatives to unilateral bond exchanges. One was opening up Bank Advisory Committees to bondholders. The negotiation with Russia on debt owed to commercial banks by the former Soviet Union was perhaps the first effort to include bondholder representatives on a negotiating committee, although it was not entirely successful. More recently, advisory committees for negotiations with several African countries have included bondholder representatives.[4] Another attempt was the organization of the Emerging Markets Creditors Association to represent the "buy side" of the private sector.[5] Proposals were made to activate the Foreign Bondholders Protective Council in the United States and its counterpart in the United Kingdom, but there was insufficient support for this step.

Restructuring Bonds versus Restructuring Bank Loans

Why is restructuring bond debt so much more difficult than restructuring bank debt? The first answer is that the ease of restructuring bank debt is more myth than reality. The process used frequently in the 1980s and 1990s was not easy from the perspective of the debtor countries. It diverted the attention of policymakers from implementing essential reforms, it resulted in deals that never seemed generous enough to voters, and it was more expensive than the Paris Club process. Nor was it easy from the creditor perspective of the G-7. Considerable arm-twisting and cajoling was required to bridge the gap between offers from the banks and requests from the debtor countries.

Still, bonds are more difficult to restructure than bank loans. First, they are designed to be more difficult. Part of their appeal to investors is their de facto seniority. Investors expect a borrower to approach its bank lenders for help before it has recourse to restructuring its bonds. Taking away this property of bonds would deprive borrowers and lenders of a choice and hence make the intermediation process less efficient. Second, bonds are designed to be held directly or indirectly by retail investors and to be highly liquid.

4. The committee that began negotiating with Côte d'Ivoire in April 2002 took the name Private Creditors Advisory Committee to reflect the participation of holders of the country's Brady bonds.

5. The "buy side" includes emerging market funds, insurance companies, and other institutional investors and asset managers. The "sell side" consists of the investment banks that arrange, as lead managers, the issuance of bonds in international capital markets.

This means that the number of holders of a single issue can be well into the thousands. The difficulty of communicating with holders has been exaggerated at times by G-7 and IMF officials, but clearly it is a bigger job than communicating with the holders of bank debt.

Significantly, institutional investors hold most of the sovereign bonds issued by emerging market countries (see chapter 3). Institutional investors usually have little discretion in their treatment of distressed assets because of their fiduciary responsibilities. They may be required to sell bonds when investors withdraw their money, when the bonds have been downgraded by a rating agency, or when the bonds become illiquid in the context of a work-out. More critically, institutional investors have almost no relevant experience in joining other creditors to negotiate a restructuring deal with a sovereign borrower that has an unsustainable amount of debt.

The Contractual Approach: A Partial Solution

An exhausting amount of material has been written since 1996 on introducing collective action clauses in emerging market bonds and on the contractual approach to improving the process of sovereign debt restructuring.[6] Nevertheless, as of mid-2003 there was still no agreement on a standard set of clauses or a list of issuing countries that should be adopting these clauses.

For many years bonds issued under English law have incorporated clauses allowing a majority of the holders of a particular issue to change the terms of payment and make the new terms binding on the minority. By custom bonds issued in the United States typically require unanimous consent to make similar changes.[7] It is permissible, however, for sovereigns to issue bonds under New York law that include collective action clauses. Thus sovereign borrowers that want these clauses face no legal obstacles in the two principal markets, New York and London. Moreover, empirical studies have not been able to find evidence that including the clauses raises the cost of borrowing significantly for emerging market issuers. The hesitation comes from issuers who do not want to be embroiled in a global policy debate between the G-7 and the financial industry.

6. Group of Ten (1996, Annex IV) remains an excellent introduction to the subject. The most recent IMF studies of bond clauses are IMF (2002b), IMF (2002c), and IMF (2003a). Excellent scholarly treatments can be found in Kenen (2001) and Eichengreen (2002).

7. The requirement of unanimous consent for changes in payment terms is in federal law (the Trust Indenture Act), which does not apply to sovereign issues. (Communication with Peter Kenen, August 2002.)

In mid-2002 both sides broadly agreed that wider use of collective action clauses in sovereign bonds could contribute to better debt workouts. The question became whose clauses, yours or mine. A G-10 working group proposed specific clauses in a report issued in September 2002.[8] A coalition of six financial industry associations began drafting an alternative set that balanced collective action options with increased investor protections—especially greater transparency. Box 12-1 summarizes the main elements of these financial industry clauses as they stood at the end of 2002.[9] In March 2003 Mexico announced that it would include collective action clauses in all of its future bond issues, instantly transforming the presumption against including these clauses to a presumption favoring their inclusion. This presumption was reinforced shortly thereafter when Brazil, South Africa, and South Korea issued new bonds with collective action clauses.

Collective action clauses by themselves, however, will never guarantee more satisfactory sovereign debt workouts, even if they are acceptable to issuers, investors, the G-7, and the IMF. They are just one tool. Other tools that are essential to success in a broad range of circumstances are various forms of official support, ways of organizing and negotiating with creditor groups, and means of fostering collaboration among the parties concerned. This is the premise of the tools-based approach to PSI suggested below.

The Statutory Approach: Overkill

Replacing the existing ad hoc approach to sovereign debt workouts with permanent machinery has a seductive appeal for all who have experienced the miseries of a debt crisis. From the perspective of the G-7 architects, the proposal put forward by the IMF for a Sovereign Debt Restructuring Mechanism represented a fundamental change in the international financial system that might be warranted by the circumstances, but also entailed substantial risks. (The main features of the SDRM, as they were described in the report of the IMF managing director to the IMFC in April 2003, are summarized in box 12-2.)

Before embracing the SDRM, the G-7 architects had to consider two questions. First, could the existing machinery be adapted to accommodate bond debt? Second, if not, was the SDRM the right kind of new machinery?

---

8. Group of Ten (2002).

9. Based on the discussion paper accompanying a press release from the six associations on December 17, 2002. The press release and paper can be found on the IIF website www.iif.com/data/public/SDRM.pdf (February 21, 2003).

Box 12-1. Elements of Model Bond Clauses Proposed by the Financial Industry

The following is paraphrased from the discussion paper issued December 17, 2002, by the Bond Market Association, the Emerging Markets Creditors Association, EMTA, the International Primary Markets Association, the Institute of International Finance, and the Securities Industry Association.

The goal is to develop and implement a marketable approach to collective action clauses that would operate in the context of an international code of conduct for crisis prevention and resolution to be applied on a case-by-case basis. New bond clauses that would help facilitate effective restructurings where unavoidable while protecting essential creditor rights are part of the approach. The model clauses would provide for:

1. *Majority action.* To permit the amendment and waiver of key bond terms by a supermajority (of at least 85 percent) of bonds outstanding (and not opposed by more than 10 percent). Key terms would include due dates for payments, the amount of principal or interest payable on any date, the currency to be used, and other substantive covenants as appropriate. Amendment and waiver could be approved by written resolution as well as at a bondholder meeting. Bonds held or controlled, directly or indirectly, by the issuer would be excluded from voting.

2. *Engagement.* To provide for the appointment by bondholders of a committee to represent bondholder interests after an event of default has occurred or the issuer has initiated restructuring discussions. The committee could adopt such internal rules as it saw fit, and engage legal and financial advisors, subject to reimbursement by the issuer.

3. *Initiation.* To require a vote of at least 25 percent of the bonds outstanding to accelerate principal following an event of default, and to provide for a supermajority vote (of at least 75 percent of bonds outstanding) to rescind acceleration.

4. *Transparency.* To require the issuer to comply fully with the IMF's Special Data Dissemination Standard, to provide rolling forecasts of inflation and of key budget components, and to disclose proposed treatment of other creditors such as domestic and Paris Club creditors. This information could be published on the websites of relevant industry associations.

Box 12-2. Key Design Features of the SDRM

The following points are paraphrased from the Report of the Managing Director to the International Monetary and Financial Committee on a Statutory Sovereign Debt Restructuring Mechanism, April 8, 2003.[1]

1. *Scope of claims.* The debtor country would determine, in light of negotiations with its creditors, whether all or some of the eligible claims would be restructured. The central government of the debtor country would be a "specified debtor." Other specified debtors could include the central bank or any local government or public sector entity not subject to a domestic debt restructuring framework. The only claims eligible for restructuring under the SDRM would be those that are against a specified debtor, arise from a commercial contract, and are not governed by the laws of the debtor country or subject to the exclusive jurisdiction of a tribunal in that country. The following eligible claims would be exempt from restructuring: (a) claims that benefit from a statutory, judicial, or contractual privilege; (b) guarantees; (c) wages, salaries, and pensions; (d) contingent claims that are not due and payable; and (e) claims held by international organizations accorded preferred creditor status in the instrument creating the SDRM.[2]

2. *Activation.* The SDRM could only be activated by a debtor country after concluding that its eligible debt was unsustainable.

3. *Provision of information.* Activation of the SDRM would require the debtor country to disclose fully to the Dispute Resolution Forum (DRF) information about the indebtedness of all specified debtors. The DRF would make this information public.

4. *Registration and verification of claims.* After providing the information called for above, a registration and verification process would take place to facilitate votes on an aggregated basis for each specified debtor. The DRF would establish the rules for this process.

5. *Limits on creditor enforcement.* Amounts due to a creditor under an approved restructuring plan would be reduced by any amounts recovered by the creditor through a legal proceeding initiated after activation. Upon request of the debtor country and approval of a supermajority (75 percent) of creditors concerned, a temporary stay against enforcement proceedings would become effective. Similarly, the DRF could order the suspension of an enforcement proceeding.[3]

6. *Creditor committees.* A representative creditor committee would address both debtor-creditor and intercreditor issues. The debtor country would pay the costs of the committee's operations.[4]

7. *General voting rules.* Proposals by a specified debtor for a stay on enforcement, priority financing, or terms of restructuring would be approved by creditors holding 75 percent of all verified claims.

8. *Priority financing.* A specified post-activation financing transaction could be excluded from restructuring with the approval of creditors holding 75 percent of all verified claims.

9. *Restructuring agreement.* A separate restructuring agreement would be proposed for each specified debtor. When a specified debtor proposes a restructuring agreement, it must disclose how it intends to treat claims not being restructured under the SDRM. Agreements certified by the DRF would become binding on registered and unregistered claims.

10. *Termination.* The SDRM would terminate automatically upon a request from the debtor country, upon a vote of creditors holding 40 percent of verified claims, or upon certification by the DRF of all restructuring agreements.

11. *Dispute Resolution Forum.* The DRF would be established in a manner that ensures independence, competence, diversity and impartiality. Its operations would be financed by the IMF. The IMF managing director would designate a selection panel of seven to eleven judges or private practitioners nominated by professional associations and international organizations. The selection panel would form a pool of twelve to sixteen candidates through an open nomination process from which a DRF panel would be selected. The pool as a whole would be approved by the IMF Board of Governors. Four members would be impaneled for each country case. The responsibility of the DRF would be limited to administrative functions (such as registration and verification of claims), resolving disputes, and suspending enforcement actions.

12. *Legal basis and consistency with domestic laws.* The SDRM and DRF could be established through an amendment of the IMF Articles of Agreement (requiring approval of 60 percent of the members with 85 percent of the voting power). Most members would need to ratify this step. Some members would need to enact domestic legislation to give the amendment full force and effect.

1. Available at www.imf.org/external/np/omd/2003/040803.htm (April 12, 2003).

2. There was no consensus on whether claims held by foreign governments and their agencies would be restructured within the SDRM or through a parallel mechanism. The instrument creating the SDRM would specify a consistent approach.

3. Many executive directors supported this feature, but a number of directors supported a more debtor-friendly version.

4. Many executive directors supported this feature, but some directors supported a more debtor-friendly version.

On the need for new machinery, the experience with sovereign debt workouts over the past fifty years—as described in chapters 5 and 6—suggested that the problem might be solved by the bondholders themselves. As the Paris Club creditors did in the 1950s and 1960s, and the commercial banks did in the 1970s, bondholders might be able to organize themselves for workout negotiations and might have sufficient incentives to do so. The formation of the Emerging Markets Creditors Association (EMCA) in 2001 and several committees of Argentine bondholders in 2002 were positive steps in this direction. At the beginning of 2003, however, holders of Argentina's bonds were hampered by two factors. One was that they lacked a counterparty to engage in discussions or negotiations. Up to this point the government of Argentina was not prepared to initiate serious contacts, although it took a step forward at the beginning of 2003 when it selected a well-known investment bank to serve as the government's debt-restructuring advisor. Behind the government's hesitation was the tortuous process of electing a government in May 2003 that would have a popular mandate to implement a comprehensive economic recovery program.

The second factor hampering creditor action to restructure Argentina's bond debt was the apparent reluctance of the G-7 architects to apply some combination of carrots and sticks to encourage the two sides to commence negotiations. This attitude contrasted with the pattern in the 1980s, where there was a high degree of collaboration between finance officials and commercial banks in the debt area, and where the finance officials intervened with commendable skill and force to persuade creditors and debtors to conclude mutually acceptable deals.[10]

One implication of the Argentina case is that as soon as a new government has a credible recovery program, the bondholders will be ready to organize themselves and engage in serious negotiations. At the same time the amount and forms of official financing to support Argentina's program, and related actions taken by the G-7 and the IMF, will have a major bearing on the terms of a deal and how quickly it is closed. A broader implication is that the "gaping hole" that worried Anne Krueger in November 2001 does not

10. In mid-2002 Pedro Malan, Brazil's finance minister, was reported to have said that "if the IMF had devoted a tenth of the time to Argentina that it spent working on sovereign bankruptcy, the crisis would be solved by now." Alan Beattie and Thomas Catan, "IMF Picks Its Way through Latin American Minefield," *Financial Times*, August 2, 2002, p. 2. This statement was made about a week before the IMF announced a $30 billion package of support for Brazil to ward off a financial crisis. Similar sentiments can be found in a remarkable address by Guillermo Ortiz, the Mexican Central Bank Governor, delivered in July 2002 at the Bank for International Settlements in Basel, Switzerland, as the annual Per Jacobsson Lecture (Ortiz 2002).

exist. When a country with unsustainable debt is in a position to make the necessary changes in its policies, creditors will work constructively to restructure their claims.[11]

Presuming a successful workout with Argentina in the second half of 2003, the global financial community will have a template for future workouts that require restructuring of bond debt. In the course of adapting the Argentina template to other cases, the existing ad hoc machinery will evolve organically, and at some point it is likely to acquire a new label. This process of refinement could be completed with only two or three cases—fewer than required to produce the London Club in the 1970s.[12]

Under two possible sets of circumstances, new ad hoc machinery of the kind suggested here might not be adequate. One possibility is a series of crises in a short period of time that represented a threat to the system—on the order of the threat associated with commercial bank exposure to developing country borrowers at the beginning of the 1980s. In such circumstances, a bolder mechanism that is more driven by the public sector may be appropriate. The ideal mechanism, however, would not necessarily resemble the SDRM. The G-7 architects may be better served by designing a mechanism specifically for the circumstances at the time.

The other possibility is that the ad hoc approach to Argentina's workout will fail for some reason that is difficult to discern now. As a result, a mechanism like the SDRM may become more appealing. By waiting until a specific problem arises, however, the basic design of the mechanism could then be tailored to address this problem. Political support for creating a new institution would undoubtedly be stronger under these circumstances.

The Tools-Based Approach: A Pragmatic Alternative

Sovereign debt crises involving countries that borrowed heavily from commercial sources have adverse impacts well beyond the crisis country. They are also complex phenomena that are not amenable to simple solutions.

One of the axioms of public policy is that multiple policy instruments are required to pursue multiple policy objectives. Applying this precept to sovereign debt workouts suggests that achieving satisfactory results will depend on having sufficient policy instruments or tools. The current approach to

11. Indeed a restructuring might be easier to conclude if the country has no outstanding debt to official agencies and no expectations of new money from official sources, including the IMF. As a consequence, however, both the country and its private investors and creditors would experience heavier short-term losses.

12. Uruguay restructured its debt in May 2003 as a condition of continued IMF support. The bond exchange carried out can be seen as a template for future cases.

workouts appears to depend on a toolkit that is too restricted. Most of the heavy lifting is done with two pieces of machinery that use a small set of tools (the IMF and the Paris Club), and one that has a relatively wide range of tools (the London Club). The London Club is in the process of evolving into a new form of creditor committee that includes bondholder representatives and may even come to be dominated by them. As a result it will end up with even more tools. The Paris Club is searching for a better way to share the workout burden with private creditors in cases where debt owed to bilateral donor agencies is relatively small. Three new tools the Paris Club could use for this purpose are proposed in the second half of this chapter.

The IMF has been active since 1995 in creating and updating its tools, but its interest in the SDRM seems to reflect some disenchantment with their effectiveness in sovereign debt crises. The IMF will necessarily remain at the center of the process of crisis resolution. Without an SDRM it will have to articulate a clearer policy on the amount of financing it will provide to restructuring countries as well as a clearer position on how it will assess PSI in the context of the programs adopted by these countries. With regard to financing, a strict access limit appears to be inconsistent with the political realities of the day. A sensible alternative would be a policy of committing exceptional amounts of IMF financing only in those cases where the debtor country is implementing an exceptionally strong adjustment program. In some cases this approach would allow the country to recover from a crisis without any restructuring of debt owed to private creditors. In other cases, even with exceptional IMF financing, the country's debt to private creditors will have to be restructured.

Apart from adding or sharpening the policies and tools associated with the IMF, Paris Club, and London Club to permit a more surgical approach to future workouts, several additional tools could be usefully developed:

—*Bilateral balance-of-payments loans.* These fast-disbursing, nonproject loans were used with some frequency in the past but fell out of favor. Like all tools, they can be misused, in this context by extending them to countries pursuing unsustainable economic policies. However, not every country can mount a strong postcrisis recovery program. It is better to support weaker programs with bilateral financing that can be rescheduled in the Paris Club if assumptions about the pace of recovery turn out to be overly optimistic. Excessive reliance on IMF financing tends to shift the workout burden to private creditors because of the IMF's preferred creditor status.

—*Reschedulable loans from the multilateral development banks.* By the same logic, balance-of-payments (or adjustment) loans from the multilateral development banks can contribute to future debt-servicing problems when extended to countries where the risks of policy slippages are substantial. The recent move to provide more IDA financing to low-income developing countries in the form of grants rather than loans reflected this concern. A parallel move for middle-income developing countries would be to open new "windows" in the development banks for loans that could be rescheduled or written down on the same basis as debt owed to Paris Club creditors. With appropriate changes in provisioning policies, such a move would not jeopardize the triple-A ratings of the multilateral development banks.

—*Public sector–private sector collaboration.* In the 1980s creditor country governments had some leverage over banks through their regulators. Trying to exert moral suasion on bondholders is like pushing on a string. A few experiments with dialogue and collaboration have been undertaken recently: the IMF's Capital Markets Consultative Group, the G-20, and Paris Club meetings with private sector representatives. Bolder experiments offer the prospect of more tangible results. One particular object of collaboration could be to ensure that effective creditor committees are in place to negotiate restructuring arrangements when countries are ready to design and implement credible recovery programs. Adoption of a code of conduct jointly produced by private and public bodies could provide a helpful roadmap.

—*Crisis prevention.* It bears repeating that much remains to be done to prevent crises and that the benefits for the world of progress in this area could easily be larger than the benefits of progress in perfecting workout techniques. Market participants would also take comfort in seeing more G-7 and IMF activity on crisis prevention and less on crisis resolution.

The tools-based approach recommended here is an ad hoc approach that may not appear sufficiently orderly. How important is it that the workout process be orderly? How can an orderly process be distinguished from a disorderly one?

The IMF seems possessed by the desire for an orderly workout mechanism, and the G-7 has to some extent bought into the notion.[13] It is not

13. The interest in having an orderly process is not new, despite the inference in many IMF documents and statements on the subject of PSI. UNCTAD and the G-77 were campaigning for a more orderly process in the 1970s. Federal Reserve Governor Henry Wallich, in the June 1978 issue of *Institutional Investor* (p. 9), wrote: "Earlier, it was not possible to foresee whether payments difficulties could be met by orderly rescheduling and refinancing arrangements or were more likely to lead to outright moratoria and default. Now, a pattern of orderliness . . . seems to be establishing itself." The first IMF paper on the subject of debt restructuring (Nowzad and others, 1981, p. 21) does not use

obvious that a workout process has to be orderly to be good. The workouts in the past thirty years can be divided, but not neatly, into two groups. One consists of cases where the crisis country had sufficient domestic political support and institutional capacity to implement a credible recovery program. The workout process in these cases tended to be relatively speedy (measured from time of payment suspension to agreement in principle on restructuring terms), and their recoveries were relatively speedy (measured from the time of agreement in principle to "normal" market access). The other group consists of cases where the crisis country had difficulty getting its act together for one reason or another. In these cases workouts tended to be protracted and recoveries halting.

The point is that creditors—both official and private—will generally bend over backward to help a country that has a credible recovery program. The G-7 and the IMF should be more concerned with helping countries formulate and implement such programs and less concerned about the process for achieving private sector involvement. Any workout that is acceptable to the debtor country and its creditors can be considered a "good" workout. Workouts that come quickly are preferable, of course, to workouts that come after a long time. But there can be many legitimate reasons for delay. Adding "orderly" as a requirement is unhelpful.[14]

The Problem with the Paris Club

Fixing the machinery for restructuring bonds would still leave an important piece of debt workout machinery that is in need of repair: the Paris Club.

The Paris Club started off in 1956 with a simple approach to burden sharing with other creditors that worked well for more than twenty-five

the word "orderly" but stresses the importance of a "viable multilateral framework." Hudes (1986, p. 451) wrote: "This article will examine the procedures used in the Paris Club and the London Club to ensure that timely, orderly, and equitable relief is provided."

14. The IMF has tended to exaggerate the orderliness of the commercial bank workouts in the 1980s. In her November 26, 2001, speech, Krueger said: "In the 1980s, restructuring sovereign debt was a protracted but generally orderly process." As related in chapter 6, the process of commercial bank debt restructuring was distinctly disorderly from 1976 to 1982. It only became relatively mechanical after 1982, when many of the deals were repetitions of previous deals with the same country. Surely after equivalent experience with bond restructuring, the process would become just as mechanical. IMF arguments in favor of an orderly approach have also inferred that the domestic bankruptcy process is orderly. Perhaps it appears so from the IMF's global perspective, but bankruptcy practitioners tend to view it as inherently messy. Moreover practitioners have been arguing hotly among themselves for years about whether their regimes are too creditor-oriented or too debtor-oriented.

years. Strains appeared during the 1980s, when the Paris Club found itself rescheduling previously rescheduled debt for a growing number of poor countries, with a snowballing effect. As a result it was forced to add debt reduction to its short list of possible treatments, but it limited this option to the poorest countries. The Paris Club was compelled to go further in this direction in the 1990s as part of the HIPC Initiative to bring debt owed to multilateral agencies down to manageable levels, but again it did so only for the poorest countries. For non-HIPCs, Paris Club operations were variations on the theme of rescheduling payments falling due during a consolidation period of one to three years.

New strains appeared in the Paris Club machinery after the G-7 launched its campaign in 1998 to curtail the amount of official financing provided to countries in crisis and to shift more of the workout burden onto private creditors. This shift is a matter of concern to the extent that it discourages private capital flows that could contribute to more rapid global growth and a reduction in income disparities between wealthy nations and poor nations. The magnitude of the impact on private capital flows is sometimes exaggerated, which tends to mire the debate about burden sharing in details.

Instead of entering the debate over the magnitude of the impact, this study proceeds from the observation that the Paris Club approach at the beginning of 2003 was backward looking in two respects.[15] First, it operated with a set of long-standing policy constraints on the restructuring techniques that could be used in operations involving the non-HIPCs, or middle-income, countries. Second, it used a test of burden sharing (comparable treatment) that was anachronistic.

Before elaborating on the features of a more forward-looking approach, a brief discussion is in order explaining why dealing with the Paris Club problem is less urgent than fixing the bond restructuring problem. The Paris Club treats a limited body of debt: debt owed to official agencies in its nineteen member countries, and by extension debt owed to the equivalent agencies in all other countries. It has no authority over debt owed to multilateral agencies (which is not restructured because they are preferred creditors) or debt owed to private creditors (principally commercial banks, bond investors, and suppliers).

Recalling the discussion about capital flows to developing countries in chapter 10, the mix over the past decade has been heavily biased toward private

15. Mohamed El-Erian suggested this image during the course of the discussion at the Paris Club's meeting with private creditors in April 2001.

flows. Cumulatively from 1990 through 2000 private flows totaled $1.9 trillion, compared with official flows of $320 billion. Barring a global economic meltdown, the proportion of private flows is likely to rise further over the coming decades, reflecting competing budget priorities and improved country performance. As a consequence the amount of debt owed to Paris Club creditors involved in sovereign workouts is likely to shrink relative to debt owed to private creditors. Instead of being the driver in the burden-sharing game, the Paris Club seems destined more often to be a passenger.

As stressed repeatedly, these remarks apply to the relatively small number of developing countries (fewer than 50) that are currently tapping international capital markets. A larger number (close to 100) remains highly dependent on official flows. HIPC debt reduction will provide plenty of business for the Paris Club over the next five to ten years, but these operations are intended to be once-and-for-all workouts. Consequently, this business too will eventually dry up.[16]

To underscore the point, because of the growing importance of private credit to the more advanced developing countries, Paris Club operations are likely to treat a relatively small share of the total debt being restructured in comprehensive debt workouts taking place in the coming years.

Three Policy Constraints

Setting aside the HIPCs and a few other poor countries, the standard debt-restructuring treatment by the Paris Club is a long-term (twelve years, for example) rescheduling of payments falling due during a defined (normally one to two years) consolidation period. The Paris Club has declined to use three tools often selected by private creditors in sovereign debt-restructuring arrangements: new money, stock restructuring, and principal reduction. Adding these tools to its toolkit would help the Paris Club play a more constructive role in future workouts involving a substantial amount of debt owed to private creditors.[17]

NEW MONEY. The main reasons for excluding new money from Paris Club negotiations were mentioned in chapter 5. The problem going forward is that for private creditors, it makes no sense to separate new money from other components of a debt-restructuring deal. This is not to say that

---

16. Another factor contributing to this outcome is the shift by donor agencies (even the multilaterals now) from loan to grant funding for the poorest countries. After the HIPC Initiative has run its course, the graduates will look creditworthy and start to borrow again. It remains to be seen how much of their borrowing will come from official sources, but it is easy to imagine a future wave of problems as the new borrowers rediscover the perils of external debt.

17. The exceptions to each of these practices have been too minor to be mentioned here.

every Paris Club operation with a middle-income country should include a new-money component. It is simply that Paris Club creditors would benefit from adding the new-money tool to their toolkit. In general, a substantial new-money component in a restructuring deal is a signal of confidence in the debtor country's prospects. In some cases actions by the Paris Club creditors to reinforce such signals can encourage spontaneous flows of private capital after a workout. These flows will make it easier for the countries to repay exceptional financing from the IMF (and other preferred creditor debt) and remain current on their rescheduled and unrescheduled debt to Paris Club creditors. The new-money option may be particularly attractive to certain creditor countries. It is also more suited for debtor countries with good prospects for rapid adjustment than for countries with poor track records.

STOCK VERSUS FLOW TREATMENT. The very first Paris Club operation involved "consolidating" principal payments falling due during a short-term period of adjustment and establishing a new long-term repayment schedule for these payments. This basic treatment continued into the 1980s, when commercial banks began rescheduling in much the same fashion. It continued through the Brady Plan era, when commercial banks agreed to debt-restructuring arrangements involving debt and debt-service reduction. And it continued in the 1990s, when bonds began to be restructured with an element of reduction, or haircut. The Paris Club creditors, however, did not experience haircuts because the stock of debt owed to them was never reduced and the interest rate charged by each creditor agency on rescheduled debt was a quasi-market rate.

Declining to consider stock treatments could be justified in a world where official creditors were doing most of the heavy lifting in a sovereign workout (because they represented the lion's share of the outstanding debt), or in a world where official creditors were providing new money while private creditors were systematically lowering their exposures. Refusing to consider stock reduction did not introduce any serious complications into the workout process. Looking forward, however, in cases where bonds are a major component of a country's external debt, the current Paris Club practice could become an obstacle to a speedy workout. One problem is that consolidating a limited set of bond payments and rescheduling them is impractical. There are only two practical treatments for bonds: extending the final maturity and adjusting the interest rate (through a vote of the bondholders), or carrying out a market-based exchange of old bonds for new bonds.

Beyond this structural problem is a problem of equity created by treating Paris Club creditors more favorably than private creditors for no financially valid reason. A further problem is that each time the Paris Club comes back to do another in a series of consolidations, the debtor country must renew its agreement to achieve comparable treatment. Doing a bond exchange three years in a row is obviously not practical. Adding the possibility of restructuring some portion of the stock of debt owed to Paris Club creditors could therefore contribute to faster workouts in some cases.[18]

RESCHEDULING VERSUS REDUCTION. In two exceptional cases the Paris Club agreed to reduce debt instead of reschedule debt owed by middle-income countries: Egypt and Poland, both in 1991. Political considerations were paramount in each case.[19] Commercial banks were required to accept comparable treatment in both cases, and they expressed strong reservations about this politicization of the debt-restructuring process. As long as private creditors are not being asked to reduce debt, the Paris Club practice of declining to consider debt reduction is not a problem. Looking forward, there could be more cases like that of Ecuador where private creditors have to agree to debt reduction.[20] As in the case of refusing to restructure the stock of debt, the Paris Club's refusal to reduce debt could become a sticking point in cases where bondholders are getting a haircut. Adding the possibility of debt reduction could contribute to faster workouts.[21]

RECAPITULATION. What is being proposed is not a bold initiative but a modest relaxation of certain historical policy constraints to give the Paris Club more flexibility (more tools). None of these new possibilities—new money, stock treatment, reduction—should be considered standard (or clas-

18. Steps in this direction were taken at the end of 2001 for Pakistan and in mid-2002 for Jordan. The Paris Club agreed to reschedule Pakistan's entire stock of eligible debt over an unusually long period of time, with a view to avoiding a series of rescheduling operations. For Jordan the Paris Club agreed to an "exit rescheduling" that consolidated precutoff payments falling due over the next five years (100 percent of these payments in the first year, stepping down to 70 percent in the last year) to be repaid on an extra-long-term schedule (Houston terms), based on the understanding that Jordan would not require further debt relief during this period and beyond.

19. The only other non-HIPC to be granted debt reduction by the Paris Club was the former Republic of Yugoslavia in 2001.

20. Argentina will present an early test. It will have roughly $50 billion of sovereign bond debt to restructure. Argentina's debt to Paris Club creditors, $9 billion at the end of 2002, was roughly the same order of magnitude as commercial bank debt. A haircut of more than 50 percent for bondholders seems inevitable. A rescheduling of Paris Club debt that involved no reduction of net present value would presumably be unacceptable to the bondholders.

21. A step in this direction was taken in 2002 in the negotiations with Côte d'Ivoire, which was eligible for HIPC debt reduction despite its high per capita income and status as a capital market borrower. Reflecting Côte d'Ivoire's relative prosperity, the Paris Club only granted Lyon terms (80 percent reduction) rather than Cologne terms (90 percent reduction). This case provides a possible precedent for reducing Paris Club debt owed by other middle-income countries.

sic) treatment. The standard would continue to be rescheduling of payments on precutoff debt falling due during a time-bounded consolidation period.

Why, one might ask, do Paris Club creditors regard these small steps as being too radical? One objection seems to be that changes of this kind would require some countries to obtain legislative authority in advance of the negotiations, which would delay these negotiations unduly. This is a particular problem for the U.S. government.[22] A broader objection may be that any greater flexibility would tend to compromise the negotiating position of the creditors in future cases. The main reason may simply be inertia and the absence of sufficient political pressure to change.

Giving the Paris Club more tools to use in its work entails some risks, but these appear smaller than in the past because of the diminishing role of lending by bilateral donor agencies. The cases the Paris Club has to deal with will be more complicated by the presence of bond debt, which cannot be sliced and diced in the same way as bank debt. Each time the HIPC program is expanded to more countries or enhanced to make it more generous, the pressure will increase from civil society to extend debt reduction to non-HIPC countries. Specific proposals along these lines have already been advanced.[23] There is no need to announce a major change in Paris Club policy. Instead Paris Club creditors could simply start using the new tools in future cases whenever they would appear to contribute to a better workout. Such an approach would be consistent with the Paris Club tradition of adapting to changing times, as it did when it began doing debt reduction for low-income countries in the late 1980s.[24]

---

22. Under the Federal Credit Reform Act of 1990, the U.S. government must have budget authority to reduce debt before it commits to doing so (before a Paris Club negotiation, for example). This requirement adds a political element to the process that can be in conflict with the underlying principle of maximizing eventual recovery. It can also introduce a substantial delay in implementing debt reduction, which could have an adverse impact on the debtor country's recovery and on burden sharing with other creditors. The result is that "the tail wags the dog." The executive branch should be given standing authority to participate in debt reduction whenever it is clearly linked to an inability to pay and to appropriate burden sharing by other creditors (both official and private). More information on the impact of credit reform on Paris Club debt restructuring can be found in U.S. Department of State (1999).

23. In April 2002 the new Center for Global Development in Washington rolled out a strong case for extending the HIPC program to Indonesia and other middle-income countries; see Birdsall and Williamson (2002).

24. Another potentially useful innovation would be to negotiate menus of options designed to match the preferences of the different creditor countries. Menus are a common feature in workouts with private creditors.

The Comparable-Treatment Principle

Comparable treatment is one of the five principles of debt-restructuring operations by the Paris Club (see chapter 5).[25] It is a simple principle with a fancy name. It requires countries benefiting from Paris Club debt restructuring to seek to obtain similar (comparable) relief from their private creditors. A more common term for the same principle is burden sharing. In every sovereign debt workout there have been and will be arguments about how to share the burden, but no group involved claims it should not bear part of the burden.[26]

The first serious test of comparable treatment came in the late 1970s, when commercial banks sought to avoid rescheduling by persuading borrowing countries to adopt strong adjustment measures and by persuading official agencies to extend sufficient amounts of balance-of-payments financing to help these countries avoid arrears to private creditors (see chapter 6).[27] Comparable treatment worked relatively well during the 1980s and into the 1990s, when bank loans were the only substantial form of commercial borrowing and the countries seeking debt relief all had large amounts of Paris Club debt. The first signs of a comparable-treatment problem accompanied the Paris Club debt-reduction operations with Egypt and Poland in 1991, noted earlier. Additional concerns about comparable treatment developed in a series of operations financed by the World Bank's IDA Debt Reduction Facility, where low-income countries bought back commercial bank debt at steep discounts through a largely involuntary process.

25. A remarkable paper on comparable treatment was produced by the IMF staff in mid-2001, discussed by the executive board in August, and posted on the IMF website on December 19, together with a summary of the board discussion (IMF 2001b). The executive board zeroed in on the choice between the current approach based on quantitative analysis and a "catalytic" approach focusing on the impact of the Paris Club's action on future flows of private capital. The summary notes that "although Directors generally did not consider the use of the catalytic approach for Paris Club reschedulings as appropriate, they confirmed the need for flexibility in requiring comparable treatment of private sector debt, including in cases where private debt restructuring could affect future market access." The "catalytic approach" dismissed by the board seems close to what is being advocated in this study, but the "flexible approach" endorsed by the board does not appear significantly different .

26. The multilateral agencies are exempt from formal rescheduling or restructuring as a matter of practice, but they invariably contribute new money and provide other forms of support such as program monitoring and technical assistance. See chapter 3.

27. Citibank executive Irving Friedman, who was personally involved in Zaire's negotiations with commercial banks in the 1970s, offered this assessment of comparable treatment in the case of Zaire: "The governments feared that the private banks would somehow induce Zaire to pay them off while leaving the governments holding the bulk of Zaire's debt. Indeed, . . . Zaire had to agree to obtain 'comparable' terms from the private banks—a caveat that impeded private bank efforts to raise new incremental credits for Zaire afterward." Friedman (1983, p. 40).

Comparable treatment became a hot issue in 1999, when the Paris Club applied it to bonds for the first time, initially in the case of Pakistan and shortly thereafter in the cases of Ukraine and Ecuador (see chapter 10).[28] Part of the heated reaction related to the relative lack of negotiations with bondholders before the bond exchange offers were announced.[29] But some fundamental problems with the basic concept of comparable treatment began to surface. These can be put under three headings: apples and oranges, the calculus of comparable treatment, and the application of comparable treatment in specific cases.[30]

APPLES AND ORANGES. A close reading of the early history of the Paris Club suggests that the qualifier "comparable" was selected over qualifiers such as "equal," "equivalent," or "similar" to allow for some differentiation between Paris Club terms and those obtained from private creditors in the same context. Indeed the record shows a systematic difference: the terms obtained by private creditors have been somewhat more favorable than Paris Club terms. Differentiation has two possible rationales. One is that the different kinds of creditors perform different functions in the process of channeling capital flows from creditor countries and debtor countries. Another is that individual credits take varying forms. Thus, for example, if Paris Club creditors extended only long-term loans and private creditors

---

28. Nigeria loomed large as a potential problem in 2000 and 2001. The case was particularly intriguing because Nigeria had accumulated huge arrears to Paris Club creditors when they cut off aid flows after a military coup in 1993. Nigeria was current on payments to commercial creditors at the time, notably on par bonds that had been offered in exchange for distressed commercial debt in 1991. From roughly equal amounts of debt in 1991 ($5 billion–$6 billion), Paris Club debt ballooned to more than $24 billion at the end of 2000 (simply because of late interest and penalty interest charges). A newly elected democratic regime was able to obtain a standby arrangement from the IMF in 2000 and return to the Paris Club for more relief. For a while it appeared that the comparable treatment requirement would force Nigeria to restructure its par bonds, but instead Nigeria's IMF-supported program went off track, and arrears to Paris Club creditors began accumulating again. With no prospect of Paris Club negotiations in the near term, concerns among bondholders about comparable treatment evaporated. At the end of 2002, however, and the approach of fresh elections, the government of Nigeria announced an auction to buy back some of its par bond debt and made a token interest payment to Paris Club creditors.

29. There was a reasonable degree of informal consultation between the investment bank selected to underwrite the deal and bondholders in the case of Ukraine, and somewhat less in the case of Pakistan. The strongest concerns about the lack of consultations were registered in the case of Ecuador, which was an especially sensitive issue because it affected Brady bonds and because it involved substantial net present value reduction.

30. Some readers may be surprised by the absence of any discussion of "reverse" comparable treatment, which includes the notion that Paris Club creditors should be forced to provide matching debt reduction whenever private creditors agree to debt reduction. The argument here is that comparable treatment no longer makes sense in either direction.

extended only short-term loans, the treatment of these two exposures would not necessarily be the same. This kind of differentiation has a parallel in domestic bankruptcy-insolvency regimes, and it appeals to common sense.

Both kinds of differentiation are alluded to obliquely in the explanation of comparable treatment provided on the Paris Club website: "Paris Club creditors do consider on a case-by-case basis whether particular factors mitigate against demanding comparable treatment of a particular creditor or debt instrument(s)." However, no explanation of the "mitigating" factors is provided, such as the different functions performed by commercial creditors and official creditors. These different functions create an "apples and oranges problem" in the sovereign debt-restructuring context. The principle of comparable treatment can magnify or minimize the differences depending upon how it is interpreted.

Commercial creditors (banks and bond investors for the most part) are performing a straightforward intermediation function between savers and spenders. They allocate credit to borrowers to earn a return that covers their cost of funds or offers an equivalent yield for an equivalent risk without regard to the purpose of the loan. If they do their business well, they make a profit, which is the main incentive for engaging in the business. By contrast Paris Club creditors (bilateral donor agencies) are, generally speaking, forbidden to lend in a way that would compete with private creditors. Their lending operations are designed to advance a range of political and social objectives such as ensuring that domestic exporters are not disadvantaged by financial support being offered by governments in other countries, helping dispose of surplus agricultural stocks, making it possible for borrowing countries to procure military equipment needed to defend themselves from external aggression, and sharing the cost of building highways and other infrastructure projects that may help countries achieve higher rates of economic growth. On the face of it, according the same treatment to these loans as to commercial loans in a sovereign workout is illogical.

In other words it is impossible to differentiate among commercial loans on the basis of purpose because they all have a single purpose: to make a profit. By contrast bilateral loans serve a wide variety of purposes, and making a profit is not one of them. Even though, from a narrow legal point of view, a borrowing country's obligation to repay is just as strong under official loans as under private loans, official creditors have always been more willing to write off their claims than commercial creditors because of their noncommercial nature. The fundamental differences between official lending and private sector lending represent perhaps the biggest unspoken mystery of the sovereign workout process. The Paris Club hides the issue, the IMF has tried to flag the issue, and the G-7 seems to be ducking the issue. Highlighting the fact that official credit and commercial credit are apples and oranges could mitigate the public controversy surrounding sovereign debt workouts. Using the comparable treatment principle to transfer the political and social baggage attached to official credit to commercial credit can only make an inherently difficult process even more difficult, unnecessarily.[31]

THE CALCULUS OF COMPARABLE TREATMENT. After decades of declining to explain how it determines whether comparable treatment has been achieved in a particular case, the Paris Club has yielded to the pressure of the transparency movement in every other aspect of crisis prevention and resolution by outlining a methodology for measuring comparable treatment. The Paris Club website offers the following introduction: "As a general rule, comparability of treatment is assessed with the effect of private treatments compared to the effect of Paris Club treatments (in terms of duration, net present value and flow relief)."

Under pressure to elaborate on how this assessment was made in specific cases, the Paris Club made a presentation on the cases of Pakistan and Ecuador during its initial meeting with representatives of the private sector in April 2001. For each case, the Paris Club terms were compared with the bond exchange terms on the basis of the cash flow relief during the consolidation period, the net present value relief (using the same discount rate assumption for each treatment), and the increase in the duration (final maturity). In addition, the sensitivity of these calculations to different discount rates was tested.

The analysis showed that the Paris Club agreement and the bond exchange with Pakistan were quite comparable based on these criteria. By contrast, the deals with Ecuador were fairly different on the basis of cash flow relief (63 percent for Paris Club debt and 44 percent for bond debt) and net present value reduction using a "risk free" discount rate (4 percent reduction of Paris Club debt and 15 percent reduction of bond debt). Despite the differences in the Ecuador case, the conclusion was that comparable treatment had been achieved. The presentation raised a host of questions, however, which the format of the meeting gave no time to explore. For example, this assessment ignored the likelihood that the Paris Club would extend additional relief to both countries in subsequent years, did not make clear whether the three tests

31. Checki and Stern (2000) provide a succinct and powerful exposition of the differing natures of commercial financing and official financing and the implications for crisis management and sovereign workouts.

were being given equal weight or different weights, and gave no indication of how far the terms could diverge before being considered noncomparable.

The methodology issue could be explored for pages. The financial industry's approach to analyzing burden sharing would be more comprehensive, coherent, and technically sound (as reflected in the analysis of "equivalency" among different menu options in Brady Plan deals). Such an exercise is beside the point, however, because there is no way of getting around the fact that Paris Club debts are apples and commercial debts are oranges.

THE APPLICATION OF COMPARABLE TREATMENT IN SPECIFIC CASES. The third fundamental problem is that the Paris Club measures comparable treatment after the fact and has no effective mechanism for promoting comparable treatment before negotiations have begun with official and private creditors. Up through the 1980s this problem was not a serious handicap. Before 1989, when both groups were engaging in debt rescheduling, the Paris Club had a looser concept of comparable treatment. After 1989, when commercial banks began doing debt-reduction deals, the two creditor groups parted company by mutual agreement (with the expectation that the official creditors would continue to provide new money and thereby increase their exposure while banks would not provide new money and thereby reduce their exposure).

Going forward, this failure to consult before negotiations will be a less tenable position. Commercial banks and bondholders are fully prepared to bear their share of the workout burden, but they expect to have an opportunity to discuss both the size of the pie and how it is divided. The arguments for prior consultations were advanced in the meetings organized by the Paris Club with representatives of the private sector in April 2001 and March 2002, but no agreement was reached on a consultation procedure. A prior consultation was undertaken on an experimental basis in connection with one Paris Club operation later in 2002, but the Paris Club made no commitment to continue the practice. If the Paris Club applies the principle of comparable treatment in future cases in ways that private creditors find objectionable, an adverse reaction must be expected at some point in some form.

A New Burden-Sharing Principle

The basic flaw in the comparable treatment principle is the absence of any consideration of how the application of the principle in a particular case will affect future flows of private capital to the debtor country. As observed earlier, the world of the future is one in which developing countries will rely increasingly on flows of private capital, individually and as a group. More-over, the multilateral agencies will increasingly depend on spontaneous flows of private capital to repay the adjustment financing they provide to crisis countries. The Paris Club creditors must be aware of this link but so far have resisted taking it into account in their approach to burden sharing.

The alternative is a forward-looking approach that stresses flexibility in the pursuit of a comprehensive solution that will help accelerate the debtor country's return to normal market access.[32] No quantitative analysis can substitute for qualitative judgment in the course of pursuing this objective. Moreover, the objective is probably impossible to achieve without mean-ingful consultations and cooperation among the Paris Club, the IMF, and private creditors. The only way to get beyond the apples-and-oranges prob-lem is through an active dialogue and negotiations on loosely parallel tracks, one case at a time. Sticking with the backward-looking, inconsistent, and provocative way of applying comparable treatment that has been followed for the past three years is no longer a viable approach.

The new formulation of the comparable treatment principle suggested here is not a radical departure from the past. It is an evolutionary step build-ing naturally on recent practices and reflecting ongoing changes in the nature of capital flows to developing countries. To help clear the air, the new Paris Club principle could adopt the phrase "burden sharing" rather than "comparable treatment." The new principle and its application in cases involving countries that have a significant amount of sovereign debt owed to private creditors could incorporate three elements:

—A requirement that the debtor country pursue debt-restructuring arrangements with private creditors to ensure that they bear an appropriate share of the losses involved in the workout.

—A commitment to engage in consultations—in advance of negotia-tions—with the debtor country, its private creditors, and the IMF to identify actions by each party that would be mutually reinforcing in promoting a speedy recovery by the debtor country and an early resumption of sustain-able flows of private capital.

—Use of the full range of financial tools available to tailor the restruc-turing of debt owed to Paris Club creditors to the circumstances of each country.

32. In the words of an IMF staff paper issued in 2001, "a perception of a relative seniority that forces private creditors to bear a disproportionate part of the risk associated with resolving solvency problems could reduce the willingness of investors to extend new credit." IMF (2001b, p. 9).

The strongest objection to this reformulation is, presumably, that it is too ad hoc and that any departure from strict (and statistically measured) comparable treatment would expose creditor governments to accusations of "bailing out" private creditors. The rebuttal is that one does not have to look at too many of the 360 agreements concluded by the Paris Club since 1956 to detect a pattern of "ad hoc-ery" underneath the veil of standard treatments. The "bailout" issue is a tougher nut to crack. Here a public education effort is required on the broad subject of crisis prevention and resolution. The public has yet to grasp the catalytic potential of official financing (including Paris Club debt restructuring) and the factors that influence private capital flows to developing countries.[33] Once this reality is understood, most likely through a series of successful cases of crisis prevention and resolution, the Paris Club should find that taxpayers value flexibility, rather than fear it.

The public education campaign could help to stress the exceptional nature of crises. Exceptional situations call for exceptional responses. It is inherently inconsistent to treat an exceptional situation with a strict rule. The only rules compatible with exceptional circumstances are variations on flexibility.

Conclusion

What is broken? What fixes make sense?

First the machinery for restructuring bond debt after a sovereign default is not broken or missing. It simply has not yet assumed a clear form. New and permanent machinery could be designed and firmly rooted in an amendment of the IMF's Articles of Agreement. The IMF has proposed this solution in the form of the Sovereign Debt Restructuring Mechanism. The SDRM looks like overkill, however. Most of the problems it is designed to address can be dealt with informally. A better fix would be to nourish efforts by private creditors to develop "organically" a workout process for bonds, as they did for commercial bank debt in the 1970s. This will take time, but not necessarily the five years required to establish the London Club process. It would also allow the G 7 and other finance officials to focus more attention on the more critical task of crisis prevention.

---

33. More and more of these flows represent money that taxpayers have entrusted to pension funds, insurance companies, and other asset managers. Consequently taxpayers should be increasingly interested in how they are treated in sovereign workouts.

Second the Paris Club machinery for restructuring debt owed to bilateral donor agencies is in need of an overhaul. The Paris Club is trying to repair broken cars with only a hammer. It could do a better job if it had a few wrenches, screwdrivers, and a hydraulic lift. The Paris Club is also stuck with a backward-looking approach to burden sharing called the comparable treatment principle. The sensible fix here is to take off the shackles and let the principle evolve naturally toward a forward-looking approach that encourages new flows of private capital, in sustainable forms and amounts, to countries that implement sound recovery programs. This is the only growth-oriented road to reducing the dependence of developing countries on official financing, a goal that taxpayers in these countries as well as in the industrial countries seem to share.

Finally, the G-7 architects and the IMF should make their actions more consistent with their rhetoric by putting new initiatives on the crisis prevention front clearly ahead of initiatives on the crisis resolution front. The benefits of preventing one crisis may be greater than the benefits of achieving marginally more orderly workouts in ten crises. In particular, the potential payoff from more active consultations and cooperation with private creditors appears to be large. As a crisis approaches, this collaboration should become more visible. The ability of the private sector to act positively and creatively to preempt a crisis has barely been explored. At the same time there will be cases where, despite the best efforts of outsiders, a country is unable to take the steps required to avoid default. In these cases an effective public-private dialogue can help to minimize the collateral damage (contagion) to other countries.

In the spring of 2003 the PSI debate entered a fifth phase consistent with the policy approach recommended in this study. With respect to the machinery for restructuring bond debt, the U.S. government adopted a new position of antipathy toward the SDRM at the mid-April meeting of the IMFC. Shortly before that meeting, the government of Mexico announced its intention to include collective action clauses in its future bond issues. These actions put the work on bond restructuring machinery on a more pragmatic track. With respect to the Paris Club machinery, the G-8 summit meeting hosted by France in June provided the political impetus for adopting a new "staged approach" to debt restructuring by the Paris Club for non-HIPCs. This initiative was announced by the G-8 finance ministers at their presummit meeting in mid-May, and it clearly represented a more flexible and forward-looking approach. Other steps in the direction of those advocated in this study are likely to be taken in the months to come.

Appendix A
"Countries Don't Go Bankrupt"

C ountries don't go bankrupt" seems to be the most frequently repeated sound bite associated with the broad subject of sovereign debt work-outs. It is everywhere. Former Citibank chairman Walter Wriston is usually cited as the originator of the quip.[1] This is almost certainly wrong; it was considered conventional wisdom in the international financial community at least a decade earlier.

Two versions of this observation can clearly be traced to Wriston. The first was in an op-ed piece by Wriston carried in the September 14, 1982, edition of the *New York Times*, about a month after the Mexican default that signaled the beginning of the 1980s debt crisis. Wriston wrote:

> If a country undertakes policies that contain a formula for solving its balance-of-payments problems over time, it will find that financing for

---

1. Anne Krueger, IMF's first deputy managing director, began an op-ed piece that appeared in *El Pais* on January 18, 2002, as follows: "Walter Wriston, former head of Citibank, famously remarked that countries don't go bust. But, over the past two centuries, more than 90 have in fact defaulted on their debts and a number have done so several times. When it announced a moratorium late last year, Argentina became only the latest example."

its investment projects and for any temporary balance-of-payments gap is almost always available; however, if the adjustment polices show no foreseeable long-term solution, financing will not be forthcoming, but *the country does not go bankrupt*. Bankruptcy is a procedure developed in Western law to forgive the obligations of a person or a company that owes more than it has. Any country, however badly off, will "own" more than it "owes." The catch is cash flow and the cure is sound programs and time to let them work. (Emphasis added.)

In June 1984, at the International Monetary Conference in Philadelphia, Wriston's biographer, Philip Zweig, recounts a variation on this theme:

Wriston once again made his pitch about countries being different from companies. "Unlike a business corporation," he told the gathering, "a country has almost unlimited assets in its people, its government, its natural resources, its infrastructure, and its national political will."[2]

An effort to track down the earliest source of this observation did not yield any clear answers. One pre–World War II variation was found in the context of a restructuring of Mexican government bonds in default arranged in 1922 by Thomas Lamont, a partner at J. P. Morgan, on behalf of a bankers' committee. In 1927 the Mexican government sought to revise the terms of a 1922 restructuring because of the country's deteriorating financial circumstances, and they were encouraged in this effort by Dwight Whitney Morrow, the U.S. ambassador to Mexico and a former partner at J. P. Morgan. According to an account of this affair, "Lamont maintained that a nation could never be insolvent since it always had taxing power. Morrow countered that a nation could reach the point where despite the taxing power it could not meet in full its obligations. He believed that Mexico had reached that juncture."[3]

Reporter Tad Szulc wrote an article about commercial bank lending to developing countries for the October 16, 1978, issue of *Forbes* magazine, which ran with the headline: "A Cliffhanger for the Banks." The subtitle for his article was, "A country, unlike a company, can't go bankrupt. So the pundits say." Unfortunately Szulc did not identify any of these pundits in his article.

2. Zweig (1995, p. 820).
3. Delamaide (1984, p. 98)

Further research revealed that prominent government officials were mak-ing the same point in the 1970s. For example, a *Euromoney* reporter in 1977 asked Henry Wallich, the Federal Reserve Board governor who followed international developments most closely, about the possibility of sovereign borrowers going bankrupt. He responded: "A country doesn't vanish from the map, though it's true that like Cuba it [can repudiate its debt]. . . . Rescheduling is always a possibility. That's happened before; it will happen again. But bankruptcy seems to me a very remote supposition."[4] A year later Wallich wrote in an opinion piece published by *Institutional Investor*:

> The borrowing countries themselves have been more aware than in years gone by of the implications of failure to meet their obligations. . . . They seem to have been able to persuade their creditors that, unlike a business borrower who may go out of business, their continuing existence as national entities assures that even in case of difficulty there will always be someone from whom the creditor can collect.[5]

Later in the same piece Wallich wrote: "Where official borrowers are con-cerned, the 'immortality' of governments and their institutions has been a protective element." Jack Guenther, who left the IMF in 1979 to join Citibank, recalls that "countries don't go bankrupt" was part of the conven-tional wisdom at the IMF when he was working there.[6]

Anecdotal evidence suggests that the optimistic view of country risk espoused by Citibank in the late 1970s and early 1980s was closely associated with Irving Friedman. Friedman, with a Ph.D. in economics and years of senior management experience at the World Bank and the IMF, was hired by Citibank in 1974 to establish a unit to assess the risk of lending to foreign countries, one of the first such units formed by a money center bank.[7] Fried-man published a number of commentaries about commercial bank lending to developing countries, but none appear to focus on the notion that coun-tries don't go bankrupt.

4. James Srodes, "Governor Wallich Wants the IMF to Advise LDC Lenders," *Euromoney*, April 1977, p. 26.

5. *Institutional Investor*, June 1978, p. 9.

6. Conversation on January 6, 2003.

7. Friedman was hired by Al Costanzo, another former IMF senior manager who joined Citibank in 1961 and became the head of overseas business in 1967 at the same time Wriston became presi-dent and CEO. Friedman in turn brought into Citibank at least one senior IMF staff member (Zweig 1995).

A lawyer's reference to this notion in the mid-1980s confirms the prevalence of the sentiment in earlier years and provides a legal perspective on the matter:

> It had become axiomatic in the 1970s to assert that sovereign states cannot go bankrupt. The 1980s have proved this axiom up to a point. Clearly there are no formal insolvency or liquidation rules that apply to sovereign states. There is no method by which the assets of a sovereign state can be distributed among the creditors. Creditors have not scrambled to obtain security for their debts as they usually do in domestic workouts. Instead the creditors have resorted to long, patient negotiations to put their debts on a more orderly footing, essentially a footing on which interest payments will be maintained.[8]

The quip about countries not going bankrupt is usually mentioned dismissively to illustrate how blind commercial banks (and other private lenders and investors) can be to the risks of doing business in developing countries. It has a kernel of truth, however, that is central to the argument in this study. It is important for policymakers, investors, taxpayers, and voters to understand the differences between sovereign default and corporate default. These are so substantial that it is wrongheaded to design a mechanism for sovereign workouts modeled on the mechanisms in use for decades for corporate workouts (such as the U.S. Bankruptcy Code).

The main differences between corporate default in a national context and country default in the international context are discussed in chapter 2. Key points from this discussion and several additional points on the matter can be summarized as follows:

—Strictly speaking, countries do not borrow and therefore cannot default. Foreign borrowing is done either by public sector or private sector entities. Defaults occur within both categories of borrower.

—Public sector borrowers can be divided into two categories. Sovereign borrowers include the national government (sovereign government) and any other entity backed by the "full faith and credit" of the national government, such as the central bank or a national oil company. The debt of these borrowers, sovereign debt, has special legal and practical characteristics. The second category, subsovereign borrowers, includes states, provinces, municipalities, and other subdivisions of the government. Depending on each

8. Clark (1986, p. 858).

country's constitution, borrowing by these entities is either backed up (guaranteed) by the national government or not. When it has not explicitly guaranteed a subdivision, a national government may nonetheless choose to intervene to protect citizens from the consequences of a default (or a state or provincial government may have responsibility or assume responsibility for a municipal or county default). Revenue-producing, government-owned companies fall in a gray area. Defaults by some are treated as sovereign defaults, and others are treated as (private) company defaults.

—Sovereign or national governments have the right (and power) to suspend payment on external debt or repudiate it without any reason. This is a fundamental attribute of sovereignty that has been exercised for centuries. As a consequence a finite risk of default is associated with the debt of every government, including the U.S. government. No debt is entirely risk free.

—Unlike companies, when sovereign governments default, creditors have no legal right to close them down or sell them to the highest bidder to satisfy their claims. Creditors have no legal right to replace governments (the equivalent of corporate managers) that fail to meet their contractual obligations.

—Creditors no longer have the military power available historically to extract payment or compensation from delinquent foreign borrowers (either in the public sector or the private sector).

—National governments have ways of obtaining funds to meet debt service obligations that corporations lack. The most important of these is the power to tax, another fundamental part of sovereignty.[9] Another is the power to sell national assets such as natural resources or state-owned companies.

—Every national government has the technical capacity (or ability) to repay all of its external debt, if not according to the original schedules in its loan contracts, then over some longer period of time. At the extreme, a country can repay its external debt by systematically impoverishing its citizens, as Romania did in the 1980s, but that is hardly a sensible solution. The technical capacity to repay supports the view that sovereign defaults reflect an unwillingness to pay, rather than an inability.

9. Makin (1984, p. 145) sums this up quite nicely, saying that developing country governments have "offered their foreign creditors remarkably little in the way of collateral beyond the implicit assurance that governments never go bankrupt because they have the power to tax. . . . But the power to tax can produce burdensome conditions that sometimes result in revolution and overthrow of governments whose successors are not disposed to honor the debts of their predecessors." Makin (p. 47) also quotes a finance minister who noted the temptation to "put off the agony of raising taxes" by borrowing abroad instead.

—In every country, there are political limits on what the national government can do to avoid default. These are determined by the social turmoil associated with specific actions such as raising taxes or cutting back on health services. Default is the only choice when these limits are reached and may be the right choice before they are reached.

—When private sector borrowers default, the bankruptcy laws (regime) of their country determine the process by which creditors can restructure their claims or gain possession of assets belonging to the borrower in partial satisfaction of their claims.

—Defaulted corporate debt is often worthless, but defaulted sovereign debt is rarely so, reflecting the special nature of sovereign borrowers. Bondholders have particularly long memories. Recently the Soviet Union and China had to conclude settlements with holders of prerevolution bonds before they could issue new bonds in certain capital markets.

In short, countries cannot go bankrupt the way private companies can. Sovereign governments can default on their debts, however, and they have done so with some regularity over the past 200 years. Furthermore, the incidence of sovereign defaults is not likely to diminish in the near term. It is difficult to predict the timing of a sovereign default because it results from policy decisions driven as much by political factors as by economic or financial ones. It is even harder to estimate recovery values because of the small number of cases and the changing geopolitical circumstances.

Appendix B
Five Milestone Cases

Chapter 6 noted that the London Club process for restructuring sovereign debt owed to commercial banks emerged organically from negotiations with five countries in the 1976–80 period: Zaire, Peru, Sudan, Turkey, and Poland. This appendix describes the experience of commercial banks with each of these countries. Statistics on the structure of the long-term external public debt of the five countries are provided in table B-1.

Zaire, 1976–80

Zaire, the third largest country by area on the African continent behind Sudan and Algeria, is blessed with rich mineral and other natural resources.[1] After gaining independence from Belgium in 1960, Zaire was a country full of promise, but it became a pawn in the cold war, in large part because of its reserves of cobalt and uranium ore. After five years of political turbulence, General Mobutu Sese Seko consolidated power over the country in 1965

---

1. The discussion of Zaire draws extensively on the cover story in the March 1977 issue of *Institutional Investor*, IMF (1980), Friedman (1983), Delamaide (1984), and Callaghy (1993).

Table B-1. Long-Term, Public Sector, External Debt of Milestone Cases, 1970–78

Millions of U.S. dollars

Country	1970	1972	1974	1976	1978
Zaire					
Total	308	573	1,343	2,377	3,684
Official creditors	222	147	311	974	1,622
Multilateral	6	30	60	116	261
Bilateral	216	117	251	858	1,361
Private creditors	86	426	1,032	1,403	2,062
Commercial banks	0	167	453	470	555
Others	86	259	580	932	1,507
Peru					
Total	856	1,053	2,221	3,666	5,455
Official creditors	373	480	774	1,289	2,505
Multilateral	148	156	152	171	258
Bilateral	225	324	622	1,118	2,247
Private creditors	483	573	1,447	2,378	2,950
Commercial banks	148	217	922	1,573	1,660
Others	335	355	526	804	1,290
Memo: Private sector nonguaranteed debt	1,799	1,787	2,128	2,436	1,830
Turkey					
Total	1,846	2,470	3,164	3,648	6,490
Official creditors	1,766	2,318	2,948	3,305	5,320
Multilateral	383	372	617	980	1,446
Bilateral	1,383	1,946	2,332	2,324	3,874
Private creditors	81	152	216	343	1,170
Commercial banks	8	33	34	135	809
Others	73	119	182	209	361
Memo: Private sector nonguaranteed debt	42	70	146	248	557
Sudan					
Total	294	361	896	1,657	2,407
Official creditors	256	310	599	1,091	1,805
Multilateral	104	105	143	240	367
Bilateral	153	205	456	850	1,439
Private creditors	37	50	297	566	602
Commercial banks	27	35	201	220	168
Others	10	15	96	346	434
Poland[a]					
Total					24,000
Official creditors					12,000
Multilateral					0
Bilateral					12,000
Private creditors					12,000
Commercial banks					12,000

Source: For Zaire, Peru, Turkey, and Sudan, World Bank, *Global Development Finance* on CD-ROM; for Poland, Delamaide (1984, pp. 73, 78).

a. End 1980 estimate.

and aligned it politically with the democracies of the West.[2] These countries responded by extending large amounts of financial support. For example, one of the world's largest hydroelectric dams (at Inga on the Congo River) and one of the world's longest transmission lines (to deliver power to the copper mines in Katanga province) were financed almost entirely by export credits. Encouraged by the strong official support, commercial investors and lenders rapidly increased their involvement in the country, sometimes supporting projects of questionable merit. These included a world trade center building in the capital. The first syndicated bank loan, in 1970, was led by Bankers Trust based in New York.[3]

The government of Zaire responded ineptly to the quadrupling of oil prices in 1973–74 and the subsequent drop in the world price of copper (its major export commodity). Arrears to banks began accumulating in 1974, and by the end of 1975 arrears to all foreign creditors exceeded $300 million. In March 1976 Zaire was able to conclude a low-conditionality standby arrangement with the IMF, setting the stage for Zaire's first Paris Club negotiations. In June the Paris Club agreed to reschedule 85 percent of principal payments due in 1975 and 1976, with repayment stretched out over ten years. The agreement included standard language committing Zaire to seek comparable rescheduling terms from its commercial bank creditors.

In April 1976 the Bank of England took the initiative to organize a meeting of banks that had syndicated eurocurrency loans to Zaire.[4] The Bank of England was concerned that a default by Zaire might adversely affect other developing countries that had borrowed in London's eurocurrency market. It hoped to arrange an orderly workout as an alternative to default. The meeting, chaired by a Bank of England staff member, brought together about a dozen agent banks for roughly twenty syndications totaling around

2. In 1997, following the overthrow of President Mobutu, the country changed its name to the Democratic Republic of the Congo.

3. Lee Lescaze and Don Oberdorfer, "Big Foreign Lender Citibank Hedges Bets in a Risky Business," *Washington Post*, April 24, 1977, p. A1.

4. Zaire and Peru initiated debt negotiations with commercial banks almost simultaneously in 1976. Three sources describe Zaire as the first debt-stressed country to engage its commercial bank creditors as a group in multilateral restructuring negotiations. The cover story in the March 1977 issue of *Institutional Investor* noted (p. 24) that "this was the first time bankers had sat down with a defaulting LDC [less developed country] to discuss debt." In an article published in the April 1977 issue of *Euromoney* (p. 33), Wells Fargo Bank executive Robert Bee wrote: "Negotiations with Zaire, which were the first with major commercial bank involvement . . . may have established a workable precedent [for debt relief negotiations]." Friedman (1983, p. 140) wrote: "Zaire was the first major developing country workout case faced by the private banks in the 1970s." Peru was more of a bilateral case because of the dominant role of U.S. banks.

$375 million and involving about 100 participating banks.[5] The fact that this meeting took place in London may have contributed to the adoption of the London Club label for the process of restructuring sovereign debt owed to banks.

Shortly after Zaire concluded its rescheduling agreement with the Paris Club, the group of agent banks telexed a request to meet with the government to find a mutually acceptable alternative to debt rescheduling that would help Zaire maintain its access to new bank loans. The two sides met in early September, in London, but the head of the Zaire delegation, central bank governor Sambwa Pida Nbagui, requested a straightforward rescheduling on terms that went beyond those agreed by the Paris Club. Specifically, he proposed restructuring Zaire's entire debt to commercial banks into a new obligation to be repaid over fifteen years.[6]

The banks did not immediately respond with a counteroffer, but they met on October 5 at the headquarters of Credit Commercial de France in Paris to consider three options that could be seen as equivalent financially (meaning the net amount of debt payments each year would be the same).[7] The "strong" option was to extend a new short-term loan of around $250 million to finance capital imports ostensibly required to sustain economic growth. This option meant Zaire would be treated as a fully creditworthy country and would make it possible for the government to avoid any refinancing or rescheduling of commercial bank debt. The "weak" option was to mirror the Paris Club's rescheduling terms, which implied a willingness to repeat the deal if necessary the following year. The "middle" option was to provide a medium-term refinancing loan to clear Zaire's arrears and to fund principal payments due through the remainder of 1976. This alternative implied a positive attitude toward further increasing exposure if Zaire's balance of payments strengthened. Citibank, the only major bank with a

5. The agent banks included Banque de Paris et des Pays-Bas, Banque Nationale de Paris, Chase Manhattan Bank, Citibank, Citicorp International Bank Ltd., Morgan Guaranty Trust Co. (the holding company for J. P. Morgan), Commerce Union Bank (from Nashville, Tennessee), Credit Commercial de France, Grindlay Brandts Ltd. (49 percent owned by Citibank), Morgan Grenfell and Co. Ltd., Société Générale de Banque (from Brussels), and Tokai Bank, Ltd. (Japan).

6. A member of the IMF staff participated as an observer in the bank meetings with the Zaire authorities, reflecting the importance the banks placed on the discipline and financing associated with an IMF standby arrangement. The IMF representative addressed technical aspects of Zaire's stabilization program and answered questions about the IMF's financing policies. The IMF's participation established a precedent that was followed in most of the subsequent bank negotiations with developing countries.

7. Paul Monnory was the host for Credit Commercial de France.

branch in Zaire, assumed a prominent role at this stage as the advocate of the strong option.

The agent banks scheduled a meeting with Governor Sambwa on October 22 in New York to convey their counterproposal. However, at a bankers-only meeting the day before, Irving Friedman, a senior executive at Citibank, surprised the other banks by announcing that he had already reached agreement with Governor Sambwa on the new-money option. (Friedman had been a senior official at the IMF and World Bank and had access to the leadership of the Zaire government that other bankers could not begin to match.)[8]

Friedman offered his approach as a model for future negotiations with debt-stressed countries. He was quoted as saying, "Our only view can be that we get paid and paid on time." The context hints at two themes that reappeared regularly in debt-restructuring operations in the 1980s and 1990s. One was the trade-off between adjustment and financing. In Friedman's words, "any country that has lost its creditworthiness has the ability within itself to restore it." The other theme was burden sharing between official and private creditors. "In the world of government lending, rescheduling does not affect a country's creditworthiness," Friedman observed. "It is often viewed as a positive method of development assistance."[9] In effect he was seeking to test the willingness of the IMF and the major donor countries to help Zaire maintain its access to commercial credit. This aggressive stance prompted the Paris Club creditors to make Zaire a test case of the burden-sharing principle. They warned Zaire against making payments to banks that would reduce bank exposure while official creditors were continuing to commit new financing to the country.

The view that developing countries could avoid debt workouts with commercial banks through a combination of strong adjustment and official support looks remarkably naïve in hindsight. In defense of this view, many experts expected that oil prices would return to "normal" levels, and others saw developing countries as the major source of future global growth as the industrial economies exhausted the gains from postwar reconstruction. A comment by an experienced banker involved in Zaire's efforts to avoid debt restructuring illustrates the attitude that motivated the banks to help Zaire find an alternative that would preserve its creditworthiness:

8. Earlier in the year Friedman had arranged a similar balance-of-payments loan for Peru. See Peru section.

9. All quotes from *Institutional Investor*, March 1977, pp. 24 and 25.

Nobody who was involved in Zaire's negotiations with the agent banks can doubt the serious desire of the Zairois to meet their obligations, or their willingness to accept sacrifices to obtain a realistic agreement on their debt, and then live up to it. Even the two Shaba invasions, which have serious political implications as well as delaying exports, do not appear to have undermined this determination.[10]

Although many of the other agent banks in the Zaire case apparently viewed the Friedman approach to be ill advised or worse, Friedman had seized the high ground, and they had little choice but to play along. Governor Sambwa was able to extract two major concessions in the negotiations the following day, and the deal was ratified in a formal Memorandum of Understanding signed at the Bank of England in London on November 5.[11]

In brief Zaire agreed to pay immediately about $40 million in interest arrears (and did so) and to remain current on future payments. The banks in return agreed to make their "best efforts" to syndicate a new loan in the amount of $250 million. Rounding off the deal, Zaire agreed to pay principal arrears and future principal payments into an escrow account at the Bank for International Settlements that would be disbursed to the banks when Citibank obtained firm commitments to the new loan. At this point Zaire's long-term public debt to commercial banks was around $470 million and to Paris Club creditors around $860 million.

The bank deal fell apart at the beginning of 1977 when a rebellion broke out in Shaba province (supported by the pro-Soviet government of Angola) and Zaire's budget and foreign exchange resources were diverted to contain the insurrection. In April, however, the political situation had stabilized enough for Zaire to obtain IMF financing under the Compensatory Financing Facility (for a shortfall in copper exports) and a new standby arrangement. This improved the prospects for concluding the new-money loan, but Zaire fell behind in making payments into the BIS escrow account.[12] Citibank floated the idea of arranging a revolving import credit facility as an alternative, but Zaire would not agree to it. The banks' hopes for avoiding rescheduling suffered a major setback in August when Sambwa was deposed as a central bank governor.[13]

10. Donaldson (1979, p. 164).
11. The Memorandum of Understanding was not a legally binding document but rather a gentlemen's agreement, similar to what would come to be known as a term sheet.
12. The amount required to trigger the new loan was $130 million, but the amount paid in never went beyond $80 million (Delamaide 1984, p. 58).
13. Another factor motivating the banks in this case was the North-South Dialogue, where some

Zaire was able to take advantage of its April IMF stand-by arrangement to reschedule principal and interest payments to its Paris Club creditors falling due in 1977. A sea change occurred in the Paris Club's attitude toward the role of commercial banks during these negotiations. At a preparatory session before the 1976 negotiations, the U.S. delegation had reported that "although there was little discussion . . . , creditors generally concurred that the [Paris Club] rescheduling agreement should make some provision for Zaire rescheduling private unguaranteed debt on terms similar to those of multilateral arrangements." The IMF representative at the same session noted that it was not possible, on the basis of information then available, to distinguish between commercial bank loans and supplier credits that were guaranteed by bilateral agencies and those that were not guaranteed, which made it difficult to estimate the amount of relief that might be available from the Paris Club.[14] In the July 1977 Paris Club agreement, comparable treatment of commercial bank creditors was mentioned in three separate paragraphs. The final reference explicitly linked another round of negotiations on payments due in 1978 to "the conclusion before then of a loan agreement with the banks." This was in effect the first major test of the comparable treatment principle since the Paris Club's initial negotiation with Argentina in 1956.[15] Despite these warnings the commercial bank loan was not concluded before the next Paris Club agreement was signed in December. The issue did not go away, however. The Paris Club creditors were more united than before on making sure that Zaire rescheduled its commercial bank debt on similar terms.[16]

In April 1978, with arrears growing and facing the loss of vital support from donor agencies, Zaire agreed to put the administration of its central bank in the hands of an expert appointed by the IMF. Erwin Blumenthal,

developing country leaders were advocating unilateral debt moratoriums on payments to commercial banks by countries facing severe balance-of-payments strains. Zaire was seen as a prime candidate for such action.

14. Based on a cable sent from the U.S. Embassy in Paris to the Department of State on April 28, 1976, and a copy of the statement made by the IMF representative at the April 1976 Paris Club meeting circulated to interested U.S. government agencies.

15. An observer at the time described comparable treatment as "difficult to comply with as well as to monitor, so it became in effect more of a desirable objective than a strictly-enforced obligation." Cizauskas (1979, p. 202).

16. From the perspective of a senior U.S. Treasury official: "From 1976 to 1980, burden-sharing between official and private creditors became a serious issue. . . . Official creditors could not afford to be seen as bailing out commercial lenders. When Zaire developed serious debt problems in 1976, the commercial banks argued that they should be preferred creditors. The creditor governments refused to accept this position and conditioned debt relief in 1979 upon 'comparable' relief from banks. The banks eventually yielded." Leland (1983, p. 108).

retired from the Bundesbank, was selected for the job. A month later there was a renewed outbreak of rebellion in Shaba province. During the year Citibank made several unsuccessful attempts to obtain Zaire's approval of a new-money arrangement. These efforts were undercut by Zaire's inability to conclude another IMF standby or to make up the shortfall in its payments to the BIS escrow account.[17] At a conference in June in Paris, Zaire's major aid donors agreed to an emergency package of food and medicine and broadly endorsed the "Mobutu Plan" for economic recovery in the medium term. In November the donors put together another emergency aid package, but Zaire's policies were still too weak to qualify for an IMF standby.

A hopeful development in this period of drift was Zaire's decision to hire a "troika" of investment banks (Lazard Frères, based in Paris; S.G. Warburg, based in London; and Lehman Brothers, based in New York) to advise on its negotiations with Paris Club and commercial bank creditors. This move established a precedent followed by numerous other debtor countries over the ensuing two decades.[18]

At some point between August 1977, when Sambwa was sacked, and April 1979, when President Mobutu balked at signing the Letter of Intent for a new IMF standby arrangement, the commercial banks concluded that their attempt to save Zaire from rescheduling was doomed to failure. A key factor was mounting evidence that Mobutu was more interested in staying in power than preserving his country's creditworthiness.[19] Another was Blumenthal's inability to establish any meaningful discipline over the country's finances in the face of Mobutu's kleptocratic behavior. Blumenthal left Zaire in June 1979 completely disillusioned.

Finally, in August 1979, Mobutu was forced to accept the IMF's conditions for a standby arrangement. That opened the door for another package of emergency aid from donor countries in November and a Paris Club rescheduling operation in December.[20] Negotiations with a steering committee of 10 banks (representing a total of 134 banks) began in October, and a rescheduling deal was reached in December around a Paris Club meeting. At that point, the banks were not optimistic about Zaire's future prospects. They agreed to replace the entire stock of Zaire's medium-term bank debt

17. Zaire shocked the bankers in August when it took funds out of the escrow account to buy military equipment.

18. The troika's first sovereign advisory job was helping the Indonesian government fix the debt problems of its parastatal oil enterprise, Pertamina, in 1975.

19. Conversation with Hamilton Meserve, June 4, 2002.

20. The Callaghy (1993) case study of Zaire focuses on these negotiations, highlighting the political maneuvering and the competition among commercial creditors.

with a single new instrument embodying terms close to the latest Paris Club terms. The final documentation was signed in April 1980.[21] The deal involved around $370 million of medium- and long-term debt, of which about $290 million was in arrears. The terms were the most favorable granted by commercial banks to any debtor country up to that point. Seventy-six percent of principal payments in arrears were to be repaid over five years. All remaining principal payments were to be repaid over ten years including a five-year grace period.

From mid-1980 to mid-1981 Zaire's performance and prospects improved sharply. That performance made it possible for Zaire to conclude a three-year arrangement with the IMF in June 1981 and a more favorable Paris Club rescheduling a month later. By the end of the year, however, Zaire was out of compliance with its IMF arrangement, and arrears to Paris Club and London Club creditors quickly reappeared. The banks signed six more agreements during the 1980s to defer principal payments in return for promises of monthly interest payments. After 1989, when banks were negotiating debt-reduction agreements with a flock of countries undertaking credible reforms, Zaire was unable to meet the minimum requirements for a Brady Plan workout.

The Paris Club also rescheduled Zaire's debt in six more operations during the 1980s. Each one expanded the definition of eligible debt and extended the repayment period a bit further. In the 1990s Zaire was not able to qualify for Paris Club debt reduction for low-income countries because of the growing antipathy toward the Mobutu regime.[22]

Peru, 1976–78

The case of Peru is noteworthy because it was the first of the debt-stressed Latin American countries handled through a formal steering committee. [23]

21. The new instrument was governed by New York law. The original syndicated loans may have been a mix of New York law and English law instruments.

22. With the end of the cold war, Zaire's aid donors lost interest, financing from the multilateral agencies dried up, and arrears to these agencies began to pile up. In June 2002, the renamed Democratic Republic of the Congo was able to obtain a bridge loan from four friendly countries to clear its arrears to multilateral agencies and to qualify for concessional loans from the IMF, World Bank, and bilateral donor agencies to pay off the bridge loan. In September 2002 the Paris Club took the first step toward HIPC debt reduction for this country by extending Naples terms. At the beginning of 2003, however, it was not clear when the country would qualify for the more generous Cologne terms. Furthermore, there appeared to be little support among the G-7 to settle the country's outstanding arrears to commercial banks through a buyback under the IDA Debt Reduction Facility.

23. The discussion of Peru draws heavily on IMF (1980), Hardy (1982), and Friedman (1983).

It also deserves special mention for being the only country in the past fifty years to have given back debt relief won from its creditors.

Peru encountered debt-servicing difficulties in the late 1960s, negotiated a standby arrangement with the IMF in 1968 (renewed in 1969 and 1970), and then rescheduled debt owed to Paris Club creditors in 1968 and 1969. Some refinancing deals were also concluded with individual commercial bank creditors. Over the next five years Peru's balance of payments improved.

After 1973, however, balance-of-payments strains developed because of excessive government spending for development projects and military equipment, together with growing subsidies for fuel and food imports. Falling prices for Peru's commodity exports (especially copper) in 1977 cut export earnings to around $1.8 billion a year against projections of more than $2.8 billion, leaving the government insufficient foreign exchange to service its external debt. (Long-term public debt to Paris Club creditors at the end of 1976 was around $1.1 billion, compared with $1.6 billion owed to commercial banks.) Commercial bank loans featured prominently in the financing obtained to cover Peru's current account deficits during the 1973–76 period, but grace and repayment periods shortened over time and spreads rose on these loans, contributing to the strains.

In mid-1976 the government approached U.S. banks for a balance-of-payments loan. They responded by forming a six-bank steering committee led by Citibank.[24] Feeling uncomfortable with their growing developing country exposure, the banks agreed in August to arrange an experimental deal (termed a balance-of-payments facility) to help Peru meet its payment obligations to the banks and avoid an outright rescheduling that would damage its creditworthiness. Citibank's Friedman masterminded the deal. Totaling $390 million, it involved a syndicate of eighteen U.S. banks ($210 million), two European syndicates ($115 million), a Canadian syndicate ($30 million), and a Japanese syndicate ($35 million). The deal was path-breaking in its multinational character and the requirement that all U.S. banks with substantial exposure in Peru participate in the U.S. syndicate.

At this point, the banks wanted to see policy reforms that would stabilize the Peruvian economy, but the government refused to negotiate a standby arrangement with the IMF. (The government was concerned that a standby would provide ammunition to political opponents who were accusing the government of mismanagement.) The government did, nevertheless, intro-

24. The banks were Bank of America, Chase Manhattan, Citibank, Manufacturers Hanover, Morgan Guaranty, and Wells Fargo. *Institutional Investor*, October 1976, p. 31.

duce a reform program of its own design to bolster its creditwhiness. As a precursor to the economic subcommittees used in Bank Advisory Committee negotiations in later years, the Peru steering committee formed a special subcommittee to monitor the program based on monthly reports prepared by the government. Still, a number of second-tier U.S. banks resisted being dragooned into the new loan, and considerable effort was required to structure it to reach the desired amount. One selling point was disbursing the loan in two tranches. Disbursement of the second tranche required the approval of banks contributing 75 percent of the loan amount, and it was understood that reaching this level would depend on better implementation of reforms by the government. The loan was finally signed and the first tranche disbursed in November. The second tranche was disbursed in February 1977, despite little evidence of improvement in policy implementation.

Peru's balance of payments deteriorated early in 1977, partly due to the failure of the annual anchovy harvest (source of Peru's substantial fish meal exports). Another factor was the government's decision at the end of 1976 to purchase thirty-six fighter-bombers from the Soviet Union for $250 million, which prompted some banks and suppliers to cut short-term trade credit to Peru. The banks warned the government that access to short-term credit could diminish further in the absence of a strong adjustment program supported by an IMF standby arrangement.[25]

In May 1977 a new finance minister was appointed who promptly adopted a reform program acceptable to the IMF. Domestic opposition to the program was fierce, however, and the minister was forced to resign two months later. Payment strains intensified. The Peruvian government finally floated the peso in the fall and implemented other measures required to obtain an IMF standby arrangement in November. Meanwhile the banks were rolling over maturing principal payments. In addition Wells Fargo Bank provided a $50 million bridge loan to help the government meet its interest obligations. Peru also requested an emergency loan of $100 million

25. The banks' insistence on IMF financing may have been motivated in part by negotiations under way to establish a new "recycling facility" in the IMF with $10 billion of resources. This facility would presumably increase the amount of financing Peru could obtain from the IMF to meet payment obligations to its creditors. The IMF membership decided in September 1977 to establish the Supplementary Financing Facility, but it did not become operational until the end of 1978 because of difficulties in obtaining approval from the U.S. Congress for the U.S. contribution. The creation of the Extended Fund Facility in 1974 and a quota increase agreed in March 1976 also expanded the scope for IMF financing to oil-importing countries in this period and thereby contributed to burden sharing.

from the U.S. Treasury's Exchange Stabilization Fund, but the request was turned down.[26] The rejection was a shock both to the Peruvian government, which was expecting substantial help from the United States for its politically unpopular adjustment efforts, and to the commercial banks hoping to avoid rescheduling.

Peruvian teams traveled to New York and European financial centers early in 1978 to obtain refinancing loans for around $300 million, but the effort was unsuccessful in large part because Peru was out of compliance with its IMF arrangement before the end of the first quarter. Around this time, to facilitate future negotiations, the U.S. bank steering committee evolved into an international steering committee by adding representatives from Canadian, Japanese, and European banks.[27] In May the Peruvian government appointed a new finance minister and a new central bank governor to implement a more stringent adjustment program. Martial law was declared to stop the riots that broke out when the program was announced.

In mid-1978, the banks agreed to roll over principal payments maturing in the second half of the year and then restructure these payments into a new loan, conditioned on Peru concluding a standby arrangement with the IMF and a rescheduling agreement with the Paris Club. A new standby arrangement, covering 1979 and 1980, went into effect in September. Toward the end of October the steering committee agreed in principle to reschedule 90 percent of Peru's principal payments falling due in 1979 and 1980.[28] In November the Paris Club agreed to reschedule Peru's debts on the same terms accepted by the commercial banks.[29] The bank deal formally closed in December.

Comparable treatment between Paris Club and London Club creditors was perfectly clear in this case and was achieved without any real controversy. Both agreements were limited to principal payments on medium-term debt, both treated payments falling due in 1979 and 1980, and the grace and repayment periods for the deferred payments were identical. The only difference was in the interest rates, which were market-based for commercial bank debt and negotiated bilaterally for Paris Club debt.

26. Similar loans had been obtained with relative ease in the 1950s and 1960s.

27. Manufacturers Hanover Bank led the new committee. Hardy (1982, p. 36).

28. The IMF was not represented in any of the negotiations between the commercial banks and Peru in the 1976–79 period, but informal contacts were made through telephone conversations or visits to Washington.

29. An agreement with the Soviet Union in early 1978 to reschedule payments due over the 1978–80 period may have helped Peru obtain its exceptional two-year rescheduling arrangements with commercial banks and the Paris Club.

To everyone's astonishment, Peru's balance of payments improved sharply during 1979 as export earnings rose almost 80 percent. The government prepaid the amounts originally due to commercial banks in 1979 and rescheduled the amounts originally due in 1980 at a lower spread over LIBOR. To maintain comparability Peru also paid in full to Paris Club creditors the amounts originally due in 1980.

Bank negotiations with Jamaica and Nicaragua during the same period reinforced some of the precedents set in the Peru case and introduced several new ones, noted in box B-1.[30]

Turkey, 1977–79

Like Argentina and Brazil, Turkey has lived at the edge of default for much of the past thirty years.[31] Time and again it has been rescued from disaster by its wealthy European neighbors and more distant NATO allies. Because of Turkey's position as a frontline state in the cold war era, successive governments could count on emergency assistance as an alternative to essential economic reforms that might have opened the door to a democratically elected but anti-West government. The first rescue package to include debt renegotiation—largely involving suppliers' credits guaranteed by official export credit agencies—was arranged in 1959. A second was arranged in 1965. Both were carried out within the framework of the Organization for European Economic Cooperation (predecessor of the OECD), of which Turkey was a member. The repayment terms on rescheduled debt were more generous than terms granted by the Paris Club, and additional support was provided in the form of balance-of-payments loans on soft terms.

The seeds of Turkey's debt crisis in the 1970s were sown when the OPEC cartel raised oil prices in 1973–74, hitting Turkey with a large terms-of-trade shock. The 1974–75 recession in the industrial countries represented one aftershock, and the Western embargo on military sales to Turkey following its invasion of Cyprus in 1974 represented a second one. Large deficits in the central government's budgets were financed by massive borrowing from the

30. The bank negotiations with Jamaica and Nicaragua are described in considerable detail in IMF (1980). Additional information is found in Friedman (1983). The summary here also benefitted from a conversation with William R. Rhodes (December 18, 2002), who chaired the committees for both countries. Argentina was having another bout of payment difficulties in 1976, too. Arrears to commercial banks emerged, but the new military government was successful in obtaining new loans in the context of comprehensive policy reforms as an alternative to rescheduling. Beim (1977, p. 724).

31. The section on Turkey draws on a conversation with Alfred Mudge, May 28, 2002.

Box B-1. The Cases of Jamaica and Nicaragua

In the case of Jamaica, arrears to commercial banks emerged early in 1977. In the middle of that year, a steering committee of North American banks was formed to negotiate a deal that would help Jamaica avoid rescheduling. A two-year IMF standby approved in August supported an adjustment program that was off track by the end of the year. As payment pressures intensified at the beginning of 1978, banks arranged a couple of bridge loans and discussions were pursued on a new-money loan from a consortium of lead banks. A three-year IMF arrangement under the new Extended Fund Facility was approved in June and shortly thereafter the banks agreed to extend a loan to refinance principal payments falling due in the 1978–79 fiscal year (the new-money loan was abandoned). This refinancing loan was formally signed in September. Jamaica also sought support from the banks for the second and third years of its IMF-supported program. For this purpose, the steering committee was enlarged to include European and Japanese banks. Agreement in principle was reached in November 1978 (a month after reaching the corresponding stage with Peru) to roll over most of the principal payments due in 1979–81 and convert them into term loans at the end of each year subject to successful implementation of Jamaica's IMF-supported program. This condition was not met because of political instability and was replaced by a rescheduling deal negotiated in March 1981.

A special feature of this case was the absence of a Paris Club operation, although there were special aid packages arranged covering the 1978–80 period. A related issue was the treatment of bank loans guaranteed by export credit agencies, which would have been rescheduled in the Paris Club. The export credit agencies eventually agreed to extend their cover to the rescheduled amounts. Strong political currents shaped this case. Shortly after being reelected in 1976, Prime Minister Michael Manley's government took control of the foreign-owned bauxite mines and relations with the United States in particular became seriously strained. After Manley's party lost to the pro-business

central bank. At the same time Turkey took full advantage of its ability to borrow from commercial banks on what appeared to be advantageous terms to finance its mushrooming trade and current account deficits. Much of this financing was obtained through the "convertible Turkish lira deposit" (CTLD) scheme introduced in 1975 to attract foreign deposits in Turkish

party led by Edward Seaga in the 1980 elections, relations with donors and private creditors quickly improved. Several more rescheduling deals were concluded between 1981 and 1991, but none involved debt reduction.

In the case of Nicaragua, borrowing from commercial banks escalated to finance reconstruction following a devastating earthquake in 1972 and to finance an extravagant development program. U.S. banks, including many small ones, provided most of this financing. When the civil war intensified in 1978, balance-of-payments strains grew, reflecting in part a drop in new bank financing. Exchange controls were introduced in September, and arrears to banks emerged in October on short-term debt and interest obligations as well as on long-term debt. The government organized an initial meeting in December to seek support from the banks . Sixty banks attended and shortly thereafter a steering committee of nine banks was formed. Formal rescheduling negotiations commenced in April 1979 after the government reached agreement with the IMF on a standby, and terms were agreed the next month on all elements except the interest rate. Meanwhile, the economic situation deteriorated rapidly in the first half of 1979 as the civil war entered its final stages. Political stability was restored when the Sandinista rebels gained control of the country in July. The new government immediately suspended negotiations with the banks and reviewed its options, which reportedly included repudiation. It quickly decided against repudiation and resumed negotiations. In September, a reformed steering committee reached agreement on a comprehensive rescheduling of outstanding bank debt, including short-term debt and arrears. The deal was exceptionally generous and included some innovative features such as deferring any portion of interest payments due above 7 percent and reducing the interest spread as a reward for good performance. This deal was also distinctive because it was not linked to either an IMF arrangement (the government had an antagonistic attitude toward the IMF) or a Paris Club operation. Nevertheless, Nicaragua was unable to stay current on its new obligations. An IDA-funded buyback in 1995 was required to clear its arrears to the banks.

banks by providing an exchange rate guarantee from the central bank.[32] At the end of 1976 Turkey's debt to Paris Club creditors was around $2.3 billion and to commercial banks less than $200 million (excluding the CTLD scheme).

32. Beyond the exchange rate guarantee, the attractions were spreads on the order of 1 3/4 percent above LIBOR and generous front-end fees.

Arrears on commercial bank loans emerged in late 1976, prompting a slowdown in new commitments from commercial banks. Political instability in Turkey contributed to delays in implementing an agreement to resume U.S. military aid and step up economic assistance. By October Turkey was effectively illiquid from the perspective of foreign bankers.[33]

Arrears to banks and official creditors reached a critical point in early 1978, prompting the government to adopt a reform program sufficient to qualify for a standby arrangement with the IMF in April and a rescheduling of debt owed to bilateral donor agencies in July. Following the precedents set in Turkey's 1959 and 1965 operations, the rescheduling was again negotiated in the OECD's "Consortium for Turkey," but it followed Paris Club rules more closely.[34] Turkey's OECD partners also came through with a large package of new aid.

In July 1978 Turkey began negotiations with a core group of eight banks—Citibank, Morgan Guaranty, Chase Manhattan, Deutsche Bank, Dresdner Bank, SBC, UBS, and Barclays—that represented more than 200 banks with Turkish exposure through the CTLD scheme. This steering committee emerged spontaneously rather than being established on the basis of specific precedents or a conscious policy decision.[35] Even though Turkey hired the Lazard-Warburg-Lehman troika as an advisor, the negotiations were protracted. One reason was that the Turkish government quickly fell out of compliance with its IMF-supported adjustment program. Another was that the banks were not prepared to commit as much new money as Turkey wanted. An equally important reason was that a daunting administrative problem had to be solved before the CTLD debt could be rescheduled: verifying the claims associated with more than 2,000 separate deposits in seven separate currencies made by approximately 250 banks.[36]

The situation came to a head in the summer of 1979. Turkey agreed to devalue the lira as part of a new adjustment program supported by the IMF. This program allowed Turkey to conclude another rescheduling agreement with OECD–Paris Club creditors in July and to qualify for another large package of OECD assistance.

---

33. "Austerity Now—and Hopes for IMF Aid," *Business Week*, October 17, 1977, p. 53.

34. The unprecedented inclusion of short-term debt in this operation illustrates the special treatment given to Turkey (Cizauskas 1979).

35. Bankers involved in this negotiation stressed its ad hoc nature and indicated that the earlier negotiations with Peru and Zaire were not considered relevant experience.

36. Mudge (1984a, p. 88).

In August 1979 Turkey wrapped up a deal described at the time as the most complicated foreign debt restructuring with commercial banks ever undertaken.[37] One of the biggest challenges in the bank negotiations was to find a position acceptable to banks with small exposures that were therefore not members of the steering committee, as well as to banks with large exposures that were on the committee.

The deal included a new-money loan (in the form of a letter of credit facility) of around $400 million from forty-odd banks, a restructuring loan to take out another $400 million of short-term deposits by fifteen banks in the Central Bank of Turkey, and a restructuring of $2.1 billion of convertible lira deposits.[38] This deal was fundamentally different from the Zaire and Peru deals because it did not affect outstanding medium-term loans. The new instruments were governed by New York law even though the negotiations took place in London. The documentation included a "comfort letter" from the IMF stating that Turkey had made all of the drawings to which it was entitled under its standby arrangement.

Turkey's last debt-restructuring operation with OECD–Paris Club creditors was concluded in July 1980. It was an exceptional three-year arrangement that deferred payments on previously rescheduled debt as well as unrescheduled principal and interest payments.

Remarkably, comparable treatment between OECD–Paris Club creditors and commercial banks did not become an issue in this case. One reason was certainly the special treatment that Turkey was able to obtain from its OECD partners. Another was the contrasting term structure of the respective bodies of debt. The OECD debt was predominately long term. The bulk of the commercial bank debt was short term in nature under the CTLD scheme. After rescheduling this entire amount in 1979, there was not much to be gained by forcing commercial banks to reschedule their relatively small long-term exposures. Moreover, by applying comparable treatment flexibly in this case, the OECD–Paris Club creditors were able to keep the door open for new loans from commercial banks as Turkey's economic performance improved.

37. C. Frederic Weigold, "$840 Million Loan Package Readied for Turkey," American Banker, July 11, 1979, p. 1.

38. The terms of the deal were improved in March 1982. Turkey managed to avoid recourse to further debt relief until the beginning of 2001, when some limited restructuring of commercial bank debt was undertaken to deal with a financial crisis triggered by political infighting.

Sudan, 1978–79

Sudan was another cold war pawn hit by high oil prices and low commodity prices in the mid-1970s.[39] It was also engaged in containing a persistent rebellion in its southern provinces. On the positive side Sudan was getting large amounts of financing from Saudi Arabia and Kuwait to support the strategic objective of transforming Sudan into the "bread basket of the Middle East."

Reflecting poor harvests as well as poor economic management, Sudan's balance of payments weakened in 1975, and arrears to commercial banks emerged. The banks were reluctant to enter into debt negotiations without more evidence of support from official creditors, such as an IMF standby arrangement and a Paris Club rescheduling. A low-conditionality standby was approved in mid-1978, but Sudan quickly fell out of compliance. Arrears to commercial banks grew steadily until mid-1979. Sudan barely avoided outright default during this period due in part to bilateral rescheduling by several donor countries and unilateral debt cancellation (linked to the North-South Dialogue) by others (including the United Kingdom).

The IMF began a new round of negotiations with Sudan in early 1979 and was able to put a three-year arrangement in place in May. This deal was supplemented by the first drawings from the IMF's new Supplementary Financing Facility and provided the basis for a relatively generous two-year Paris Club rescheduling operation in November.

In June 1979 Sudan initiated debt-relief discussions with individual commercial banks. Citibank once again played a leading role, this time in the person of John Botts, but was no longer pushing the new-money approach. Sudan's economic prospects were so bleak that it was widely viewed as a basket case. The only practical objective for the banks was to defer principal payments and hope that Sudan would be able to keep up with its interest payments. A formal steering committee, eventually representing around 115 banks with various kinds of exposure, was formed and held its first negotiating session in October 1979 in London. Agreement in principle was not reached until November 1980, after Sudan hired an investment bank advisor. Even then, the formal rescheduling agreement was not signed until December 1981.

39. The importance of the Sudan case has been stressed by only a few practitioners. The case of Côte d'Ivoire, beginning around 1977, may be just as important because the negotiations centered in Paris and established precedents for subsequent deals with numerous French-speaking countries in Africa.

The law firm of Coward Chance in London was selected to prepare the documentation to implement the agreed terms because it had, from the beginning, drafted the documents for syndicated eurocurrency loans arranged by Citibank under English law. The documentation developed for the Sudan deal provided a model for a number of subsequent deals. Some of the technical issues tackled included the treatment of debt for different purposes and the treatment of secured debt. The law firm of Surrey & Morse in London advised the government of Sudan.

The 1979 London Club rescheduling with Sudan was a Band-Aid. The commercial banks, stuck with about $1 billion of exposure (including short-term claims), deferred principal payments in agreements concluded in 1982, 1983, and 1984. Subsequent governments were distracted by the rebellion in the south and unable to implement essential economic reforms. Sudan accumulated very large arrears to the IMF and became (together with Liberia, Zaire, and Zambia) one of the deadest of the world's deadbeat countries during the 1990s.[40]

The Paris Club creditors received no better treatment despite continuing to extend new loans and grants to Sudan. Paris Club operations in 1979, 1982, 1983, and 1984 rescheduled more than $1.5 billion of debt cumulatively. Arrears piled up exponentially when aid flows were eventually curtailed.

Poland, 1980–81

The commercial bank rescheduling agreement with Poland in 1981 drew on many of the practices developed in earlier deals.[41] It also addressed some new issues and incorporated some innovative solutions that helped banks in subsequent negotiations with other countries.

Poland's debt difficulties originated in the economic modernization program undertaken by the communist regime of Edward Gierek during the 1970s. The government borrowed heavily from export credit agencies in the OECD countries and commercial banks eager to support this manifestation of cold war détente. As an oil importer with weak macroeconomic management, Poland used external borrowing increasingly to finance budget

40. Relations with the IMF improved temporarily in 2001, and preliminary steps were taken toward an operation to clear Sudan's arrears to the IMF. These accounted for half of the roughly $3 billion of arrears on the IMF's books at the end of 2002.
41. Some of the material on Poland is drawn from Delamaide (1984).

deficits rather than capital investment in the industrial sectors. In 1979 a syndicated loan for $500 million was oversubscribed by $50 million.

In 1980 Poland's prospects deteriorated sharply. Severe balance-of-payments strains developed as a result of a change in the Soviet Union's trade policies with its COMECON (Council for Mutual Economic Assistance) partners. Implicit subsidies were slashed as the Soviet Union acted to protect its own international liquidity. Another factor was a more skeptical attitude toward détente among the G-7 countries. To obtain another large syndicated bank loan in 1980, the Polish government had to seek a partial guarantee from the West German government.[42]

In the meantime a coalition of labor unions and the Catholic Church gathered strength despite periodic episodes of repression by the government. A worker strike at the Gdansk shipyard in August 1980 gave birth to the Solidarity movement. As the government struggled to contain civil unrest, it turned to debt restructuring to ease balance-of-payments strains, concluding an initial rescheduling with Paris Club creditors in April 1981. General Wojciech Jaruzelski introduced martial law in December 1981 to prevent demonstrations for religious and intellectual freedom from getting out of hand. The OECD countries responded by abruptly stopping the flow of new credit and refusing to negotiate further Paris Club support.

Poland's debt crisis was the first "systemic" case. First, the amount of commercial debt involved was around $12 billion, four times the size of Turkey's (the biggest case up to that point). Second, based on years of observing the efforts made by the Soviet Union to protect the strong credit ratings of all Soviet bloc borrowers, commercial lenders expected that the Soviet Union would intervene to prevent a commercial default by any of its COMECON partners. This implicit protection was called the "Soviet umbrella." The Polish leak in the umbrella raised doubts about commercial bank lending to all communist countries. Out of a total of $50 billion owed by these countries to both official and private creditors at the end of 1976, $30 billion was owed to commercial banks.[43]

The bad news was delivered to the banks at a meeting in a guild hall in London (Plaisterers' Hall) in March 1981. The messenger was Jan Woloszyn, a senior official at Bank Handlowy, the agency used by the Polish government to manage its external borrowing. Representatives from most of the 500–600 banks that had participated in one or more of Poland's syndicated

42. Carvounis (1984, pp. 154–55).
43. "The New Sophistication in East-West Banking," Business Week, March 7, 1977, p. 40.

loans were in attendance.[44] To simplify the negotiation process, a multinational task force was formed with representatives from 50 banks. The law firm of Coward Chance in London was selected to advise the task force, which had its first meeting in July in Zurich, hosted by Swiss Bank Corporation. Autwin Klapper from Creditanstalt in Vienna chaired the task force. Because 50 banks were unwieldy, a working group of twelve banks headed by Klapper did most of the preparatory work. These included Citibank, Bank of America, Barclays, Lloyds, BNP, Dresdner, and Bank of Tokyo. Meetings of the working group were held at the headquarters of the participating banks in rotation.

An important development in this case was the formation of the first formal economic subcommittee, functionally similar to the informal subcommittee created for Peru in 1976. Gabriel Eichler from Bank of America was selected to chair it. This step was necessitated by the fact that Poland was not a member of the IMF at the time. Consequently the banks had no alternative for assessing Poland's future debt-servicing capacity or linking their rescheduling to essential reforms. Nor could they condition their agreement on a Paris Club operation; the official creditors refused to negotiate with the Jaruzelski government as a way of expressing their distaste for martial law.

Several practices were firmed up in this case. The banks insisted that interest arrears be cleared before the rescheduling would go into effect. They also insisted that short-term loans (360 days or less) be excluded from rescheduling to ensure that vital trade flows would not be interrupted. To keep Poland on a short leash, the rescheduling window was limited to one year.

Various technical issues were sorted out that provided precedents for subsequent deals. The loans at stake had been made in as many as forty different currencies. Formulas for converting debt into seven major currencies, each with a different interest rate, were developed. Banks were restricted in the amount of switching they could do from one currency into another, except that all banks could switch freely into U.S. dollars. The cutoff date was a contentious issue because some loans had closed immediately before the Plaisterers' Hall meeting, and the participants argued that these should not be tampered with. Some bond debt was outstanding, but the general view was to avoid compromising Poland's capital market access (a potential source of funds to service outstanding debt to banks). Bondholders were

44. A last-ditch effort by Woloszyn to arrange a $1 billion jumbo loan had flopped in January, prompting some banks to cut short-term lines of credit.

given the option of rescheduling on the same basis as bank debt or escaping the process. New money was another key element of the deal. However, it was disguised by recycling interest into a revolving trade facility and arranging a "voluntary loan."

The negotiations with Poland were long and bumpy. The Polish negotiators argued that there was insufficient foreign exchange to clear arrears up front, and they continued to mount. The task force concluded an agreement in April 1982 on rescheduling terms for Poland's 1981 principal payments and immediately began discussing rescheduling terms for 1982 payments. In five subsequent deals, almost all principal payments falling due through 1987 were rescheduled, and some interest payments were recapitalized. In 1988 the entire stock of commercial bank debt was restructured. In 1994, following the collapse of the Iron Curtain, a Brady Plan exchange was carried out.

The Paris Club held out until July 1985 to avoid rewarding the Jaruzelski government for its suppression of democratic forces.[45] Follow-on rescheduling agreements were concluded in November 1985, December 1987, and February 1990. In April 1991 an exceptional operation was carried out to reward Poland for its role in ending the cold war. In this operation Poland's outstanding Paris Club debt was reduced by 50 percent in net present value terms. By force of the Paris Club's comparable treatment principle, commercial bank creditors were required to write down their claims despite evidence that Poland did not have an external financing gap to justify such relief.

45. Poland had applied for membership in the IMF early in the decade, but little progress was made during martial law. By mid-1985, however, support was growing for Poland's application, and it formally joined the IMF in June 1986.

References

Allen, Peter T., and Daniel C. Peirce. 1997. "Poland: The First Investment-Grade Brady Bonds." In *The New Dynamics of Emerging Markets Investment: Managing Sub-Investment Grade Sovereign Risk*, edited by Michael Pettis, chapter 10. London: Euromoney Publications.

Bartholomew, Ed, Ernest Stern, and Angella Liuzzi. 2002. *Two-Step Sovereign Debt Restructuring*. New York: J. P. Morgan.

Beim, David O. 1977. "Rescuing the LDCs." *Foreign Affairs* 55 (4): 717–31.

Birdsall, Nancy, and Brian Deese. 2002. "Delivering on Debt Relief." *CGD Brief 1*. Center for Global Development, Washington (April).

Birdsall, Nancy, and John Williamson. 2002. *Delivering on Debt Relief: From IMF Gold to a New Aid Architecture*. Washington: Center for Global Development and Institute for International Economics.

Bitterman, Henry J. 1973. *The Refunding of International Debt*. Duke University Press.

Bogdanowicz-Bindert, Christine A. 1985. "World Debt: The United States Reconsiders." *Foreign Affairs* 64 (2): 259–273.

Boote, Anthony, and Kamau Thugge. 1997. "Debt Relief for Low-Income Countries and the HIPC Initiative." Working Paper 97/24. International Monetary Fund, Washington (March).

Borchard, Edwin M., and William H. Wynne. 1951. *State Insolvency and Foreign Bondholders*. Yale University Press. Reprint. Beard Books, Washington, 2000.

Boughton, James M. 2001. *Silent Revolution: The International Monetary Fund, 1979–1989.* Washington: International Monetary Fund.

Bowe, Michael, and James W. Dean. 1997. *Has the Market Solved the Sovereign-Debt Crisis?* Princeton Studies in International Finance 83. Princeton University, International Finance Section (August).

Brau, E., and others. 1983. "Recent Multilateral Debt Restructuring with Official and Bank Creditors." Occasional Paper 25. International Monetary Fund, Washington.

Buchheit, Lee C., and G. Mitu Gulati. 2000. "Exit Consents in Sovereign Bond Exchanges." *UCLA Law Review* 48: 59–84.

Buiter, Willem C., and Anne C. Sibert. 1999. "UDROP: A Contribution to the New International Financial Architecture." *International Finance* 2: 227–47.

Callaghy, Thomas M. 1993. " Restructuring Zaire's Debt, 1979–1982." In *Dealing with Debt: International Financial Negotiations and Adjustments Borrowing*, edited by Thomas J. Biersteker. Westview Press.

Camdessus, Michel. 1984. "Governmental Creditors and the Role of the Paris Club." In *Default and Rescheduling Corporate and Sovereign Borrowers*, edited by David Suratgar. London: Euromoney Publications.

Carvounis, Chris C. 1984. *The Debt Dilemma of Developing Nations: Issues and Cases.* Quorum Books.

Checki, Terrence J., and Ernest Stern. 2000. "Financial Crises in the Emerging Markets: Roles of the Public and Private Sectors." *Current Issues in Economics and Finance* 6 (13): 1–6.

Cizauskas, Albert C. 1979. "International Debt Renegotiation: Lessons from the Past." *World Development* 7(2): 199–210.

Clark, Keith. 1986. "Sovereign Debt Restructuring: Parity of Treatment between Equivalent Creditors in Relation to Comparable Debts." *International Lawyer* 20 (3): 857–65.

Clark, Keith, and Martin Hughes. 1984. "Approaches to the Restructuring of Sovereign Debt." In *Sovereign Lending: Managing Legal Risk*, edited by Michael Gruson and Ralph Reisner. London: Euromoney Publications.

Cline, William R. 1995. *International Debt Reexamined.* Washington: Institute for International Economics.

Cohen, Benjamin. 1989. "LDC Debt: Is Activism Required?" In *Third World Debt: The Search for a Solution*, edited by Graham Bird. Edward Elgar.

Commission on International Development (chaired by Lester B. Pearson). 1969. *Partners in Development.* Praeger Publishers.

Council on Foreign Relations. 1999. *Safeguarding Prosperity in a Global Financial System: The Future International Architecture.* Report of an Independent Task Force. Washington: Institute for International Economics.

———. 2000. *Roundtable on Country Risk in the Post-Asia Crisis Era: Identifying Risks, Strategies, and Policy Implications.* Key Recommendations from Working Group Discussions, October 1999–September 2000. www.cfr.org/public/pubs/Country-Risks_Recom_Report.htm.

Dammers, Clifford. 1984. "A Brief History of Sovereign Defaults and Rescheduling." In *Default and Rescheduling Corporate and Sovereign Borrowers*, edited by David Suratgar. London: Euromoney Publications.

Delamaide, Darrell. 1984. *Debt Shock: The Full Story of the World Credit Crisis*. Doubleday.

Dillon, K. Burke, and others. 1985. "Recent Developments in External Debt Restructuring." Occasional Paper 40. International Monetary Fund, Washington.

Dimancescu, Dan. 1983. *Deferred Future: Corporate and World Debt and Bankruptcy*. Cambridge, Mass.: Ballinger Publishing Company.

Donaldson, T. H . 1979. *International Lending by Commercial Banks*. Wiley and Sons.

Eichengreen, Barry. 1988. "Resolving Debt Crises: An Historical Perspective." Discussion Paper 239. London: Centre for Economic Policy Research (June).

———. 2000a. "The EMS Crisis in Retrospect." Working Paper 8035. Cambridge, Mass.: National Bureau of Economic Research (December).

———. 2000b. "Is Greater Burden Sharing Possible?" In *Reforming the International Monetary and Financial System*, edited by Peter B. Kenen and Alexander K. Swoboda. Washington: International Monetary Fund.

———. 2002. *Financial Crises:And What to Do About Them*. Oxford University Press.

Eichengreen, Barry, and Richard Portes. 1989. "After the Deluge: Default, Negotiation and Readjustment during the Inter-War Years." In *The International Debt Crisis in Historical Perspective*, edited by Barry Eichengreen and Peter H. Lindert. MIT Press.

———. 1995. *Crisis? What Crisis? Orderly Workouts for Sovereign Debtors*. London: Centre for Economic Policy Research.

Friedman, Irving. 1977. *The Emerging Role of Private Banks in the Developing World*. New York: Citicorp.

———. 1983. *The World Debt Dilemma: Managing Country Risk*. Washington and Philadelphia: Council for International Banking Studies and Robert Morris Associates.

Gitlin, Richard A. 2002. "A Proposal: Sovereign Debt Forum." Presentation at the U.N. Financing for Development Conference, Monterrey, Mexico, March 19, 2002.

Group of Seven Finance Ministers. 1999. "Report to the Cologne Economic Summit." June 18–20. www.g7.utoronto.ca/g7/finance/fin061999.htm (8/2/02).

Group of Ten. 1996. *The Resolution of Sovereign Liquidity Crisis*. Washington: International Monetary Fund.

———. 2002. "Report of the Working Group on Contractual Clauses." Washington (September 26). www.imf.org/external/np/g10/2002/cc.pdf (May 22, 2003).

Group of Thirty. 2002. *Key Issues in Sovereign Debt Restructuring*. Washington.

Group of Twenty-Two. 1998. *Report of the Working Group on International Financial Crises*. www.bis.org/publ/othpol.htm (August 23, 2002).

Haldane, Andy, and Mark Kruger. 2001. "The Resolution of International Financial Crises: Private Finance and Public Funds." www.bankofengland.co.uk/financialstability/boeandboc.pdf (August 23, 2002).

Hardy, Chandra. 1982. *Rescheduling Developing Country Debts, 1956-1982*. Washington: Overseas Development Council.

Harrison, Glennon J. 1989. *Rescheduling International Debt*. Washington: Library of Congress, Congressional Research Service.

Hawn, Robert V. 1984. "The Re-negotiation of the Official International Debt: Whose Club Is It?" *University of California Davis Law Review* 17 (3): 853–89.

Holley, H. A. 1987. *Developing Country Debt: The Role of the Commercial Banks*. London: Routledge & Kegan Paul for the Royal Institute of International Affairs.

Hudes, Karen. 1986. "Co-ordination of Paris and London Club Rescheduling." In *International Borrowing: Negotiating and Structuring International Debt Transactions*, edited by Daniel D. Bradlow, 2d ed. Washington: International Law Institute.

Independent Commission on International Development Issues.1980. *North-South:A Program for Survival*. (The Brandt Commission Report). MIT Press.

Institute of International Finance. 1996. *Resolving Sovereign Financial Crises*. Report of the Working Group on Crisis Resolution. Washington.

———. 1999a. *Report of the Working Group on Financial Crisis in Emerging Markets*. Washington (January).

———. 1999b. *Steering Committee on Emerging Markets Finance: Special Report*. Washington (April).

———. 1999c. *Summary Report on the Work of the IIF Steering Committee on Emerging Markets Finance*. Washington (June).

———. 2001. *Survey of Debt Restructuring by Private Creditors*. Washington (April).

———. 2002. *Action Plan of the IIF Special Committee on Crisis Prevention and Resolution in Emerging Markets*. Washington (April).

International Financial Institution Advisory Commission. 2000. *Report*. Washington: United States Congress. Available at www.house.gov/jec/imf/meltzer.htm (May 26, 2003).

International Monetary Fund. 1980. "Debt Restructuring by Commercial Banks—Recent Experience of Some Fund Members." SM/80/275. Washington (December 31).

———. 1980–2001. *Annual Report*. Washington.

———. 1993–2002. *World Economic Outlook*. Washington.

———. 1993–2001. *International Capital Markets*. Washington.

———. 1999a. *IMF Policy on Lending into Arrears to Private Creditors*. Washington (June 14). www.imf.org/external/pubs/ft/privcred/index.htm (August 24, 2002).

———. 1999b. *Involving the Private Sector in Forestalling and Resolving Financial Crises*. Washington (March 17). www.imf.org/external/pubs/ft/series/01/index.htm (August 24, 2002).

———. 2000. *Involving the Private Sector in the Resolution of Financial Crises—Standstills—Preliminary Considerations.* Washington (September 5). www.imf.org/external/np/pdr/sstill/2000/eng/index.htm (August 24, 2002).

———. 2001a. *Involving the Private Sector in the Resolution of Financial Crises—Restructuring International Bonds.* Washington (January 11). www.imf.org/external/pubs/ft/series/03/index.htm (August 24, 2002).

———. 2001b. *Involving the Private Sector in the Resolution of Financial Crises—The Treatment of the Claims of Private Sector and Paris Club Creditors—Preliminary Considerations.* Washington (June 27). www.imf.org/External/NP/psi/2001/eng/index.htm (August 24, 2002).

———. 2001c. *Official Financing for Developing Countries.* Washington.

———. 2002a. "Assessing Sustainability." Washington (May 28). www.imf.org/external/np/pdr/sus/2002/end/052802.htm (February 8, 2003).

———. 2002b. *Collective Action Clauses in Sovereign Bond Contracts—Encouraging Greater Use.* Washington (June 6). www.imf.org/external/np/psi/2002/eng/060602a.htm (August 31, 2002).

———. 2002c. *The Design and Effectiveness of Collective Action Clauses.* Washington (June 6). www.imf.org/external/np/psi/2002/eng/020602.htm (August 31, 2002).

———. 2002d. "The Design of the SDRM—Further Considerations." Washington (November 27). www.imf.org/external/np/pdr/sdrm/2002/081402.htm (December 22, 2002).

———. 2002e. "Fund Policy on Lending into Arrears to Private Creditors—Further Consideration of the Good Faith Criterion." Washington (July 30). www.imf.org/external/np/sec/pn/2002/pn02107.htm (December 30, 2002).

———. 2002f. *Sovereign Debt Restructuring Mechanism—Further Considerations.* Washington (August 14). www.imf.org/external/np/pdr/sdrm/2002/081402.htm (December 22, 2002).

———. 2003a. "Collective Action Clauses: Recent Developments and Issues." Washington (March 25). www.imf.org/external/np/psi/2003/032503.htm (April 19, 2003).

———. 2003b. "Crisis Resolution in the Context of Sovereign Debt Restructuring: A Summary of Considerations." Washington (Janaury 28). www.imf.org/external/np/pdr/sdrm/2003.012803.htm (April 5, 2003).

———. 2003c. "Proposed Features of a Sovereign Debt Restructuring Mechanism." Washington (February 12). www.imf.org/external/np/pdr/sdrm/2003/021203.htm (April 5, 2003).

———. 2003d. "Report of the Managing Director to the IMFC on a Statutory Sovereign Debt Restructuring Mechanism." Washington (April 8). www.imf.org/external/np/omd/2003/040803.htm (April 12, 2003).

Kearney, Christine A. 1993. "The Clubs: London and Paris." In *Dealing with Debt: International Financial Negotiations and Adjustment Bargaining*, edited by Thomas J. Biersteker. Westview Press.

Kenen, Peter B. 1977. "Debt Relief as Development Assistance." In *The New International Economic Order: The North-South Debate*, edited by Jagdish N. Bhagwati. MIT Press.

———. 2001. *The International Financial Architecture: What's New? What's Missing?* Washington: Institute for International Economics.

———. 2002. "The International Financial Architecture: Old Issues and New Initiatives." *International Finance* 5 (Spring): 23–45.

Klein, Thomas M. 1973. "Economic Aid through Debt Relief." *Finance and Development* (September): 17–20, 34–35.

Kraft, Joseph. 1984. *The Mexican Rescue.* New York: Group of Thirty.

Krueger, Anne O. 2002. *A New Approach to Sovereign Debt Restructuring.* Washington: International Monetary Fund.

Kuhn, Michael G., and Jorge P. Guzman. 1990. *Multilateral Official Debt Rescheduling: Recent Experience.* Washington: International Monetary Fund.

Lane, Timothy, and others. 1999. "IMF-Supported Programs in Indonesia, Korea, and Thailand: A Preliminary Assessment." Occasional Paper 178. International Monetary Fund, Washington.

de Lattre, André. 1999. *Servir aux Finances.* Paris: Comité pour l'histoire économique et financière de la France.

Leland, Marc E. 1983. "Rescheduling from a United States Perspective." In *Rescheduling Techniques: An International Conference on Sovereign Debt.* London: Group of Thirty and Oyez IBC Limited.

Lomax, David F. 1986. *The Developing Country Debt Crisis.* St. Martin's Press.

Macmillan, Rory. 1995. "Towards a Sovereign Debt Work-out System." *North Western Journal of International Law and Business* 16 (1): 57–106.

Makin, John. H. 1984. *The Global Debt Crisis: America's Growing Involvement.* Basic Books.

McDonald, John W., Jr. 1982. "The North-South Dialogue and the United Nations." Occasional paper. Georgetown University, Institute for the Study of Diplomacy, Edmund A. Walsh School of Foreign Service, Washington.

Mentré, Paul. 1984. "The Fund, Commercial Banks and Member Countries." Occasional Paper 26. International Monetary Fund, Washington.

Mudge, Alfred. 1984a. "Sovereign Debt Restructuring: A Current Perspective." In *Default and Rescheduling: Corporate and Sovereign Borrowers*, edited by David Suratgar. London: Euromoney Publications.

———. 1984b. " Sovereign Debt Restructure: A Perspective of Counsel to Agent Banks Advisory Groups and Servicing Banks." *Columbia Journal of Transnational Law* 23 (1): 59–74.

———. 1988. "Country Debt Restructure: Continuing Legal Concerns." In *Prospects for International Lending and Rescheduling*, edited by Joseph Jude Norton. Matthew Bender.

———. 1992. "Country Debt Restructure, 1982–87: An Overview." In *Current Legal Issues Affecting Central Banks*, vol. 1, edited by Robert C. Effros. Washington: International Monetary Fund.

Mussa, Michael. 2002. *Argentina and the Fund: From Triumph to Tragedy.* Washington: Institute for International Economics.

Newman, Peter, and others, eds. 1992. *The New Palgrave Dictionary of Money and Finance.* Macmillan Press.

Nowzad, Bahram, and others. 1981. *"External Indebtedness of Developing Countries."* Occasional Paper 3. International Monetary Fund, Washington (April).

Ortiz, Guillermo. 2002. "Recent Emerging Market Crises—What Have We Learned ?" Per Jacobsson Lecture delivered at the Bank for International Settlements, Basel, July 7, 2002. www.bis.org/events/agm2002/sp020707.htm (August 9,2002).

Peterson Commission. 1970. *U.S. Foreign Assistance in 1970's: A New Approach.* Report to the President from the Task Force on International Development. Washington: Government Printing Office.

Putnam, Robert D., and Nicholas Bayne. 1984. *Hanging Together: Cooperation and Conflict in the Seven Power Summit.* London: SAGE Publications.

Raffer, Kunibert. 1990. "Applying Chapter 9 Insolvency to International Debts: An Economically Efficient Solution with a Human Face." *World Development* 18 (2): 301–11.

Rhodes, William R. 1983. "The Role of the Steering Committee: How It Can Be Improved." In *Rescheduling Techniques: An International Conference on Sovereign Debt.* London: Group of Thirty and Oyez IBC Limited.

———. 1989. "A Negotiator's View." In *Solving the Global Debt Crisis:Strategies and Controversies,* edited by Christine A. Bogdanowicz-Bindert. Harper and Row.

Rieffel, Alexis. 1984. "The Paris Club: 1978–1983." *Columbia Journal of Transnational Law* 23 (1): 83–110.

———. 1985. "The Role of Paris Club in Managing Debt Problems." *Essays in International Finance* 61. Princeton University, International Finance Section.

Robinson, James D., III, and Andrew H. Bartels. 1989. "Comprehensive Approaches for Solving the Debt Crisis." In *Solving the Global Debt Crisis: Strategies and Controversies,* edited by Christine A. Bogdanowicz-Bindert. Harper and Row.

Rogoff, Kenneth, and Jeromin Zettelmeyer. 2002. "Bankruptcy Procedures for Sovereigns: A History of Ideas, 1976–2001." *IMF Staff Papers* 49 (September): 470–507.

Sachs, Jeffrey. 1986. "Managing the LDC Debt Crisis." In *Brookings Papers on Economic Activity:2,* edited by William C. Brainard and George L. Perry. Brookings.

———. 1988. "Comprehensive Debt Retirement: The Bolivian Example." In *Brookings Papers on Economic Activity: 2,* edited by William C. Brainard and George L. Perry. Brookings.

———. 1995. *Do We Need an International Lender of Last Resort?* Harvard University Press.

Sevigny, David. 1990. *The Paris Club: An Inside View.* Ottawa: The North-South Institute.

Surrey, Walter Sterling, and Peri N. Nash. 1984. "Bankers Look beyond the Debt Crisis: The Institute of International Finance." *Columbia Journal of Transnational Law* 23 (1): 111–30.

Trichet, Jean-Claude. 1989. "Official Debt Rescheduling: The Paris Club." In *Solving the Global Debt Crisis: Strategies and Controversies,* edited by Christine A. Bogdanowicz-Bindert. Harper and Row.

United Nations. 1977. *Proceedings of the United Nations Conference on Trade and Development, Fourth Session, Nairobi* (Volume I: Report and Annexes). New York.

————. 1980. *Report of the Trade and Development Board, Volume II (Twenty-First Session).* United Nations Conference on Trade and Development. General Assembly, Official Records: Thirty-Fifth Session (A/35/15). New York.

————. 1981. *Proceedings of the United Nations Conference on Trade and Development, Fifth Session, Manila* (Volume I: Report and Annexes). New York.

United Nations Center on Transnational Corporations. 1989. *International Debt Restructuring: Substantive Issues and Techniques.* UNCTC Advisory Studies, Series B, No. 4. New York: United Nations.

United Nations Conference on Trade and Development. 1975. *Debt Problems of Developing Countries. Report of the Ad Hoc Group of Governmental Experts on Its Third Session.* TD/B/545/Rev. 1. Geneva.

United Nations Conference on Trade and Development. Trade and Development Board. 1978a. *Elaboration of Detailed Features for Future Operations Relating to Debt Problems of Interested Developing Countries: Note by the UNCTAD Secretariat.* (Intergovernmental Group of Experts on Debt and Development Problems of Developing Countries.) TD/B.AC.28/2. Geneva.

————.1978b. *Report of the Intergovernmental Group of Experts on Debt and Development Problems of Developing Countries.* TD/B/AC.28.3. Geneva.

————. 1985. *The History of UNCTAD, 1964-84.* New York.

U.S. Department of State. 1999. *User's Guide to the Paris Club: A Guide to How the U.S. Government Reschedules Official Debt.* Office of Monetary Affairs, Economics Bureau (December).

U.S. National Advisory Council, Department of the Treasury. 1956–1998. *Reports on International Monetary and Financial Policies to the President and to the Congress.* (Quarterly, semi-annual, or annual).

U.S. House Committee on Banking, Finance and Urban Affairs. 1977. *Hearing before the Subcommittee on Financial Institutions, Supervision, Regulation and Insurance.* March–April. Washington: GPO.

Wagner, Rodney B. 1989. "The LDC Debt Problem." In *Solving the Global Debt Crisis: Strategies and Controversies,* edited by Christine A. Bogdanowicz-Bindert. Harper and Row.

Walker, Mark A., and Lee C Buchheit. 1984. "Legal Issues in the Restructuring of Commercial Bank Loans to Sovereign Borrowers." In *Sovereign Lending: Managing Legal Risk,* edited by Michael Gruson and Ralph Reisner. London: Euromoney Publications.

Watson, C.M, and K. P. Regling. 1992 "History of the Debt Crisis." In *Current Legal Issues Affecting Central Banks,* vol.1, edited by Robert C. Effros. Washington: International Monetary Fund.

Wellons, Philip A. 1987. *Passing the Buck: Banks, Governments, and the Third World Debt.* Harvard Business School Press.

Wertman, Patricia A. 1989a. *The "Brady Plan" and the Third World Debt Problem.* Washington: Library of Congress, Congressional Research Service.

———. 1989b. *An International Debt Authority: A Brief Overview.* Washington: Library of Congress, Congressional Research Service.

Winkler, Max. 1933. *Foreign Bonds, An Autopsy: A Study of Defaults and Repudiations of Government Obligations.* Reprint. Manchester, N.H.: Ayer Company, 1976.

World Bank. 2002. *Global Development Finance—2002.* Washington.

Yianni, Andrew. 2002. "Proposed New Approach to Sovereign Debt Restructuring." *Central Banking* 12 (February): 78–88.

Zweig, Phillip L. 1995. *Wriston: Walter Wriston,Citibank and the Rise and Fall of American Financial Supremacy.* New York: Crown Publications.

Index

policy preferences, 101–02; international institutions and, 15n8; sovereign immunity and, 13. *See also* Sovereign debt restructuring; Sovereign Debt Restructuring Mechanism

Basel Committee on Banking Supervision, 34, 166, 261n1

Behavior of economic agents: asymmetrical information effects, 10; consumption and investment, 9–10; herd behavior, 10–11; moral hazard, 10; saving and lending, 10

Bilateral agencies, 53n4; commercial bank lending practices and, 105; lending policies and practices, 35; Paris Club workout policies, 73

BIS. *See* Bank for International Settlements

Bloom, Rick, 122–23b

Blumenthal, Michael, 201n18

Bond debt: Argentine default, 216–19, 270–71; borrower's perspective, 39–40; challenges in restructuring, 264–65; collective action clauses, 223, 227, 230, 237, 257, 258, 259, 265–66, 267b, 287; comparable treatment issues, 280–84; country risk premium, 40; debt reduction in *1980s* crises, 165–66; Ecuador, forced restructuring, 212–13, 242, 263–64; emerging market bonds, 192–94, 192n2; future of international machinery, 5, 19–20, 148, 266–71, 287; future of sovereign debt restructuring, 7, 223; G-7 policy, 189, 264, 283; G-*10* recommendations, 223; growth trends, 5, 19, 37, 74, 130–31, 192, 262–63; historical development, 96, 194–97; IIF restructuring recommendations, 246–47; IMF restructuring recommendations, 245–46; institutional investment in, 265; international institutions for restructuring, 2; London Club and, 96, 264; maturity structure, 37–38; in Mexican crisis of *1994*, 4–5; nature of investor risk, 38, 39; Pak-

istan, forced restructuring, 211–12, 236–37, 263–64; Paris Club workout policies, 74–75, 94; policy issues, 2–3, 5, 189, 262–63; restrictions on restructuring, 37; secondary markets, 38, 40; source of profit in, 38–39; in sovereign workouts, 37, 40; special features, 37–40; Ukraine, forced restructuring, 212, 263–64

Borrowing: characteristics of mature democracies, 50b; debtor categories in sovereign workouts, 20, 21b, 41; economic theory of, 10; foreign, 16–17; hierarchy of borrowers in sovereign default, 42–44; nature of bond financing, 39–40; by public sector enterprises, 42; repudiation of previous government's debt, 52; sources of market failure, 10–11; by sovereign authorities, 42; by subsovereign entities, 42

Brady, Nicholas, 150b, 170

Brady Plan, 19, 37, 74, 115; accomplishments, 150, 170, 171b, 176–77, 188; Brady bonds, 192, 213; bond status in debt hierarchy, 193; criticisms of, 152; Ecuador deal, 213n36; London Club process, 120, 128, 129; main features, 150–51b, 152, 156, 170–72; negotiations, 174–76; new money support, 173–74; objectives, 150–51; official enhancements, 172–73; options for restructuring, 172; origins, 150b, 152–53, 168–70; participants, 155–56; U.S. participation, 151–52

Brandt, Willy, 147

Brandt Commission, 147

Brazil, 51b, 54n6, 98, 195, 235; crisis (*1998–99*), 213–15; current status, 218; debt crisis (*1980s*), 165–66; London Club negotiations, 112–14, 122–23b, 128; Paris Club and, 58; Real Plan, 213–14

Bretton Woods system, 7; accomplishments, 2; adaptability, 1–2; limitations,

2; origins, 1; procedural reforms
(*1970*s), 3. *See also* International Monetary Fund; World Bank
Bridge loans, 126n46; and *1980*s debt crisis, 158
Buiter, William, 248–49
Burden sharing, in sovereign debt restructuring, 2–3; Argentina (*2001*), 215–16; bonds and, 189; Brazil (*1999*), 214–15; forced bond restructurings (*1999*), 210–13; G-7 approach, 55, 57–58, 60–61; goals, 55; IIF recommendations, 226–27; local currency issues, 16; London Club principles, 110; Paris Club approach, 7, 57, 60–61, 72–75, 262, 283–86; private sector costs, 54–55; and *1980*s debt crisis, 3–4, 160–61; taxpayer costs, 53–54
Burns, Arthur, 101
Bush (G. H. W.) administration, 168–69

Camdessus, Michel, 145n36, 198, 244
Canada, 24, 183
Capital account liberalization, 225–26, 235–36
Capital flows of *1990*s, 189, 190–92, 191b, 225, 275–76
Cardoso, Fernando Henrique, 214
Cavallo, Domingo, 216, 217
Center for Global Development, 279n23
Central banking systems, 50–51b
Chapter *9* bankruptcy (U.S. Code), 15
Chapter *7* liquidation (U.S. Code), 14
Chapter *11* restructuring (U.S. Code), 14–15
Chase Manhattan Bank, 117
Checki, Terence, 174n51
Chile, 99b, 129, 162, 166
China, 46, 139, 191
Citibank, 97–98, 117, 159, 165
Cleary, Gottlieb, Steen, & Hamilton, 76–77n30, 117n38
Clifford Chance, 117
Cline, William R., 152–53, 170
Clinton administration, 228

Cohen, Benjamin, 169b
Collective action clauses, 223, 227, 230, 233, 237, 257, 258, 259, 265–66, 267b, 287
Commercial banks: as borrowers in sovereign debt restructuring, 43; Brady Plan provisions, 150b, 151b, 152; in Brazilian *1999* workout, 214–15; debt crisis of *1980*s, 3–4, 150–51, 155, 156–57, 158–59, 162–63, 164–68; debtor country reporting systems, 100n10; emerging market capital flows, 191; foreign lending practices, 36, 38; goals of sovereign lending, 106; history of international lending, 96–102; as lenders in sovereign debt restructuring, 36–37; lending in developing countries, 19; losses in *1990*s crises, 210–11; Paris Club workout policies, 74; post–Soviet Russian debt, 209; risk management, 36, 84, 111; role of London Club, 2, 95, 96, 102–03; in South Korean crisis, 206–07; World Bank financing of debt buy–backs, 30. *See also* London Club; Private creditors
Commission on International Development, 133, 181
Conference on International Economic Cooperation, 139, 140–42
Consumption behavior, 9–10
Contract law, 45–47
Corporation of Foreign Bondholders, 196
Corrigan, Gerald, 174n51
Costanzo, Al, 98
Côte d'Ivoire, 114n33, 166n32, 278n21
Council on Foreign Relations, 238, 249
Creditor Reporting System, 22
Crisis management: Brazil (*1998*), 213–15; Bretton Woods system, 2; crisis prevention, 47–49, 220, 226, 230, 260, 273; current policy issues, 5, 6; G-7 role, 26–27; IIF recommendations, 226–27, 234–39; incidence, 19n11; in *1990*s, 188–89, 210–11; oil shocks of *1970*s, 100; Turkey (*2001*),

226–27, 234–39, 247–48; G-7 and, 238, 247–48, 261; G-10 recommendations and, 226, 227; private sector losses, 210; on restructuring of private debt, 246–47; on Sovereign Debt Restructuring Mechanism, 257–58

Institutional investors, 265

Inter-American Development Bank, 31, 34; and 1980s debt crisis, 163

Interest payments: commercial bank syndicated loans, 107; debtor country adjustments in workouts, 49; economic theory of debt contracting, 10, 11; forms of debt restructuring, 13–14, 65b; London Club rates, 102–03, 112, 128–29; market vs. market-based rates, 128–29n51; origins of 1980s debt crisis, 154; Paris Club workout policies, 74, 86, 88

International Bank for Reconstruction and Development, 33. See also World Bank

International Debt Commission, 59, 142–46

International Debt Management Authority, 168

International Development Association, 30, 33, 272–73

International Finance Corporation, 33–34, 190

International lending, generally: benefits, 11; commercial creditor concerns, 13; debt swaps, 89; debtor country adjustments and, 49–52; enforcement mechanisms, 12–13; evolution of international machinery and policy, 3–5, 11; fundamental concepts, 6; importance of contracts, 45–47; international institutions for debt restructuring, 2, 6, 21b; political context, 53; role of commercial banks, 96–102; sources of market failure, 10–11. See also Bankruptcy regimes, international; Bond debt; Sovereign debt restructuring; specific types of lending institution

International Monetary Fund (IMF), 25; antiglobalization demonstrations against, 244; Argentina, refinancing, 60–61b; Argentine default (2001) and, 217–18; Art. VIII, sec. 2(b), 234; authority to block litigation, 234, 237; balance-of-payments projections, 77–79, 120; Brady Plan provisions, 172–73; Brazil and, 218; burden allocation in workouts, 55; capital market relations, 232–33; Capital Markets Consultative Group, 232, 273; comfort letter, 125; consolidation period limitations, 86; crisis prevention efforts, 47, 48, 287; criticism of, 28–29; economic principles, 1; Ecuador, workout, 213; financial losses in workouts, 53–54; future of sovereign debt restructuring, 5, 7, 272, 273–74; G-7 and, 25, 29, 53; G-10 recommendations for, 224; G-22 recommendations for, 230–32, 233; gold sales, 139; HIPC Initiative and, 66, 185, 186; IIF and, 237, 238, 247–48; international bankruptcy treaty, 18; international debt statistics, 21; jurisdiction over capital movements, 225–26; lending into arrears, 173; lending practices, 32–33, 224, 231–32, 237; London Club and, 112, 115, 117, 120; and 1980s debt crisis, 155, 158, 159–60, 163; origins of, 1; Pakistan, bond restructuring, 211–12, 236–37; Paris Club and, 64–65, 64b, 70, 71, 77–79, 115; politics and financing decisions, 111–12; preference for orderly workouts, 273–74; as preferred creditor in sovereign workouts, 32; on private sector involvement, 224, 232–34, 236, 239, 240, 242–46, 247–48; Reports on the Observance of Standards and Codes, 232; roles and responsibilities, 27–29; Russian monetary crisis and, 208, 209, 210; Sovereign Debt Restructuring Mechanism, 5, 29, 114n32, 250, 251–59, 272, 286; Special Data Dissemination Stan-

Organization of Petroleum Exporting
Countries, 100
Ortiz, Guillermo, 270n10

Pakistan, 40, 52, 135, 197; bond restructuring, 211–12, 236–37, 263–64; Paris
Club and, 58–59, 71n21, 278n18, 283
Paris Club, 6–7; Ad Hoc restructuring
terms, 90–91; Agreed Minute, 81,
91–92; analytical framework, 77–79;
Argentina and, 59, 60–61b, 216,
278n20; and Asian crises, 204–05;
bilateral agreements, 91–92; bond debt
policies, 74–75, 94; burden-sharing
approach, 7, 72–75, 262, 283–86; case-
by-case principle, 69–70, 114; Chile
and, 99b; classic restructuring terms,
90; Cologne terms, 185–86; comparable treatment, 72–75, 94, 115, 240, 246,
280–84; concessional and nonconcessional loans, 87; conditionality, 70–71,
115; consolidation period, 86; contract
cutoff date, 85–86; de minimis creditors, 88–89; debt reduction, 84–85, 91,
93–94, 274–75, 278; debtor country's
bilateral commitments and, 91–92;
decisionmaking model, 70, 114; features of workout agreements, 88; fees,
82n37; future of international debt
restructuring, 5, 91, 94, 276; goodwill
clause, 89–90; guaranteed credits,
85n42; HIPC debt restructuring policies, 4, 57, 60–62, 65–68, 180, 182–83,
184, 274–75, 276; Houston terms, 90;
IMF and, 64–65, 64b, 70, 71, 77–79,
115; imminent default, 69; Indonesia,
debt rescheduling, 134, 204–05; interest payment policies, 74, 86, 88; limits
on debt restructuring, 85–86, 275;
London Club vs., 87, 103–6, 114–15,
119–20, 125, 128, 129; London terms,
184; Lyon terms, 185; lower-middle-
income country debt restructuring,
90; membership, 64; middle-income
country debt restructuring, 84, 94;

multiyear agreements, 89; Naples
terms, 184; negotiating process, 75–82,
143n30, 146–47; new-money commitments, 82–83, 104–05, 125, 276–77;
Nigeria, restructuring, 281n28; and
1980s debt crisis, 155; nonconsolidated debt, 87; in North-South
Dialogue, 138, 143–47; nondiscrimination, 75n28; number and scope of
interventions, 67, 75; observers, 64–65;
ODA loans, 87, 88, 89; offshore
accounts, 88n44; opportunities for
improvement, 262, 272, 276–79,
285–87; origins and development, 2, 5,
19, 56–57, 58–62, 93–94, 96, 274–75;
Pakistan, bond restructuring, 211, 212,
236–37, 278n18, 283; politics and
financing decisions, 112; post-Soviet
Russia and, 209, 210; press release, 81;
principles, 68–75; private sector debt
in restructuring, 85, 92–93, 275–76;
procedural reforms (1970s), 3, 59, 68;
purpose, 2, 19, 58, 59; repayment periods, 87–88; secretariat, 62; solidarity
principle, 72, 114–15; in sovereign
debt restructuring, 18, 21b, 35, 67;
stock and flow treatments, 83, 277–78;
structure and operations, 7, 59, 62,
63b, 68, 79; swaps, 89; Toronto terms,
184; tour d'horizon sessions, 77; trade
credits protection, 85; transparency
of operations, 65, 81–82, 238, 283;
UNCTAD participation, 138–39;
U.S. and, 68n16, 80n36
Pearson, Lester, 133
Peron, Juan, 216
Peru, 58, 89n47, 102, 138n18
Peterson, Peter, 238
Peterson Commission, 133n5
Philippines, 99n8
Poland, 102, 112, 278, 280
Political contexts: Argentine economy,
215–16; Asian economic crises,
207–08; bilateral lending agencies, 35;
causes of default, 52; concerns about